ULSTER UNIONISM AND
BRITISH NATIONAL IDENTITY
SINCE 1885

ULSTER UNIONISM AND BRITISH NATIONAL IDENTITY SINCE 1885

James Loughlin

PINTER

London and New York
Distributed in the United States by St. Martin's Press

PINTER
An imprint of Cassell Publishers Limited
Wellington House, 125 Strand, London WC2R 0BB, England

First published in 1995

Distributed exclusively in the USA by St. Martin's Press, Inc.,
Room 400, 175 Fifth Avenue, New York, NY 10010, USA

British Library Cataloguing in Publication Data

A CIP catalogue record for this book is available from the British Library

ISBN 0 86187 845 0

Library of Congress Cataloging-in-Publication Data

Loughlin, James.
    Ulster unionism and British national identity since 1885 / James Loughlin.
    p.   cm.
    Includes bibliographical references and index.
    ISBN 0–86187–845–0
    1. Ulster (Northern Ireland and Ireland) – Politics and government.
2. Nationalism – Great Britain – History – 20th century.   3. Northern Ireland
– Politics and government – 1969–.   4. Ireland – Politics and government – 20th
century.   5. Ireland – Politics and government – 1837–1901.   6. National
characteristics, British.   7. Irish unification question.   8. Home rule (Ireland)   I. Title.
DA990.U46L688   1995
941.608–dc20   95–3881
                                                                                CIP

Typeset by Mayhew Typesetting, Rhayader, Powys
Printed and bound in Great Britain by Biddles Ltd, Guildford and King's Lynn

CONTENTS

To
Caroline, Carmen and Ann

PREFACE

This work is not another history of the Ulster question, a subject that has now been well covered by historians. Rather, it is an attempt to explore one of the most fundamental problems that history has thrown up, namely, the Ulster Unionist understanding of their national identity and its place in the wider British context. Accordingly, the major developments that provide the landmarks of Ulster Unionist history since the 1880s are employed here to identify distinct phases within which the subject is examined.

Further, Unionist identity is explored in three separate, though related, contexts: party politics, monarchy and 'national imagining'. These contexts, it can be argued, are not of equal significance, that what happens in the party political sphere is of much greater importance than the Unionist relationship with monarchy, or the extent to which Northern Ireland can be assimilated to changing metaphors of British national identity and territory. But while the importance of party politics is acknowledged, it is impossible to deal adequately with this subject in that context alone. For example, the monarchy represents the supreme embodiment of British nationality and has historically provided Ulster Unionists with an ideal state, or model, of national identity – a model that they would like to replicate in the party political context, and against which the complexities and duplicities of that context are assessed. Also, while these two contexts are formally distinct, with the monarchy being 'non-political', nevertheless, not infrequently the meaning of royalty and royal occasions for Ulster Unionists has been determined by what was happening in the party political context – something that was apparent, for instance, in the period following the signing of the Anglo-Irish Agreement (AIA) in November 1985.

Again, the developing process of how the British nation has been imagined since the late nineteenth century may appear rather marginal to the political conflicts that have determined the fate of the Unionist community. But ideas of the nation's identity, it can be argued, were of importance for Unionists in a period when Westminster's disengagement from Ireland was under way and when the island, north and south, was increasingly seen as a place apart. Such ideas defined the parameters of 'belonging' and the extent to which they excluded Ulster made it all the easier for the region's constitutional position to be made a question of party political negotiation.

As the rift between Ulster and Britain developed over this period, their relationship was often defined in terms of the extent to which the regional particularity of the North approximated to generalized and mythic definitions of Britishness, supposedly representative of Britain as a whole. With this in mind, a major theme of this study is the relationship between the local sphere of everyday life and that of the national sphere of public life, a theme intended to clarify the issues involved in accommodating Ulster's regional distinctiveness with wider British concerns. Relatedly, this study rejects the idea of defining Britishness *only* as indicating an over-arching, homogeneous identity representative of all the regions of Britain. The term 'British', as Keith Robbins has suggested, can, given the variety of national and regional groupings within the Kingdom, imply diversity no less than uniformity.

Thus the approach taken to the question of national identity in this study is wide, attempting to take account of the several dimensions of the subject. It has been influenced, to varying degrees, by the recent work of a number of writers who have taken British national identity as their subject. In addition to Keith Robbins, among others, they include Tom Nairn, Patrick Wright and Martin Wiener.

Note on Terminology

This study often employs terms such as 'Ulster' and 'the mainland' in accounting for the North's relationship with Britain. These terms are often considered politically contentious. They are used here for convenience in explaining the Unionist outlook. They should not be seen as indicating an endorsement of Unionist arguments.

ACKNOWLEDGEMENTS

This work originated in a preliminary study of Ulster Unionism funded by the Economic and Social Research Council (Ref. No. RE/00/22/33/94), undertaken in 1987 when I was a Research Fellow of the Institute of Irish Studies, Queen's University Belfast. For both his backing of the original project and his general helpfulness during my time at the Institute, I would like to thank Professor R.H. Buchanan.

For assistance willingly given at various stages in the preparation of this study thanks are also due to Beverley Cole of the National Railway Museum, York; Toby Haggith of the Imperial War Museum, London; Joseph Canning of the Irish Studies Library, Armagh; Paul Rowlandson, University of Ulster; the Ulster Tourist Development Association; the staffs of the British Library; British Library Newspaper Division at Colindale; House of Lords Records Office; Cambridge University Library; Birmingham University Library; Public Records Office, Kew; Public Records Office of Northern Ireland; Berkeley Library, Trinity College, Dublin; Magee College Library; Central Library (Irish Section), Derry; Linenhall Library, Belfast. I would also like to express my appreciation to the following for granting me interviews: David Trimble, Dr Laurence Kennedy, Dr Ian Paisley and Rev. Martin Smyth. For permission to quote from materials in their possession, I would like to thank the Deputy Keeper of Records, Public Records Office of Northern Ireland, and Viscount Craigavon.

Professor T.G. Fraser, Head of the School of Politics, Philosophy and History at the University of Ulster, was of considerable assistance, both in making materials available and in enabling me to obtain a period of study leave to complete the research and writing of the project. Financial support was provided by the Research Sub-Committee of the Faculty of Humanities.

On a more personal note, I would like to thank Catherine and Allan Preedy for their hospitality during many – often impromptu – research trips to London. My wife, Jacinta, was highly considerate of the project and the demands it made on my time, while my daughters, Caroline and Carmen, provided invaluable assistance in preparing it for publication.

INTRODUCTION: NATIONALITY, MYTH
AND IDENTITY

Nationalism has been described as the fusion of patriotism with the consciousness of nationality, when love of country – an emotion involving fondness, sympathy, fidelity and loyalty – is channelled through the perspective of the nation, its history, population, territoriality, political institutions, cultural interests and ambitions (Hayes 1960: 2, 9–10). Of these elements, history is undoubtedly one of the most important. History, or more exactly a nationalist myth which unfolds the story of the nation, performs essential functions. For example, it shapes perceptions of national identity and characteristics; it gives meaning to 'national prestige'; and generally, it contextualizes the nation's place in the world. As one leading commentator on nationalism has put it, without such myths it is difficult to see nationalities surviving for any length of time (Smith 1992: 22). Given the centrality of myth to national identity, close analysis of its properties is needed.

The term 'myth' used in this context does not, of course, mean fantasy or complete fiction. It means rather 'an interpretation of what the myth maker believes (rightly or wrongly) to be hard fact'. Thus a given account can be identified as a myth 'not by the amount of truth it contains, but by the fact that it is *believed* to be true . . . and it is generally accepted as true if it explains the experience of those to whom it is addressed and justifies the practical purposes they have in mind (Tudor 1972: 17, 138). The ability of myth to function in this way is fundamentally conditioned by the form of communication it embodies at the level of mass understanding; a level demanding clarity and simplicity. Roland Barthes described this property of myth when he argued that it purified human acts:

it makes them innocent, it gives them a natural and eternal justification; it gives them a dignity which is not that of an explanation but of a statement of fact . . . it abolishes the complexity of human acts, it gives them the simplicity of essences, it does away with all dialectics, with any going back beyond what is immediately visible, it organises a world which is . . . without depth.   (Barthes 1973: 142–3)

For our purposes Barthes's 'simplicity of essences' will often be adapted to 'stereotypes', for, as a specific form of myth, national myth is essentially a discourse of stereotypes: stereotypes of historical development; stereotypes (favourable) of group self identity and of others (often negative); and stereotypes of national mission and destiny. Taken together they present a world-view that is easily comprehensible at the lowest common denominator of mass perception.

The national myth, however, while perceptively simplistic is yet dynamic in character. At its centre is an oscillation between threat and reassurance, specified in how the myth presents the history of the nation – a chosen people – as a recurring tale of danger and deliverance. Further, in times of perceived national danger the past can function as the repository of a golden age of national existence which it is the duty of contemporary national leaders to reconstitute.[1] Thus the myth is not disinterested or devoid of political motive in the way that it deals with the national past. Its perspective is present-centred, its purpose instrumental. The notion of 'lessons' is central to it: 'myth tells us what we ought to do and what we have to avoid, what we should fear and what we should hope' (Heller 1975: 7). It does this, moreover, within a context that provides a *total* explanation of group existence: 'The end result of existence is *this* existence; "once upon a time" is "here and now" . . . "man" is identical with the clan or tribe of the myth' (ibid.: 6).

In other words, the myth encompasses the total world-view of the group, and in so doing makes no distinction between past, present or future. Essentially, it embodies an ahistorical enclosed outlook, denying the possibility of change in history. The past provides lessons of conduct for the present and the future; the acceptance of those lessons presupposing the existence of an unchanging environment.[2]

One of the most vexed problems associated with the study of national myths lies in defining their influence at the popular level. The gap between the public sphere within which national myth is effective and the private sphere of personal experience can be difficult to overcome, especially as different vocabularies are often employed in these contexts. The vocabulary of national myth, being a language of public discourse, is usually inappropriate for personal use. Why that is so has been graphically described by Frederick Hertz (1951: 46):

The development of a national ideology often leads to a differentiation in the rules of conduct which implies almost two different characters in the same person, a private character in regard to private affairs and a national character in national affairs. . . . People may be peaceable and humanitarian in their private affairs and ruthlessly aggressive in national matters, especially in such as affect the so-called national interest and honour.

Nationalist ideologues can attempt to bridge the gap between the public and private spheres by incorporating the latter within the national framework; for example, by giving 'a national significance to local or sectional facts such as old customs, popular ballads, folk dances, etc.' (ibid.: 19). At another level, connections between the two spheres can be sought in the influence of crises, especially those involving external threats, in crystallizing national issues at the mass level and, in the process, effecting a homogeneity, however temporarily, between these spheres in such a way that the private sphere is largely swallowed up in the national. The speed with which this can happen[3] suggests the existence of a subliminal national consciousness in people otherwise apolitical. It is likely that even those for whom national identity is not usually salient are yet, without knowing it, 'bound by numerous invisible bonds to the nation. Without knowing it they are imbued with the elements of national ideology.' (ibid.: 23). Some insights into the nature of the 'invisible bonds' Hertz refers to are provided in Patrick Wright's more recent work on 'everyday historical consciousness' (1985).

Drawing heavily on the work of Agnes Heller, Wright argues that everyday life is understood in terms of 'stories'. Even when told of times past they 'are judged and shaped by their relevance to what is happening now, and in this sense their allegiance is unashamedly to the present'. Further, stories are assessed and appreciated 'in terms of their *authenticity*', which, of course, is different from objectivity and 'true knowledge'. Authenticity and truth may collide and if this happens it is the account of the original 'authentic' story that will prevail; abstract truth will be resisted in the face of what is experienced, felt and believed to be true (Wright 1985: 14–15).

Wright makes these points as part of a sophisticated study of historical consciousness in everyday life, but what is important to note for our purposes is how his definition of the mode of everyday understanding conforms essentially to that embodied in national myth; in the preference for authenticity over abstract truth, in the tendency for stories to be present-centred – shaped by current need – and further, in that the stories of everyday life will encapsulate the 'verisimilitude of everyday life'. Or to put it another way, as with the stories of national mythology, they express the nature of the world of which they are a part: 'The authentic story is . . . *evocative* in character' (ibid.: 15).

Thus it can be argued that the ability of national myth to invest everyday life in times of national crisis is facilitated by the fact that both spheres of existence – the national/public and the local/private – employ essentially the same modes of understanding. Moreover, while everyday life *per se* stands outside or apart from national life, it is, nevertheless, impinged on in certain respects by central institutions of the national myth in uncontroversial ways. Perceived and accepted, such institutions as the office of national leadership, the national flag and the national territory, while existing apart from everyday life, nevertheless constitute some of the most important parameters within which everyday life takes place. Not surprisingly, in periods of national crisis these institutions can become the most popular foci of national identity.

In this context the idea of the national territory is especially potent as it embodies three of the most important kinds of motives that bind human groups together – traditions, interests and ideals: 'The territory is regarded as a heritage of the national past, and is the basis of the whole present existence of the nation, while its further development forms an ideal in the future' (Hertz 1951: 18–19). Moreover the national territory, a *natural* territory which to a large extent produces the nation (ibid.: 146), encourages the idea of the naturalness of national consciousness.

If less essential than territory as foci of national identity, flags nevertheless have great potential for engendering national sentiment, linking as they do national emotion with a country's status and power (Firth 1975: Ch. 10); and while the same can be said for the office of national leader, where this institution is a monarchy, its symbolic national function can be more complex than that of an elected politician, finding responses 'in a set of ideas of a diffuse moral kind about . . . social relationships, family life and institutional patterns focused upon and epitomised in the person' of the monarch (ibid.: 89). Most importantly, and as a recent study confirms (Billig 1992), the person and family of the monarch can provide the means for the most spontaneous, uncomplicated and effective linking of the national and everyday spheres of existence.

The discussion so far has been concerned with outlining the conceptual framework within which this study will generally be pursued. Thus it has identified abstractly the central features of national myths and some of the means through which they can become influential at the mass level. It has, in particular, assumed the existence at this level of an ideologically and ethnologically homogeneous people. However, as we shall see, the application of this explanatory framework to the complex realities of the United Kingdom in this period is by no means simple. An ideologically and ethnologically homogeneous people, for example, does not exist. Neither, for much of this period, is it possible to identify one, overarching national myth to which all of the people subscribed.[4] Again, the study of specific cases necessitates the examination of issues that need not arise at the abstract level, such as the means available for the dissemination of political propaganda and who controls them; specific forms of discourse on identity and their fluctuation in popularity; changes in the nature of national myths; changes in the national leadership; and especially, the evolving political contexts and crises that crystallize national identity. Accordingly, the structure of ideas on national myth and identity outlined here cannot be applied rigidly to the subject matter of this study. Rather it provides a broad context which informs the discussion on fundamental issues.

Notes

1. These characteristics have been identified in both English and Irish national myths (Loughlin 1990b: 9–15).
2. At a general level this aspect of myth is expressed in the arguments of those Ulster unionists who continue to define the 'Papal threat' in seventeenth-century terms.
3. For a relevant example, see Calder 1991.
4. This is reflected in Keith Robbins's statement (1990: 7), that there was, in the nineteenth century, no 'single all-purpose name' for the United Kingdom, 'Britain' being increasingly unacceptable for the purpose.

1

THE UNITED KINGDOM: CRISIS AND NATIONAL IDENTITY IN THE 1880s

As Britain entered the 1880s it faced a crisis of social, economic and political proportions. For many commentators, especially Conservatives, the symptoms of national disintegration itself were perceived. Accordingly, the language of patriotism formed an important part of their response to that crisis. This chapter explores the nature of late nineteenth-century British patriotism and the terms within which it was articulated.

I

As an example of how myth shapes a critique of current realities by reference to a past golden age, A.V. Dicey's assessment of late nineteenth-century Britain is instructive. Dicey, whose work was infused with a highly developed sense of pride in the excellence of British institutions – 'He taught us to strike our chests as free-born Britons . . . and to pity the poor Frenchman', recalled a former student (Jowitt 1951: 28) – identified the 1830s as a period of ideal national cohesion, from which time could be traced 'the disintegration of beliefs . . . the breaking up of established creeds, whether religious, moral, political or economical' (Dicey 1905/ 1952: 38–9). This was especially evident in popular attitudes to the constitution:

Faith . . . in the English Constitution was, fifty years ago, the common characteristic of all our statesmen. This was a creed of no sudden growth, it was enforced by the arguments of Hallam, it colours every page of Macaulay. It explains Wellington's celebrated declaration that the nature of man was incapable of creating, by any effort, institutions of such paramount excellence as the constitution England enjoyed under the unreformed Parliament of 1830. The Whigs never desired . . . to do more than to repair the revered fabric of the Constitution. Many of them held that the policy of reform was nothing more but the strengthening of the original foundations on which rested the institutions of England. . . . Both [Lord John] Russell and Palmerston believed, and acted on the belief, the Frenchmen, Germans or Italians might all of them put an end to any grievances under which they suffered by the adoption of the form of Government which existed in England. . . . This was, in the main, the creed of at least two generations. . . . But from 1830 onwards attacks began to be made on popular faith in the English Constitution.   (ibid.: 440–41)

The contrast Dicey made between the ideal constitution of the past and the stability it represented and the uncertainties of his own time, was a constant theme of Tory and Unionist complaints about what they defined as the 'tendency' of the age.[1] Matthew Arnold's view of the social and political condition of England in the 1880s was no less pessimistic than Dicey's.

Indeed we are at the end of a period, and always at the end of a period the word goes forth: 'Now is the judgement of this world.' The 'traditional existing, social arrangements', which satisfied before satisfy no longer; the conventions and phrases which once passed without question, are challenged.   (Arnold 1882/1891: xi)

The historian, Goldwin Smith, voiced similar views in an article entitled, 'The Political Crisis in England', which explained more fully the depth of that crisis.
    Smith focused on a central concern of the Right, namely, the growing disjunction between the 'constitution' – a term which he correctly identi-fied the mythic properties of by describing it as believed to be 'rather occult', a 'hollowed word . . . a mystical standard by which all political claims could be tried and all mystical excesses could be restrained' – and the 'nation'. Smith believed this was the culmination of a historical process in which

England has had a balance of forces which, oscillating more or less through her history, has now been finally upset, the Crown having been divested of all authority, the House of Lords of all but a suspensive veto, while supreme power is vested in the House of Commons, or in an electoral caucus. . . . British democracy is unprovided with safeguards against revolution.   (Smith 1894: 104–5)

The crisis in England, according to Smith, was demonstrated most obviously in the 'falling off' in the 'character' of the House of Commons; in particular, it had lost 'independence, order and dignity' (ibid.: 112). Smith detected among 'public men' a 'fatalistic belief that they are being swept along by the irresistible current of inevitable change and that there is nothing for it but surrender', a situation he compared to 'the eve of the French Revolution' when comparable 'revolutionary forces . . . hurried France into the abyss' (ibid.: 112–13). The most serious aspect of the crisis was the Irish question: 'Let the upholders of party government trace . . . the process by which a proud and mighty nation has been compelled to surrender to a contemptible conspiracy to give Ireland a separate parliament' (ibid.: 117).
    The apprehensions of Dicey, Arnold and Smith about constitutional decay were widespread. Nor is this surprising, given that school histories in the first half of the nineteenth century subscribed generally to the view that the pre-1832 constitution was perfect and could only be changed for

the worse (Chancellor 1970: 50). And as Smith's comments indicate, these anxieties took on a greater urgency from the beginning of the 1880s with the Irish question once more assuming a serious aspect as the land war got under way, and as demands for the extension of the franchise became vociferous. In the year that the great franchise reforms of 1884–5 were completed and which tripled the British electorate, Sir Henry Maine, the eminent jurist and philosopher, penned one of the most articulate statements of English Conservatism, *Popular Government* (1885), a work which associated the advance of democracy with the loss of material prosperity and 'national greatness' (Feaver 1969: 230). Maine also saw in recent trends in British politics 'many similarities with France on the eve of the French Revolution' (ibid.: 222). The most authoritative statement of these views, however, was made by Lord Salisbury in his article, 'Disintegration', contributed anonymously – though the authorship was soon known – to the October 1883 issue of the *Quarterly Review*. Salisbury's article was intended to rally 'constitutional forces' to combat the activities of Joseph Chamberlain, then considered a radical demagogue, and by so doing to establish the Tory Party as the party of national unity.

The essay is an example of highly effective political propaganda. Sharply focused, it identified the Tories as the party of the English nation and the Liberals, though in office, as traitors, effectively, who did not represent the national will in the way that they dealt with social classes. Salisbury simplified the complex issues of the day into a conflict between 'unity' and 'disintegration', and central to his assessment of the crisis facing the country was the supposed disjunction between the 'constitution' and the 'nation'. Again the point of departure was a previous golden age, with which the present sad state of affairs was compared:

What we require in the administration of public affairs . . . is the spirit of the *old constitution* [my italics] which held the nation together as a whole, and levelled its united force at objects of national import, instead of splitting it into a bundle of unfriendly and distrustful fragments. The danger we have to face may be summed up in a single word – disintegration.

This was manifest, not only in domestic politics, 'in the estrangement of classes that make up the nation', but in the loss of large portions of the British Empire. Liberal 'theorists' had conspired to undermine 'the respect in which the superiority of the English race is held' by the natives in India; patriotism was no longer strong: 'the national impulses which used to make Englishmen cling together in the face of every external trouble are beginning to disappear' (Salisbury 1883 in Smith (ed.) 1972: 342–3). Salisbury drew an analogy between the political constitution and the human constitution, with the former dying of the disintegration malady, the most serious symptom of which was the Irish problem which Liberal politicians had exacerbated (ibid.: 357, 366–7). Yet significantly for future Tory policy on Ireland, Salisbury warned that 'all that was Protestant, loyal and industrious in Ireland' could not be left to the mercies of Nationalist agitators: 'If we have failed after centuries to make Ireland peaceable and civilised, we have no moral right to abandon our post and leave all the penalty of our failure to those whom we have persuaded to trust in our power' (ibid.: 374).

Taken collectively, the mythic characteristics of these arguments are clear, not only in the contrast between the perceived present crisis of state and nation and a past golden age which provided the model for the saviours of the nation to aim at, but also in the reduction of historical complexity to a simplified conflict of opposing forces, with the implication that the supposed loss of national dignity, prestige and power was due to the action of traitors, not only within the state but actually in power, and whose removal from office would set the country back on the road to national greatness. The widespread currency of such arguments derived substantially from their source in the forms of discourse within which issues of identity and nationality were debated in late nineteenth-century Britain.

II

Perceptions of British nationality in this period were heavily influenced by established traditions of historical understanding; traditions, such as those at Oxford, which were essentially mythic in their tendency to screen out problematic complexity in favour of the 'lessons' of history for England's national progress: 'the long evolutionary process which had ended in making England top nation.' (V.H. Galbraith on Bishop William Stubbs's approach to history, quoted in Soffer 1987: 80). It was history which took the nation as its subject, the progress of which was charted in a national narrative about high politics and the constitution, and which was 'taught as a demonstration of national character, free institutions and moral obligations' (ibid.: 79–80). And while change had to be taken account of, it was expected 'to occur in accord with well-delineated traditions established as the constitution had been perfected' (ibid.: 83).

The relationship between national character – a preoccupation of the Victorians (Collini 1985: 33) – and the constitution was central to both academic and political perceptions of the nation, and especially to Conservative patriotism. In its modern form this understanding had been shaped by Edmund Burke in his nationalist polemic against the French Revolution, *Reflections on the Revolution in France* (Burke 1790/1868). Burke 'hijacked' the Glorious Revolution from its base in the Whig/Liberal tradition – where it had been associated ideologically with individual liberty and the overthrowing of arbitrary monarchic and aristocratic power – and used it to underpin a Tory historicist view of the English nation (Thompson 1986: 52). In this respect he provided a telling example of mythic reorientation in the face of crisis. For Burke, concerned to enhance the legitimacy of the existing social and political order in the face of external threat, argued that the revolution did not mark a chasmic break in English history, but was, in fact, made to 'preserve our *ancient* constitution of government which is our only security for law and liberty'

(Burke quoted, ibid.: 52). But most significantly, Burke – in articulating a conception of history centring on an organic theory of society, belief in the aristocracy as a governing class, and in the state as a great spiritual entity uniting the living and the dead (Burke 1790/1868: 101, 112–20) – firmly enmeshed the 'constitution' in both the realms of the public sphere of national affairs and that of the private and familial:

People will not look forward to posterity who never look backward to their ancestors . . . the people of England well know, that the idea of inheritance furnishes a sure principle of transmission. . . . In this choice of inheritance we have given to our frame of polity the image of a relation in blood; binding up the constitution of our country with our dearest domestic ties; adopting our fundamental laws into the bosom of our family affection . . . always acting as if in the presence of canonised ancestors. (ibid.: 42–3)

Burke's concept of the nation established a 'foundation myth' for Tory patriots in the formative period of modern British nationality, the period of the Twenty Years War with revolutionary France. (For the most recent and imaginative account of this period in the shaping of modern British nationality, see Colley, 1992a.) This concept of the nation became the dominant one during the nineteenth century, being built on and developed by leading Conservatives to meet the challenge of popular democracy. Disraeli, for example, in explaining the process of national formation, was to make a fundamental distinction between 'nation' and 'people'. While a people was 'a species', he argued, only a civilized community was 'a nation'; and a nation was 'a work of art and a work of time'. More specifically, it was the product of 'original organisation', climate, soil, religion, laws, customs, manners, historical accidents and the character of prominent citizens:

These influences create the nation – these form the national mind, and produce in the course of centuries a high degree of civilisation. *If you destroy the political institutions which these influences have called into force, and which are the machinery by which they constantly act, you destroy the nation* [my italics]. The nation in a state of anxiety and dissolution then becomes a people.
(Disraeli, *The Spirit of Whiggism*, quoted in Hertz 1951: 29)

Disraeli's was the most important influence shaping Tory national patriotism in the nineteenth century, and this quotation could stand as a neat encapsulation of the outlook of commentators such as Maine and Salisbury, as well as those of 'old' Liberals like Arnold, Dicey and Goldwin Smith who came to take the same view of the state of the nation. It was an élitist view, desiring to concede full national membership only to an aristocratic and class élite. In the longer historical view it can be seen as the nationalism of the dominant group that had formed the State's ethnic core; and which, through its control of the State, was able to define politically and culturally the nature of national identity. In this context it is important to note that the conception of national identity articulated by Tory commentators in the nineteenth century drew upon a long established matrix of beliefs embedded in British popular opinion. Of these Protestantism was undoubtedly the most important. It was, for example, the break with Rome and the Reformation that followed that provided England with a national church and the religion that came to define the particular identity of Englishmen (Smith 1992: 55). In the 1870s Lord Salisbury expressed a widely held view when he argued that the Reformation had had a profound formative influence on the character of the English people: Protestantism had invested the English people with moral virility and independence, so much so that the Catholic practice of confession was not only theologically repugnant, but actually foreign to the English national character (Best 1967: 136–7). Certainly popular Protestantism constituted an important element of Tory nationalism in the nineteenth century and was used ruthlessly at times to inflame opinion against Irish Catholic immigrants in Britain (Kirk 1980: 64–106).

Protestantism also integrated well with widespread stereotypes about the racial character of the English people. The credibility of national stereotypes rested on the view – widely held in the nineteenth century and only gradually losing its hold in the twentieth – that nations had specific characters that could be objectively identified. In England's case the belief that the modern English were essentially of the same blood as the race of conquering Teutons that invaded Britain from northern Germany after the fall of the Roman Empire – a race of superior stock and outstanding character, and possessing a form of parliamentary assembly, the Witenagemot, the prototype of the English Parliament – was widely accepted; as was the view that these racial origins largely explained England's national and imperial greatness in the modern world. The section on England in the *Encyclopaedia Britannica* (1878), for example, spoke in highly personalized terms of an ideologically homogeneous national being, 'we English', that had colonized southern Britain, expelled the indigenous Celts, and imposed a distinctive English language, political and social system; and while these may have developed and changed greatly down the centuries, they did so without ceasing to be fundamental aspects of the 'one and the same English nation'.[2]

This interpretation was not the preserve of any one political faction. It appealed right across the political spectrum, including staunch Gladstonian Liberals no less than diehard Tories. Ideas of race were essential, for example, to the arguments of the most influential imperialist texts of the period, Sir John Seeley's *The Expansion of England* (1883/1920) and Sir Charles Dilke's *Greater Britain* (1869) – works expressing concern for the maintenance of England's world-wide Empire in the face of economic and expansionist competition from foreign competitors, especially the USA, Russia and Germany. Seeley, for example, advanced the view that in sixty years Russia and the USA would surpass in power the states 'now' called great (Seeley 1883/1920: 340–50), and that if England wanted to retain its membership of the great power league it must recognize and act on the lesson of its historical development, namely its unparalleled expansion. Seeley, recognizing that unlike Russia and the USA England lacked a native land mass as the basis of its imperial greatness, focused instead on the 'vital' bonds of nationality, blood and religion as the foundation of unity and imperial expansion of England (ibid.: 346–7, 359–9). Seeley, it should be noted, used the term 'England' as many Englishmen did in this period, to describe the United Kingdom as a whole – 'in these islands we feel ourselves for all purposes as one nation, though in Wales, in Scotland and in Ireland there is Celtic blood, and Celtic languages utterly unintelligible to us are still spoken' (ibid.: 59). Accordingly, in this context, greater Britain was seen as 'an extension of the English state . . . and of the English nationality'; and, in a period when modern communications had greatly reduced the disuniting tendencies of vast distances, the prospects for increasing unity were extremely good and should be taken advantage of (ibid.: 54, 349). With this in mind 'Englishness' had to mean something more than the narrow élitist culture of Oxbridge educated gentlemen, even if they remained the carriers of the dominant strand in the national culture. The concept of Englishness had to expand to include the English people as a whole, to be found, as Seeley forcefully argued, where English people were to be found; and to be defined in terms of a checklist of traits associated with the English race, namely: governing capabilities, respect for law and order, emotional stability, energy and determination, worldly success and Protestant religion.[3] Such arguments became highly influential in the late nineteenth century, not only because of Seeley's propagandist skills but because science appeared to endorse them:

it gave the weight associated with ordered empirical data to widely circulating ideas which seemed to conform to Victorian domestic realities and experience of the wider world. It appeared to confirm the inevitability of racial conflict, the validity of generalising about group characteristics, the desirability of racial purity . . . and the justice of imposing European civilisation on the hunting economies and cultural crudities of 'savagery'.   (Bolt 1984: 131)[4]

The arguments of Seeley and Dilke stimulated and justified an aggressive imperialist mood in Britain in the 1880s, one that became more extreme as the struggle for Africa intensified. It was a mood the Tory Party encouraged and capitalized on as Gladstone's second ministry staggered through a series of imperial blunders and, in the process, appeared to demonstrate that Liberal patriotism had failed the test of practical politics (Loughlin 1986: 48–9). With Gladstone's fall from office over the Home Rule crisis of 1886 and the onset of the Conservative hegemony that was to last almost twenty years, this was a period in which Liberal patriotism was of little influence; however, it is still important to take account of. As we shall see, it would re-emerge in the Edwardian period to provide a powerful justification for the radical Liberal legislation that provoked the third Home Rule crisis.

The Liberal patriotism of the late nineteenth century had its roots in the radical patriotism of the eighteenth century, a patriotism which also looked back for the origins of the English constitution to the old Teutonic assembly – the Witenagemot. In this period one of the chief ideological weapons used by radicals complaining of the corruption of the Whig oligarchy that controlled the Government was the theory of the 'Norman yoke' – the belief that the Norman invasion had destroyed the constitutional freedoms enjoyed by Saxon Englishmen and imposed a lasting tyranny on the people in the form of the existing ruling class of crown and aristocracy, a tyranny it was their duty to overthrow (Newman 1987: 77, 189–91). However, with the ascendancy gained by the patriotism promoted by Burke and his Tory successors, radical patriotism diminished in influence; by the 1870s it was incorporated within Liberalism and seen increasingly as out of touch with the age (Cunningham 1989: 77). The trouble with Liberal patriotism was its earnestness and lack of emotional dynamics. In foreign policy its thrust was the pursuit of peace and international conciliation, subjects on which it was difficult to arouse public excitement – especially so in the 1880s when it was associated with the failures of Gladstone's imperial policy.

Tory patriotism, on the other hand, drawing more explicitly on a potent mix of popular Protestantism, race and class prejudice and xenophobia, was a more aggressive strain and seemed more appropriate to the times. In truth the potency of Tory patriotism derived from its ability to transcend formal political allegiances. In his thorough study of the Home Rule Parliament of 1886, W.C. Lubenow demonstrated, for example, how on coming into office the Liberal Government and Party immediately supported the outgoing Tory Government's high-handed annexation of Upper Burma (Lubenow 1988: 148–9). Perhaps the most striking example of the influence of Tory patriotism in this period is the career of Joseph Chamberlain. Chamberlain made his reputation in the 1870s and early 1880s as the most virulent critic of the Tory establishment, with a Liberalism conceptualized firmly within the radical patriotic tradition; however, he converted to Unionism during the first home rule crisis and increasingly adopted the aggressive race patriotism of the Tory Party. His rhetoric also became increasingly anti-Catholic, reflecting the importance this sentiment still had as a factor in British national identity (Loughlin 1992: 207–19).

The belief that Roman Catholicism was incompatible with British nationality was one that would find expression well into the twentieth century. In the nineteenth century it was stimulated partly by the emergence of the Oxford Movement, but more so by the development of Irish Catholic nationalism:

popular Protestantism was emphatically British in flavour . . . for Britain as a whole seemed a Protestant bastion against Roman ambitions. Each disturbance by the Catholics of Ireland, from O'Connell's campaigns of the 1840s to Parnell's in the 1880s served to reinforce this stance.   (Bebbington 1982: 501–3)

British popular Protestantism, moreover, and the imperialism it was associated with and encouraged, also acted to deter the development of Celtic nationalism (ibid.). Its underpinning of a common national identity could also proceed despite a range of conflicts and tensions between the British churches on a range of organizational, social and theological issues.[5]

Nevertheless, while the Protestant element in British national consciousness was important – at its most intense in the decades up to mid-century it could be said to have effectively linked the realms of national consciousness and everyday experience – it *gradually* began to lose its popular influence from the late 1870s onwards (Best 1967: 138–9), as Protestant religious observance diminished under pressure from rationalism, hedonism, economic change and new methods of historical inquiry.[6] For our purposes, developments in historical inquiry have a special interest.

The fundamentalist emphasis on a literal interpretation of the Bible had been an essential foundation of popular Protestantism and, by extension – given the centrality of the Reformation experience to its development – of the British national myth at the popular level. The development of a critical historiography after the mid-century, however, was to seriously erode this aspect of the myth. The distinguished Protestant theologian, Dr George Salmon, claimed it was the main reason why, in the 1880s, there was a serious falling off in the numbers of young men coming forward who were willing to take up 'the struggle' with Rome:

Modern conceptions of the proper attitude of mind of an historian require him to enter impartially into the feelings of his characters. . . . No wonder, then, that we can find apologies, too, for Roman Catholic persecutors, and believe that many a judge who sent a heretic to the stake may have been a conscientious good man, fulfilling what he regarded as an unpleasant duty.   (Salmon 1890: 3)

The integrity of myth, we noted, was largely dependent on its ability to invest its audience with the relevance of its lessons; in this context, the belief that the persecution suffered by Protestants during the Reformation was a reliable guide to what they could expect if Catholics got the upper hand in the United Kingdom in the future. But, as Salmon's comments indicate, the influence of critical historiography, in replacing mythic authenticity with something approaching true knowledge, was having the effect of divesting religious conflict of its emotional charge. In the process, it was also releasing the Reformation controversy from the realm of politics into that of history, and with it an important element of the British national myth. This was, of course, a gradual process, and the popular influence of Protestantism in the 1880s and 1890s was nowhere more clearly indicated than in Lord Salisbury's advice to Queen Victoria, that the Duke of Clarence's intended marriage to the daughter of the Comte de Paris should be discouraged on the grounds that the anti-French and anti-Catholic elements in British national feeling were so strong that popular allegiance to the throne could be adversely affected if it went ahead (Salisbury to the Queen, 9 Sept. 1890 in Williamson (ed.) 1988: 327).

Nevertheless, Salmon's comments indicated accurately enough the future demise of popular Protestantism; and one of the clearest indicators of how clerical disillusionment with religious controversy could be disseminated among the public at large was in how celebrations of one of the greatest Protestant/national anniversaries – Guy Fawkes Day – changed in this period. Until 1859 the occasion was celebrated in Anglican churches with a reminder that Fawkes represented a Roman Catholic threat to the State, thus associating Roman Catholics with treason (Colley 1992b: 317). Thereafter, however, it increasingly lost its national significance, being stripped of many of its anti-Catholic overtones until the eve of the First World War when it was largely the secular occasion we know today, focused around a range of local issues (Storch 1982: 71–99). Yet in the late nineteenth century these indications were worrying for Protestant patriots, especially so as they seemed to be associated with a corresponding rise in the influence of Roman Catholicism. Between 1840 and 1900, the Catholic population in Britain doubled, from 700,000 to 1,500,000 and prominent Catholics started to appear in government ranks (Chadwick 1970: Ch. 8). For many patriotic Britons the Catholic revival was seen as a serious threat to 'our national destiny' (Paton 1893: ii, 556).

But the demise of popular Protestantism was only one aspect of a more widespread crisis facing the established social and political order in late nineteenth-century Britain. That crisis was manifest most strikingly in the sudden and dramatic collapse of British and European agriculture in the late 1870s, due partly to a massive influx of cheap foreign goods from North and South America and the Antipodes. From then until the mid-1890s the United Kingdom experienced an economic recession that stimulated the rise of agrarian struggle and militant nationalism in Ireland, and mass unemployment, riots and labour radicalization in Britain (Hobsbawm 1969: Ch. 9; Cannadine 1990: 1–31). Against this background, Gladstone's great extension of voting rights to the working classes, entailed in the franchise reforms of 1884–5, was viewed by right-wing commentators with deep foreboding. The fears of many that Britain could be facing a state of affairs not unlike that of France on the eve of the Revolution found expression in A.V. Dicey's description of radicalism: 'New radicalism is the child of old Jacobinism and exhibits with slight change the familiar traits of its parent.' (Dicey 1888: 486). In this context the increasingly anxious appeals to national patriotism, as a solution for the nation's ills, made by establishment spokesmen is easy to understand. At the same time, however, and reflecting Britain's diminishing role as a world industrial power, the image of the nation itself was undergoing change.

III

In the 1850s, when England was the world's predominant industrial power, national pride focused primarily on the country's material achievements. Indeed, this was almost the defining characteristic of British nationality. It was a sentiment that acted as a powerful antidote to national divisions. People, as Francois Bedarida argues, were comforted by it and revelled in it, disparaging the foreigners unlucky not to have been born English. Hector Malot wrote in 1862 that 'the Englishman' had such an idea of his superiority in all things 'that his pride cannot understand how the matter could be even worth discussing. For him this superiority is like the light of the sun, and those who are not used to it must be dazzled' (quoted in Bedarida, 1979: 92–3). A form of this sentiment was perceived even among the British working class. Karl Marx wrote that the 'ordinary English worker' felt himself in relation to the Irish worker, 'a member of the *ruling nation*. . . . He cherishes religious, social and national prejudices against the Irish worker. His attitude towards him is much the same as that of the "poor whites" to the "niggers" in the former slave states of the U.S.A.' (Marx and Engels 1971: 93–4).

Nowhere was the spirit of the age better represented than in T.B. Macaulay's massively influential *History of England* (1848–61). Macaulay's work was infused with an arrogant English nationalism; indeed it was intended, less as a serious work of history, than as a great patriotic statement. Centred on the period of the 'Glorious Revolution', it was a moral fable of the English nation and its survival in the face of Roman Catholic threats to the monarchy and the constitution, the latter described as a 'just and holy thing' (Macaulay 1848–61/1907: 10). Macaulay celebrated, chauvinistically, the industrial and material achievement of mid-Victorian Britain and his work was typically mythic in its present-centred use of history to establish contemporary political lessons, especially in its appeal to the racial and religious prejudices of 'the average Englishman' (Henderson, introduction to Macaulay 1907: xiv–xvi). By the 1880s, however, as England experienced the end of the mid-Victorian industrial boom, the subsequent depression in trade and agriculture and the social problems associated with modernization – high unemployment, the degradation of industrial slums, popular democratic and socialist agitation – a conservative reaction developed. Macaulay's *History* would continue to inform political argument into the 1880s – as we shall see, it was especially influential among Ulster Unionists – but the pride in industrial achievement as a national characteristic it reflected would diminish greatly.

Based on the cultural values of the aristocratic élite – to which *new* economic élites were keen to adapt – and whose *cultural* hegemony was not significantly affected by its gradual loss, as a class, of political control, a transformation in how the nation was imagined took place. Its specific form was a transmutation of the nation as an industrial power into a rural arcadia: a timeless and unchanging environment, the repository of authentic English values. Arcadianism was not simply the preserve of Tories, Radicals and Socialists had their own versions. But the Tory version was the most influential. Propagated by prominent Conservatives such as Lord Tennyson and Alfred Austin, it sketched out a mythic ideological landscape within which the Tory conception of the constitution, idealizing the hierarchical, rural social structure, was conceptualized (Wiener 1987: Chs 1 and 2). This idealized rural landscape was the necessary environment for a political conception of the nation centred on the stability of the constitution – Church, Crown, Lords and Commons.

This rural vision, moreover, was all the more appealing because it carried no political risk. In England the countryside had long been integrated into national life. There was no rural society distinct from the 'national' society based in the cities.[7]

As an identity for the nation the rural ideal, based on the home counties, came to effectively displace the industrial image of the mid-century as the most influential conception of the nation, and it carried with it important implications. For example, industrial England was conceived as dynamic and 'young'. Samuel Smiles could claim in 1861 that 'everything in England is young. We are an old people, but a young nation. Our trade is young; and the civilisation of what we call "the masses" has scarcely begun' (quoted in Wiener 1987: 43). The ruralist vision of the 1880s, in rejecting industrialization, also rejected the idea of national youth in favour of the attractions of tradition:

The discovery was made that England was, after all, an *old* country, with a precious heritage in danger of obliteration. . . . An elite separating itself from the sources of dynamism in existing society and striving to adapt itself to an older way of life promoted a change in collective self-image from that of a still young and innovative nation to one ancient and peculiarly stable.   (ibid.)

The ruralist conception of the nation, moreover, carried with it connotations of organic wholeness and authenticity that the image of industrial society, a clearly 'manufactured' society could not. Donald Horne speaks of two competing metaphors of the nation in this period, 'Northern' and 'Southern':

In the *Northern Metaphor* Britain is pragmatic, empirical, calculating, serious and believes in struggle. Its sinful excess is ruthless avarice rationalised in the belief that the prime impulse in all human beings is a rational, ruthless self interest.

In the *Southern Metaphor* Britain is romantic, illogical, muddled, divinely lucky, Anglican, aristocratic, traditional, frivolous, and believes in order and tradition. Its sinful excess is a ruthless pride, rationalised in the belief that men are born to serve.
                                                              (Horne 1969: 22–3)

Both metaphors assumed that 'Britain is best' but it was the southern metaphor that came to predominate, with its seductive idea that national success was due fundamentally not to sustained effort but to a unique cultural inheritance: 'It was not for what they did but for what they were that destiny had rewarded them so lavishly' (ibid: 23).

The victory of the southern metaphor, it has been argued, went together with the devaluation of both the locales and the qualities that had made the industrial revolution. Such places became 'provincial'; provincialism being defined not simply as remoteness from the capital city but much more as

remoteness from one approved style of life. Working-class and lower-middle-class suburbs might be provincial, whereas much of the countryside is not. Rural villages, or ancient cathedral towns that happen to be far from London, are not provincial. 'Things that are rural or ancient', as Horne observed, 'are at the very heart of southern English snobberies, even if they occur in the North. *Provincialism is to live in or near an industrial town to which the industrial revolution gave its significant modern form*'.   (Wiener 1987: 42)

But though it was displaced from its central position as an image for the nation *at home*, the industrial idea still predominated in the imperial and colonial sphere where it was important for the nation to be seen as dynamic and thrusting. And this sphere came to be of crucial importance for the prosperity of Britain in the late nineteenth century, as the loss of economic competitiveness in the European context was compensated for with a drive for imperial markets. Certainly from 1876, with the crowning of Queen Victoria as Empress of India, imperialism centred on an aggressive English nationalism.[8] Monarchism, moreover, was important, not just to the imperial identity of the British, but, increasingly, to the national identity of the United Kingdom itself.

IV

This development was not immediately apparent in the mid-1880s. A.V. Dicey, for example, was to write of it from the longer perspective of 1914 with some surprise as an important change in 'political habits and conventions unconnected with any legal innovation'. The now

established habit of any reigning King or Queen to share and give expression to the moral, . . . the humane, the generous and the patriotic feelings of the British people . . . can fairly be attributed to Queen Victoria as an original and a noble contribution towards national and imperial statesmanship.
                                                        (Dicey 1885/1914: I)

It was, significantly, he noted, a development that coincided with and tended to counter the divisive growth of the party system (ibid.: ci–cii). However, Dicey's description of this development as an altruistic contribution to the national interest by Queen Victoria need not be taken too seriously. As David Cannadine argues, in this period Britain was an urban, industrial, mass society, with class loyalties and class conflicts set in a genuinely national framework for the first time: 'In such an age of change, crisis, and dislocation, the "preservation of anachronism", the deliberate ceremonial presentation of an impotent but venerated monarch as a unifying symbol of permanence and national community became both possible and necessary'. Moreover, with developments in the media such as the emergence of a working class, conservative and patriotic yellow press, and new photographic and printing techniques, it became possible for great ceremonial occasions to be described with 'unprecedented immediacy and vividness in a sentimental, emotional, admiring way which appealed to a broader cross-section of the public than before' (Cannadine 1983: 121–3). In effect, the preservation of the monarchy as the master symbol of national community was increasingly developed mythically: 'all criticism of the monarch in the domestic press disappeared in the desire to present the sovereign as the pure essence of the nation' (ibid.: 123).

Thus, if Protestantism, as a major element of national identity that integrated the national sphere of public life with that of everyday experience was gradually on the wane, as it was in this period, the monarch, Queen Victoria, was ideally suitable as a substitute. Indeed, a vital element in the restoration of the Queen in public esteem, following the brief resurgence of republicanism in the early 1870s, was her role as mother of a large family. A serious illness affecting the Prince of Wales at the end of 1871 was the trigger for a mass public reaction in her favour (Martin 1962: 49). Walter Bagehot's discussion of the monarchy helps us to understand why this transformation in public attitudes was so easily effected. He points, for example, to the ease with which the public can assess the mind and will of a single individual; something that is easily and empathetically done in the case of a mother faced with the serious illness of a child. In the same context, there was the Prince of Wales's marriage, a 'brilliant edition of a universal fact' and likewise compelling public attention. But the real importance of the monarch in this respect was constitutional:

we have whole classes unable to comprehend the idea of a constitution – unable to feel the least attachment to impersonal laws. Most do indeed vaguely know that there are some other institutions besides the Queen. . . . But a vast number like their minds to dwell more upon her than upon anything else, and therefore she is inestimable. A republic has only difficult ideas in Government; a Constitutional Monarchy . . . has a comprehensible element for the vacant many, as well as complex laws and notions for the inquiring few.

(Bagehot 1867/1976: 82–5)

To Bagehot's explanation for the popular attachment to monarchy in this period we can add Tom Nairn's more recent work on the British monarchy. Highly critical of Bagehot's celebration of deference as a national characteristic, among other things, Nairn persuasively argues that while the monarchy represented, and still represents, a fundamentally anti-democratic oligarchy it is difficult to remove it because to attack the structure is to appear almost treasonable, to attack national identity itself.[9] Nairn points up the centrality of 'familialism' to it, and how this has worked to promote a sense of community from above, as against the dangerously disturbing potentialities of *ethnic* nationalism. Thus, he acutely observes, this monarchic state nationalism has always worked best when ethnic nationalism was weakest. In fact, its purpose was largely to marginalize such forms of nationalism:

what followed under Victoria is . . . this: Britain couldn't do without a 'nationalism', in the sense of an ideological armour for coping with modernity. But it had to have a strongly dissembling one, a national identity simultaneous above *and* below all that – an undoctrinaire formula bridging directly from the popular to the transcendent, from the 'ordinary' to the supernally grand and ethical . . . a pseudo-nationalism fostering 'community' from above and bestowing a sense of 'belonging' without the damnable nuisance of ethnic and rudely democratic complaint.   (Nairn 1988a: 183)

There was, in fact, a fundamental and inverse relationship between the lack of real political power the monarch could exercise and the vast increase in the social influence of the monarchy. In this respect, Frederick Engels argued that in England 'the social aspect has gradually prevailed over the political one and has made it subservient. The whole of English politics is fundamentally social in nature' (quoted ibid.: 207–8). So much did this state of affairs depend on the monarchy, the 'subjective apex', that if it was removed the whole artificial constitutional structure would collapse:

The English Constitution is an inverted pyramid; the apex is at the same time the base. And the less important the monarchic element became in reality, the more important did it become for the Englishman. Nowhere is a non-ruling personage more revered than in England. The English press surpasses the German by far in slavish servility.   (quoted, ibid.: 203–4)

The truth of Engels's observations on the social importance of the monarchy was reflected in the politics of Joseph Chamberlain. From the early 1870s, when he briefly supported and then dissociated himself from the small republican movement in Britain, Chamberlain, until he converted to Unionism in 1886, made a trenchant critique of established institutions. He was, however, always careful to avoid explicit criticism of the monarchy; indeed he argued that political reform would greatly strengthen the ties that bound the monarchy in the people's affections (Loughlin 1992: 212).

Nevertheless, while popular affection for the monarchy was strong, the specific meaning the monarchy had for the industrial working class is problematic. It has been suggested that while the 'familial' aspect of royalty made it relevant to the working class 'at the most immediate and personal level', they were otherwise generally indifferent to it: that while they apparently accepted the monarchy and the social hierarchy of which it was the apex, it was, nevertheless, 'utilized within a dense and inward-looking working-class culture which . . . created and sustained its own values and meaning within that hierarchy' (Baker, thesis, 1978: 5). But if the influence of the monarchy functioned so as to neutralize any potential working-class threat to the established order, there was another social group – the lower middle class – that believed that order to be already in the process of collapse and for whom the monarchy was much more emotively symbolic. This sector, socially and politically conservative, was concerned to 'reassert a system of values that was breaking down. . . . [In particular] the verities of religious faith . . . were not only being questioned but were undergoing wholesale abandonment'. For this social group, salvation lay in the creation of a national patriotic consensus (Price 1977: 90–94). Not surprisingly, it responded most enthusiastically to the concerns expressed about contemporary politics by Dicey and Salisbury. And what is striking about its patriotism is the fundamentally mythic nature of its expression: 'appeals to British rights that were never defined, to inherent British superiority that was never explained, to British valour that was extolled above all other virtues' (ibid.: 95). It was this mentality that was mobilized in opposition to Gladstone's Home Rule scheme of 1886 – ironically, a measure which, by reforging the constitutional arrangements of the United Kingdom, sought to strengthen British nationality.

V

The complexity of the United Kingdom as a 'national' community in this period makes the imagining of it highly problematic. The existence, by the mid-1880s, of a radical nationalist movement in the south of Ireland meant that British nationality was not coterminus with the borders of the state. But even for those groups that accepted it, there was no consensus on its nature. There was no single national myth to account for the experience of all of the people; rather, two party-based myths – Liberal and Conservative – existed, together with a developing royal myth of national identity which, though it served to legitimize the hierarchical social vision at the heart of Conservatism, yet functioned to convey a sense of the United Kingdom as a national community in a more effective way than either of the party-based myths. Again, two different images of the nation existed in this period, one northern/industrial, the other southern/rural.

The process of national imagining, moreover, has to take account of the vocabulary of identity in any given period – in this period, especially, the language of late Victorian religious and race theorizing – and fluctuations in the applicability of identities: an important consideration in regard to the expansion of 'Englishness' in the 1880s. Yet again, there is the consideration that conditions of crisis will intensify, for those groups that feel themselves to be most directly threatened, the process of imagining the national community – enhancing its mythic properties by screening out to a greater extent than might otherwise have been the case the complexity of political realities. In sum, then, the process of imagining the British national community in the mid-1880s is a dynamic and complex, rather than static, process. It is in this context that the question of Ulster Unionism's membership of the British nation must be considered.

Notes

1. For a stimulating analysis of such arguments in ancient Greece, the USA and England, see Finley (1975: 34–59).
2. Gardiner, *et al.* (1878: 248–344). For an argument stressing the relevance of the 'earliest constitution' of England to contemporary political conditions, see

Freeman (1872/1906: ix–x). Such arguments were also widespread in school history textbooks (Chancellor 1970: 50–51).

3. For a nuanced discussion of Englishness, see the articles by Colls and Dodd (Colls and Dodd (eds) 1986: 1–61).

4. The employment of such arguments in the Irish context is well documented. See Curtis Jr (1973); Lebow (1976). On their application to other subject European nationalities, see Kiernan (1972: 28–30).

5. See the discussion on relations between the churches in Britain in Robbins (1988: Ch. 3).

6. For a useful discussion see Ensor (1936: 137–43, 305–10, 527–31). Even Scottish Protestantism lost much of its anti-Catholicism in this period (Bruce 1985: Ch. 1).

7. See Blondel (1963: 24–6). On the political and economic limitations this development both reflected and enhanced see Nairn (1977: 28–44). On the limitations of 'ruralism' as a *total* explanation of British economic decline, see Hobsbawm (1969: 183–94).

8. This nationalism was to a large extent centred on the City of London. As Britain faltered as a manufacturing power, the City aggressively promoted imperial federation to facilitate its domination of markets in the Empire (Smith, thesis, 1985: 234, 265–6).

9. See Nairn ('Republicanism', *New Statesman*, 11 March 1988). This point was also made at the turn of the century by the French writer, Emile Boutmy (1904: 188–9): 'Royalty is not only the image of authority but the author and symbol of national unity. Without it, in the past, the incongruous elements of which the nation is composed would never have mingled with one another'.

2

HOME RULE, ULSTER UNIONISM AND THE INTEGRITY OF THE NATION 1886–1910

Convinced that his Home Rule scheme of 1886 would effect the integration of Irish nationality with a wider imperial patriotism, Gladstone was ill-prepared – politically and ideologically – to deal with the negative reaction of Ulster Unionists to his plans. Allied with a Parnellite Party insisting on the existence of a one-nation Ireland and persuaded by his reading of the 'nationalist' activities of the Volunteer movement in Ulster in the late eighteenth century, Gladstone took the view that Ulster Protestants were fundamentally nationalists and would readily accept Home Rule once it was established (Loughlin 1986: Chs 5, 6, 9, 10). Consequently his Home Rule scheme failed to deal adequately with their apprehension of being ruled by a Dublin parliament which, they imagined, would be controlled by the despotic Roman Catholic Church. Also, in failing to deal with Ulster Protestant fears he provided the Unionist movement with one of its strongest arguments against Home Rule – the existence of a staunchly British community in the north of Ireland whose interests and physical well-being should not be sacrificed to the demands of rebellious Irish Nationalists. But what did it mean to argue that Ulster Protestants were British?

I

The view that crises work to enhance the relevance of national myths for a community is borne out by an examination of the political crisis occasioned by Gladstone's Home Rule plans of 1886. It heightened, almost to hysteria, the apprehensions of Tories and supporters of the status quo about the security of civilized order itself. Their caste of mind was well expressed by Lady Sophia Palmer, daughter of the Earl of Selborne: 'We all lost a great deal of time when we learned the 10 commandments – to rejoice in the Magna Charta and ached our heads over Adam Smith – Fawcett, and even J.S. Mill! It is all disproven – and we have to unlearn and learn anew.' (Palmer to Sir Arthur Gooden, 6 April 1886, quoted in

Lubenow 1988: 69). The anxieties of the establishment were reflected at the popular level.

Political controversy crystallized and stimulated the anti-Irish and anti-Roman Catholic prejudice that was still a significant element of British popular opinion in the 1880s. Less than a week after Gladstone introduced his Home Rule Bill, Lord Harrowby wrote: 'the depth and intensity of feeling excited by the Separatist scheme is beyond anything we have seen. An anti-Roman feeling is on the verge of rising.' (Harrowby to Lord Carnaervon, 12 April 1886, quoted ibid.: 268–9). Nor was this prejudice confined to Conservatives. Wilfrid Blunt wrote of the Liberal Party that the plea made from the constituencies to the Party's central office was, 'give us a Jew if you like but not a Catholic', and put Gladstone's defeat at the general election of 1886 down to 'the No Popery cry [which was] almost as strong an argument with Radicals as with Tories.' (Blunt diary, 16 June, 17 July 1886, quoted ibid.: 269). The following quotation from a pamphlet distributed by T.H. Sidebottom, the successful Tory candidate at Hyde, and intended to inflame the rising tide of popular sectarianism, was not exceptional:

Q. Have the Irish ever had Home Rule and how did they behave?
A. They murdered every Englishman and Protestant they could lay their hands on in 1641. They were set on by the priests, who said that the killing of them was a meritorious act. Altogether they killed in that year 150,000 Protestants – men, women and children.   (Quoted in Loughlin 1986: 173)

What is noteworthy about this question, apart from its naked appeal to Protestant prejudice, is how it reflected the Unionist tendency to emphasize the 'English' identity of Ulster Protestants as their importance to the anti-Home Rule case was recognized. In this context common 'Anglo-Saxon' racial characteristics were allied to a common Protestantism as the basis of that identity; and this racial identity was clarified by invidious comparison with the supposed characteristics of Irish Romanist Celts. E. Ashmead-Bartlett's explanation of 'What Separatism Means', for example, drew heavily on popular Anglo-Saxon racialism. The lazy, lawless 'Celt', he argued, had never been 'an imperial or ruling race'; however, in the east of Ulster 'where the descendants of . . . Saxon colonists are the bulk of the population, the only really prosperous and law-abiding portion of Ireland [exists]. . . . There, a race of British blood and of the Protestant faith are the mainstay of the British connection', as well as being the most progressive and civilizing element among the Irish population.[1] Such arguments, of course, did not by any means constitute the whole of the Unionist case against Home Rule. Nevertheless, they were an important element of that part of the Unionist case that focused on national identity and, like all good propaganda, they drew on a discourse that, in a period of aggressive imperialist expansionism, had wide popular resonance.

'Ulster', in fact, had impinged prominently on the British popular consciousness during the land war of 1879–82, when it appeared to be a bastion of British civilization, free of the anarchy and agrarian crime that was seemingly endemic in the Celtic and Roman Catholic south (O'Brien 1880: 44–5). In this respect it appeared to validate the popular English self-image at a time when the term 'English' was widely applied to communities of supposed Anglo-Saxon race. Matthew Arnold, writing in 1882, could describe 'the Protestant north' of Ireland as representing English middle-class civilization 'in full force' (Arnold 1882/1891: 48). It was very much in this light that Arnold wrote to Goldwin Smith on 18 January 1886, when it became clear that Gladstone would introduce a Home Rule Bill, complaining that the scheme would 'merge Ulster in Celtic Ireland' when *it should be kept distinct as a centre of natural Englishism and loyalty* [my italics] (see Haultain (ed.) printed sources, 1913: 175–6). John Beddoe, in his seminal work *The Races of Britain*, subscribed substantially to the view that the population of Ulster was racially superior to that of the rest of Ireland: 'For ages . . . the Ulster men [have] . . . differed by their manly and vigorous character from their soft and treacherous countrymen in the south' (Beddoe 1885/1971: 146). Paradoxically, even when Unionist public figures sought to argue that the United Kingdom should not be broken up by conceding Irish Home Rule because the races of the kingdom had intermixed to such an extent that no pure Irish race existed on which to base a separate Irish nationality, they still sought to retain the idea of the racial separation of Ulster from the rest of the island.[2]

To a considerable extent, the influence of such ideas about Ulster in Britain can be explained by the account of the province given in Lord Macaulay's massively influential and patriotic work, *The History of England* (5 vols, 1848–61) – a work that was to have enormous influence among Ulster Unionists also, in terms of shaping their understanding of their British identity. Macaulay, for instance, in describing the differences between the civilized 'Englishry' (Macaulay 1848–61/1907: 42) and the 'aboriginal' population in the seventeenth century, used language that within twenty years would be both the common currency of late Victorian imperialism and of debate on the Ulster question:

the same line of demarcation that separated religions separated races. . . . On the same soil dwelt two populations locally intermixed, morally and politically sundered. . . . They sprang from different stocks. They spoke different languages. They had different national characters as strongly opposed as any two national characters in Europe. They were in widely different stages of civilisation. The relation in which the minority stood to the majority resembled the relation in which the followers of Cortez stood to the Indians of Mexico. . . .

The great predominance of numbers on one side was more than compensated by a great superiority of intelligence, vigour and organisation on the other. The English settler seems to have been, in knowledge, energy and perseverance, rather above than below the average level of the population of the mother country. The aboriginal peasantry, on the contrary, were in an almost savage state. They never worked till they felt the sting of hunger. They were content with accommodation inferior to that which, in happier countries, was provided for domestic cattle. . . . The dominion which one of these populations exercised over the other was the dominion of wealth over poverty, of knowledge over ignorance, of civilised over uncivilised man.   (ibid.: 206–7)

Macaulay, moreover, had little hesitation in applying this perspective to contemporary Ulster:

Belfast has become one of the greatest and most flourishing seats of industry in the British isles. A busy population of a hundred thousand souls is collected there. The duties annually paid at the Custom House exceed the duties annually paid at the Custom House of London in the most prosperous years of the reign of Charles the Second. Other Irish towns may present more picturesque forms to the eye, but Belfast is the only large Irish town in which the traveller is not disgusted by the loathsome aspect and odour of long lines of human dens far inferior in comfort and cleanliness to the dwellings which, in happier countries, are provided for cattle.
                                                                              (ibid.: 502–3)

Macaulay also gave the Ulster Protestants a prominent role in his lengthy discussion of the battle of the Boyne and exulted over the outcome of the siege of Derry: it was a contest between nations and the victory lay with the nation which, though interior in number, 'was superior in civilisation, in capacity for self government, and in staunchness of resolution' (ibid.: 498–510).

In short, Macaulay, popularly regarded as the greatest of English historians, gave the Ulster Protestants a major role in the most important events associated with the most influential of British national myths, the Glorious Revolution. And it is hardly surprising that a community so lavishly praised in Macaulay's History should be excessively influenced by it. As the volumes of the History came off the presses, the sections relevant to Ulster were extensively quoted in the loyalist press[3], while the extent to which it informed Unionist politics was clearly indicated during the first Home Rule crisis. In 1886 speculation was rife as to whether Lord Wolseley, commander-in-chief of Crown forces in Ireland and a direct descendant of the Wolseley Macaulay described as having routed the Jacobite forces at Newtownbutler – 'These historical facts were well known to a large part of the Ulster population . . . [and were] recalled with great significance' – would dare to attack Ulster Protestants who might oppose the implementation of home rule on Ulster (McKnight 1896: ii, 146; see also Bullock n.d. [1931]: 188–93). And when, in Parliament, the Ulster Orange leader, William 'Ballykilbeg' Johnston, claimed in the face of Nationalist derision that Belfast was prosperous because it was Protestant, he declared that the proof was to be found in Macaulay's History.[4] But while Nationalists might ridicule such views they did, in effect, recognize Macaulay's influence on Ulster Unionist opinion. When Justin McCarthy won the Derry city seat at the general election of 1886, the Nationalist Party organ, United Ireland, used McCarthy's success as part of an argument rejecting Macaulay's claims on the racial superiority of Ulster Protestants to the 'native Irish' (United Ireland, 30 October 1886). Even today the Ulster sections of Macaulay's History are being employed to support the Unionist case (see Lucy (ed.): 1989a). Macaulay did make some strictures about how the 'Englishry' abused their 'superior civilisation', especially the excesses which sometimes accompanied the siege of Derry commemorations. But, as one Protestant minister to whom Thomas McKnight mentioned this replied, in Ulster such criticisms were of little consequence (McKnight 1896: i, 10).

The credibility of Macaulay's Ulster arguments was enhanced by the fact that visitors to the province had little difficulty in finding 'empirical' evidence that appeared to validate them. Travellers coming to Ulster, especially from the south, were often struck by its 'English' appearance, a legacy of the plantation and the progressive industrialization of north-east Ulster in the nineteenth century.[5] Just as the English rural landscape that was to become so integral a part of perceptions of English national identity in the late nineteenth century was not a natural wilderness but one shaped and ordered by human activity (Lowenthal 1991: 7–10), so the Ulster landscape that denoted the region's 'Englishness' was not an uncultivated terrain but one largely shaped by the Protestant people. Thomas McKnight, proceeding northward to take up the editorship of the *Northern Whig*, was impressed by the fact that as the train entered the province 'the landscape gradually improved. It began to show signs of energetic industry, of busy and prosperous life such as was powerfully wanting among the much more romantic scenery of the south and west' (McKnight 1896: i, 6). McKnight, of course, was a Unionist, but his account was mirrored by other, politically disinterested, sources. A neutral French visitor in 1886 was similarly impressed:

If you did not know beforehand that you are entering a new Ireland through Enniskillen, an Ireland Scotch, Protestant manufacturing, a glance through the carriage window would suffice to reveal the fact. . . . Another symptom . . . is the aspect of the landscape; no more uncultivated fields, no more endless bogs and fens . . . all gives the impression of a properly cultivated land.
                                                    (Grousset 1887/1986: 271–2)

F.F. Moore put it more succinctly when he wrote that Ulster 'was like a piece hacked out of Britain between the Tweed and the Tyne' (Moore 1914: 70). Unionists were, of course, proud of the distinctive character of the province, reading into it proof of their superior qualities as a community to southern Irishmen[6] and substantive evidence of their claim to an 'English' identity, a claim Pascal Grousset found being strongly made by members of the Belfast business class in 1886 who were vehemently opposed to Gladstone's attempt to 'deprive us of our rights as British subjects. . . . We shall repeat that we are Englishmen and we will not be anything else' (Grousset 1887/1986: 291–2).

As this comment suggests, underlying the Ulster Unionist position was the perception, noted in Chapter 1, of the close relationship between nationality and the constitution, a perception common among British right-wing commentators, and one which saw constitutional change as inevitably impacting on national identity. In this context, for Ulster Unionists, the Act of Union was their cornerstone of the British constitution, one that guaranteed, not only freedom from oppression by Catholic Nationalists, but the means by which they could legitimately identity themselves as British – the terms 'British' and 'English' being virtually interchangeable in this period. As one commentator put it, 'the Union brought [Ulster Unionists] . . . into full communion with the great national life which they had a right to share and opened up to them a part in the great future of what we . . . call the English nation.' (Harrison 1888: 100–101). Or, as a delegate to the Irish Presbyterian General Assembly in 1890 expressed it, despite their specific problems with Westminster administrations, it was still great 'to be an Englishman in the wider sense of the term.'[7] At the same time, however, it is worth looking more closely at the particular concept of 'English' identity that was being appealed to. While Ulster could provide examples of an ordered rural landscape that set it apart from the rest of Ireland, it was not its rural aspect that provided the dominant image of the region, but rather its impressive and developing industrial character. As such, this persona assimilated to the 'northern' metaphor of Britain described by Donald Horne (see Chapter 1, pp 15–17). The characteristics that made Britain great according to this metaphor – pragmatism, empiricism, shrewdness and Puritan bourgeois enterprise – were exactly those that characterized the stereotype of the 'hard headed' Ulster Protestant. But while the 'northern' metaphor may have been the dominant image of Britain when Macaulay was writing his great patriotic *History*, it had, by the 1880s, become devalued in favour of the 'southern' metaphor, based on the home counties and emphasizing rural community and 'organic' wholeness.

It is important not to place too much significance on this point, but it is, nevertheless, noteworthy that at the very time that the Ulster Protestants' membership of the United Kingdom was being put in question, the image of the British nation they naturally identified with was losing much of its influence. It still retained its significance in the wider imperial sphere, but that dimension of Britishness was clearly less substantial and secure. It is also worth noting that while the language of race and religion largely provided the terms with which Ulster Unionists asserted their British identity, it would be wrong to assume that their concept of identity was always sharply delineated. In fact, a study of Unionist speeches delivered over the period of the first Home Rule crisis and focusing on how they expressed their identity revealed a complex picture. Beyond abstract notions of Britishness and imperial 'heritage' and 'status', the discourse on identity often displayed a quite bewildering range of associations of ideas, with race, class and national distinctions often ambiguously and confusedly employed in the same speech. The term 'nation', for example, could be used to refer to the Ulster Unionist community and the population of Great Britain, while others used this term to refer to all the peoples of the British Isles (see Loughlin 1986: 153–4, 295–6). Nevertheless, if no sharply delineated consensus on national identity emerged from the study – and in this context it is important to remember that Unionist speakers were not giving replies to specific questions on their concept of nationality – what was identified was a repertoire of terms which was employed to explain their identity, with the significance of any one or more of them being determined by specific political contexts. Thus, for instance, when Michael Davitt claimed that Ulster Unionists were only alien settlers in Ulster, neither Celtic by race or habit, ethnicity and race were the concepts employed by the *Belfast News-Letter* in making its reply (ibid.: 160). For the purpose of this study, however, the central focus of which is the national identity of Ulster Unionists, an attempt has been made to provide greater depth to our understanding of their perceptions of Britishness through a survey of editorial opinion in a wide range of Unionist papers, covering local, British, imperial and foreign affairs.

II

Whether true or not, British provincial papers in the nineteenth century were believed to have great influence with the communities that they served. Their coverage traditionally had given prominence to national rather than local issues. But from the 1870s the nature of their content gradually changed until, by the turn of the century, the position common today was reached, whereby local interests greatly predominated (Jackson 1971: 11–15). What was true of the provincial press in Britain was also true of Ulster, with the exception that, among Unionist papers at least, the preoccupation with national, imperial and foreign affairs persisted until well after 1914. And even if they did not carry the influence with their readership that the press in Britain was supposed to, the view taken here is that, as organs of opinion embedded in the life of their communities, they at least generally reflected the world-view of their readers.

In conducting this survey, the assumption was made initially that newspapers in the Unionist 'frontier' areas of west Tyrone, Fermanagh, Londonderry, Down and Armagh would express a more acute anxiety on issues of identity and nationality – because of their vulnerability – than those in the eastern Unionist heartland. This assumption proved to be wrong. As it turned out, there was no appreciable difference on these issues across Unionist Ulster as a whole, while the terms employed to give meaning to national identity were also the same.

Indeed, one of the most striking features of editorial comment during the Home Rule controversies of the Gladstonian period was how the associated discourse of race, religion and Englishness that was employed by Unionist politicians and public figures in their references to the Ulster question resonated in the local press. The Armagh newspaper, the *Ulster Gazette*, for example, expressed a widely shared view when it argued (10 April 1886) that Home Rule would entail a war of 'race and religion' in Ireland and that we are 'one with England'.[8] The *Tyrone Constitution*, in disparaging Irish Home Rule 'Celts' (21 May 1886, see also issue for 29 December 1893), called on the English people to keep their obligations to 'their brethren here'. It agreed with the *Tyrone Courier* that Irish Celts hated anything 'in the shape of a Saxon' (see issues for 10 April, 21 May 1886). The *Witness* expanded on the theme of racial difference by pointing out supposed similarities in the social habits of Irish Catholics and the Maori natives of New Zealand: 'Like Paddy they are idle, voluble, rollicking, emotional, hospitable, ready to fight and kiss at a moment's notice'.[9]

Again, in the local press, as in Unionist discourse generally, identity with the population of Britain went together with the view that nationality and the constitution were inextricably linked. Despite Gladstone's claim that Irish Home Rule was compatible with a wider British identity, the emphatic conclusion of the Unionist press was that a separate constitution for Ireland meant the creation of a separate nation and that under it they would 'cease to be Britons'.[10] As the *Ballymena Observer* expressed it (21 July 1893), 'Ireland a nation' did not exist because 'Ireland being now submerged in the larger life of England has no claim to the autonomy of a nation; and . . . has more than her fair share of partnership with England'. This paper also expressed an opinion as common in Ulster as it was among Unionists in Britain, namely, that a distinction was to be drawn between the 'misguided electorate' that had put Gladstone in office and the real English nation whose willing consent to their being subjected to nationalist tyranny it was 'absolutely incredible' to contemplate.[11] It was to enhance his claim to be the 'true' representative of the real English nation that Lord Salisbury, on his visit to Ulster in 1893, informed Unionists that the minister who recommended James I to 'plant Ulster' was an ancestor of his own (*Newtownards Chronicle*, 27 May 1893). Indeed, the historical resonance of the Home Rule issue had already been brought home to Unionists in June 1892 when the bones of Protestants believed to have been massacred in Portadown during the 1641 rebellion were unearthed during the construction of a quay in the town (see *Belfast Newsletter*, 23 June 1892; *Witness*, 24 June 1892).

Salisbury's remarks and the Portadown discoveries informed an already well-established Unionist historical sense of community, something the loyalist press exploited ruthlessly in 1886 to whip up popular Protestant passions against Gladstone's first Home Rule scheme (Loughlin 1986: 161–4), and which itself was only a more extreme rendering of a view of Ulster Protestant history that 'was relentlessly rehashed at Orange church and political meetings throughout the nineteenth century' (Hempton 1990: 245). Thus the claim recently made, that it was only during the period of the third Home Rule crisis (1912–14) that 'an Ulster history was discovered and elucidated in anti-home rule tracts' (Jackson 1989: 14–15), is hardly credible.[12]

The Gladstonian phase of the Home Rule struggle was one which saw the emergence of the intense commitment of British Unionist leaders to the Ulster cause, and which lasted until the outbreak of the First World War. In the period 1886–92, all the Unionist Party leaders – Lord Hartington, Salisbury, Arthur Balfour and Joseph Chamberlain – visited northern Ireland and pledged their commitment to the Ulster Unionist cause (Loughlin 1986: 279). Of these leaders, however, it was Joseph Chamberlain who identified himself most closely with Ulster Unionism and who was most enthusiastic in promoting their 'English' identity.

Strongly influenced by Dilke's *Greater Britain* and Seeley's *Expansion of England*, Chamberlain, like Seeley, argued that historical development was in the direction of large state entities that would submerge and supersede the small nationalities within their boundaries. Thus, in the United Kingdom, the separate nationalities of Welsh, Scots and English were now merely local divisions of the developing British/English imperial race. Ireland, of course, posed a serious obstacle to the complete merger of the state's nationalities, but Chamberlain preferred to argue that, viewed in the longer historical perspective, this would be seen to have been a temporary problem: history would take care of it. Moreover, to compensate for the rejection of British nationality by Irish Catholic Celts, there was in Ulster an Anglo-Saxon, Protestant community, industrious, law abiding, enthusiastically British and whose virtues, as Chamberlain would frequently argue, contrasted markedly with the supposed racial inferiority, agrarian criminality and business incapacity of the population of the southern provinces. Not surprisingly, Chamberlain was highly popular in Ulster where the Protestant population was naturally keen to support his claim that they were an authentic part of the British nation (Loughlin 1992: 208–19).

Throughout this period Protestantism provided one of the most enduring and easily exploitable bonds of identity between the Unionists of Ulster and the population of Britain. And loyalist papers were keen to report evidence that Protestantism was taken as seriously in Britain as in the north of Ireland.[13] Moreover, a number of religiously centred controversies arose in this period that allowed that element of Britishness to crystallize, issues such as Arthur Balfour's proposed Roman Catholic university for Ireland, ritualism in the Church of England, [14] and the Roman Catholic Eucharistic Congress of 1908, when the prospect of Roman prelates processing through the streets of London in ceremonial robes and carrying the Eucharist provoked widespread popular Protestant opposition. So intense was the opposition that the Asquith Government felt compelled to conciliate it by forcing the processionists to obey remnants of the penal laws that prohibited such processions. The controversy caused considerable embarrassment for Asquith's Government when the Catholic Archbishop of Westminster, Cardinal Bourne, published his correspondence with the Government on the issue, which indicated its initial willingness to permit the procession.[15] It also allowed the extremist Protestant Alliance to revive age-old fears about the threat to British national security posed by the Papacy, fears that resonated easily with the beliefs of Ulster Protestants. Indeed, the Independent Unionist MP for South Belfast, T.H. Sloan, was actively engaged in the campaign against the procession, while Ulster loyalist opinion rejoiced in its outcome (*Belfast News-Letter*, 14–18 September 1908).

However, while religious controversies allowed Ulster Unionists to assert their Britishness, they did so in circumstances that were necessarily problematic. That identity could be much more completely expressed when directed, in classically nationalist terms, against the alien other. That context allowed Ulster Unionists to forget the difficulties of their relationship with the rest of the United Kingdom in the simplified imagining of a homogeneous British nation pitted against external enemies. The commentaries in the local Ulster Unionist press on a range of international issues in this period demonstrate a patriotic world-view at one with that of Conservative Unionism in Britain.

Gladstone, for example, was blamed for forcing the country to pursue an insane foreign policy that entailed national humiliation: 'instead of exhibiting the robust courage for which England has long been famous we have shown ourselves to be weak, irresolute and vacillating' (*Tyrone Courier*, 1 December 1884).[16] The ambitions of England's traditional enemy, France, aroused similar heated passions: 'we' were on the eve of serious trouble because of French aggression in Siam. While France was getting greedy, 'this country' had given away her right to a say in the matter (*Witness*, 28 July, 8 September 1893). Ulster Unionist opinion on England's other, and more threatening enemy in the late nineteenth century – Russia – was even more bellicose. Russia was observed to be getting too close to 'our own doors' in India (*Witness*, 21 January 1898). In view of the Russian threat, the *Ballymena Observer* (6 January 1899) declared:

As an island power we have a right – and indeed it is a necessity to our national existence – to be all powerful at sea. Our naval supremacy does not menace any other power. It only protects our own shores. . . . England is bound to maintain her naval supremacy.

When, in the same month, Czar Nicholas II made peace overtures to improve Anglo-Russian relations, the *Newry Telegraph* (28 January 1899) reacted thus:

As a nation of shopkeepers we have no desire to see our relations with our neighbours disturbed at any time. A nation cannot prosper and war at the same time. On selfish grounds alone we favour peace, but taking the high ground of the most Christian nation in the world[!] we are wedded to peace.

Nevertheless, Anglo-Russian relations continued to be unfriendly and Ulster Unionist opinion reacted accordingly. When Japan, a British ally, emerged victorious from the Russo-Japanese War of 1904–5, the *Cookstown News* (31 December 1905) produced a free commemorative souvenir poster of Admiral Tojo, commander of the Japanese forces, describing him as the 'Nelson of Japan'.

In the context of their ultra-patriotic concern for British national interests, it is worth noting that Ulster Unionists adopted a xenophobic attitude to the supposed 'alien menace' threatening Britain at the turn of the century. Hatred of Russia did not, apparently, induce sympathy for the victims of anti-Semitic pogroms in Russia, significant numbers of which sought refuge in Britain. Although the Jewish refugees congregated mainly in industrial areas such as Manchester, Leeds and, especially, the East End of London, the loyalist press – taking its cue from the hostile nativist reaction in Britain (on the response to the Jewish influx in Britain, see Lebzelter 1981: 88–104; Panayi 1993: 10–11) – reacted as if they had all suddenly arrived in Belfast. The *Ballymena Observer* (2 January 1903), in reporting the case of a Jew arrested for theft, railed against the 'evils of allowing alien criminals to enter this country unrestrictedly'. The *Down Recorder* (12 December 1903) praised the introduction of an aliens bill to stem the flood of 'criminal aliens', and when this measure was proceeding through its parliamentary stages the *Portadown News* (1 October 1904) commented that, while it approved of the use of cheap Chinese labour in South Africa,[17] it could not accept the 'immigration of impoverished foreigners into this country with the design of underselling British labour'.

The most important focus of loyalist patriotism in this period, however, arose with the outbreak of the Boer War. Loyalist support for the war, moreover, was enhanced by the presence of the Irish nationalist enemy within, and which was active in support of the Boers. Loyalist support took a variety of forms, with Orange lodges in all parts of the north forming volunteer companies for service in South Africa, though their services were politely refused by the War Office. However, 'Patriotic Days' and public meetings to maintain support for the war effort; the organizing of 'War Funds' by local councils for the relief of the relatives of those killed or wounded in the conflict; and lectures on the implications of the conflict for the Empire, all were characteristic of the Ulster Unionist response to the conflict.[18] Shortly after its outbreak, virtually every Unionist newspaper in Ulster threw its support behind the Government, their collective attitude being expressed in a *Belfast News-Letter* editorial (13 October 1899): 'It is we who are being attacked, and the object aimed at is to drive us out of South Africa.'[19] Of all the regions of the United Kingdom, Ulster appears to have given the most enthusiastic support to the war effort (Meehan, thesis, 1992: 40). Moreover, the large numbers of Irish Catholics fighting in Irish and British regiments allowed at least some Unionists to proclaim, in this specific context, a greater pride in their Irishness (see ibid.: 39–40) than was evident during the Home Rule crises of 1886 and 1893, when the fear existed of being associated with the nationalist Irishness of the south and west of Ireland.

The intensity of the Ulster Unionist commitment to the war effort is partly explained by their close relationship with Joseph Chamberlain, the Colonial Secretary whose aggressive approach to the South Africa issue did much to provoke hostilities (see Judd 1968: 162–71), and a hero to Ulster Unionists because of his enthusiastic commitment to their cause. They proved to be no less strongly committed to Chamberlain's tariff reform campaign that followed hard on the heels of the Boer War and which was intended to bind the Empire together. Again, virtually every Ulster Unionist newspaper supported it. The *Banbridge Chronicle* (19 September 1903) expressed the fundamental concerns of northern Unionists and the hopes they invested in Chamberlain as follows:

In the business of imperial federation in fiscal matters with our extensive and progressive colonies, he will have on his side the instinctive and deep-rooted feelings of kinship that distinguishes Britons on both sides of the globe and which he has the principal means of bringing to the surface in times of stress.[20]

This period provided many occasions for Ulster Unionists to give expression to their British national identity. Historians, however, have been largely reluctant to accept that they were, or are, 'truly' British. The range of debate has been wide, covering, for example, race and ethnicity as factors in national identity, the Ulster–Britain relationship, and the primacy loyalists gave to the province's affairs.

III

One of the most influential recent theories on the identity of Ulster Unionists has been D.W. Miller's 'contractarian' thesis (Miller 1978), which argues that the defining characteristic of the loyalists' relationship with Britain, was, and is, not a common nationality – Miller defines Ulster Protestants as a community having no nationality – but the belief that a civil 'contract' existed between themselves and successive British governments, to the effect that, in return for colonizing and 'civilizing' Ulster, their rights, especially the right not to be handed over to their enemies, had to be respected by the authorities in London. The merits of Miller's argument I have discussed elsewhere (see Loughlin 1986: 154–8) and do not intend to discuss them at length here, except to state that while enough evidence exists to establish this notion as an element in loyalist thinking, there is little to support the view that it was the central focus shaping their relationship with Britain – a conclusion supported by a more recent and extensive analysis of the Ulster Protestant world-view in the nineteenth century (see Hempton and Hill 1991). Likewise, neither is there much support, either in my own work or in that of Hempton and Hill, for the contention that an Ulster nationalism – focusing on Ulster as a separate national territory with a unique history, traditions and culture differing from other national groups – developed in the late nineteenth century.

The most recent proposition that such a nationalism, or a version of it, did exist has been made by Alvin Jackson. Jackson suggests that a separate 'Ulster nation' did exist in this period – 'a cohesive, Protestant and particularist community' in the north-east of Ireland – and supports his argument by reference to A.D. Smith's *Theories of Nationalism* (1983), which outlines the constituent elements that go to make up a nation (Jackson 1989: 10–13). His argument, however, is fundamentally flawed by an omission under the heading of 'collective sentiments', namely, the elementary condition of national existence that the community concerned has a subjective consciousness of itself as a separate nation – and, as stated, for this virtually no evidence exists in the case of the Ulster Unionist community. As a culturally distinct community Ulster Unionists can be defined as an ethnic *group*, but an ethnic group is not necessarily the same thing as an ethnic nationality, as the history of Ulster Unionism so clearly demonstrates.

The rejection of British nationality by loyalists is also taken up by D.G. Boyce. Boyce argues that despite the fact that they were conscious of being part of a Protestant majority in the United Kingdom as a whole, something which might have persuaded them to present themselves as British or West British,

> they were frustrated by the fact that a sizeable portion of the population of the United Kingdom sympathised with the Irish parliamentary party . . . a British government in a British parliament threatened to turn Protestant majority status into Protestant minority disadvantage. . . . Northern Protestants, with their clear (sic) territorial area, their greater concentration of population, had a better opportunity to look after themselves.   (Boyce 1986: 232–3)

Though they were loyal, they might have to oppose 'a decision of the British government and legislature'. Hence it was only to the Crown that they gave true allegiance (ibid.: 233). Alvin Jackson, arguing along similar lines, acknowledges that while Unionists did make British patriotic speeches in 1886 these did not reflect 'a coherent [British] identity' but 'merely . . . ephemeral political needs' (Jackson 1989: 9). Jackson also stresses the extent to which Ulster Unionists were alienated from both of the major British political parties – in the Conservative and Unionist case because of certain pieces of legislation associated with the 'policy' of 'constructive Unionism' (ibid.: 14). Moreover, they had little interest in mainland British interests, being primarily concerned with those of northern Ireland. Nor, as their evident concern with Irish and local Ulster issues shows, were they really interested in the Empire, about which they talked so much:

> Irish loyalist MPs posed as imperialists but, in attacking the proposals of the Home Rule Bills, the true nature of their imperialism, and of the gulf separating them from British Conservatives became quite apparent. If Conservatives and Liberal Unionists thought of Home Rule primarily as a threat to Empire, then loyalists were unequal to the detachment which a similar point of view demanded from Irishmen: they thought of Ireland fundamentally in terms of local partisan division, and exploited imperial rhetoric partly as a ready source of communication with English Conservative sentiment. Thus, the focus of loyalist concerns on the Empire had little to do with broader concerns of imperial unity. . . . In 1886 the Irish Unionist interest in imperialism probably owed more to a perception of the state of British opinion one year after the death of Gordon, and in the midst of continuing colonial warfare in Egypt and Burma, than to any truly deep-rooted faith in Empire.   (Jackson 1989: 120)

Jackson, indeed, goes further and also suggests that neither did they have any real interest in the union with Britain and would, in fact, have preferred complete Irish independence to Home Rule (ibid.: 122–3). For the Ulster Unionists to qualify as *truly* British, he argues, it would have to be demonstrated that they 'were committed to an unpragmatic expression of principle at this time – since it may otherwise be contended that their speeches merely reflected ephemeral political needs' (ibid.: 9). Thus, for

Boyce, the Liberal Party alliance with Irish Nationalists effectively denied Ulster Unionists the possibility of identifying themselves as really British. Jackson reaches the same conclusion from a wider perspective, adding Ulstercentrism and lack of interest in British and imperial affairs to alienation based on disenchantment with both Liberal and Tory Parties, while setting the further condition that a true British national identity could only have existed among Ulster Unionists had it been based on 'principle' and devoid of self-interest.

There are, however, serious reservations that need to be considered in regard to these arguments. First, the view that Liberal Party activity alienated Ulster Unionists from British nationality is hardly persuasive. As demonstrated in Chapter 1, there was in Britain in the late nineteenth century not one, but two influential myths of national identity associated with the two major parties. There was, thus, no British political consensus on national identity. Indeed, the Unionist case against Liberalism from 1886 – outlined in Chapter 1 and which, as we shall see, was very much to the fore in the crisis over the third Home Rule Bill – was the denial that Liberal administrations supported by a 'mechanical' majority of disparate interests represented 'authentically' the 'will of the nation'. In this respect, a more accurate context within which to assess Ulster loyalist attitudes to British nationality than that which posits an alienation between loyalism and an abstract mainland British identity, is one which recognizes the divisions in Britain on the subject, and which, in fact, allowed Ulster Unionists to identify easily enough with the Conservative and Unionist position on the subject. Certainly there is nothing either in the loyalist speeches against Home Rule in this period, or in their pamphlet literature, to suggest an alienation from British nationality. As for the argument that British patriotic speeches by loyalists in 1886 were motivated merely by temporary political needs, this is hardly supported by the evidence of sustained interest by the Ulster Unionist press in British national and imperial issues over the whole period from 1886 to 1905.

Undoubtedly the most important point raised by Jackson in this respect is his claim that a lack of British identity among Unionists is demonstrated by their preoccupation with local Ulster affairs and unconcern for issues affecting people in Britain. There is, first of all, a conceptual problem with this claim. Unionists who see Ulster as British would have difficulty accepting its validity. But more importantly, it can in fact be argued that, in focusing on local affairs instead of 'national' issues, Ulster loyalists were representative of, rather than different from, communities in Britain.

In her study of national and local issues in east Sussex and the Lancashire spinning towns in the period 1906–10, Grace Jones has shown that while the election addresses of both Liberal and Unionist Parties stressed much the same issues of fiscal reform, Chinese labour, education, licensing, Home Rule, reform of the House of Lords and social reform, they were given a different order of priorities in different constituencies. But most significantly, 'they were presented not so much in national terms as in a way that would appeal to local needs and interests'. Thus, free trade and tariff reform were the most important issues in both areas in

1906, being fought out in Lancashire in terms of their effect on the cotton industry, and in Sussex on the basis of their implications for the agricultural interest, the building trade, and the hotel and lodging interests (Jones, thesis, 1965: 13–14). Again, while in Lancashire – which had a substantial Irish Roman Catholic population – Home Rule was often a burning and emotive issue, in Sussex it 'proved to be largely irrelevant'. Tory attempts to raise the issue met with a disappointing response: 'Ireland and the Irish were too far away to arouse a sustained interest' (ibid.: 20).

What was true of these issues was true of other issues such as work-men's compensation, ritualism, trade unions and education: *local* interests and concerns determined their relevance (ibid.: 21, 64–7). Thus despite the recurrent imperial and international crises of the Edwardian era, British foreign policy was among the least popular subjects: 'Matters of local importance almost always received precedence' (ibid.: 377, 402). Jones's findings are largely mirrored for Great Britain as a whole in Henry Pelling's important work on the social geography of British elections, which points up the importance of regional and local factors in deter-mining election results (Pelling 1967: 414–18). Localism, then, clearly had a primacy over national issues in British politics, and in this context localism in Ulster can hardly be cited as evidence of non-Britishness. What was distinctive about Ulster was merely the *nature* of its localism.

However, while neither in Ulster nor in Britain did great national issues impinge on the population to the extent of undermining the primacy of local concerns, in Ulster's case it can be argued that the consciousness of British identity was more present at the local level than in Britain, because the issue of national identity was of recurrent concern to a Unionist community whose existing membership of the United Kingdom was repeatedly under threat from Liberal and nationalist Home Rulers. In other words, British nationality was a *local* issue in Ulster. Thus, whereas, as outlined in the Introduction (pp. 3–4), connections between the separate spheres of national/public and local/private life in general are made substantially through similar modes of understanding, in northern Ireland those spheres and modes of understanding were not separate but inextricably meshed.[21]

Relatedly, Jackson's claim that Ulster Unionists could only be considered truly British if that identity was expressed in terms of 'unpragmatic principle' is also highly suspect. To argue thus is to set standards of national membership that not only do not apply in the British context but hardly apply to any community in any national context.The self-interest of groups is invariably an important element in their national identification. In the United Kingdom, Scotland is the outstanding example of the relationship between self-interest and the willingness to embrace British nationality (Brand 1978: 64–70), while its importance generally both to British nationality and the stability of the British state in the eighteenth and early nineteenth centuries has been convincingly argued by Linda Colley (1992a) – 'unpragmatic principle' is little in evidence.

The self-interest of groups suggests the uniqueness of the various regions within the United Kingdom that were subsumed under the term 'British'. It is an important point to bear in mind and especially to set against the rather simplistic conception of the Ulster–Britain relationship that posits an opposition between unique Ulster interests and a Britain homogeneous both in ideology and interests. The complexity of Britain in the nineteenth century in these respects has been incisively explored by Keith Robbins (1988: 97), who points out: 'What it meant to be "British" admitted of no straightforward answer: everything depended upon context. Diversity in the spheres of broad culture, language and religion . . . could not be denied.' In this context Ulster's specific character and interests *per se* were no more a disqualification for British identity than that of any other region in the United Kingdom. What was singular about Ulster, of course, was its geographical position within the Kingdom and especially its being subject to the competing national claims of Unionists and Irish Nationalists. And here the perceived bonds of British identity that all regions of the kingdom might claim to have in common were naturally of more importance to Ulster Unionists than they were to the various regions of Britain. The problem for Ulster loyalists, however, was that over this period the bonds of identity of most importance to them began to weaken significantly.

IV

If, as Martin Wiener has argued, Britain had the opportunity mid-century to develop as a 'new' industrial nation – a development, it has been suggested, that occurred in Scotland in the late nineteenth century and which allowed Irish Catholic immigrant communities to develop as part of a new Scottish industrial nation (McCaffrey 1991: 117–18) – then Ulster, given its predominantly industrial persona could, arguably, have developed as more 'authentically' British than was the case with the hegemonic ruralist and southern English metaphor of the nation that became established in the mid-1880s. Ulster, of course, shared the same fate in this respect as other industrial regions of Britain; however, their membership of the British state was not under threat and they could merely remain invisible in the process of national imagining. Ulster Unionist anxieties about their constitutional security, on the other hand, placed a premium on publicity and persuading public opinion in Britain to take on board their concerns; however, those anxieties also fuelled an intense sectarian spirit at the very time that, as we have noted (Chapter 1, pp. 13–14), popular Protestantism was in the process of gradually losing its hold in Britain. Thus, over this period, as Protestantism followed industrialism as a diminishing characteristic of national identity in Britain, Ulster increasingly enhanced its reputation as a rather bleak industrial environment, peopled by narrow-minded, sectarian philistines. Accordingly, as Britain progressively left its sectarian past behind, it became easy to identify these characteristics as peculiar to Ulster and devoid of any representative British dimension. The only opportunity that existed in this period for the industrial persona of Ulster to become integrated into a national identity of a similar kind for Britain as a whole lay with Joseph

Chamberlain's campaign for tariff reform – which, as we have noted, Ulster Unionists supported enthusiastically. Chamberlain's campaign, Martin Wiener has argued, 'offered an activist, urban, industrial version of Conservatism that promoted economic reform', but was unacceptable to a Party imbued with a pastoral concept of the nation and repelled by industrial materialism (Wiener 1987: 99). It would be sixty years before Ulster Unionists would have another opportunity to ideologically integrate the north of Ireland with a similar national image of Britain (see the discussion of Terence O'Neill's attempt to modernize Ulster in line with Harold Wilson's vision of a progressive Britain experiencing the 'white heat of technology', in Chapter 8).

Furthermore, the concept of Englishness articulated by Seeley and Chamberlain at the height of the struggle for Africa in the 1880s – which defined it largely in terms of Anglo-Saxon race and Protestant religion – and which was easily extended to Ulster, fell distinctly out of favour following the military disasters of the Boer War; while the pseudo-scientific race theorizing that underpinned it increasingly lost academic respectability.[22] Certainly, by 1914 the racial division of 'Saxon' and 'Celt' had lost all scholarly credibility. H.J. Fleure, in his contribution on the races and languages of the British Isles for the *Oxford Survey of the British Empire* exclaimed: 'the rubbish about Saxon and Celt that is so familiar . . . [is] only an obstruction to study and good feeling' (Fleure 1914: 298). Even in Ulster, where the *Ulster Journal of Archaeology* began publication in 1852 with a ringing endorsement of Ulster Anglo-Saxon superiority to inferior Irish Celts (Hume 1852), its credibility was undermined. Indeed, now J.M. Dickson, in 'Notes on Irish Ethnology', argued that it was the Protestants who were really Celts, a much superior breed to the 'aboriginal black Irish' whom had racial affinities with 'the lower type of Spaniard' and African native.[23] Clearly, despite the discrediting of the Saxon–Celt dichotomy, it was apparently still important to establish a racial basis for Ulster's 'superiority' to the southern Catholic Irish.

To the growing divergence between Ulster Unionists and the population of Britain on subjects on which they were formerly united may be added the unsuccessful attempts of the former to assert their Britishness by identifying their struggle with the foundation myth of modern British nationality – the Glorious Revolution. For Ulster loyalists, it was the military struggle in Ireland that gave the Revolution meaning, explaining why they had 'freedom, religion and laws', and sometimes being used to excuse sectarian excesses. The *Witness* (15 January 1892), for example, could admit the existence of Orange bigotry, but justify it on the grounds that 'the historical memories' to which Ulstermen clung fanatically sprang 'from one of the most momentous struggles for constitutional freedom that the world has ever seen'. On the occasion of the Ulster Unionist Convention of 1892, Thomas Sinclair, leader of the Ulster Liberal Unionists, sought to base their opposition to Home Rule on the principles of the 'Revolution of 1688', while the *Belfast News-Letter* (18 June 1892), reflected the Ulster Unionist view of their community's contribution to the Revolution as follows: 'If there had been no Londonderry and no

Enniskillen and no Newtonbutler two hundred years ago . . . there would have been no independent United Kingdom today'. However, despite Macaulay having placed Ulster Protestantism at the heart of the revolutionary experience, it failed to register as an integral part of the revolutionary myth. In Britain the Revolution's defining characteristic was its peaceful nature. British commentators tended to focus on events in Britain in 1688, ignoring the subsequent violence in Ireland – something that was also true of the tercentenary celebrations of the Revolution in 1988. The events Ulster Unionists revered were seen, if at all, as external aspects, rather than essential elements, of the myth – a tendency, moreover, that could only have been reinforced by the increasingly sectarian image of Ulster in Britain in this period. The divergence of Ulster and Britain in this respect, moreover, was reflected in the strategies pursued by the Tory Party to market patriotism in the late nineteenth century.

It says much for the adaptability of the Tory Party, faced with a greatly extended electorate and the gradual demise of traditional forms of patriotism, that they reacted so quickly and so inventively in seeking new ways of investing everyday life with a national patriotic dimension. The means they used to do this was the Primrose League, a supposedly non-party but effectively Tory organization that devoted itself to stimulating a patriotic consciousness through the promotion of crown, country and Empire. Martin Pugh has succinctly described its activities:

The League sponsored a great array of social activities that were easily accessible to ordinary people, in this way successfully embedding the Conservative cause in the routine social life of many communities. It proved enormously successful in convincing large numbers of middle and working-class people to identify a common interest with the ruling parliamentary elite as members of a British patriotic nation increasingly under threat from outside and to regard their political opponents . . . as, at best, feeble friends of Britain's enemies or, at worst, traitors.
(Pugh 1988: 259)

On the religious issue, especially, the League avoided militant Protestantism and went out of its way to encompass the full range of Christian belief: 'None but atheists and opponents of the British Empire were excluded from membership: Nonconformists, Catholics and Jews were all welcome' (Pugh 1985: 83). For Roman Catholics, membership of the League provided a convenient point of entry into mainstream Conservative politics and also served to diminish the 'No Popery' image of the Party. The presence of Catholics also helped to counter the argument that the Party's Irish policy consisted simply of the coercion of Catholics by a Protestant majority (ibid.).

Part of the League's success was undoubtedly due to its ability to tap into the growing popular preoccupation with tradition, of which the ruralist concept of the nation was one of the most important indicators. The League, for example, employed a range of medieval terms, such as 'tribute' instead of 'dues', 'habitations' instead of 'branches', while members who paid more than one guinea in membership fees were known as 'Knights' or 'Dames'. And while claiming to be above 'party', it proved able to exploit effectively the Home Rule issue in the 1880s to the Tories' advantage. Its membership rose from just over 11,000 in 1885 to exceed one million by 1891, with substantial yearly increases thereafter (Robb 1942: 57–8). The League can, thus, be seen as a successful attempt to market a Conservative-oriented conception of British patriotism at a time when Protestantism, formerly so central to British nationalism and so well exploited by Conservatives, was losing its popular influence. Certainly the League sought to keep extreme Protestant organizations such as the Orange Order at arm's length, denying that its principles were the same and officially refusing to co-operate with it (ibid.: 196) – though the Orange Order was, apparently, one of the models on which the Primrose League was based (ibid.: 37). Tory sensitivity to the embarrassment that its connection with the sectarianism of Ulster Unionism might occasion was reflected in the care taken in selecting Ulster speakers for campaign work in Britain: the possibility of Ulster bigotry offending English sensibilities was to be avoided at all costs (see Buckland 1973: 40–44). So far had the divergence between Ulster Unionist and mainland British conceptions of British national identity proceeded by the end of this period that, as one recent commentator has argued, Protestant Belfast's integration of religion and politics, in going beyond the British understanding that fighting for religion was out of date, effectively placed it beyond the British national pale: 'Belfast was no longer a British, but an Irish city'.[24] In this respect, it is also worth noting that the idea that Ulster was not authentically British had been, undoubtedly unintentionally, conveyed in the arguments of the agrarian reformer and Liberal Unionist MP for South Tyrone, T.W. Russell. For the purpose of gaining influence with Unionist leaders such as Joseph Chamberlain and Arthur Balfour, Russell consistently and apparently successfully, pressed the argument that the loyalty of Protestant tenant farmers in Ulster to the union with Britain could only be secured if substantial land reforms were enacted, otherwise the province would be lost to Irish nationalism. The fact, however, was that quite apart from their enthusiastic British self-identity, the fear and loathing of the Roman Catholic Church among Ulster Protestants was such that there was never any prospect of a mass conversion to the overwhelmingly Catholic Nationalist Party (see Loughlin 1990a). Ironically, though, while their intense anti-Catholicism may have ensured their loyalty to Britain, as we have seen, it was also, to a significant extent, responsible for preventing their being accepted in Britain as authentically British. Yet it is also important to note that there was another context for the expression of national identity where this consideration appeared not to apply. That context was provided by royal occasions.

V

The context of royal ritual could be described as a 'purified' one for the demonstration of national identity: uncomplicated by party political issues, identity could be communicated with a clarity and immediacy not possible otherwise; an identity, moreover, that could register simultaneously at the level of everyday experience and at the national level. It was a context defined, less by action, than by perception and by highly regulated contact between monarch and subjects. Erving Goffman has argued that if 'perception' is a form of 'contact and communion' then 'control over what is perceived is control over contact that is made'. Accordingly, restrictions placed upon contact, especially the maintenance of social distance, provide a way in which awe can be generated and maintained in the audience, a way in which the audience 'can be held in a state of mystification in regard to the performer' (Goffman 1971: 74). Such techniques of mass manipulation were central to the successful execution of royal occasions. Nevertheless, the *meaning* of a royal event was one that emerged less from the focus of mass attention – the royal person – than from the spectators. As Sir Frederick Ponsonby, assistant secretary to Edward VII, informed the King of Norway: 'The monarchy is really the creation of each individual's brain. . . . People invest the monarch with every conceivable virtue and talent' (Ponsonby 1951: 194).

This aspect of monarchy, however, had an enhanced importance for Ulster Unionists. The significance of the monarch as the master symbol of British nationality was bound to have a special meaning for a community whose membership of the United Kingdom was perceived to be constantly under threat. Thus, while the context of royal ritual *per se* lay outside the party political realm, it makes sense, for our purposes, to define this context as the *immediate* context. In a way that did not apply in Britain, certainly to anything like the same extent, party politics constituted a *secondary* context which, though it did not usually impinge explicitly on the former, could yet influence significantly the meanings that were read into it. For example, as we shall see, royal occasions allowed Ulster Unionists to demonstrate their loyalty and Britishness in a thoroughly respectable manner – while at the same time allowing them, at least temporarily, to redeem a reputation for bigotry and violence that they had acquired through the assertion of loyalty in the party political sphere.

We saw in Chapter 1 (pp. 17–19) that by the mid-1880s the reshaping of the monarchy to meet the needs of a changing social and political environment had largely taken place. The monarch had become transformed from the head of society to the most important representative of the nation, while her large extended family had helped to establish the royal family itself as a focus of loyalty. Unionist Ulster was affected by these developments no less than Britain but given its political anxieties there was, it is reasonable to argue, a greater intensity to their attachment and, especially, a greater inclination to project their own intense Protestantism on to the monarch. In fact, Queen Victoria shared many of the religious and political prejudices of Ulster Unionists.

There is evidence, for example, that though she was the constitutional embodiment of United Kingdom nationality, she did not regard Irish Catholics as really part of it. A persistent refusal over many years to establish a royal residence in Ireland, for which no persuasive reason was given, was motivated, apparently, by the fear that the Prince of Wales or some other leading member of the royal family might 'go native', become attached to the Irish and emerge as the focus of an alternative centre of power to herself. She was 'so afraid lest any of them be taken up by the Irish as to throw Balmoral into the shade' (Lady Augusta Stanley, quoted in Roby 1975: 151). During the second Home Rule controversy she questioned the legitimacy of Gladstone's parliamentary majority as a basis for introducing Home Rule: 'the majority of the British nation feel very strongly the way in which the small Irish majority is used to force through a measure so repugnant to their feelings and so fraught with danger to the constitution'. Gladstone, however, pointed out in reply, that the Irish represented only one part of a majority across the whole kingdom: 'This is a united Parliament and a United Kingdom' (Buckle (ed.) 1931: ii, 290–1). The Queen, in fact, was virulently unionist and conservative across the broad range of political issues in general and made little secret of it (Pugh 1985: 72–80).

On the Ulster question, specifically, she agreed with Lord Tennyson that one of the worst aspects of Gladstonian Home Rule was its 'betrayal of the loyalists of Ulster' (Lee 1904: 493). For their part, the Ulster Unionists were confident of the Queen's opposition to Home Rule, and correctly divined evidence of this in her delay in sending for Gladstone to form a government.[25] While taking care not to bring the monarchy directly into the party political arena, the Tories used it in their anti-Home Rule campaign. One leaflet contained an illustration of the royal standard with the Irish harp ripped out, to demonstrate the 'national mutilation' that Home Rule would entail. This was a clever ploy and one that would not have worked with the Union Jack, from which the Cross of Saint Patrick could have been removed without conveying any sense of 'national mutilation' whatever.[26] Thus, although the monarchy was formally non-political in the party sense, given the passions aroused by the Home Rule issue, it was unlikely to escape political involvement. This was clear from the beginning of this period when, in 1885, Edward, Prince of Wales made a much publicized visit to Ireland, a visit Nationalists interpreted as intended to strike a blow at Parnell's authority.[27]

For Ulster loyalists the visit was viewed largely as an indicator of British identity, as judged by the reaction to the Prince of the populations in the localities he visited. Keen to validate the opinion common among Unionists generally that Parnellite politicians did not 'authentically' represent Irish national opinion, they saw evidence of this in the favourable reception given to the Prince in areas that had formerly been centres of strife; while the Ulster dimension of his visit afforded an opportunity for the expression of Anglo-Saxonist views on the supposed racial differences between northern and southern Ireland and, especially, the close familial relationship between loyalists and the population of Britain: 'we regard our English and Scottish neighbours . . . as our kin beyond the narrow channel' (see *Belfast News-Letter*, 27, 24 April 1885; *Weekly Northern Whig*, 18 April 1885). What was characteristic of the loyalist response to this and subsequent royal visits, however, was an intense focus on every gesture and utterance of the royal visitor. And what was remembered long after Edward left the province was his comment on the 'determined spirit of enterprise and perseverence' he saw in the north, which 'I hope is characteristic of our race and which overcomes all difficulties in the way of success'; a statement loyalists interpreted as a coded criticism of nationalist Ireland, whose problems would be solved by following the loyalist example (see *Belfast News-Letter*, 24 April 1885). But equally important for Ulster loyalists was what might be termed the politically redemptive dimension to the visit. Conscious of their negative political image in Britain, it was hoped that their warm reception of the Prince, as contrasted with the chilly reaction of Parnellite Nationalists, would help to repair their reputation:

Henceforth the press of Great Britain will know us better, and let us hope the knowledge acquired will be employed to describe more correctly in future the conduct of the men of the north. . . . ill-treated and discouraged, they are still friends of the Crown and supporters of the Union.[28]

This royal visit took place before the Liberal conversion to Home Rule in 1886. Succeeding royal events – such as the Golden Jubilee celebrations in 1887 of the Queen's accession to the throne – taking place in the context of the struggle against Home Rule, took on an enhanced significance for Ulster loyalists as occasions on which to affirm their British identity.[29] One of the most important royal occasions of the period was Queen Victoria's visit in 1900, undertaken as a token of appreciation for the substantial Irish contribution to the struggle in South Africa. That contribution fuelled the belief that Ireland was not really committed to Home Rule, and for unionists in Britain and Ireland the warm popular reception of the Queen was taken as evidence to this effect.[30] This wishful thinking persisted and was given further credibility when the former Prince of Wales, now Edward VII, made his coronation visit to Ireland in 1903.

Several factors worked to make this visit special. It began on the day that the Wyndham Act[31] received its third reading in the House of Commons, and it was widely believed both that the King was partly responsible for its enactment and also had an open mind on the Home Rule question. Moreover, when Pope Leo XIII died shortly after the visit began, the King had Dublin Castle mark the event with a lowering of flags at the same time as it was made known publicly that he was to entrust Cardinal Logue with a letter of condolence to the College of Cardinals in Rome. Furthermore, the King's evident enjoyment of the occasion also encouraged popular support and helped to make it a success (Lee 1925/ 1927, i: 161–70). Edward did appear to have a different attitude to the Irish question in general than his late mother; however, the difference was not as deep as it seemed. Certainly, he did not share her marked Protestant prejudices, but on Home Rule and other political questions his views, like hers, were strongly conservative and unionist (Hardie 1970: 85–7); though, of course, this was not publicly bruited and thus did not affect his reception in Ireland, The King's evident rapport with the nationalist population caused some concern about its effect on Ulster Protestants, but on its conclusion the visit would be seen instead as having 'stilled sectarian passions' (*The Times*, 30 July 1903).

The Ulster Unionist press, in fact, saw Edward's reception in southern Ireland as a vindication of their own hopes that the visit would show evidence of the great loyalty to the throne of the Irish people when allowed to express their own views unhindered by the 'mercenary agitator'.[32] In the words of the *Belfast News-Letter* (21 July 1903), the visit hopefully marked the beginning of a period of peace and contentment when the majority of Catholics would 'settle down . . . and make the best of their heritage as British subjects'. In this way it would be demonstrated that 'the United Kingdom is really one'.[33] Nevertheless, as the King undertook his visits in Ulster, the Unionist disposition to glory in a more pure form of national patriotism than was evident elsewhere in Ireland asserted itself. Ulster's loyalty was not a mushroom growth: 'The loyalty of the Imperial province . . . does not rest on self-interest . . . land purchase acts or education grants. It is the same whether smiled or frowned upon; and often it has had more frowns than smiles.' Moreover, the King's presence allowed for the construction of a self-congratulatory frame of reference within which to interpret the warm reception he received in southern Ireland. The King's apparent advice to the Irish nationalist community when he visited the province as Prince of Wales in 1885 – that if they followed the north's example their problems would be solved – was recalled as advice that seemed to have been heeded: 'It is because many of them are coming to see this that there is a brighter outlook for the country as a whole' (*Belfast News-Letter*, 27 July 1903). In this context, the King's description of the relations of the nationalities of the United Kingdom as being those of friendly rivalry 'in the paths of peace and within the bounds of Imperial greatness' was readily accepted. Indeed, it even allowed Ulster Unionists to reclaim an Irish 'nationality' that the nationalist campaign for Home Rule had hitherto inhibited Unionists from asserting: 'Politics do not constitute nationality' (ibid., 28 July 1903; see also *Weekly Northern Whig*, 1 August 1903).

Edward VII's Irish visit of 1903 provided probably the most important occasion of this period for Ulster loyalists to assert their British identity; and if much of their assessment of its meaning consisted of wishful thinking, it was not entirely fanciful. The visit had taken place almost twenty years since Lord Salisbury had, in 1886, inaugurated 'twenty years of firm government' in Ireland; government that was intended to undermine the demand for Home Rule by dealing with the 'real' grievances of the Irish people – especially land problems – and eliminate crime by the stern implementation of the law. In that time, the Nationalist Party had split, the second Home Rule Bill had been defeated, and a significant range of Irish reforms – culminating in the Wyndham Act which effectively solved the land question – had been implemented. With the Unionists having held office for all but three years of that period and the Home Rule issue no longer a prominent feature of Liberal politics, the construction placed on Edward's visit by Ulster loyalists was not wholly at variance with reality. Furthermore, it is also likely that the expansion of the role of the monarch in this period – from head of a social élite to the most authentic embodiment of British nationality – also enhanced the Ulster Unionist sense of national belonging, as the following comment from a leading article on the death of Edward in the *Fermanagh Times* (26 May 1910) suggests:

To-day the Royal family is an integral factor of the nation's social life. Its members are trained to the full in the routine of professions which are recognised items in the nation's programme of work; their lives are lived in intimate contact with every phase of the nation's life; and they form a personal acquaintance with our people beyond the sea.

Nevertheless, while their relationship with monarchy allowed Ulster loyalists to demonstrate their British national identity to advantage, even here developments were taking place that indicated the breach that was emerging between their conception of Britishness and that developing in Britain. In fact, even during Edward's visit in 1903 signs of that breach were detected.

For instance, while no public protest emerged from Ulster against Edward's acknowledgement of Pope Leo XIII's death – such would only have damaged the Ulster Unionist cause – private resentment does seem to have been expressed, with the King acquiring the nickname 'Popish Ned' (Leslie 1966: 130). Further, while Sir George Wyndham and Sir Anthony MacDonnell were made to pay for the devolution crisis of 1904–5,[34] rumours circulated in the north that the King had supported the devolution proposals (Good 1919: 286). Here again, these rumours did not result in public criticism of the King, something that Ulster loyalists sought to avoid at all costs, even when – most trying of all – members of the royal family renounced Protestantism on marrying into European Catholic royalty. When in May 1906 the King's daughter, Princess Ena of Battenburg, married King Alphonso XIII of Spain, the Orange Order, expressing confidence that the King had done his utmost to prevent the 'apostasy', declared that it would be unfair to place upon his shoulders 'the sins and delinquencies of all the members of the Royal family' (see *Belfast News-Letter*, 13 July 1906). In cases such as this it was much more tempting to divert anger away from the King and on to his representatives – in the case of the Spanish marriage, Lord Londonderry, who was accused of being a 'flunkey' (*Cookstown News*, 23 June 1906). Certainly, it would appear that *public* respect for the King was significantly greater in Ulster than in other parts of the United Kingdom, where it was by no means uncommon for him to be insulted.[35]

VI

This chapter has argued that to accurately assess the question of the British identity of Ulster Unionism we have to dispense with the notion of one homogeneous national identity impinging externally at the local level of everyday experience; that the relevance of national ideology at that level was determined by a process of negotiation conditioned fundamentally by local needs and interests. That ideology, moreover, was dynamic rather than static in character, i.e., the relative importance of elements within it was likely to be shaped by political issues and the contexts within which they emerged, as the controversy over the Eucharistic Congress of 1908, and the way it revived and crystallized Protestantism as an element of national identity demonstrated. At the same time, however, it was also seen that while Ulster Unionism experienced national identity in much the same way as other regions of the United Kingdom, breaches did emerge over this period between conceptions of Britishness in Ulster and in Britain, even if they were not apparent in the non-party political context of royal ritual. It will be argued in Chapter 3 that the pre-war crisis in the United Kingdom in the years 1910–14 was fundamentally about national identity and that its seriousness can be gauged by the extent to which the 'neutral' monarchic sphere of national identity became conflated with that of party politics.

Notes

1. These statements were delivered as part of a speech entitled 'What Home Rule Means', delivered in Town Hall, Westminster on 22 February 1887. It was later reproduced for mass circulation as a Unionist pamphlet. See *National Union Pamphlets 1887–90* (1891).

2. See Sir John Lubbock's comments in the debate on race and British nationality that took place in the letter columns of *The Times* in 1887 between, for the Liberals, James Bryce and for the Unionists, Lubbock, T.H. Huxley, Sir John Beddoe and the Duke of Argyll (*The Times*, 18, 19, 21, 28 March; 3, 9 April; 2 May 1887).

3. See, for example, *Belfast News-Letter* (5 January 1849): 'We are authorised to state that the second edition of this valuable and interesting work [vol. 1] will be published in London this day. Mr. Hodgson [bookseller] begs to inform those subscribers whom he was most reluctantly obliged to disappoint in supplying their orders . . . [he] would soon be able to supply orders.' For examples of press comment on later volumes, see *Weekly Northern Whig* (24 March 1851); *Belfast News-Letter* (19–22, 25–6 December 1855; 19 March 1861); *Portadown News* (24 March 1861).

4. Newspaper Cutting, 1892 in Johnson diary (Public Record Office (PRONI), D880/2/40). In this context it is worth noting that Macaulay wrote at a time when it was widely believed that historians could write absolutely objective history. Thus Macaulay wrote 'The' history, rather than 'A' history, of England.

5. This is usefully pointed out by Patrick Buckland (1973), though he does not discuss the 'Britishness' of Ulster Unionism.

6. For a study of Ulster Unionist speeches against Home Rule in 1886 which clearly identifies this sentiment, see Loughlin (1986: 295–6).

7. See Davey (1940: 62–3). An emphasis on maintaining their 'British heritage'

was a major theme in Ulster Unionist speeches in 1886 (Loughlin 1986: 295–6), and evident in their pamphlet literature (Hempton 1990: 245).

8. See, for example, *Tyrone Courier* (19 June 1886); *Newry Telegraph* (9 February 1886, 2 March 1893); *Ballymena Observer* (27 February 1886, 3 February 1893).

9. *Witness* (15 January 1892). For more evidence of the extent to which this view prevailed, see Moore (1914: 26–8); and on the significance of racial division in Ulster generally, Bullock (n.d. [1931]: 132) and Smith (1925: 77–9).

10. *Banbridge Chronicle* (10 April 1886); *Witness* (12 February 1893); 'A Statutory Nation', *Edinburgh Review*, CCXXVIII (April 1893), 565–86.

11. *Ballymena Observer* (19 June 1886); also issues for 20 March, 17, 24 April, 22 June 1886 for more in a similar vein. The *Newtownards Chronicle* (16 September 1893) argued that only the House of Lords really represented the nation against Gladstone's 'mechanical majority' in the Commons.

12. There is evidence that Ulster Unionists, already in the Gladstonian period, saw Ulster as a separate entity within Ireland. See, for example, the *Ulster Gazette* (25 February 1892) on the importance of loyalists organizing to prevent Nationalists 'entering Ulster', and similar comment in *Witness* (21 May 1886) and *Newry Telegraph* (20 March 1886).

13. See, for example, the report of the protest campaign led by the eminent constitutional expert, Sir William Anson, against plans by Oxford town council to erect a statue in honour of Cardinal Newman (*Witness*, 5 February 1892).

14. See Gailey (1987), Jackson (1989: 88, 176–92, 324). For examples of loyalist press opinion on ritualism, see *Strabane Chronicle* (15 July 1900); *Belfast News-Letter* (13 July, 1 October 1900).

15. For a thorough account of the controversy from the Catholic perspective, see Oldmeadow (1940: i, Ch. 47).

16. Support for an aggressive British foreign policy was common in the loyalist press. Thus there was strong support for the annexation of Upper Burma in late 1885, and the opportunities it provided for 'planters' to exploit 'cheap Coolie labour'. See *Witness* (1 January 1886); *Tyrone Constitution* (1 January 1886); *Banbridge Chronicle* (2 January 1886); *Newry Telegraph* (5 January 1886).

17. The issue of cheap 'Chinese labour' – Chinese labourers used in the diamond mines to undercut wage rates given to white men – was used effectively against the Tories at the general election of 1905.

18. On Ulster Unionist support for the war effort, especially in Londonderry, see the work of my former student, Catherine Meehan (1992: 38–40).

19. The *Newry Telegraph* (27 September 1899) declared: 'we must either be paramount or leave the country'. For other examples of the aggressive British nationalist spirit on the war that infused the Ulster loyalist press, see *Londonderry Sentinel* (19 July 1899); *Newtownards Chronicle* (8 July, 23 September, 28 October 1899); *Ballymena Observer* (1 September, 27 October 1899); *Coleraine Chronicle* (27 September, 7 October 1899); *Down Recorder* (14, 28 October, 11, 18 November, 2 December 1899); *Portadown News* (11 November 1899); *Fermanagh Times* (28–9 January, 12 February 1903).

20. The enthusiasm for tariff reform was evident also among Ulster Unionist MPs (Jackson 1989: 112); unlike the Tory Party in Britain which was in turmoil over the issue.

21. For an important study of a rural community showing how its everyday life was influenced by national issues, see Harris (1972). For a succinct personal

illustration, see Lynn Doyle's [Leslie A. Montgomery] description of his childhood fears of home rulers (quoted, Loughlin 1986: 163). See also Bullock (n.d. [1931]: 127).

22. The credibility of these ideas was undermined, in particular, when they were tested against social reality. Thus, an ambitious attempt to undertake an 'ethnographic' survey of the United Kingdom in the 1890s, based largely on racial categorization, was a dismal failure. See Urry (1984: 83–105).

23. Dickson's 'Notes on Irish Ethnology' was a series of several short pieces which appeared over the four years from 1896 to 1900 and was the most substantial work on the subject in Ulster in this period.

24. See Sybil Gribbon's stimulating article on Edwardian Belfast (1987: 219); also Young (1907: 25–7): 'the religious bigotry of the north of Ireland must be experienced to be credited'.

25. See Meehan (1992, thesis: 43); also *Ulster Gazette* (2 January 1886), which argued that under Home Rule there would be 'no Queen and no Queen's laws'.

26. Illustration entitled 'The Old Flag and the New' in *National Union Pamphlets* (1891). However, despite their use of royalty as a weapon against Home Rule, Unionists had little compunction in using Gladstone's support for the Unionist position on Civil List payments as anti-Radical propaganda. See also Pugh (1985: 75–6).

27. *Annual Register 1885* (1886: 196–8). For a comprehensive account of the visit, see Lee (1925: i, 237–41).

28. *Belfast News-Letter* (27 April 1885); *Weekly Northern Whig* (25 April 1885). Reflecting the pre-Home Rule conflict between Liberals and Tories in Ulster this newspaper argued that the Ulster reception for the Prince would demonstrate that Orange bigotry was not representative of its people, as often thought in Britain (*Londonderry Standard*, 27 March 1885). See also issues for the period 22–9 April 1885).

29. *Belfast News-Letter* (21, 27 June 1887). For a more restrained reaction, though agreeing in essentials, see the Liberal Unionist *Londonderry Standard* (27 June, 6 July 1887). The Diamond Jubilee of 1897 brought forth similar reactions. See *Belfast News-Letter* (23 July 1897).

30. *Weekly Northern Whig* (14, 21 April 1900); *Derry Standard* (4, 6, 27 April 1900). For an exhaustive chronology of the visit, see McCarthy (1901: 463–506). The *Ulster Gazette* (14 April 1900) rejoiced that 'Ireland was true to the core to Her Majesty personally and to the majesty of our empire that is unequalled on the earth'.

31. This measure, which virtually solved the land question, was intended to, and succeeded in, inducing landlords to sell large tracts of land, by awarding the seller a 12 per cent bonus in addition to the price agreed with the tenants.

32. See, for example, *Banbridge Chronicle* (1 April, 22, 25 July 1903); also *Ulster Gazette* (25 July, 1 August 1903); *Tyrone Constitution* (24 July 1903).

33. *Belfast News-Letter* (22, 23, 27 July 1903); *Weekly Northern Whig* (25 July 1903); *Ulster Gazette* (25 July, 1 August 1903); *Tyrone Constitution* (24 July 1903).

34. The crisis arose when the Under-Secretary at Dublin Castle, Sir Anthony MacDonnell, and Lord Dunraven, a leading mover of the land settlement in 1903, sought to extend the co-operation between Unionists and Nationalists on which that settlement was based, to the area of Irish government. They proposed a moderate measure of devolution which, however, infuriated right-wing Unionists, especially Ulster loyalists, who suspected a sell-out to Irish

Nationalists. The resulting furore brought about the removal of MacDonnell and the resignation of Wyndham, the Irish Chief Secretary.

35. See diary entry, 21 June 1902 (Vincent (ed.) 1984: 67), describing how Edward's friendship with prominent Jews had led to jeers of 'King of the Jews' while on a visit to Aldershot; also, report of a physical attack on the Prince of Wales in Glasgow in September 1908 (ibid.: 114).

3

THE CRISIS OF NATIONAL IDENTITY AND THE ULSTER PROBLEM 1910–14

As the debate on the third reading of Asquith's Home Rule Bill opened in mid-January 1913, Leo Amery noted regretfully that 'not a soul throughout these debates ever says anything to suggest that he feels the United Kingdom is really a nation and that Irish nationalism in any shape or form means the end of United Kingdom nationalism' (diary entry, 15 January 1913 in Barnes and Nicholson (eds), 1980: 92). At moments like this Amery brought himself face to face with the contrast between the claims of national myths and the political reality they were supposed to describe. The problem, fundamentally, Amery concluded, was the failure to invent 'a single name for the United Kingdom in 1800' and to abolish 'the Irish Vice-Royalty' (ibid.). There was something in part of this argument at least. More politically disinterested commentators than Amery – a radical enthusiast for Alfred Milner's British imperial nationalism – likewise noted the lack of a national name for the United Kingdom state capable of engendering 'emotional associations' (Wallas 1908: 80). The problem of national cohesion as defined by Amery, however, was chiefly a Unionist concern and reflected anxieties felt across a range of political issues, and greatly intensified since the accession of the Liberal Party to power in 1906.

I

As the radical programme of the Liberal Party unfolded, culminating in Lloyd George's controversial budget of 1909, the apprehensions of right-wing Unionists that Liberal rule represented a 'Jacobin' tendency towards national decay and disintegration intensified. Supporting evidence was held to exist in the range of problems facing Edwardian society – 'racial' fitness, the labour question, the women's movement, education, deterioration of the family, Jewish control of national finance and the influx of 'riff-raff' from abroad that polluted public morals, hygiene and culture with their foreign ways. There were also external threats, economic and military, from Russia and America, but mostly Germany. Finally, and from 1910 most acutely, there was the Irish question, threatening both constitutional and imperial disintegration (see Porter 1982: 128–44). The Liberal Government, moreover, not only lacked the *will* to deal with these problems, but given that its majority from 1910 was 'mechanical' – that is, based on a diversity of groupings temporarily united and each with its own political agenda hardly less threatening to the nation than Home Rule – *could not* do so as it did not represent the 'nation'. This is a point worth emphasizing, for the crisis of 1910–14 was fundamentally a crisis of national identity, at the centre of which were competing concepts of English/British nationality and debate over what it meant to be British, especially the terms on which membership of the national community could be assumed. Liberals no less than Unionists were capable of conceptualizing their politics within a patriotic tradition and vocabulary (see Chapter 1, pp. 11–12).

Defenders of Lloyd George's redistributive 'Peoples' Budget' of 1909, for example, employed a radical patriotic vocabulary that extended back to Thomas Paine and beyond to the Levellers of the seventeenth century (see Asa Briggs, quoted in Kuklick 1984: 62); a vocabulary, indeed, that even Joseph Chamberlain employed extensively before his break with Gladstone over Home Rule in 1886 (Loughlin 1992: 210–11). In this context it is worth noting that the second general election of 1910, turning on the issue of the House of Lords' veto, was fought by the Liberals on the slogan 'Shall six hundred peers rule six million Englishmen?' (Smith 1912: 26). More specifically, in his famous Limehouse speech of 30 July 1909, Lloyd George, in justifying his land tax proposals, cleverly attacked rural land-lords for having failed in their 'traditional duty' by the people and the country (Riddell 1934: 224); that is, in the paternalistic duty ascribed to them in the Tory 'organic' conception of the nation. Moreover, Lloyd George's speeches, especially on foreign policy, could be aggressively nationalistic,[1] as could his conception of Wales's place within the United Kingdom. He argued vigorously, though unsuccessfully, for the symbolic recognition of Wales as a separate entity within the United Kingdom by the incorporation of the 'Arms of Wales' in the royal coat of arms (Fitzroy 1925: ii, 428–9, 433). At the same time though, his concern for the British national interest as opposed to party political interests moved him, in co-operation with Winston Churchill, to propose a government of national unity to Unionists in mid-1910; a proposal that came to grief chiefly because Arthur Balfour both feared a revolt of Party veterans in Tory ranks and was himself unwilling to compromise on Home Rule (Shannon 1988: 156–8). In fact, the Unionist movement was already in deep turmoil over the perceived disaster facing the country – turmoil exacerbated by the multiplicity of factions within its ranks offering conflicting advice as to a remedy; by the movement's political impotence in opposition; and by the apparent failure of the nation to respond to its warnings of national disaster.

The strands of right-wing opinion in the Edwardian period are by no means easy to delineate clearly. The problem of maintaining traditional bases of support while being sufficiently 'progressive' to meet the needs of the times produced a variety of organizations – the Navy League, National Service League, the Anti-Socialist Union and the Tariff Reform League – and a wealth of advice for national regeneration. Broadly speaking, the pre-war Right in Britain has been divided into two strands: (i) the 'Old Right', consisting of the traditional landed élite and including both the diehard peers opposed to the Liberal abolition of the Lords' veto on legislation and more cautious members of the landed élite such as Lord Salisbury and Arthur Balfour; and (ii) the radical, or 'New Right' of the Leagues, largely professional middle class in composition – though some diehard peers could be included – opposed nearly as much to traditional Unionist Party managers as to radical Liberalism and preoccupied with national efficiency and internal stability (see Kennedy 1981: 11–12). Geoffrey Searle has described their development and objectives thus:

the first ten years of the century saw the emergence of a circle of social imperialists, who were agreed upon the necessity of imperial unity, tariff reform, compulsory military service and a 'constructive' approach to social reform which could unite people of all social classes. (Searle 1981: 29)

Nevertheless, general agreement on objectives and unity – based on opposition to the Parliament Act, Irish Home Rule and the flawed leadership of Arthur Balfour – might obscure, but did not obliterate, internal differences within the radical Right. These were exhibited most clearly in the opposition between scientistic Milnerites – emphasizing 'the technocratic and managerial elements latent in the creed of social imperialism and national efficiency', keen on a 'national settlement' of party conflict in the interests of the country and prepared to accept federalism as a solution to the Irish question – and a second group which included Lord Willoughby de Broke and which found its voice in Leo Maxse's *National Review*. This group bitterly opposed, both any suggestion of a deal with Liberal ministers, especially Lloyd George, and a federalism or 'home-rule-all-round' as an Irish settlement (ibid.: 32–3).

That the Conservative Party lacked an integrated and consistent political ideology (on this subject see Fair and Hutcheson Jr 1987: 549–78) undoubtedly facilitated the debate within Unionist ranks, a debate which only became resolved in the period 1910–14 – and not as a result of intellectual synthesis, but under both the immediate pressure of the third Home Rule crisis, with the intensifying and narrowing of political debate that it entailed, and the adjustments made by the party leadership to attract electoral support. To this end contentious issues such as tariff reform and compulsory military service were jettisoned. Nevertheless, while much of the radical Right's specific agenda was abandoned, it did, in a wider context, achieve considerable success. It succeeded especially in investing the Party leadership with its own heightened patriotic consciousness (Kennedy 1981: 12), and thus did much to establish the emotional context that gave Conservative Party support for Ulster Unionism's militant rejection of Home Rule credibility. In the longer term, it was influential in enabling the Tory Party to present itself as the 'national' party: 'the only party capable of preserving the nation from internal and external threats' (Coetzee 1991: 164). Thus, while both Liberals and Unionists could articulate their arguments in nationalist terms, it was the achievement of the radical Right to make British nationalism a preoccupation of the Tory Party to a much greater extent, and more convincingly, than was possible for the opposing coalition of Liberals, Labour and Irish Nationalists.

II

To appreciate adequately the nature of the crisis in British politics as seen by the Unionists, it is necessary to focus on the relationship between the constitution and national identity, especially on the belief that the constitution – unwritten and evolving in a 'commonsense' way according to need – was a reflection of British national character. A.F. Pollard expressed a widely-accepted view when he stated: 'Parliament . . . has been the means of making the English [British] nation and the English state. It is really coeval with them both' (Pollard 1920: 4–5). In this context, the 'destruction' of the 'old constitution' supposedly effected under Liberal rule since 1906 and culminating in the Parliament Act of 1911 became a metaphor for the 'decay' of national character itself. This view was pervasive throughout the Tory Party, among diehards and moderates alike. Imbued with an essentially hierarchical social view derived from Burke and Disraeli, reflected in a constitution composed of King, Lords and Commons, each with its own legitimate constitutional role, the Party saw Asquith's Parliament Bill – and his evident intention to 'coerce' the King into creating enough Liberal Peers to ensure the bill's enactment – as a revolutionary act by a 'Jacobin' government that effectively destroyed the existing constitution. The idea of constitutional destruction as necessarily entailing an attack on national life itself is well expressed by Willoughby de Broke, whose critique of Liberal policy covered its supposed effects on both everyday and national life. The Parliament Act of 1911 had not only 'attacked the institutions of the country' but had 'made war upon the manners and customs of the people' (Willoughby de Broke 1914: 776–7). Willoughby de Broke had long been calling for a 'national' party to redress the disasters brought about by Liberal legislation , a party inspired 'by the purpose of preserving and elevating the national character' (Willoughby de Broke 1912a: 413), and saw in the prospect of the King giving the royal assent to the Home Rule Bill as the moment at which 'the honour of England' would be lost. Yet that could still be prevented and like many British Nationalists of the period he could see in the struggle against Home Rule the opportunity to reinvigorate the national fibre: 'character is more important than things. The real value of the Home Rule struggle will be to stiffen the sinews, summon up the blood, and show all the enemies of England at home and abroad that they still have to reckon with the old spirit' (ibid.: 417–19).

As illustrated in the publication, *Rights of Citizenship: a Survey of*

Safeguards for the People (1912), to which he contributed together with other leading Unionist public figures – F.E. Smith, the Marquess of Lansdowne, the constitutional experts Sir William Anson and A.V. Dicey, Viscount Midleton, Sir Robert Finlay, Lord Hugh Cecil and the Earl of Selborne – his perception of the crisis was widely shared. In particular, all took the view that 'the national will acting through parliament' (Willoughby de Broke 1912b: 46) no longer existed. What prevailed now was the dictatorial power of the House of Commons, which itself was 'in the hands of a small clique [the cabinet] which has cheated the people of every vestige of effective control over the national policy' (Smith 1912: 27). In this scenario the House of Lords constituted, not a selfish class interest as argued by Liberals, but the representative and guardian of the nation: the Lords, thus, represented, while the House of Commons mis-represented, 'the will of the nation' (Dicey 1912: 86). *Rights of Citizenship* was a classic statement of the Unionist national myth, a myth expounded all the more frenetically given their exclusion from power.

In fact, what greatly exacerbated Unionist anxieties as the constitutional crisis developed was evidence of the contrast between the local, everyday concerns of a large section of the British public and Unionist patriotic concerns. As we saw in Chapter 2, there was evidence of this in the period 1906–10. By 1912 it was clear that the public had, by and large, lost interest in the Home Rule question – the *raison d'être* for the existence of the Unionist movement. Walter Long, for example, reported from Bradford, Bristol and Newcastle-upon-Tyne in 1912 that the public was apathetic on the issue, with little prospect of a revival of interest.[2] Public apathy on Home Rule was reflected in the difficulty A.V. Dicey had in finding a publisher for his most recent anti-Home Rule work, and when *Fools' Paradise* did appear in 1913 it lost money (Cosgrove 1980: 240, 245). Public apathy on the Home Rule issue would remain an enduring problem for Unionists; a problem, moreover, all the more keenly felt by a party that saw itself as representing the nation and whose attempts to deal with it exhibited a tendency to imagine the nation in accordance with the dictates of the Unionist national myth rather than adjust the myth to the prevailing reality.

Despite its evident failure to respond to their warnings about the national peril entailed in the government's Home Rule plans, references to the 'nation' in Unionist speeches exhibit a conception of the average citizen as nationally minded, soundly conservative at heart, but, nevertheless, vulnerable to the duplicities of Liberal politicians and prone at times to 'irrational actions'. During the first general election of 1910, Arthur Balfour described the House of Commons as having been elected in 1905 by a community 'under the influences that, in moments of excitement, dominate all communities', but whose 'sober, reflective, common sense' would, if Liberal reform of the House of Lords were effected, no longer be consulted on important constitutional questions (*The Times*, 7 January 1910). During the second election of that year he contrasted the Liberal 'revolution' with the interests of 'the ordinary, quiet, law-abiding, law-loving British citizen, whatever his politics', that were being entirely thrown to one side (*The Times*, 30 November 1910). Were it not for the Liberal deception of the electorate, the national patriotism of the masses would easily come to the fore; as Lord Selborne put it: 'Take off the coat and the Englishman will be found to be exactly the same man underneath whether he be a peer or a dock labourer.'[3] Other Unionists, however, argued that the problem of the nation lay substantially in the intellectual limitations of the working class: 'The simple-minded working man or farm labourer cannot, of course, picture to himself the complex and delicate organisation and solidarity of a world-Empire.'[4] The arch-imperialist, Leo Maxse, indeed, accused his fellow Britons of a total lack of imagination and abysmal ignorance of everything outside the United Kingdom (Porter 1982: 140). But Maxse was capable of expressing more specifically his view of where the core of the problem lay, and this was in the 'Celtic fringe'.

According to Maxse – contradicting, incidentally, the favoured Unionist concept of a homogeneous British nation extending, at least, throughout the British mainland – the election of the Liberal Government dependent on Irish, Welsh and Scots interests had 'delivered a once great Imperial Power, trussed and helpless' into German hands. Under Liberal rule, Britain was reduced to 'an island in the German ocean, governed by Scotsmen, kicked by Irishmen and plundered by Welshmen' (Maxse quoted in Morris, 1984: 227). Maxse's views reflected a significant strand of opinion among English Tories – one that naturally more often found expression privately rather than publicly – namely, that the only true 'Anglo-Saxons' resided in the English heartland and only they could be relied on to safeguard national and imperial interests. In the fraught context of the third Home Rule crisis it was not unusual to find the British 'Celtic fringe' being discussed in terms normally reserved for the traitorous south of Ireland (see, for example, 'The Problem of Wales', Sale 1913: 507–18). Indeed, even at the outset of this period there is evidence of paranoid fears among Unionists of a pan-Celtic uprising in the United Kingdom. The following entry for 19 November 1910 from the journal of David Lindsay, Unionist chief whip in the years 1911–14, gives a good impression of this frame of mind:

John Gretton [Baron Gretton, MP for Rutland] who has extraordinary means of securing subterranean information which has seldom proved wrong gives this memorandum.
'There is a widespread movement on foot among the Celtic elements of the U.K. to assert predominance over the Anglo-Saxon. An understanding exists between the principal Irish, Welsh and Scotch parties to co-operate at the right time. They are careful to sow discontent in the army so as to alienate the Celt from discipline, and at least persuade him to refuse to turn on his kinsman.'
We are all familiar with the anti-military movement in Ireland, and it exists in a sporadic fashion in Wales. Hitherto Scotland has been immune, and I doubt whether this propaganda would ever gain much popularity there. The danger, however, exists, and the best method to combat this tendency should be carefully thought out, though there is great difficulty in meeting what is in effect the hidden working of a secret society.   (See Vincent (ed.) 1984: 169)

Lindsay had great confidence in his informant as a source of 'advice on all sorts of subjects about which you would expect nobody to know anything' (ibid.). His journal entry is also interesting both as an illustration of the continued influence of popular racial stereotypes, at least in private if not public political discourse, and of how a period of crisis could invest such ideas with a credibility they were unlikely to have had in more settled circumstances. But what is most interesting about Lindsay's commentary on the treacherous political inclinations of the non-English population of the United Kingdom is the absence of any mention of the Ulster Protestant community. This calls to mind Matthew Arnold's description of them in the 1880s as authentically 'English' (see Chapter 2, p. 24), an idea which, it seems, was still influential in this period.

Of course, Unionists claiming to represent the nation could not afford seriously to entertain, and certainly not to act on, the belief that large sections of the country's population were alienated from British nationality. Rather, it was more congenial to conceive of the 'Englishman' as an uncomplicated figure, naturally conservative and patriotic. One reason why Lord Selborne rejoiced at Bonar Law's bluntness of language during the Home Rule crisis – 'to mean what you say and say what you mean' – was because 'the English are a simple people and your attitude of mind is one that they will thoroughly comprehend and appreciate' (Selborne to Law 19 December 1912, in Boyce (ed.), 1987: 93–4). It was largely for this reason that the proposal to solve the Home Rule problem by referendum found favour with Unionists: it would cut away the influence of political agitators and place a great political issue directly before a politically conservative nation (see Selborne 1912) – an option, indeed, considered by Chamberlain, Salisbury and Balfour during the second Home Rule crisis in 1893 (see Loughlin 1986: 328, footnote 4). It was this need to communicate horizontally with the masses – as 'Englishmen' – that led 'progressive' Rightists such as Amery, Lord Roberts and Rudyard Kipling to favour universal compulsory service as a means of overcoming the alienating influences of social hierarchy, though they usually proved incapable of breaking their own attachment to such ideas (Searle 1981: 30–31).

The belief that the electorate was 'simple' and imbued with an uncomplicated patriotic impulse encouraged a correspondingly simplistic remedy for the problems facing Unionists. As J.L. Garvin, editor of the *Observer* and the Unionist movement's most influential propagandist, put it, the attention of the voters waned easily 'and must be seized and fixed in spite of themselves', something that could only be done by simplistic messages strongly communicated – messages that would appeal to what Garvin considered the most important concerns of the voters. Among these were:

a They dread dimly an Imperial and Social catastrophe. That dread has got to be developed and defined in their minds. The argument that the nation is prepared for is that the Radical-Socialist method means revolution, chaos and peril, while the Unionist party stands for power, union and security.

b The average Englishman loathes favouring the foreigner and wants him to be taxed. . . .
c The country responds strongly to every form of the appeal 'Britons hold your own.'
d It wants the fleet to be placed on a footing of unassailable superiority.
e It wants Imperial Union and Commercial equality.
f And above all it wants to combine social progress with national security.
                    (Garvin to J.D. Sandars, 29 November–1 December 1909,
                    Memo. on campaign literature, quoted Scally 1976: 371–4)

As always, what was being expressed here was the Unionist conception of what the nation *should* want. As will be seen, their conception of English national identity and modes of behaviour would exert a significant influence on Unionism as the constitutional crisis developed. But the major problem for the Unionists in 1910–11 was to devise a programme or central idea that was truly 'national', and, though they would eventually focus on the Ulster question, there was initially much disagreement within Unionist ranks about the appeal of the issue for the British people, for it was then apprehended that the concerns of Ulster Unionism were losing their relevance for the people of Britain.

III

The accession of George V in July 1910 was associated with a development that historians have usually regarded as politically insignificant, but which, for the purpose of assessing the shared national identity of Ulster Unionists with the population of Britain, is noteworthy: namely, changes in the royal Declaration of Accession removing references attacking the Mass and the adoration of the Virgin Mary as 'superstitious and idolatrous', references that naturally gave great offence to Roman Catholics (Oldmeadow 1944: ii, 47–8). Calls for change had been made at the Eucharistic Congress of 1908 and the issue became urgent on the death of Edward VII, not least because the new King, offended by the bigotry of the Declaration, informed Asquith that he would refuse to open Parliament unless the Declaration was suitably amended (Nicholson 1952: 162).

The prospect of amendment, however, brought forth both extreme Protestant objections to any form of dilution and moderate Protestant reservations based on the difficulties of finding a suitable alternative (Bell 1935/52: 614–17; Oldmeadow 1944: ii, 51–3). Unionist opinion, with the surprising upsurge of popular Protestantism that the Eucharistic Congress of 1908 had initiated in mind, expected a repeat performance on this occasion. David Lindsay's record for 20 July 1910, shortly before a bill amending the Declaration to a simple affirmation of fidelity to the Protestant succession was enacted, is instructive in this respect:

Trouble is brewing about the Declaration Bill. Scotland is apparently up in arms. Nonconformists in the H. of C. who don't care a fig about the Roman Catholics are furious at the proposal that the King shall pronounce himself a member of the

C. of E. Ulster is of course rampaging. All the Protestant societies are preparing for the fray and doubtless members are getting anxious about the future. Tullibardine [J.G.S. Murray, Marquess of Tullibardine, MP for Perthshire] had nearly 500 letters and postcards in the course of one day. This is the kind of problem which is far-reaching in results and I notice that a lot of our new men fail to realise how serious the matter is from an ordinary electoral aspect. People fancy we are no longer animated by the old No-Popery cry, and that our old-fashioned bigotry is dead. No greater mistake: it is merely dormant.   (See Vincent (ed.) 1984: 162)

Robert Sanders recorded that MPs on both sides of the house were much perturbed by the Declaration Bill: 'The No-Popery drum is being beaten very hard. . . . Very lucky thing that the Liberal Party has to make the alteration' (diary entry, 26 July 1910 in Ramsden, (ed.) 1984: 22).

Nowhere was the opposition stronger than in Ulster, where any alteration in the Declaration was regarded as the thin edge of the wedge of Roman advancement. What was equally worrying was the complicity of the Unionist front bench in the Government's nefarious scheme (see *Belfast News-Letter*, 13 July 1910); a scheme, moreover, that had been sprung on the nation and which Ulster Unionists were convinced originated with Irish Nationalists who had made it the price of their keeping the Liberals in power (*Weekly Northern Whig*, 16, 23 July 1910). Projecting their own intense Protestantism on to the Liberal leaders, Unionists found it difficult to conceive of a British government making such changes except under duress. The County Down MP, W.J.M. McCaw's account of Asquith's speech in the Commons explaining the proposed alterations emphasized the Prime Minister's supposed sense of humiliation: 'when he sat down, after making his statement, he hung his head as if he keenly felt the shame and disgrace of the act which he had been compelled to perform' (McCaw, speaking at Ballynahinch, 12 July 1910, ibid.). Needless to say, given the strength of their allegiance to the King, of which Protestantism was one of the strongest bonds, it seems never to have occurred to Ulster Unionists that the initiative for change came from him. The closeness of the bond between ruler and subject, as seen from the Ulster Unionist perspective, was illustrated in the opinion expressed by Colonel M'Calmont, MP for East Antrim, speaking on 12 July 1910 to Orangemen at Larne: King George was 'worthy of all honour, and in honouring the King they were honouring themselves' (*Belfast News-Letter*, 13 July 1910).

It was only to be expected that in making the case against the proposed changes in the Declaration of Accession Ulster Unionists would cast doubt on whether they were 'in accordance with the public mind' (*Belfast News-Letter*, 28 July 1910; *Weekly Northern Whig*, 30 July 1910. Indeed, this was a question which worried the leaderships of both main parties. It motivated Asquith to prevent any opportunity for a public controversy to arise on the subject. More specifically, he was concerned not to repeat the mistake of 1908, when a controversy over the public display of the Blessed Sacrament was allowed to develop over a period of several weeks. With the support of opposition leaders, the Declaration Bill was rushed through its parliamentary stages in late July, leaving the Ulster Unionists helplessly arguing that the House of Commons was 'going to make a great Constitutional change in defiance of the will of the people' (*Belfast News-Letter*, 29 July 1910); while the role of the Unionist Party leadership in the Bill's enactment provoked comment on the strains placed on Protestantism within the Party (*Belfast News-Letter*, 30 July 1910).

The perception that Protestantism was increasingly losing its relevance in the Unionist conception of the political interests of the nation was well founded. Sir Joseph Lawrence, a prominent tariff reformer, wrote to Arthur Balfour in June 1908 describing a new class of Tory Unionist that had recently emerged, one that was 'lukewarm or indifferent on questions that, twenty years ago, used to hold first place in our affections. I mean such matters as Religious Education, the House of Lords, and so on' (Lawrence to Balfour, 13 June 1908, quoted in Coetzee 1991: 161). Indeed, it was noted that on the conclusion of the debate on the Declaration Bill in the Commons the opposition came only from 'Ulster and Liverpool and a few Cornish members on the Radical side' (Sanders, diary entry, 29 July 1910, in Ramsden (ed.) 1984: 22); and once enacted the Bill was soon forgotten by the public. In fact, by early November 1910 it was possible to see the Declaration controversy as a litmus test of the political relevance of popular Protestantism – one that had decisively demonstrated its diminishing significance. Accordingly, in this context, the Ulster question – a mainstay of Unionism since 1886 – was also seen to lose its relevance as a great national issue. David Lindsay, soon to take up the post of Unionist chief whip and who had expressed great concern about a popular Protestant reaction to the Declaration Bill, interpreted its failure to emerge as diminishing significantly the importance of Ulster to the Unionist cause:

the Ulster members are firing blank cartridges about Devolution, banging the Orange drum, and denouncing in future those of us who may concede something to nationalism. *In point of fact these friends of ours do not occupy the secure foothold they held ten or twenty years ago.* [my italics] England is bored about Home Rule, but in view of recent legislation less hostile than ever. The passage of the R.C. University Bill and the Accession Declaration Bill show that the Orange mob is less sensitive than before, and William O'Brien [Nationalist MP taking a conciliatory approach to Ulster Unionism] is a fitful guarantee that the northern spirit will not be without sympathy in the South. All these things tend to reconcile England to Home Rule.

(diary entry, 7 November 1910, in Vincent (ed.) 1984: 166)

Certainly in this period, before the Ulster crisis really developed, and when discussions were in progress between both main parties on the possibility of a national coalition to deal with great issues such as Home Rule, there was reasonable justification for Lindsay's views. F.E. Smith, later a strenuous supporter of Carsonite resistance to Home Rule, was also, at this time, dismissive of the importance of Ulster as a national issue: 'he urged that we ought to surrender whatever the government may demand about Irish Home Rule, on the ground that there must be give and take, and that we owe less to the Ulster Unionists than to larger issues at home'.

Smith argued that as the Home Rule quarrel was now 'dead' the Unionist Party would lose few supporters by accepting it: 'We should still be a united party with the exception of our Orangemen: and they cannot stay out for long. What allies can they find?' (see Lindsay, diary entry, 19 October 1910 in Vincent (ed.) 1984: 165; Smith to Austen Chamberlain, late October 1910, quoted in Hyde 1953: 280). Walter Long's opinion at this time was that 'the Carlton Club was full of Home Rulers', meaning supporters of Home-Rule-all-round.[5]

The consideration being given to this proposal, in which all the national groups of the United Kingdom would have parliaments under the suzerainty of the imperial Parliament at Westminster, is significant for a number of reasons. With reference to Ulster, it implied both that no fundamentally distinctive Ulster 'national' interests existed and that the province's identity was primarily Irish. However, it also suggested that a separate parliament for Ireland was not inconsistent with British nationality – a central tenet of Gladstone's Home Rule argument. The validity of this argument had its source in the role of the state as a maker – or in this case, a re-maker or modernizer – of the nation. It is clear that in the political context of 1910 – as for Gladstone in the 1880s – the acceptability of the proposal depended on the demonstrably superior power of the centre of state authority – Westminster – over the subordinate parliaments. Austen Chamberlain would have preferred the term 'Provincial Councils' rather than 'Parliaments' to describe the proposed devolved assemblies (Chamberlain to F.E. Smith, 21 October 1910 in Chamberlain 1936: 284), but, as he was later to explain it to Willoughby de Broke, under either name the essential condition of the system would be fulfilled: 'we should remain *one nation* in the same sense that Canada is one nation [because] . . . the Parliament at Westminster would be unquestionably supreme' (Chamberlain to Willoughby de Broke, 23 November 1913, HLRO, WB/6/9). From within the Liberal Party, Winston Churchill agreed with Chamberlain's concern for the supremacy of Westminster but demonstrated this from a different premise, arguing that, in the Irish case, the financial dependency of their parliament on Westminster would mean that there could effectively be no Irish 'nation': 'as long as they accept a subsidy . . . we can always bring them to heel by witholding supplies' (memo. of conversation with Churchill, 27 November 1913, in Chamberlain 1936: 576; on Churchill and Ireland generally, see Bromage 1964: Ch. 2). However, what also gave credibility to the 'federalist' solution to the Irish problem was belief about the beneficial influence of Unionist legislation in Ireland since 1886.

Recent work on 'Constructive Unionism' has doubted whether such a policy was ever actually pursued (Gailey 1987) and that, if it was, it certainly failed in its supposed intention of 'killing Home Rule with kindness'. Nevertheless, while this is abundantly clear with the benefit of historical hindsight Unionist arguments in 1910 reveal no admission that this was so. In fact, Unionists were prepared to argue that their legislation had made an important impact on the Irish, leading them to accept their position in the United Kingdom. It was a repeated refrain of Arthur

Balfour in this period, for instance, that the Union gave full freedom to the Irish people; that the evolution of the United Kingdom had demonstrated its ability – as evidenced in the case of Scotland – to resolve national conflicts; and that with the substantial record of progressive legislation enacted for Ireland to build on, the Irish too would come to accept the constitutional status quo (see Shannon 1988: 165–8). Arguing from the rather different perspective of support for Home-Rule-all-round as a solution to the Irish problem, J.L. Garvin also claimed that Unionist legislation had indeed created 'a new and quieter Ireland' – an Ireland that was more prosperous, with substantial social benefits, and which had developed '*unbreakable financial links*' with Great Britain. New conditions had produced a 'new psychology' among large sections of Irishmen who were 'about to form . . . a majority'. Garvin deduced evidence of this in the pro-imperial tone of Redmond's speeches, assuming – quite erroneously – that this was due less to Redmond's personal beliefs than to the force of the new Irish public opinion, that was sympathetic to Britain, being brought to bear. In this context, he argued, there was no real danger to be anticipated from conceding Home Rule on the Canadian provincial model. The time was also opportune, given that a new generation of British electors, knowing little of the struggles of the 1880s and incapable of being energized by the passions of that period, were more amenable to Home Rule. Further, by comparison with the 1880s present Irish difficulties were 'as water unto the wine of wrath that was', posing no greater danger to the Empire than 'our own anti-Naval, anti-militarist and Socialist factions'. Garvin even suggested that 'under Federal Home Rule on the Quebec model' Ireland would 'send a *majority* of Conservatives to help defend in the Imperial Parliament nearly all we care for' (Garvin to Balfour, 20 October 1910, in Chamberlain 1936: 279–81).

The broad ideological context of arguments such as Balfour's and Garvin's was provided by the work of J.R. Seeley, who saw the future in terms of large empire states, of which development the evolution of the United Kingdom was seen as an example. In this context, Unionists, especially tariff reformers anxious to consolidate the British Empire, could easily persuade themselves that they were working with the grain of history towards a state of affairs in which all the national groups of the Kingdom would place a pre-eminent value on their status as British nationals.

At this point, some recent comments on British nationality relevant to this issue need to be assessed, in particular, Alvin Jackson's criticism of my 'definition' of 'British Nationalism' as being so 'flaccid' that 'it might conceivably include those Nationalists who professed themselves content with Gladstonian home rule' (Jackson 1989: 10). In fact, *no* definition of British *nationalism* as a conceptual framework was made in the work he refers to (Loughlin 1986). Such a narrowly focused approach would have been of limited explanatory value. As that work showed, the debate on national *identity* was wider, more complex, often ill-focused and incoherent in expression, and defying simplistic categorization. A useful indication of its nature is provided by one of the major nationality issues that the book, among other things, set out *purposely* to assess, namely, the Gladstonian conception of British patriotism, which was *intended* to include Irish nationalism. However, as I point out (ibid.: 183) – something Jackson ignores – there were problems with Gladstone's conception of British patriotism. His need to interpret Irish nationalism as compatible with British patriotism dictated a more pallid conception of it than the much more aggressive version that found expression in the Irish nationalist speeches. They were, in fact, fundamentally incompatible and it was the case that British patriotism, for most Liberals and Nationalists, remained conceptually flaccid, as any attempt to specify too exactly, too often and too openly what it meant to be 'British' would have brought that incompatibility to the fore.

But, more importantly for our present purposes, a lack of precision about British nationality was also evident in Unionist propaganda. As we noted (see pp. 27–8), among Ulster Unionists there was certainly no consensus on the use of terms such as 'nation' and 'nationality', while – as is evident from Martin Pugh's account of the Primrose League (1985) – the need for an ostensibly non-party organization to draw support from as wide a range of public opinion as possible determined a conception of British patriotism virtually devoid of intellectual content. In fact, by focusing mainly on national personages, institutions and occasions, the British public was invited merely to celebrate its national being and achievements. This state of being – aided by twenty years of constructive government – was one that many Unionists wished to believe Ireland was also historically determined to arrive at; and one that necessitated neither the rejection of Irish nationalist struggle nor patriotism. The former could be accepted as legitimate provided it was confined, as in Scotland, to a past epoch that had been superseded by the evolution of the British State. The latter, again on the Scottish model, would be denuded of its separatist, mobilizing dimension and exist as a statement of being fully consistent with the more important British identity. The hopes of those who shared this view of how the Irish problem could be solved, however, would be confounded both by the permeation of the Unionist Party by the extreme nationalist obsessions of the radical Right and, relatedly, by the political developments that were initiated with the accession to leadership roles within Ulster and mainland British Unionism, respectively, of Edward Carson and Andrew Bonar Law.

IV

Carson became leader of the Irish Unionists in November 1910 to direct their opposition to Home Rule in the hope of maintaining the existing constitutional framework of the United Kingdom of Great Britain and Ireland. He saw no inconsistency between pride in his Irish identity and an intense embracing of British nationality (see Boyce 1989: 145–57). Indeed, Carson was well described by one acquaintance as 'another example of that curious historical fact that so many ferocious patriots are apt to be of alien origin.' (Biron 1936: 215). Of the ferocity of his British patriotism there can be little doubt. Carson was one of those for whom national myth and personal life were inextricably intertwined. On being presented to Queen Victoria – 'seeming to embody in her person and her [Indian] attendants the breadth and majesty of the British Empire' – at a garden party during the Diamond Jubilee celebration of 1897, he was so overcome with emotion that he went behind a tree and wept, thinking that this 'was the girl to whom Melborne and Wellington knelt, the woman of whom Palmerston was afraid, to whom Disraeli made love: and now she was going to speak to me.' (quoted in Marjoribanks 1932: 282).

Already in early June 1909, well before the threat of Home Rule emerged, Carson, appalled by Liberal legislation, especially on taxation, was detecting 'a gradual decay of the body politic' (Carson to Lady Londonderry, 6 June 1909, quoted in Hyde 1953: 245); a perception enhanced over the following year by the speedy progress of 'Socialism' and the unconcern of the 'people' (Carson to Londonderry, 6 November 1910, ibid.: 280). The failure of the Unionist cause to make any significant progress at the general elections of 1910 provoked a mood of near hysteria, while he also came to the depressing realization, as had other Unionist leaders at this time, that the new generation of Unionists seemed to care little about the Home Rule question: 'I do not see much sign of younger men taking up the work.' (Carson to Londonderry, 13 January, 25 June 1911, ibid.: 285). For Carson, the fundamental problem lay both with 'the people', who were too well off and fond of pleasure to care about anything except amusing themselves, and lack of leadership at national level (ibid.: 285). Convinced that 'the nation (like a woman) loves a strong man', Carson was increasingly inclined to see the solution to its 'shocking state' in the rule of such a person, for whom 'the country is calling out' (ibid.: 209). His spirits rose, however, in early 1912, when the Unionist Party under Bonar Law's leadership was pledged to support Ulster's resistance to Home Rule:

It is impossible to believe that everything great and tending to greatness is going to be wiped out in an old valiant country like England. I should not wonder if there is a great reaction even amongst the poorer people and that they would realise that a body politic ought and must be a harmonious whole or it will cease to exist. How I *long* to see home rule defeated. . . . I cannot bear the hypocrisy of so-called political toleration.
                    (Carson to Londonderry, February–March 1912, ibid.: 388)

As his letters illustrate, Carson, even in private life, thought about politics primarily in terms of national myth. Complex realities were reduced to simplistic stereotypes; difficult problems seen as amenable to solution by 'strong' action. This, perhaps, was the most significant aspect of his thinking at this time – the proto-fascistic urge to violent solutions through the leadership of the strong man: the representative individual who, by a triumph of the will, would authentically embody the national spirit and crush the revolutionary designs of 'Jacobin' Liberals and their Irish nationalist and socialist allies.[6] Nor was Carson unique in thinking in these terms. His views, in fact, were representative of many members of the radical Right in Britain and abroad before 1914, those who despaired of the Conservative establishment and craved the simple solution of the national autocrat (Fest 1981: 185–6). In this context, it is also worth noting that the view of Carson and his Ulster followers which sees their activities as narrowly localized and self-interested, and thus 'non-British', needs, in this context as in those previously discussed, to be modified.

Evidence from the Ulster Unionist press for the period 1910–14 demonstrates a concern about the Home Rule issue, but located firmly within the context of the overall British Unionist programme. The political advertisements and cartoons of the Ulster Unionist press during the second general election of 1910, for example, were the same as those appearing in Britain, and which gave the Home Rule issue no greater prominence than imperial union, tariff reform and naval strength, despite the fact that the result of the January election of 1910 had left the Liberal Party dependent on nationalist support to stay in power, and that the price of that support would be the introduction of a Home Rule Bill. Throughout the period of the third Home Rule crisis the Ulster Unionist press presented the Home Rule issue as one of a number of British issues it was concerned about. Despite the local excitement about the outcome of the second general election of 1910, for instance, the *Fermanagh Times* (29 December 1910) found time to rail against crimes committed by 'criminal aliens' who had abused 'the hospitality of our shores'.[7] It was, of course, in their own interests to emphasize their wider British identity at this time: nevertheless, as this study has shown, Ulster Unionist concern with British interests was hardly a short-term ploy designed to curry favour in Britain, but had for a long time been a major and enduring theme in their press. This is not to suggest that Home Rule was not the most important issue for Ulster Unionists; it most certainly was. But what needs to be properly established is the ideological framework within which it functioned. Obvious as it may seem, it is still worth pointing out that the loyalist struggle was intended, as the *Portadown News* (25 May 1912) put it, to safeguard their present position as 'an integral portion of the British nation' – a nation the *Lisburn Standard* (3 January 1914) accurately enough described as being 'composed of one composite people which has yet certain local differences'. It is also worth noting that the Ulster Covenant itself was not, as it has sometimes been seen, a 'natural' reflection of a community ideology, but a carefully crafted document put together by the Ulster Liberal Unionist leader, Thomas Sinclair, and designed to appeal to a mainland British audience (Lucy (ed.) 1989b: 6). Even when the Ulster crisis was at its most intense, in late 1913, James Craig was insistent that although organized to resist the imposition of Home Rule on Ulster, the Ulster Volunteer Force (UVF) would nevertheless be readily despatched to supplement the British Territorials if the threat of foreign invasion arose (account of Craig speaking at Norwich, Lady Craigavon diary, 13 November 1913: PRONI, D1415/B/38). As Carson explained repeatedly to Bonar Law, what the Ulster Unionists objected to most of all 'was being treated differently from the people of England and Wales' (Law to Arthur Balfour, 7 November 1913: BL, Add. MS 49693).

Certainly it is true that a 'two nations' argument was utilized by Unionist spokesmen in speeches and publications,[8] but the case was made rhetorically, to assert Ulster's claims to separate treatment: no Unionist speaker developed a substantial argument to give body to the claim. Carson's opinion on Ulster's national identity was expressed in the statement that he wanted the Union Jack displayed on loyal houses throughout England, Wales and Scotland on 'Ulster Day' in 1912 to demonstrate that Ulster was a 'part of their own loyal community' (*Portadown News*, 28 September 1912). In February 1914 he declared his keenness for 'Ireland a nation', along with 'England a nation' and 'Scotland a nation', but they all became 'a greater nation when they were mingled together' (see *The Times*, 19 February 1914).

V

The constitutional crisis in Britain crystallized in 1911 when it became known, following the failure of the constitutional conference and the Liberal victory at the second general election of 1910, that the King had agreed to create sufficient Peers to enable the government to enact the Parliament Bill that would amend the House of Lords veto on Commons' legislation to a two-year suspensory power, thus opening the way to Irish Home Rule (on the royal dimension especially, see Ponsonby 1951: 281–3). For the Unionists, increasingly convinced that a constitutional 'revolution' was in progress, the Parliament Bill provided the final confirmation, especially so when it became known that the monarch's support for the government was reluctant and that Asquith appeared to have taken advantage of the new King's inexperience. Thus, an unscrupulous government representing one estate of the realm had manipulated another in order to destroy the powers of the only estate – the Lords – that could effectively thwart 'Jacobin' legislation. This interpretation of events was used by Unionists to legitimize their own defiance of Parliament thereafter. With the constitution in abeyance, they were merely taking action the 'nation' required and which was necessary to restore it; and this included attempts to employ the King for the purpose.

The involvement of the King in politics was fraught with difficulties for the institution of the monarchy; in particular, it could seriously compromise the monarch's ability to embody and project a form of national identity untainted by party politics. Anxieties on this score exercised the King's mind greatly during his discussions with Asquith on the possible creation of Liberal Peers; and it was only to avoid a possibly greater constitutional crisis that he acceded to the Prime Minister's wishes (Ponsonby 1951: 282). Nevertheless, throughout this period all parties claimed loyalty to the King while at the same time arguing that his complying with their wishes was the only 'national' course of action. Lord Hugh Cecil, for instance, in his statement of the Conservative creed published in 1912, sought to make the case for the active involvement of the monarch in politics to save the monarchy from the fate of an 'inoperative ornament . . . sinking slowly away from being the centre of loyalty. . . . An active monarchy would incur the enmity of many, but it would enjoy the respect which in the long run is only given to acknowledged power' (Cecil 1912: 226). More startling was the advice of the eminent constitutional lawyer, A.V. Dicey, who contradicted his own teaching and urged the intervention of the King in politics under any circumstances, to prevent the enactment of Home Rule (Cosgrove 1980: 241, 249–51, 255) – a policy supported by both Bonar Law and Arthur Balfour, who wanted the Government dismissed and the Home Rule issue placed before an electorate they construed as naturally supportive of their position on the subject.

For Ulster Unionists, the role of the King in the constitutional crisis produced confusion and ambivalence. Proud of their loyalty to the throne, they were, nevertheless, discomfited by his agreement to Asquith's request for the creation of Liberal Peers to enact the Parliament Bill, and, at the same time, unable and unwilling to publicly criticize him. They tended to sympathize with his position as a constitutional monarch lacking real power and, with the passage of the Parliament Act, no effective second chamber to rely on for support; while, at the same time, expressing concern that he 'must be King of all his people and not the tool of a chance majority' (see speech of Sir James Stronge at Tynan, Co. Armagh, 12 July 1914 in *Portadown News*, 18 July 1914). A great many must have felt like Carson, who sought to brand Asquith as disloyal to the King for accepting the hospitality of Dublin Corporation which had refused it to the King when he visited the city in 1911 (see *The Times*, 29 July 1912), while privately complaining of the King's obsession with '"constitutionalism" which he translates into doing everything his P.M. tells him. What a good King!'[9]

Following the passage of the Parliament Act, however, the most immediate problem for Unionist leaders in Britain was how to reshape their policies to increase popular support; and given the accession of Bonar Law – who had close family ties with Ulster – to the leadership of the Unionist Party it was almost inevitable that the Ulster problem would form the centrepiece of Unionist policy. In this context, Law hoped that the bonds of race and religion that Ulster Unionists could claim to have in common with the population of Britain could be exploited to energize the population there in support of his Party.

That Ulster Unionists organized so effectively to resist the imposition of Home Rule has tended to diminish in importance the wider British dimension to their struggle, but that dimension was vital. Without support in Britain Ulster Unionists would, undoubtedly, still have rebelled violently against Home Rule, but it is hardly likely that the excluded area – if such would have emerged – would have been anything like the present six-county area. The importance of mainland British support to the success of the Ulster loyalist campaign was reflected in the reaction of their leaders to the news that Bonar Law was unequivocally supporting them. As Carson rather optimistically expressed it in the Commons, their movement was strong precisely because it had behind it the 'whole force of the whole Conservative and Unionist party' (see Peel 1914; Ch. 10; also Lady Craigavon Diary, 28 July 1912 (PRONI, D1415/B/38), for a similar reaction by Craig). Law was of the same opinion: 'it was really the certainty of British support which made the strength of the Ulster resistance' (Law to Balfour, 15 October 1913: BL, Add. MS 49693). Nevertheless, a major question mark existed over the extent to which the Ulster question could, or should, be promoted as a truly 'national' issue. To what extent could the perceived bonds of race and religion between the north of Ireland and Britain be made effective now as bonds of identity?

In fact, support in Britain for Ulster Unionism was not quite as strong as Law and Carson wished to think. Law's support for the Ulstermen caused serious reservations in leading Tory papers such as the *Daily Telegraph*, *Morning Post, Standard* and *Spectator*, something which caused Law to tone down his extremist rhetoric, at least for a while (Peel 1914: Ch. 10). As for race, it had largely fallen out of fashion as an element in the discourse on British identity by this time. It is worth noting in this context, that it played little part in Carson's Unionist arguments even though he seems personally to have accepted the idea of race as an integral element of nationhood and, especially, that the Celtic race in Ireland was an inferior element of the population: 'The Celts have done nothing in Ireland but create trouble and disorder. Irishmen who have turned out successful are not in any case that I know of true Celtic origin' (Carson to Sir John Marriott, 6 November 1933, in Hyde 1953: 49). For Bonar Law, it was mainly their common Protestantism, that, in the event of the government physically suppressing Ulster Unionist opposition to Home Rule, would arouse patriotic support in Britain for their cause:

I told him [Asquith] that in my opinion, at bottom one of the strongest feelings in England and Scotland was Protestantism, or dislike of Roman Catholicism, and that if Protestants of Belfast were actually killed, then in my belief, the effect in Great Britain would be not only that the Government would be beaten but they would be mowed under.
(Law to Balfour, 15 October 1913: BL, Add, MS 49693)

However, Law's prognosis was overly simplistic. Even the most enthusiastic United Kingdom Nationalist in Britain could set conditions on the extent to which support for Ulster should be taken. A.V. Dicey, for example, argued that if Home Rule was passed without an appeal to the people Ulster's case would be strengthened, but if Ulster opposition degenerated into bigotry and attacks on Catholics then he would abandon Ulster (Cosgrove 1980: 242). In this view Dicey appears to have reflected wider British Unionist opinion (see Hewins 1929: i. 291). Indeed, it would seem that serious efforts were made to convince British sympathizers that the UVF was keen to assert a wider British identity in preference to a narrow local Orangeism[10], though a recommendation by Lord Hugh Cecil to Fermanagh Orangemen at Enniskillen on 18 September 1912 – that as a means of reducing religious antagonisms they should merge 'their religious parties in the life of the wider community' – singularly failed to impress (Dangerfield 1935/61: 112–13).

Constitutionalists such as Dicey, however, while accepting Ulster Unionists as members of the British national community, were impelled to accept the proposition, as did Unionists in Britain generally, that a favourable verdict on Home Rule by the 'nation' at a general election would mean that Ulster's national membership would be endangered (Cosgrove 1980: 242). Dicey thus recognized possibly different qualities or states of national membership for 'Englishmen' and Ulstermen respectively, especially so when he suggested that while the latter might be justified in rebelling against a Home Rule Bill that had been approved by the electorate, this could not be the case for Englishmen (Dicey to Lord Milner, 6 March 1914, ibid.: 253–4). Implicit also in this argument were differing views of what the national interest of the United Kingdom really was; and this issue came increasingly to the fore among Unionists as the implications of what unlimited support for the Ulster loyalists could mean.

Moreton Frewen, though a fervent supporter of the Ulster cause as 'the real key to the political citadel', one that would 'cradle the new movement to which this crisis must give birth', yet shrank from the prospect of armed resistance to Home Rule being extended to England: 'we none of us dare indulge that temper; we are too near to Berlin' (Frewen to Walter Long, 24 August 1911: PRONI, Londonderry papers: D2846/22/1). A more comprehensive statement of the danger to the national interest that an obsession with Ulster might entail was delivered by Austen Chamberlain. He pointed out that Ulster alone could not defeat Home Rule: if Ulster was excluded from the operation of the Home Rule Bill, the Ulstermen would not fight and the Bill would still be implemented. But, more seriously, any attempt to extend armed resistance outside Ulster would have disastrous consequences for the country:

If officers throw up their commissions and troops refuse to fire home rule is dead. But a great deal else is dead also. I won't dwell on the danger of foreign complications, real though they be, but how then will you meet another general strike? It is not civil war which is the greatest evil but anarchy.
(Chamberlain to Willoughby de Broke, 23 November 1913, HLRO: WB/6/9)

These reservations were reflected generally among that sector of British public opinion sympathetic to Ulster and which was asked to support Willoughby de Broke's British League for the Support of Ulster and Lord Alfred Milner's British Covenant, which envisaged armed resistance to defeat Home Rule. Accordingly, the British League failed to muster mass support even among Unionists; and while the British Covenant did, according to Walter Long, eventually attract nearly two million names by the outbreak of the Great War, it only did so because it had been denuded of any commitment to military or illegal activity. Moreover, despite public demonstrations of unity, there remained fundamental differences between constitutional Unionists such as Austen Chamberlain and the self-confessed

British 'race nationalist', Alfred Milner, who lacked respect for parliamentary traditions (see Gollin 1964: Chs 6–7).

More specifically, it can be argued that what inhibited many from following Willoughby de Broke and Milner – or at least was useful in rationalizing their timidity by those who lacked the courage of their convictions – was the view that to do so would be to act in ways inconsistent with English national character. A.V. Dicey warned Milner that if any attempt was made to use the army to prevent the implementation of Home Rule, 'the English public . . . the ordinary Englishman' would not accept it (Dicey to Milner, 6 March 1914, ibid.: 198–9). Lord Robert Cecil likewise argued that what would work in Ulster would not succeed in England because of the Englishman's inherent hatred of illegality: 'With their habitual tolerance they do not apply their standards to Ireland . . . [but] if Englishmen announced their conditional intention to break the law it would be I am sure bitterly resented here' (Cecil to Leo Amery, 18 January 1914, in Rodner 1981: 80). According to the Unionist chief whip, David Lindsay, Milner was 'too inexperienced in the interpretation of the average Englishman's ideas' (Diary entry, apparently mid-January 1914, in Vincent (ed.) 1984: 323). These opinions lend support to Russel Ward's observation on the myth of national character – that while, as a people's idea of itself, it may be an absurdly romanticised and exaggerated stereotype, it nevertheless 'springs largely from a people's past experiences, and often modifies current events by colouring men's ideas of how they ought "typically" to behave' (Ward 1958: 1). However, as the differences between Unionists on the advisability of military action to defeat Home Rule suggest, it was possible to interpret the dictates of national myth in quite different ways. Indeed, the tendency of the militarists to suggest that only their policies were authentically English could annoy those who disagreed with them. Baron Delamere, for instance, in refusing to support Willoughby de Broke's plans wrote: 'You said I was an Englishman. I am but not perhaps in the same way as you. I don't think you ought to imply that no one is an Englishman unless they agree with your party in every detail of its work' (Delamere to Willoughby de Broke, 8 February 1914: HLRO, WB/8/81).

Nevertheless, it has still to be borne in mind that while serious disagreements might exist among Unionists on the proper tactics to adopt in opposing Home Rule, they were broadly united in their conception of national identity. Milnerites may have been more prepared to identify themselves as *British* Nationalists, committed to the concept, however flawed, of the United Kingdom as one national community and prepared to fight to maintain it, as opposed to those who identified more with a specifically *English* national identity which dictated modes of behaviour that ruled out illegality. These differences, however, could exist within the same ideological framework. Certainly, as discussed earlier, both sections of Unionists believed – or wished to believe – in the beneficial effects of past Tory legislation for Ireland, legislation that was gradually reconciling Ireland to its place within the United Kingdom. This argument was pressed, especially as the Home Rule crisis intensified, by Arthur Balfour.

Balfour argued that the Irish, since they had developed no native self-governing institutions, could hardly claim that a separate Irish nationality existed before the English invasion of Ireland; that Irish nationalism had developed historically in opposition to English repression, but that the remedial legislation of the last thirty years had gradually worn away the alienation on the basis of which that nationalism developed. Good government in the future would leave Ireland fully integrated with the rest of the United Kingdom. Balfour did not mean by this that Ireland would lose its national identity; rather that it would develop along the same lines as Scottish nationality, with pride in local traditions co-existing harmoniously with a wider British nationality. It was this healthy development that Asquith's Home Rule Bill would bring to a halt.[11] Balfour put this case repeatedly and when, in 1914, it was clear that Home Rule for nationalist Ireland was inevitable, he sought to validate it as far as possible through the exclusion of Ulster (see Shannon 1988). Certainly, with the 'Curragh Mutiny' of March 1914 and the Larne gun-running episode of the following month, the prospects of the government being able to impose a solution on Ulster faded. By mid-1914 then, the chasm that had existed between the respective Liberal-nationalist and Unionist positions in 1912 had been reduced to one of defining what size the excluded area of Ulster should be, for how long exclusion should last, and by whom and in what circumstances negotiations to decide this could be arranged.

At this point the King, who by October 1913 had clarified his conception of his role as a possible mediator in the Ulster crisis, took the initiative (Fair 1971: 39). Since then, he had made it clear to Conservatives that calls for him to dismiss his ministers and appoint others (Unionist), and to place the Home Rule Bill before the electors, would not be acted on. At the same time he pressed on Asquith the difficulties of his position. Attempts by the King to initiate negotiations on Ulster between Law and Asquith in late 1913 had brought forth meetings but no agreement. By the summer of 1914, however, when the Nationalists had accepted the principle of exclusion and with the Home Rule Bill having completed its final passage through the Commons in April, an atmosphere more conducive to compromise emerged. Meetings between the party leaders prompted by the King resumed on May 2 and produced a decision to enact an amending bill to take effect simultaneously with the Home Rule Bill, with the purpose of excluding Ulster from its operation while a final settlement was arranged. For the King this decision implied the recognition by the party leaders that 'they are dealing not with a mere party question, but with one of national and constitutional importance' (ibid.: 40–7); and it was to effect a final settlement along 'national' lines that the King was inspired to convene a formal conference of all the parties to the crisis in July 1914. That the conference was arranged through the King was politically useful to both Redmond and Bonar Law, who could claim that they were only attending at the monarch's command, and thus no weakening of their positions was entailed (ibid.: 48–50).

For Ulster Unionists, the King's initiative was a new departure which re-established his role as a focus of true national identity following the uncertainties of the recent past. If his action was unprecedented, the *Belfast News-Letter* (21 July 1914) argued, it was because there was 'no precedent to the situation in which the Government now stands to the King and to the country in seeking to pass the Home Rule Bill into law'. The only power that now stood between the country and the 'autocracy of the Government' – since the Parliament Act had so distorted the balance of the constitution – was the King. In this context, the King was only discharging his responsibility in circumstances 'grave and perilous to the peace and welfare of the nation' (ibid.). And when the King, in a speech to the conference, referred to the danger of 'civil war', this was taken as an acceptance by the King of the Unionist view of the crisis: 'By lifting the whole question out of the atmosphere of party controversy, and presenting the situation as it really is in its reality, the King has done a great service to the country' (ibid.: 22 July 1914).

Ulster Unionist opinion on the conference was a combination of hope of it producing a solution with a rather greater expectation that it would – as it did – fail, in which case a dissolution of Parliament was anticipated with the issue being settled by the electors; an outcome that Unionists fully expected to produce a decision in their favour (ibid.; *Weekly Northern Whig*, 25 July 1914). At any rate, the Ulster Unionist leadership appears to have resigned itself, by the end of the conference, to the fact that the King's involvement in the political process would go no further in their interest than it already had. When, following its conclusion, James Craig had an audience with the King, his reply to the monarch's request for advice on his future course of action was strictly orthodox – that he should abide strictly by the advice of his ministers – though Craig would still have to advise Ulstermen to oppose Home Rule so as to prevent their being put 'out of Great Britain' (Craigavon diary, 22 July 1914; PRONI, 1415/B/38). And it was with trepidation that Unionists watched as Asquith appeared intent, despite the failure to reach a settlement of the Ulster problem, to pass the Home Rule Bill into law regardless and despite the monarch's warning of civil war (*Belfast News-Letter*, 24 July 1914). Accordingly, it was with some serious misgivings about the future that Ulster loyalists gave practical effect to their British identity by pledging support for the British war effort when the outbreak of hostilities heralding the Great War shifted national attention away from Ireland.

Notes

1. See Riddell (1934: 21). Riddell congratulated Lloyd George on his Mansion House speech of 21 July 1911 for showing 'the Germans that Radicalism was not inconsistent with nationalism.' Lloyd George also effectively used appeals to patriotism and the national interest to bring an end to a rail strike in 1911 (Morris 1984: 292–3).
2. Walter Long to Bonar Law, n.d. 1912 (HLRO, Law papers, Box 26/1/23). See also Sanders diary, 19 June 1912 (Ramsden (ed.) 1984: 47): 'the country is lethargic about home rule'.

3. Draft letter to the *Morning Post* (July 1912), quoted in Searle (1981: 30); also Selborne (1912: 198–232).

4. Anon. [O.J. Eltzbacher], *Drifting* (1901: 39), quoted in Porter (1982: 139–40); also Lindsay diary, 18 November 1910 (Vincent (ed.) 1984: 168–9): 'politics as such are outside their [the electorate's] ken, and beyond their intellectual grasp'.

5. The issue of federalism and the Irish question is comprehensively discussed by Kendle (1989); however, Kendle is not primarily concerned with the question of national identity.

6. It is easy to see Carson's leadership of the Ulster Unionists as the logical working out of his private sentiments in this period. However, the translation of the private sphere of personal sentiment into the public sphere of political action was complicated for Carson by his legal background and personal insecurities. As the most recent biographical study (Jackson 1993: Ch. 4) persuasively argues, the pace of extremism in Ulster Unionist politics was set less by Carson than by his followers. It seems that Carson, convinced that in Asquith he faced a leader both personally and politically weak, thought that the best way of preventing violence was to prepare convincingly for it (Hyde 1953: 244, 309).

7. See, for example, *Cookstown News* (17 December 1910; 16 March, 2 November 1912; 13, 31 January, 28 February, 21, 23, 28 March, 4 April 1914); *Fermanagh Times* (6, 13, 27 January, 10, 17, 24 February, 3, 24 March, 21 April, 26 May, 8, 15 December 1910); *Ulster Gazette* (23, 30 March 1912; 7, 10 February 1914); *Tyrone Courier* (3, 22 January, 5 March, 30 July 1914); *Lisburn Standard* (3 January 1914); *Larne Times* (2 March, 18 May, 17 August, 2 December 1912; 25 April 1914).

8. For references to 'two nations' in Ireland by Bonar Law and Carson, see *The Times* (29 July 1912); and by Thomas Sinclair (*Belfast News-Letter* 10 April 1912). These arguments were repeated by Law and Sinclair in their contributions to the collection of Unionist essays edited by Rosenbaum (1912). Probably the most widely referred to 'two nations' argument is that by W.F. Moneypenny (1913).

9. Carson to Londonderry, 27 March 1912 (Hyde 1953: 311). For his part, Asquith's attitude towards the King was condescending (Brock and Brock (eds) 1982: 43, footnote 2).

10. See Good (1919: 148–9); L. Cope Cornford to Lady Londonderry, 4 June 1912 (PRONI, Londonderry papers, D2846/1/7/20). For a useful commentary on how Ulster Unionism was 'marketed', see Jackson (1992).

11. See Balfour at Nottingham (*The Times* 1 February 1913) and London (19 February 1914); and in Rosenbaum (ed.) (1912: 42–3). The argument was published separately as *Nationality and Home Rule* Balfour (1914).

4

ULSTER, WAR AND BRITISH NATIONALITY
1914–21

To thoughtful British Nationalists the outbreak of the First World War not only proved a welcome lance to the boil of Irish and domestic social conflict, but also indicated that it could be the means to permanently eliminate their causes. A.V. Dicey, profoundly affected by the rapidity with which the domestic political environment had been transformed, exulted: 'I am glad to have lived [to] witness this splendid outburst of national spirit' (Dicey to St Loe Strachey, 25 October 1914, in Cosgrove 1980: 268). Dicey had 'no idea how much a just war, to those who felt it just, was a cause of a new national unity.' (Dicey to W.P. Kerr, 16 November 1914, ibid.). What the war might offer in this respect was more explicitly detailed by Winston Churchill in a letter to Bonar Law intended to dissuade him from rebelling against the Government's plan to place Home Rule – though its operation would be suspended for the duration of the war – on the statute-book, something which Law regarded as breaking the party truce on the implementation of contentious legislation in wartime:

Our plan prevents anything being done – except the sentimental satisfaction of having an inoperative bill on the statute-book – till the war and the [subsequent] election are both over. . . . And why sh[oul]d we want to fight at all? No one can tell how parties will emerge from this war. And once the old flags of the Victorian era have been hung up, new principles of action must prevail. I am sure if you think about it at all, you will see that the concession to the Irish of the sentimental point . . . is a prudent and necessary measure wh[ich] all parties sh[oul]d take in common. It will rally to the Empire forces wh[ich] otherwise are utterly estranged. It will remove from party warfare the principal obstacle to a real unity of political action.
    Never can the Ulstermen who have put aside their weapons to aid the Belgians, and have gone to the front to serve the country be the object of coercion to put them under Home Rule. Never can Englishmen look upon Irishmen as traitors and rebels, if in this struggle they bear a loyal part and shed their blood willingly and generously with our own men.
    It will be a new world. Don't bar it out.
                    (Churchill to Law, 14 September 1914, in Gilbert 1971: iii, 79)

Thus Churchill hoped that the war effort – participation in a common struggle – would result in the reshaping and consolidating of British national identity across the whole United Kingdom; and this is consistent with academic opinion on the process of 'nation making'. Of all the factors that shape national identity, warfare is recognized as having a central role, especially 'as a mobiliser of ethnic sentiments and national consciousness . . . [and] a provider of myths and memories for future generations.' (Smith 1992: 27). As we shall see, this was also the role Carson hoped the Great War would perform for Ulster Unionists – consolidating beyond question their membership of the British nation.

I

The outbreak of war in 1914 against Germany, an external foe, created, in classically nationalist terms, both internal cohesion and uncomplicated patriotism, the focus of which – embodied in the slogan 'For King and Country' – was the national community and territory with the monarch as its head and embodiment. Indeed, for his part, George V sought deliberately to exhibit in his public persona 'what he believed to be the essential equity of the British character.' (Nicholson 1952: 249). Yet while the exhibition of assumed British national characteristics – especially those of restraint and equanimity – by the sovereign was doubtless important, a rather more aggressive strand of the national personality was needed for the prosecution of the war. This strand was embodied in the personality of Lord Kitchener, who was appointed Secretary for War on the outbreak of hostilities. Kitchener was an almost mythic 'war god' in the eyes of both the public and politicians: 'in all matters to do with land warfare his omniscience, his infallibility, were taken for granted . . . his arrival . . . spread the same sort of general, indefinite confidence as that generated more than a quarter of a century later when Churchill became prime minister.' (Reader 1988: 105).

But it was not just his successful imperial exploits that gave Kitchener credibility as a war leader; his personal bearing was also impressive. Osbert Sitwell has left a memorable description of Kitchener as an embodiment of the English imperial identity:

the realisation of an ideal of Kipling's . . . every trait of his appearance, his blue eyes and the cut of his features . . . proclaimed him to be English: not an English leader of the patrician type, such as Wellington, but one from the class that had, since the Reform Bill [of 1832], monopolised power. And you could, in the mind's eye, see his image set up as that of an English god, by natives in different parts of the Empire which he had helped to create and support, precisely as the Roman Emperors had formerly been worshipped. Within a few months . . . vast posters showed Lord Kitchener pointing into perspectives in space . . . and, below, the caption 'He wants you!'   (Sitwell quoted in Magnus 1958: 276–7)

Kitchener's public appeal was greatly facilitated by the pre-war consciousness of imperial and national greatness that permeated popular culture and which helped impel a million volunteers to take up arms within two months of the outbreak of war (Reader 1988: 108; Simkins 1988: xv); and also, quite possibly, by the political energies associated with domestic and Irish crises. It has been suggested that, while the outbreak of war defused these crises, the energies they generated did not dissipate but were refocused onto the external German foe. Exploited and exacerbated by right-wing Unionist newspapers and journals, they contributed to the most frenzied invasion scare the United Kingdom had seen since the Napoleonic era (Moon, thesis, 1968: 586). One enterprising propagandist, Ian Colvin – later Carson's biographer – sought to enlist traditional British religious and national prejudices in the war effort by claiming that the Spanish Armada in 1588 had been a Teutonic conspiracy, planned, paid for and largely manned by Germans (ibid.: 58).

Certainly, this atmosphere could only have assisted the patriotic integration of the British people who, it has been observed, were sufficiently and self-consciously united enough during the war to demonstrate that a 'British nation' did exist and would survive despite the existence of a variety of internal divisions (Robbins 1988: 174–5). Yet, as Robbins also notes, it is quite another and more difficult thing to establish just what the population thought, specifically, it was fighting for. It was, he points out, a Scottish Archbishop of Canterbury who wrote to a Welsh Prime Minister in 1918 rejoicing in the victory of 'England' (ibid.: 182). Moreover, while the poets and populace of southern England might be motivated by the need to defend 'village England' from the marauding Hun (see Dakers 1987: 11–14), the image of 'the leafy lane and the thatched cottage' was less potent the further north 'one went from Watford' (Robbins 1988: 180). It will be argued here that one way to approach this problem in general is from the perspective of the relationship between the spheres of the 'national' and the 'everyday'. But it is important, first, to note how the incorporation into the British Army of divisions from the various national groups of the United Kingdom was effected.

II

The first problem for Kitchener was to decide whether it would be best to recognize any localized national divisions at all, or, as he clearly preferred, to place them all in the same army that would recognize no national label at all other than its Britishness. He was warned of the dangers of internal national divisions in September 1914 by H.A. Gwynne, editor of the *Morning Post*, who was concerned that 'national or semi-national forces' would be difficult to change, if change was needed, 'without arousing a considerable amount of local feeling which might reach the government and result in government pressure being brought to bear on you.' (Gwynne to Kitchener, 24 September 1914: BL, Balfour Papers, Add. MS, 49797).

Nevertheless, the pressure for the formation of ethnic or national armies was considerable, and not least from the government itself in the person of

Lloyd George, who recalled the martial history of the Welsh – 'the race who faced Normans for hundreds of years in their struggle for freedom' – to make the case for the formation of a Welsh Army Corps. This proposal, however, was not favoured by Kitchener who thought the existing Welsh regiments 'always wild and subordinate', needing to be stiffened by an infusion of English and Scottish troops (Simkins 1988: 96–7). The formation of the Corps was authorized, but considerable antagonism between Lloyd George and Kitchener arose over the right of Nonconformist ministers to accompany Welsh regiments as chaplains, and an unauthorized prohibition on the use of the Welsh language by soldiers. Lloyd George vented his anger in a letter to Winston Churchill: 'You might imagine we were alien enemies who ought to be interned . . . until we had mastered the intricacies of the English language sufficiently to be able to converse on equal terms with an East End regiment.' (Lloyd George to Churchill, 29 October 1914, ibid.: 98–9).

Yet for all the difficulties Lloyd George faced, his Welsh Army Corp was authorized, something resolutely refused when John Redmond requested a similar formation for the Irish National Volunteers (INV). From an Irish Unionist background, Kitchener had no sympathy with Irish Nationalists and replied to Redmond's proposal that the Volunteers be armed to defend Ireland, thus releasing troops for the war effort in France, with the suggestion that the Volunteers should enlist in established Irish regiments while British territorials could be drafted into Ireland for the country's defence; something which Redmond envisaged as easily having disastrous results (Gwynn 1932: 366–7). Significantly, the difficulties encountered by Lloyd George and Redmond in having their nationalities represented distinctively in the British armed forces were not experienced by Carson and the Ulster Unionists.

The contrast between the apparent enthusiasm with which Kitchener incorporated the UVF as a distinctive Ulster division of the British Army and his treatment of Redmond is often commented on. Quite apart from their military capabilities, Kitchener would have sympathized with their Unionist politics, but another consideration is worth bearing in mind. Unlike the Welsh and the Irish Nationalists, their British patriotism was not complicated by ethnic nationalist considerations. A community whose historic role was that of holding Ulster for the English/British State, their support for the war effort once the Home Rule issue had been dealt with – and even then not to their satisfaction – could confidently be assumed. Indeed, it was apparent that many were prepared to enlist regardless of Carson's efforts to obtain a guarantee that the UVF would only be available on the assurance that their service for the crown would not be exploited to betray Ulster on the Home Rule issue (see Colvin 1936: iii, Chs 2–3; Falls 1922: Ch. 1; McNeill 1922: Ch. 22). Obviously, not all were inspired by unadulterated patriotism: the prospect of adventure in what was widely believed to be a short war was attractive, while in a narrowly political context, an enthusiastic commitment to the war effort would be further leverage in their demand not to be submitted to Dublin rule (see the insightful assessment in Orr, 1987: Ch. 2). Bonar Law, indeed, promised the Ulster Unionists during a speech in the Ulster Hall in September 1914 that given the way 'advantage has been taken of your patriotism' – referring to the formal implementation of the Home Rule Bill – his conditional support for their cause before the war was now unconditional (McNeill 1922: 237). In any event, it would hardly have done for the Ulster Unionists to have appeared less committed to the war effort than Redmond's Nationalists. Some indication of the hopes and expectations of the Ulster Protestant community at the outbreak of the war can be gleaned from their newspapers.

Carson's advice to the Ulster Unionist Council on 3 September 1914, that they must now make a distinction between the Prime Minister as a party leader and 'the Prime Minister as the representative of the whole British nation' (ibid.: 232), was unnecessary as far as the organs of Ulster Unionist opinion were concerned. As we have seen, they had long made the distinction between internal conflicts focused on the specific interests of their community and external conflicts affecting the British nation as a whole, and with which they naturally identified. Thus, on the outbreak of hostilities, the loyalist press, despite the fact that the Home Rule question was still unresolved, easily switched attention from that issue to the wider national context.

At the beginning of August the *Derry Standard* (3 August 1914), argued that it was impossible for the nation 'to play the part of an impartial observer. Honour and interest alike demand that Britain should not desert friends upon whom a quarrel has been forced. The nation cannot afford to see France again beaten to her knees.' The *Larne Times* (8 August 1914), pointed out that 'the conflict with Germany had to come sooner or later. That section of our people which never believed in the danger of German aggression, has had its eyes widely opened.' Even the *Belfast News-Letter* (3 August 1914) swung immediately behind the Government. The *Lisburn Herald* (8 August 1914), indeed, marvelled at the speed with which party differences were swept away: 'Just now, at any rate, none are for party, but all are for the State. . . . In this district as everywhere throughout the land a deep feeling of patriotism is being manifested.'[1] In fact, as it had so many times in the past, in this period of national crisis Ulster Unionist opinion, as reflected in its press, was uncritically behind government policy. There was also the added prospect, as the *Cookstown News* (8 August 1914) pointed out, that the war might provide a solution for Ireland's internal divisions. It applauded the fact that both the UVF and INV had joined in support of the war effort, though the nationalist attempt, initially, to restrict their involvement to the defence of Ireland prompted the *Ulster Gazette* (22 August 1914) to declare: 'They will die for Ireland but not for England. Not so the Ulstermen.' And while this paper regarded the formal implementation of the Home Rule Bill as a 'betrayal', it consoled itself with the knowledge that after the war Ulster's soldiers would be better trained to resist any attempt to impose Home Rule on the province (ibid.: 19 September 1914). Nevertheless, while Ulster Unionists gave allegiance to the British nation in a period of great crisis primacy over their domestic quarrel with the Asquith Government, significant differences existed between the Ulster Protestant troops and troops from the British mainland in the expression and content of their common patriotism.

III

Comparing French patriotism with British patriotism as exhibited by soldiers on the western front, J.G. Fuller has remarked that, unlike the French, the British lacked an overt or enthusiastic patriotism (Fuller 1990: 35). This was not because they did not have an authentic patriotism, but because it was of an essentially different kind:

Often it took the form of a deep if quiet affection for the localities from which the men came, and for the symbols of their culture. . . . Their 'Anglia Irredentia' lay in the football fields and factories, the Music Halls and Seaside excursions that they talked of, and now hoped to see once again.   (ibid.: 35)

Underpinning the soldiers' outlook, however, was a supreme confidence 'in their feelings of national superiority' over every other country in the world. This was expressed in a kindly but marked contempt for all foreigners: 'this was the one great factor in their make-up as soldiers.' (ibid.: 36). Fuller argues that several elements contributed to this belief in national superiority: the insularity of an island people; generations of economic pre-eminence under Victoria; whig teachings about 'the special providence at work in British history'; the consciousness of imperial and military success promoted by boys' papers and the popular press; and pride of race and belief in Anglo-Saxon destiny (ibid.: 36–8).

What is noteworthy in Fuller's discussion of the patriotism of British troops is that the elements of nationalist ideology appear to exist at a level that is almost subliminal, while the institutions of everyday, local, civilian experience became the primary foci of patriotic attachment. In this respect, it recalls how the national appeals of political parties in the Edwardian period – discussed in Chapter 2 (pp. 35–6) – only found a ready popular response if they were meaningful in the context of local issues; and that this situation differed substantially from that in the north of Ireland where national identity assumed a much greater salience in the community's affairs. So too was this the case in wartime.

The factors that Fuller identifies to explain the nature of the British soldiers' patriotism, of course, applied also in the Ulster Unionist case, namely, Victorian economic pre-eminence, imperial achievements and pride in their 'Anglo-Saxon' identity and destiny. However, their history – especially the experience of recurrent threats to their constitutional position – lent these factors much greater urgency and relevance. Indeed, the loyalist sense of betrayal on the enacting of the Home Rule Bill found expression, briefly, in demonstrations of antagonism towards the King. His picture was booed when it appeared in Belfast cinemas and walk-outs occurred in Protestant churches during the playing of the national anthem (see Foy, thesis, 1986: 201), the King being focused on, apparently, because his signature was necessary for the Bill's enactment and was deeply offensive to a community with an especially deep affection for the monarch and prone to interpret his approach to the Home Rule question as being very close to their own. Ever sensitive to popular feeling, George V redressed the situation, to some extent, by making a point of reviewing the Ulster Division shortly before it embarked for France and warmly congratulating its commanders on what a fine division the UVF had made (Falls 1922: 21).

What, perhaps, best illustrates the difference between the patriotism of soldiers from Britain and those from Ulster is the significance of a sense of divine mission in both. For soldiers from Britain this was a general belief in 'a special providence at work in British history'; however, for Ulster Unionists that 'special providence' was much more explicitly subscribed to, investing their attitude to the war with the dimensions of a jihad. Their particular construction of the British national myth was one in which the Deity actively intervened on behalf of the Ulster Protestants, a 'chosen' people. J.W. Good has recorded an example of this form of thinking on the outbreak of war:

I have heard a clergyman in an address designed to show that at every crisis God had miraculously intervened to save Ulster Unionists, quote as proof of his argument the fact that when the whole world believed home rule to be inevitable Germany marched her forces across the Belgian border. To drench continents in blood in order to save the political prestige of a fraction of the population of an inconsiderable province does not strike the ordinary mind as a miracle of grace, but it is an excellent example of how the theory of a chosen race works out in practice.
(Good 1919: 145)

Good was not overly sympathetic to the Unionist cause, but his argument is corroborated by sources that were. Cyril Falls, who shared the Ulster Division's wartime experiences, wrote: 'the old sense of the alliance of the "Bible and the Sword" was reborn in these men' (Falls 1922: 16). The Division's most authoritative historian also notes the literal belief of the Ulstermen that God was on their side, something which they thought had been demonstrated by the success of the Larne gun-running episode (Orr 1987: 29–30). Theirs was the belief of 'simple men': 'religion was near and real to them . . . a part of their daily lives' (Falls 1922: 17).

Not surprisingly, to English officers and chaplains, familiar only with soldiers who were indifferent or contemptuous of official religion and inclined to place more faith in lucky charms (Fuller 1990: 155–7), the intense Protestantism of the Ulstermen came as something of a shock: 'The General commanding the 4th Division, to which the 36th was attached . . . spoke of his astonishment at finding so many Ulstermen reading their Bibles.' (ibid.: 16). An English Anglican chaplain wrote thus of the Bible reading in the 36th Division: 'What I learned from these [prayer meetings] was that the simple approach – almost childlike in a way – they had to the ways of salvation, was better, by far, to the teachings of any theological college.' (quoted in Orr 1987: 57). The religious dimension was but one aspect, though probably the most important aspect, of loyalist identity. Thus, although a Division of the British Army and well integrated into it – Bonar Law made an unsuccessful attempt to have his son enlisted in it (Craigavon diary 1 October 1914: PRONI, D1415/B/38) – the Ulster Division was quite distinctive, influenced by national patriotic notions to a greater extent than others. Relatedly, those fighting on the home front in Ulster showed a similar commitment. Thus, while workers in Britain, especially in south Wales and Clydeside, were prepared to strike to protect their industrial rights and wages (Taylor 1965: 39–40), this was not the case in Ulster.

H.S. Morrison, in his celebration of Ulster, emphasized its wartime contribution and especially that of the Orange Order and the Apprentice Boys. As Morrison put it, the significance of the loyalist organizations for the war effort was that their 'patriotism and religious influence produced an atmosphere in which Pacifism, Socialism, Atheism and industrial unrest in time of crisis cannot survive.' (Morrison 1920: 137). Belfast workers had laboured throughout the war for 'the national well-being' (ibid.: 147). Moreover, Ulster Unionists were to the fore in urging the implementation of conscription to Ireland. James Craig argued that the problem in Ireland was due to the ignorance of the people who had not been trained to bear their fair share of the nation's burdens: 'The people . . . are not so well trained in the obligations of British citizenship as they should be.' Craig, speaking during the second reading of the Military Service Bill, argued that were the Bill not implemented in Ireland he would thereafter refuse to identify himself as Irish; 'it will either have to be Britisher or an Ulster-man.' (*Hansard 5*: vol. 77 (17 January 1916), cols 48–9). Nevertheless, both Bonar Law and Augustine Birrell, in rejecting the implementation of conscription in Ireland, argued that, while nationalist Ireland may not have as developed an imperial British sentiment as other parts of the United Kingdom, its voluntary contribution to the war effort under Redmond's leadership was greater than at any time in the history of Anglo-Irish relations and was proof that imperial patriotism was consistently growing there (Birrell, ibid.: vol. 76 (16 January 1916, cols 1563–5); Law, ibid.: vol. 77 (17 January 1916), cols 55–6). This argu-ment, of course, was to be rudely shattered by the Easter Rebellion of 1916 and its consequences.

IV

Insofar as the Rising had an immediate effect on Ulster it was largely in offering Unionists another occasion to demonstrate their British nationality in circumstances far from uncongenial. The Rising was viewed as militarily inept (Adam Duffin to Dorothy Duffin, 25 April 1916: PRONI, Duffin Papers, Mic. 127/17); a treacherous act in time of national danger, but one which also allowed the UVF to demonstrate its loyalty by co-operating with the British Army to preserve order in the north (Foy, thesis, 1986: 213–14), thus crystallizing their British nationality in the public mind. The *Larne Times* (29 April 1916), which constantly harped on the theme of imperial greatness, declared that 'all the Sinn Feiners in Ireland could no more sink the Empire than a fly could sink a battleship.' The *Witness* (28 April 1916), argued that the war had been a supreme test of the 'soundness' of the bonds of empire, a test which the Empire had passed, the Dublin Rising notwithstanding: 'Every nation has its section of disaffected citizens, who live upon their real or fancied wrongs, who are ready at any opportunity to pursue a policy of crime and plunder in order to bring the accepted order of things to ruin.'

Significantly, unlike the period of the third Home Rule crisis, when Unionists contrasted the 'unrepresentative' nature of the Westminster Government with 'true' national interest, the war had transformed the climate of loyalist press opinion to such an extent that not even nationalist rejection of conscription could, as the *Banbridge Chronicle* (22 January 1916) put it, 'disturb the spirit of unity and common endeavour which reflects at Westminster the fixed mind of the country.' (see also *Fermanagh Times*, 13 January 1916; *Newry Telegraph*, 20 January 1916). Accordingly, the *Banbridge Chronicle* (29 April 1916) was confident, following the Easter Rebellion, that the Government had the situation well in hand. There was also, however, the inclination to describe the soldiers killed by the Dublin insurgents as having been killed by rebels 'more treacherous than our German enemies. The nation cries for retribution.' (*Tyrone Constitution*, 28 April 1916). For its part, the Orange Order found itself in the novel position of angrily refuting a claim in the *Daily Mail* that the Commander-in-Chief of the Dublin rebels, James Connolly, was an Orangeman: 'He is not, and never was, a member of the Loyal Orange Order.' (*Tyrone Constitution*, 12 May 1916). Significantly, no Ulster loyalist paper made any connection between the paramilitary example set by the UVF in 1913 and the events in Dublin in 1916. The Rising was used instead to counterpoint Ulster loyalty: 'The north stands pre-eminently by itself apart. It has its own conceptions of national duty as well as of honourable citizenship.' (*Fermanagh Times*, 18 May 1916).

By this time, the enthusiasm of nationalist leaders and followers for the war effort that was evident in 1914–15 – suggesting real comradeship between nationalists and Unionists – had dissipated, and the Unionist paper that, in the wake of the Easter Rebellion, continued to have hopes that the common struggle against Germany would dissolve Ireland's internal political divisions was a rare exception.[2] Unionists, rather, found much to criticize in Lloyd George's attempt, in the wake of the Rising, to solve the Home Rule question. Nevertheless, the speedy failure of the attempt ensured that their commitment to the war effort would not be impaired. As the loyalist sacrifice on the first day of the battle of the Somme demonstrated, the strength of that commitment could not be faulted, though its consequence, ironically, was that the Division's unique ethnic character was destroyed.

V

The Ulster Division was unique in that it represented, not just a military formation, but the political demonstration of a community's commitment to King and country. The Ulster Unionist MP, William Moore's boast that they were part of the English garrison (Callan, thesis, 1984: 2) was meant literally. In this respect, it is worth noting that recruiting propaganda which urged Irish women to send their men to 'fight for Ireland' did not always go down well in the north: it 'introduced the national concept which did not always rest easily with the political notion of "Ulster".' (ibid.: 148). Moreover, the 'Ulster' that the Division's soldiers imagined was, of course, Protestant, and it is not surprising to find that only ten of the Division's soldiers were Roman Catholic; that Catholics were actively dissuaded by recruiting officers and Unionist politicians in Belfast from joining it; and that sectarianism not infrequently characterized the activities of its soldiers (ibid.: 144–6). On the other hand, it has been argued that their strict religious observance – which was the other side of their sectarianism – helped to smooth the relations of the Ulster Division with the inhabitants of Seaford on the Sussex coast among whom it was billeted prior to its embarkation for France (Orr 1987: 79). It is also likely that their religious commitment helped them to cope with the trauma of life on the western front.

In a wider, though related, context, George Mosse has argued that the slaughter of the war was made digestible largely through the process of mythologizing the war experience:

Those concerned with the image and continuing appeal of the nation worked at constructing a myth which would draw the sting from death in war and emphasise the meaningfulness of fighting and the sacrifice. . . . The aim was to make an inherently unpalatable past acceptable, important not just for the purpose of consolation but above all for the justification of the nation in whose name the war had been fought.   (Mosse 1990: 6–7)

The transformation involved refashioning the memory of the war into 'a sacred experience' which provided the nation with a new depth of religious feeling, putting at its disposal ever-present saints and martyrs, places of worship and a heritage to emulate (ibid.: 7). Thus was the war experience legitimized and glorified.

Mosse is referring here to how the memory of the war was shaped in the post-war years. For Ulster Unionists, however, and especially the soldiers of the Ulster Divisions, it can be argued that the process of mythologizing the war experience began in August 1914. As we have noted, loyalists embarked on a national struggle already imbued with a myth of divine intervention guiding their actions. Moreover, the first day of the Somme battle – 1 July – Unionists noted, was the anniversary of the battle of the Boyne and this carried enormous symbolic import for the Division:

In no formation was religious feeling deeper than in the Ulster Division, all ranks felt that they were engaged in a Holy War under Divine guidance and protection, and the remembrance that that day was the anniversary of the battle of the Boyne filled every Ulsterman's heart with a certainty of victory.

(Official History of the War, quoted in Colvin 1936: iii, 182–3)

Like the Boyne, the Somme battle was to be fought along the banks of a river – the Ancre – and there seemed to the Division's soldiers 'a predestination in the affair' (Falls 1922: 51).

Suitably inspired, the Division made a determined assault on the enemy, breaking through to the fifth line of the German trenches before being beaten back – due largely to the failure of accompanying Divisions to the left and right to reach their objectives – with massive casualties, 5,000 dead and wounded (Colvin 1936: iii, Ch. 19; Orr 1987: 199–200). It was an impressive, but militarily useless offensive, nevertheless, the process of mythologizing the event began immediately. Descriptions of the battle in the Ulster Unionist press emphasized national glory and sacrifice to the exclusion of the reality of mass slaughter. The *Larne Times* (15 July 1916) spoke of the Division having won 'imperishable laurels, and joined the ranks of the immortals of the British Army'; henceforth, to Ulstermen, the first of July would 'be a day of sacred memories'. By their sacrifice 'for the liberties of England' the Ulster Division had demonstrated the reality of their commitment to membership of the British nation – 'one with Britain heart and soul'. In their struggle for the 'defence of British honour and freedom . . . we may be sure that the pride of race, of sentiment, of tradition, of glorious opportunity thrilled them to a man, arousing manly ardour and quickened the pulses of all.' (ibid.). *The Witness* (14 July 1916), in its account, declared: 'We believe the nation's call and God's call are one.' The *Tyrone Constitution* (14 July 1916), reflected the self-centred mythology of Ulster Unionism's view of its place in the United Kingdom: 'today the whole United Kingdom and the entire civilised world is singing with glory which Ulstermen have won anew.' Describing the Somme battle erroneously as 'one of the greatest victories of the war', the Ulster Division's exploits were employed both to validate the actions of the UVF in 1913–14 in preparing to defy militarily the treacherous Liberal Government's Home Rule proposals, and also to integrate Ulster Unionism within the British national myth of the Glorious Revolution by tracing a direct link between 1688 and 1916. Both were great occasions when Ulster Protestants struck blows for 'civil and religious liberty' (ibid.). The *Fermanagh Times* (13 July 1916) also described the Ulster Division's actions at the Somme as the ultimate expression of British national identity, while the *Newry Telegraph* (11 July 1916) saw their sacrifice as an expression of their 'determination to live up to and if necessary to die for the declaration "No Surrender"', which for many had 'almost a sacred significance'.

The glorification of the war experience by the civilian press on the home front was, of course, not unique to Ulster; it was a common feature of the British press generally (see Winter 1985: 285–6). But while the home presentation of the war in Britain was often in stark contrast to the realism of commentaries produced by the soldiers themselves (ibid.), the greater national ideological commitment of the Ulster Division suggests that the difference between Ulster's war and home fronts may not have been quite as large as in Britain. As the sentiments expressed by these papers – the emphasis on the Somme experience as a sacrifice that would integrate Ulster more closely as an element of the British nation – indicate, Ulster Unionists had their own separate agenda that war service was expected to fulfil (Orr 1987: 197; see also the insightful discussion in Kennedy 1988: 26–7, 32). Certainly Carson would stress Ulster's role in the common British struggle in the difficult period that followed the end of the war, to illustrate the injustice of attempting to force Ulster to accept Dublin rule:

In the whole conduct of the war you can find no difference between the North-East of Ulster and any part of Great Britain. They fought as you did, they sympathised as you did, they grieved with you, they rejoiced with you. . . . Believe me, they have proved a great asset for you in the late war, in their shipyards and in their factories and in their Volunteers at the Front. Why now you should ask them to accept a Parliament if they do not want it, I cannot understand.

(Carson speaking on the Government of Ireland Bill, quoted in Hyde 1953: 440)

The Ulster Unionist contribution to the war effort, of which their exploits at the battle of the Somme were so important an element, was recounted in a publication by a Belfast 'Citizens' Committee' based at the City Hall, complete with endorsement of their contribution by Lord French, Admiral Sir David Beatty, Field Marshal Haig and even by Winston Churchill, the Secretary of State for War (Citizens' Committee 1919/1991). The ultimate endorsement, however, came from the King who, in regretting that he would not be able to accept an invitation 'from my loyal Ulster subjects' to visit Belfast before the Armistice, recalled 'the deeds of the 36th Ulster Division': 'Throughout the long years of struggle which have now so gloriously ended the men of Ulster have proved how nobly they fight and die.' (quoted in Hyde 1953: 433).[3] So effective was the mythologizing of the Somme experience and so central a place did it occupy in Ulster Unionist ideology thereafter, that, unlike Britain, where the war experience began to be critically assessed in the early 1920s, it was fifty years before any sustained critical assessment took place in Ulster (see Orr 1987: 217–19).

VI

At the war's end the unity of the Empire – always a more firmly and securely integrated entity as imagined in loyalist myth than it was in reality – came close to the Ulster Unionist ideal. It had, during the war, reflected Leo Amery, achieved a greater measure 'of effective Imperial unity in its direction than statesmen had ever contemplated before.' (Amery 1955: ii,

327). That unity, however, was not to last. It was achieved only by the perceived magnitude of the threat posed by Germany and its allies. With the elimination of that threat the imperial 'national interest' that underpinned it disappeared. Thereafter, a combination of lack of aims, will and imperial imagination at the centre, coupled with the desire of the Dominions to go their own way – thereby rejecting the roles of constituent parts of an imperial entity directed from London – confounded the ambitions of imperial Nationalists such as Amery (see the discussion in Grainger 1986: 322–6).

Most leading politicians in London were preoccupied with, and had a London-centred conception of, British national interests; and as Ulster Unionists were soon to realize, definitions of the national interest arrived at in London depended on an evolving political context in which the relevance of Ulster Unionism was largely a matter of political chance. Their expectation that a common wartime struggle against an external foe would consolidate their position as a part of the British nation may have been, as we have noted, consistent with the conclusions of theories of nationalism that acknowledge the importance of struggle in nation building. Its weakness in the British context, however, was that the bonds of identity holding Ulster within the British 'national family' were – compared to those that held the communities of Britain together on the same land mass – fragile. British Ulster, as an imagined community, was complicated by lack of geographical clarity and the claims of a competing national community, the demands of which the Government in London was under increasing pressure to accept. There was, moreover, an increasing will in London to make a settlement with the Irish Nationalists. Further, this development could not be explained away as the result of the machinations of a radical anti-national Liberal administration, for the war period had seen the Conservative Party achieve a position of dominance in the Government Coalition. The reasons for this are succinctly put by John Ramsden:

The war validated the anti-German tone of the Tariff campaign, the calls for a stronger navy, the demands for national service, and the defence of the army. If Unionists were validated by the war, not just in its taking place but in its nature, then by the same token Liberals were exposed. The war took away the unfortunate necessity, as Unionists saw it, to play with fire [on Ulster] in the national interest; but it did not materially alter their view of themselves. If the war brought them more into line with the popular feeling, then it was not because they had changed but because popular opinion (or at least the Liberal-Labour part of it) had at last seen the light.   (Ramsden 1987: iii)
    Opposition to Home Rule had been canalised into a patriotic war. . . . In the shared community of sacrifice the party had undoubtedly widened its community of interest with the British people. . . . The party, therefore, reaped the benefit of its national identity.   (ibid.: 115)

The war, thus, created a context which made the apocalyptic political outlook of Unionist extremists in the pre-war period relevant to the concerns of the mass of the British people. The view of both A.V. Dicey and Carson, that the war presented the country with the prospect either of victory or 'national death' (Cosgrove 1980: 259; Colvin 1936: iii, 61), was merely a slightly more extreme version of their pre-war propaganda, but only the war made it relevant to the mass of the British people and representative of British public opinion. Indeed, so much did the war allow the Ulster Unionists to assert their British identity that, despite their fraught relationship with the London government in the post-war period, James Craig was asked by Lloyd George to act as one of 'eleven Commissioners in England in connection with arrangements being made in the event of a General Strike'. The offer, which Craig accepted, would have entailed his being responsible, presumably, for defeating the objects of such a strike in an area of the north of England that included Northumberland, Durham and Cumberland – regions where such a strike would have been vigorously implemented (see Craigavon diary, 28 March 1920: PRONI, D1415/B/38).

For his part, Carson's patriotic enthusiasm found expression in his work as chairman of the Aliens Watch Committee, supporting the claim 'of the British-born to the birthright of his nationality' and working to strengthen the British Nationality and Status of Aliens Bill (Colvin 1936: iii, 363). In fact, such was Carson's enthusiasm for the war effort and so strong was his criticism of the government's failure to conduct it properly that he was able to establish a following in Parliament of about 100 MPs which exerted considerable political influence. Apart from the Ulster Unionist members, 'it overlapped with Lord Milner's [following] and included most of the leadership of the pre-war Unionist Social Reform Committee and the leadership of the Tariff Reform League – Leo Amery, F.E. Smith, F.S. Oliver, J.L. Garvin', and had considerable support in the press (Scally 1975: 276). With Lloyd George and Milner, Carson – under the mantle of patriotism and efficiency – sought full powers of compulsion to implement a social imperialist order that would replace traditional Liberalism and Conservatism and nullify the threat of post-war socialism (ibid.: 278–9). The underside of wartime nationalism, however, in which politicians with Ulster Unionist connections such as Lord Charles Beresford and Ronald McNeill and sympathizers such as the anti-Semitic William Joynson-Hicks were involved, was the encouragement of pogroms against the German community in Britain (see Panayi 1993: 89–90). In fact, an atmosphere of anti-Germanism was created which induced the King to abandon the royal family's Teutonic titles and adopt the English name 'Windsor' (see Nicholson 1952: 309–10).

The spring of 1916 was the period in which Carson's political influence appears to have been at its height. When the first Coalition Government led by Asquith faced intense criticism from Walter Long for lack of 'sacred fire' in prosecuting the war, there was widespread popular reaction, much of it focused on the idea of a 'Saviour' who would head a government of 'National Unity' to deliver victory for the nation. It says much for Carson's national prominence at this time that virtually all demands of this sort proposed a leadership that included him and Lloyd George (Scally 1975: 284). Just at this point, however, the Irish question, in the form of the 1916 Rising intervened to diminish that state of 'authentic' national belonging with the people of Britain that Ulster Unionists seemed on the brink of achieving.

In particular, Carson's national prominence suffered a fatal setback with the onset of the prolonged civil strife that followed the Rising. This had

the effect of permanently parochialising the Ulster Unionists, bringing a corresponding ebb in the overall strength of the Tariff Reform movement of which they made up a large and aggressive part. Carson's growing stature as a national and political figure was immediately diminished; he was too deeply committed to what could now only be regarded as a sectional issue. His name was noticeably less prominent after April [1916] in discussions about a 'truly National Government' . . . from this moment onward the Ulster contingent in Westminster became a force of almost unrelieved reaction, its leaders forever tainted with the fanaticism which most of the English attached to the whole island.   (ibid.: 295)

Thus, despite the confidence expressed by the Ulster Unionist press that the Easter Rising served to counterpoint their own loyalty and enhanced their British identity, its effect in Britain was quite otherwise. Moreover, the marginalization of the Ulster question in Britain proceeded, as was demonstrated at the end of the war when Tory opinion in Britain became increasingly reconciled to the idea of Ulster's inclusion in a Home Rule settlement for Ireland. In this context, it is worth noting that while the war functioned to expand Tory patriotic concerns among the population of Britain, it also served to dissolve the ideological construction within which those concerns were expressed in the pre-war period; namely, the opposition between a Tory 'organic' nation and a revolutionary 'Jacobin' Liberal Government based on an anti-national 'mechanical' majority composed of disparate elements – the ideological construction that had done so much to enhance the importance of the Ulster issue to Unionists in Britain. The war experience demonstrated the national loyalty of all classes in Britain.

After the war and despite frequent press reporting of the Ulster problem, the development of the struggle between crown forces and Irish Republicans shifted attention to the south of Ireland: 'there were no pressure groups lobbying on behalf of Ulster or against her; no crusading politician waved the Ulster Unionist banners.' (Boyce 1972: 103). Indeed, Ulster's unhelpful attitude during the Irish Convention of 1917 – when its representatives refused any concession in the direction of Home Rule during a crisis in the prosecution of the war – was received unfavourably in Britain, even by Conservatives. By 1918, and viewed from the perspective of the national interest as defined in London and without much reference to the Ulster Unionist interest, it was possible to see the northern Unionists as disloyal. When Carson told the British public in a speech on 12 July 1919 that he would call out the UVF if any attempt were made to deprive Ulster of her rights, the response in the British press was hostile – a feeling which sectarian attacks on Catholics in Belfast intensified. At the same time, however, Conservatives in Britain could not deny past pledges given to the Ulstermen. A partition settlement was clearly the price of peace in the north and was conceded by the Government of Ireland Act of 1920 (ibid.: 106–8).

To British observers – especially Lloyd George who sought to persuade the northern loyalists in 1921 to formally accept Dublin rule in the context of a settlement whereby Ireland would retain her imperial membership and thus Ulster her British identity – the refusal of Ulster Unionists to compromise may very well have seemed unreasonable. Nevertheless, it can be argued that there were real differences in the substance of British national identity as experienced in northern Ireland as a part of the United Kingdom, as opposed to northern Ireland as part of an all-Ireland dominion ruled from Dublin, even if, under Lloyd George's proposal, the north would still retain the self-governing powers conceded under the Government of Ireland Act (on this episode see Boyce 1972: 157–62). British national identity represented by allegiance to the King – the foundation of Lloyd George's proposal – could only be authentically experienced within a national community that willingly demonstrated its allegiance, and loyalists had never accepted that this was true of Nationalists, even when they were led by the pro-imperial John Redmond. But, more importantly, since the development of the British nation had historically been a state-directed enterprise, the idea that British identity could be authentically experienced if one's community lay outside the constitutional framework of the United Kingdom was not likely to be convincing. Although loyalists may not have framed their argument in this way, the idea it expresses can be identified as early as 1886 in the case they made against Home Rule; namely, that any breach of the Act of Union would entail a diminishing of their 'British heritage' (see Loughlin 1986: 296). It is important to note in this context that, for Ulster loyalists – whatever divergence in religious values and culture that separated them increasingly from the population in Britain – British national membership was evidenced in equality of treatment with the population there. Thus, when Carson considered federation as a settlement of the Irish question in February 1918, one of the conditions that he set was that it should be a 'true federation' – i.e., there should be 'constitutional equality' between the nations that were to constitute the federal units. In this context, the Ulster problem could be settled either by making Ulster a unit or 'by providing for its particular needs within another unit.' (Carson to Lloyd George, 14 February 1918, in Colvin 1936: iii, 325–7).

Similarly, James Craig, in June 1918, made the case for partition on the ground that 'Ulster would be on the same footing as England'; and if membership of the United Kingdom was denied her, she should be left in a position to chart her own political course and, in particular, to ensure that it conformed as closely as possible with the policy 'of the Mother country'. Likewise Ulster would strive 'to retain British traditions, British currency, British ideals and the British language, and in this way render the disadvantages entailed by her separation from Great Britain as slight as possible.' (Craig to Lloyd George, 11, 17 November 1921, quoted in Boyce 1972: 160).

Home Rule was thus accepted initially by Ulster Unionists with reluctance, though they soon came to appreciate its advantage for securing their constitutional position. Moreover, by insulating Northern Ireland from uncongenial liberal developments in mainland British life, it would ensure that Ulster's brand of Britishness did not come into conflict with that in the rest of the United Kingdom – something which, it is arguable, could not have been done so effectively were Northern Ireland just another region of the Kingdom ruled from Westminster.

VII

Having accepted Home Rule, Unionists were concerned to have their constitutional position as a part of the United Kingdom clarified publicly. In this context, the visit of George V to Belfast on 22 June 1921 to open the new Northern Ireland Parliament was viewed as having enormous symbolic import. For its part, the London Government also had hopes of the King's visit as a harbinger of peace in Ireland and, advised by General Smuts, Premier of South Africa, drafted a speech that included an offer of negotiations to the Irish Republicans (see Nicholson 1952: 348–54). The importance the London Government attached to the King was, no doubt, fuelled by intelligence reports on 'Revolutionary Organisations' in the United Kingdom which claimed that, in this period of industrial and social disorder, the monarchy was one of the most important bonds of national cohesion.[4]

It was certainly in this light, but with a view to their own special circumstances, that Unionists viewed the King's visit. In a reflective editorial on the day of the visit, the *Belfast News-Letter* (22 June 1921) accounted for north-east Ulster's intense loyalty as being due to 'a frontier mentality', to the fact that 'we labour under a sense of detachment from the centre of national life and government, and . . . this feeling engenders in us a fonder and keener appreciation of what the Sovereign stands for as the binding link in the nation and the Empire.' Consequently, explicit loyalty played a greater part in the public life of the north-east and in shaping opinion on questions of high politics. Accordingly, the King's visit would not only confer distinction on the new Parliament but signal

to the whole world that our acceptance of the new status in no way weakens the link between us and the Crown, and that the gift of self-government under our own Parliament does not depreciate our connection with Great Britain and the Empire. We shall remain in full possession of all the rights and privileges of citizenship of the United Kingdom and of subjects of the King. Therefore we welcome King George and Queen Mary today not only out of loyalty to their persons and to the Crown and Constitution, but they have graciously set the seal of their presence upon our new Parliament and thereby brought it in visible among the Parliaments of the Empire which acknowledge their rule.

(see also *Weekly Northern Whig*, 25 June 1921; Colvin 1936: iii, 283)

The King, apparently keen to underline the special nature of the occasion and his own commitment to his Ulster subjects, made a point of informing Craig that he came to Belfast despite the fact that 'his entourage was very much against it' (Craigavon diary, 22 June 1921: PRONI, D1415/B/38). The success of this royal visit was a pointer to the future relationship between British monarchs and their Northern Ireland Unionist subjects; a relationship in which their British identity would be periodically confirmed in contexts largely devoid of the party political complications associated with the Irish question in the past.

Notes

1. See also *Lisburn Standard* (7 August 1914); *Down Recorder* (8 August 1914); *Lisburn Herald* (15 August 1914). The *Ulster Gazette* (5 September 1914) declared: 'We are out to fight the world's braggart.'
2. One such was the *Newry Telegraph* (27, 29 April 1916), which reported local co-operation between UVF and INV detachments in safeguarding public buildings during the Rising.
3. However, the massive German offensive on the western front in the spring of 1918, which at its height looked as if it could succeed, prompted both the *Ulster Gazette* (20 April 1918) and the *Larne Times* (20 April 1918) to suggest that Ulster should accept Home Rule if that was the price of getting Ireland's full support for the war effort. As the *Larne Times* put it: 'The prosecution of the war is the only thing that matters at the present moment . . . home rule is parochial.'
4. See Directorate of Intelligence, *A Survey of Revolutionary Feeling in the Year 1919* (PRO, CAB24/96/CP462), pp. 4–5; Report no. 48: 'Report on Revolutionary Organisations in the United Kingdom', 30 March 1920 (PRO, CAB24/103/CP1009).

5

PROJECTING THE PROVINCE: HOME RULE, ULSTER AND BRITISHNESS 1921–39

While Ulster Unionists had, in 1921, won the struggle to retain their membership of the United Kingdom, there was a constant concern to consolidate that position and to give expression to their British identity. For a community almost paranoid about the nationalist threat from southern Ireland and informed by a press given to exaggerating those aspects of southern society to which it took exception (Kennedy 1988), this was never going to be an entirely calm and reflective process. Nevertheless, once in government Unionists had much greater facilities than in the past for constructing an image of Northern Ireland as authentically British, and in this they were assisted by a close relationship with leading British politicians and the monarchy, as well as close contacts with tourist and commercial organizations.

I

In fact, the Ulster Unionist relationship with Tory politicians was much closer in this period than is often recognized. They could be assured of the constant support of the Conservative right-wing and, increasingly from the mid-1920s when Stanley Baldwin was in office, from government ministers as well. Winston Churchill, for example, made a gradual movement back from Liberalism to Conservatism after the Great War, a movement reflected in a strongly developing sympathy for Ulster loyalism and its policies (Canning 1985: 69; Gilbert 1979: companion vol. v). There were personal as well as political reasons for this development. In 1921, following the death in a railway accident of a first cousin, Lord Herbert Vane Tempest, Churchill inherited the Garron Tower estate in County Antrim. The property, whose mansion was gutted by incendiaries in 1922, yielded an income of about £5,000 a year (*Cookstown News*, 3 March 1926), a considerable sum in the inter-war period when Churchill had to work consistently at journalism to maintain his lifestyle; and he took a keen interest in his property (see Craigavon diary, 28 February 1926: PRONI, D1415/B/38).

Churchill's support for the Unionist regime, having crystallized in the early 1920s, remained unchanged thereafter. He consistently defended the regime from criticism and was instrumental in demonstrating the political significance of the Ulster question within Tory ranks in 1931, when, in reaction to the Statute of Westminster – which to many Tories threatened imperial disintegration – he dwelt at length on the supposed threat to Ulster, thereby instigating a Diehard amendment intended to safeguard Ulster's interests which attracted fifty-two Tory votes (McEwan, thesis, 1959: 344). Churchill, moreover, was glad of Ulster loyalist support during his wilderness years in the 1930s. Of a silver cup – engraved with quotations from speeches on Ulster by his father, himself and his son Randolph – sent by Lord Craigavon as a Christmas present in December 1938, Churchill wrote to his wife: 'I wish some of the dirty Tory hacks, who would drive me out of the Party, could see this trophy.' (Gilbert 1979: v, 1029). Not surprisingly, his sympathy for the Unionist regime found expression in his influential history of the Great War (Churchill 1923–31). The passage from volume four, *The World Crisis: the Aftermath*, about the 'dreary steeples' of Fermanagh and Tyrone emerging once again at the war's end, a passage oft quoted by historians of the Ulster question, suggests an objectivity on the subject that did not exist. More telling is the following:

In Ulster, Sir James Craig stood solid as a rock. Imperturbable, sagacious, above hate or anger, yet not without a lively sentiment, steady, true, unerring, he brought his people at length out from the midst of indescribable miseries and difficulties back to daylight and civilisation.

(Churchill 1929: 319; see also Bromage 1964: Ch. 5)

As well as Churchill, with his recently acquired Ulster interests, there were other influential members of Baldwin's Government of 1924 who had personal contacts with Northern Ireland, interests which Craigavon – who together with Lord Londonderry were the Ulster politicians with most influence among Tories (Canning 1985: 54–5) – was keen to exploit. The Attorney-General, Sir Douglas Hogg (Lord Hailsham), for instance, had family links with Ulster dating back to the 1690s. His son, Quintin Hogg (the present Lord Hailsham) expressed the family's Ulster background thus: 'Mine is an Ulster family and . . . we have never forgotten our origins.' (Hailsham 1975: 237; see also Craigavon diary, 17 January 1928: PRONI, D1415/B/380). Like Churchill, Hailsham would act as a powerful brake on any attempt to investigate Unionist practices in Northern Ireland. This was true also of Viscount Cave, the Lord Chancellor, the presiding judge in the trial of Sir Roger Casement in 1916 and who had spoken against the Anglo-Irish Treaty of 1921 (Canning 1985: 71–3); and of Ronald McNeill, Lord Cushendun, author of *Ulster's Stand for Union* (1922), Financial Secretary to the Treasury from 1925–7 and thereafter Chancellor of the Duchy of Lancaster. Furthermore, there was Sir W. Mitchell Thompson, MP for a Scots seat and former MP for Down, who was appointed Post-Master General in 1924 (see *Impartial Reporter*, 20

November 1924). An Ulster ancestry could even be found for Stanley Baldwin, whose maternal great-grandfather, according to the *Impartial Reporter* (21 August 1924), was born in Ballinamallard, County Fermanagh, in 1761.

However, strong support for Ulster Unionism existed within the Government even among those without personal links with the North. This was especially true of Sir William Joynson-Hicks – 'Jix' – the Home Secretary. Joynson-Hicks was a virulent anti-Semite, who exemplified in his outlook the world-view of Tory Diehards. Convinced of a world-wide Jewish conspiracy against the British Empire, he displayed an intense national chauvinism against 'aliens' – especially Jews, Germans and communists (Cesarani 1989: 461–82). He had both the firm support of Baldwin (ibid.: 475–7) and the friendship of Craigavon (Craigavon diary, 2 July 1929: PRONI, D1415/B/38). That friendship was reflected in Craigavon's delight when Joynson-Hicks agreed to come to the North and lay the foundation stone for the Stormont parliamentary buildings in 1928 (ibid.: 19 May 1928). In Joynson-Hicks, the minister responsible for Westminster-Northern Ireland relations, Craigavon had a supporter who was prepared to refuse any plea from opposition quarters in the North to investigate complaints against his government. As Jix wrote to Craigavon: '"I know my place", and don't propose to interfere.' (quoted in Buckland 1979: 261; see also McMahon 1984: 211–12). Indeed, far from interfering in Northern Ireland's affairs, he thought the Unionist regime could have some lessons in government that might be applied to Britain. When an agitation arose in Scotland against the immigration of Roman Catholics from the Irish Free State, Joynson-Hicks wrote to his opposite number in Belfast, Sir Dawson Bates, inquiring as to what policies he pursued to deter immigration from the South (Joynson-Hicks to Bates, 1 September 1928: PRO, HO45/13634/432707).

Tory support for Ulster Unionism was demonstrated clearly in the early years of the northern regime, when it mobilized to ensure that the Boundary Commission – provided for under the terms of the Anglo-Irish Treaty of 1921 to finalize the borders between Northern Ireland and the Irish Free State – did not result in anything more than minor rectifications. Freed from the pressures that constrained them to acquiesce in attempts to persuade Ulster loyalists to accept unity with the South in 1919–21, Tories in Parliament, together with important organs of Tory opinion such as *The Time* and the *Daily Telegraph*, now placed great importance on the bonds of common identity they shared with Ulster Unionists, as well as the strategic importance of Northern Ireland. Thus, in contrast to his liberal attitude in public to the Irish question and especially to partition (see p. 99), Baldwin privately acknowledged the strength of pro-loyalist feeling in the Party when, as the Boundary Commission set about its work, he wrote to Edward Wood (later Lord Halifax): 'If the Commission should give away counties, then of course Ulster couldn't accept it and we should back her.' (Baldwin to Wood, 6 September 1924, quoted in Canning 1985: 86). There was, however, also a strictly Party dimension to Tory support for Ulster Unionism. Given the narrow margins of victory and defeat at general elections in the 1920s, the thirteen Ulster Unionist MPs constituted an important element of Conservative support.[1] Tory concern to maintain close links with Ulster Unionism is reflected in the yearly procession of leading Party personalities as guest speakers at the annual meetings of the Ulster Unionist Council.

In 1933, for example, the young Quintin Hogg used the occasion to reject Eamon de Valera's calls for an end to partition and to affirm the common British identity of Ulster Protestants with the people of Great Britain: 'British subjects are not for sale. We can never be a party to bartering away the allegiance of our fellow-subjects.' (*Londonderry Sentinel*, 28 August 1933). As Hogg recalled many years later, he was then, and remained, 'a British nationalist' (Hailsham 1978: 28). Hogg was followed in 1934 by the Postmaster-General, Sir Kingsley Wood, who asserted that the bonds of identity and political allegiance that bound Ulster and Britain together were unbreakable, and that as Postmaster-General he would do all he could to provide ever more effective communications between the two parts of the United Kingdom (ibid.: 20 January 1934). As Joseph Chamberlain's son, the Chancellor of the Exchequer, Neville Chamberlain, received an especially enthusiastic welcome in 1935; and took the opportunity to recall his father's efforts in securing Ulster's place within the United Kingdom. He affirmed his own commitment to the Union with the words, 'We are still one nation.' (ibid.: 19 January 1935). Similar messages were conveyed by the Minister of Agriculture, W.S. Morrison, in 1936 (ibid.: 22 February 1936), and by Sir Douglas Hacking, the Financial Secretary to the Treasury in 1937, who also conveyed Baldwin's love and esteem for Craigavon (ibid.: 16 January 1937).

As Ulster Unionists were aware, such high profile visits from leading Conservatives brought Ulster 'prominently and most favourably into the public eye' (ibid.: 20 January 1934). They are also important in the context of the question of Westminster's ultimate responsibility for the policies of the Northern Ireland government. The period covered by the speeches cited here – 1933–7 – was one in which Craigavon and other members of his Government made explicit in public speeches the sectarian nature of the regime, when vicious riots frequently occurred, and when the National Council for Civil Liberties publicized political abuses by the Stormont regime in Britain. Yet, as the speeches cited here indicate, the Tory leadership not only failed to take action, but in affirming the common British values and nationality of Ulster and Britain without a word of criticism, it effectively condoned Stormont's policies. For its part, the Craigavon Government and Unionist press organs in Northern Ireland gave effect to their British nationality chiefly by following uncritically the Baldwinite line in national, imperial and foreign affairs. Craigavon, for example was keen to act on Baldwin's behalf when trade unions in the North announced an extension of the General Strike of 1926 to Northern Ireland, by offering protection against victimization to anyone who wished to remain at work. Baldwin, however, anxious not to become involved in Northern Ireland's affairs, advised him that any announcement on the issue must be made in his own capacity as Prime Minister of Northern Ireland (see exchange of letters between Baldwin and Craigavon, 11 May 1926: PRONI, CAB 23/53). Again, Ulster Unionist opinion was behind Baldwin when demands were made for his resignation (*Larne Times*, 28 March 1931), and in his decision to join the National Government with the Labour leader, Ramsay MacDonald, in 1931 (*Tyrone Constitution*, 28 August 1931; *Larne Times*, 29 August 1931). It is also worth noting that the varieties of fascism that emerged in this period and which hoped to draw support from established right-wing parties, had less success in the North of Ireland than they did in Britain.[2]

Yet, close as the links between Ulster Unionism and the Tory Party were, and despite the affirmations of common identity regularly expressed by leading Tories, the reassurance provided for Ulster Unionists was limited. Past experience had demonstrated how changing political circumstances – indeed, how changing concepts of the national interest – could diminish the salience of their common identity with Ulster Unionism for Conservatives; and there was always the possibility that changing political fortunes in the future would have the same effect. Indeed, in 1938 Neville Chamberlain, who had so ringingly endorsed Ulster's membership of the British nation in 1935, became convinced that ultimately 'there would have to be a united Ireland just as there was a united Canada' and was quite prepared to negotiate the end of partition – though, of course, he could not coerce Ulster.[3] At the same time, and despite the existence of a powerful coterie of Conservatives concerned to defend Ulster interests (McMahon 1984: 211–12), the threat of national 'expulsion' was something loyalists felt was always close at hand. Our understanding of why that was so is enhanced by an examination of the wider political and ideological context within which influential conceptions of British national identity were articulated in this period.

II

In his concise assessment of the political influence of the British Right in the inter-war period, G.C. Webber points up its lack of ideological coherence: 'there was . . . no single [defining] right-wing attitude towards society, the economy, the state or the outside world.' (Webber 1986: 133). Combining old-fashioned aristocrats, individuals (often writers) of peripheral status, rising businessmen anxious to consolidate their social position and avert social revolution, and working-class supporters of fascism, what essentially united these groups was their anxiety about imperial decline, social disintegration, constitutional imbalance and economic change – and their belief that the Conservative Party was unable or unwilling to defend their interests properly (ibid.: 133–4). If the context of right-wing patriotic ideas is widened sufficiently we could also include Ulster Unionism, which generally shared the Right's patriotic concerns, especially its imperialist outlook. Certainly Ulster's defenders within the Tory Party, such as Joynson-Hicks, Churchill and Hailsham, saw Ulster as one among a number of national issues that caused anxiety; and one which, given de Valera's anti-partitionist rhetoric in the 1930s, allowed them to unite and concentrate their efforts. In fact, the Ulster Unionist concern to consolidate their membership of the British nation can be seen merely as their particular dimension of the Right's general concern that the 'British way of life' be maintained against threats from enemies such as Germany, Bolsheviks, Jews, or Irish, Indian and Egyptian nationalists (ibid.: 56; Webber, however, takes little account of Ulster).

This outlook, of which anxiety about the decay of 'national character' and spiritual malaise was also a part, provoked a three-fold response from the Right, namely: the promotion of 'integrating myths' combining ruralism, religion and cultural renaissance, with the purpose of re-establishing social solidarity. What, in fact, the Right intended was to re-establish the Toryism of the mid-nineteenth century. It was, however, an attempt that was bound to fail, largely because the values they sought to preserve had been gradually weakened by changing patterns of economic and social behaviour (ibid.: 57). Nevertheless, since a re-establishment of nineteenth-century Tory values was really the only means by which the increasingly anachronistic Britishness of Ulster Unionism could have been made more relevant in the wider British context, an examination of this attempt, especially in its religious dimension, will enhance our understanding of the difficulties facing loyalists in promoting their conception of British national identity.

It is not surprising to find that an anxiety about the state of Protestantism in Britain activated at least some of Ulster's most staunch supporters on the mainland. Joynson-Hicks, for example, was a leading opponent of the discussions taking place in 1924 between Cardinal Mercier and Church of England clerics – the Malines Conversations – on the issues that divided their two churches (*Weekly Telegraph*, 16 February 1924). Like Joynson-Hicks, William Ralph Inge, Dean of Saint Paul's Cathedral and an influential commentator on national affairs,[4] also opposed the Malines Conversations, on the grounds that they were destructive of the Reformation settlement (*Impartial Reporter*, 17 January 1924). Inge's views on Ireland were typical of those held by the Right. He regarded the loss of southern Ireland as shameful and thought the Catholic Irish much inferior to the Ulstermen: 'a good stock'.[5] Relatedly, he regarded Romanism as incompatible with 'true' loyalty and saw it as foreign to English national character (Inge 1927: 68–9).

What gave urgency to the attempts of Rightists such as Joynson-Hicks and Inge to restore or stabilize Protestantism as a central element of national patriotism was that, while church attendance in general was decreasing, the number of practising Roman Catholics was increasing. Indeed, the leading exponents of religious conservatism in this period tended to be groups of right-wing Catholics, sympathetic to Corporatism and Italian fascism (Webber 1986: 62–3). Thus, increasingly, Ulster Unionism's natural base of common identity with Britain was a diminishing one. Only occasionally did special circumstances arise to contradict this trend. One such occasion was the controversy in the late 1920s over the revision of the Book of Common Prayer. This had been in progress since before the Great War and was intended to give greater latitude to the Anglo-Catholic practices and doctrines of which most of the Anglican clergy now approved. The revision was completed in 1927 and generally welcomed by the clergy. It was less welcomed, however, by some of the laity and when the revised Book was presented to Parliament it failed to find a majority in the Commons, despite being overwhelmingly endorsed by the Lords.

The endorsement of the upper House had been given despite the vehement opposition of Carson (Colvin 1936: iii, 434–6); and the significance Ulster Protestants attached to the issue is illustrated by the fact that the recently ennobled Lord Craigavon chose to make his debut in the Lords on the issue and in support of Carson (Hyde 1953: 480). That the opposition case was accepted in the Commons was mainly due to the efforts of Hailsham, Joynson-Hicks and Sir Thomas Inskip who whipped up a head of no-popery fever (see Williamson (ec.) 1988: 212–13). Significantly, this majority was composed of a minority of English MPs with the main body of the opposition coming from Wales, Scotland and Ulster (Somervell 1935: 407–8). The majority for rejection was over thirty votes, of which the Ulster Unionist contingent of thirteen votes was, accordingly, a significant contribution.

But while on this occasion Ulster Unionist opinion apparently chimed with that of British political opinion, it was the exception to the rule of increasing divergence of interest. A.J.P. Taylor did not exaggerate excessively when he described the outcry demanding rejection as 'the echo of dead themes' (Taylor 1965: 259) as the very different parliamentary fate of the Roman Catholic Relief Bill of 1926 indicated.

This measure was intended to remove vestiges of the penal laws, such as a ban on church bells, and, more importantly, to place Roman Catholic charities on the same footing as others in terms of exemption from taxation. But despite the fact that Inskip and Joynson-Hicks sought to arouse anti-Romanist sentiment against the measure, on this occasion they failed resoundingly. On the report stage of the bill, the Ulster contingent – voting against the measure despite the fact that it would not apply to Northern Ireland where equality of religious treatment was guaranteed under the terms of the Government of Ireland Act – together with mainland opponents, accounted for only some thirty-six votes against, compared to 168 votes in favour. The bill passed its third reading without a vote (see Oldmeadow 1944: ii, 299–300). The extent to which popular attitudes to Roman Catholicism had moved from the mid-nineteenth century is indicated by the fact that, over the inter-war period as a whole, some forty Roman Catholics sat as Tory MPs (McEwan, thesis, 1959: 37). Moreover, at the same time as the religious ties of identity between Ulster and Britain were waning, the dominant concept of national identity, embodied in Baldwinite patriotism in the inter-war period, was not such as could easily accommodate Ulster loyalism.

III

Much has been written about Stanley Baldwin's articulation of Englishness/Britishness as an arcadian concept, focused on southern England, and extolling and invoking nostalgia for a supposedly authentic, rural, 'organic' existence deemed culturally superior to modern urban, industrial life.[6] Its ideological roots can be traced to Burke's *Reflections on the Revolution in France*, with its integration of the genetic family in the local sphere of existence with that of the 'national' family in the public sphere (see Chapter 1, pp. 8–9). The appeal of the 'organic' ruralism that Baldwin articulated – enthusiastically marketed, ironically, in a period when the proportion of Conservative MPs actually connected with 'land' as the basis of their livelihood dropped to one tenth in 1939 from one-quarter in 1914 (McEwan, thesis, 1954: 415) – lay in its projection of peace, consensus and harmony to set against the trauma of war and the immediate post-war experience of industrial conflict and urban social dislocation.[7] Moreover, the potency of ruralism's public appeal lay in its ability to resonate against the general experience of 'the turmoil of modern everyday life' (Wright 1985: 86–7). Accordingly, it lent itself easily as a repository, or site, for the articulation of national characteristics. On these there existed a broad consensus across the political spectrum. For example, the national character as presented by the socialists, George Orwell and J.B. Priestley – the latter actually a defender of industrial Britain – among other influential commentators, included tolerance, individualism, balance, compromise, a sense of humour, equanimity, social homogeneity and kindliness; with humour, tolerance and emotional restraint constituting central strands (see Richards 1988: 55–60). That these were precisely the characteristics evident in Baldwin's national myth-making indicates that both Left and Right in Britain drew on a common and well-established ideological fund of national characteristics.

But Baldwin was concerned not only to articulate the British national character in general, but to present himself as the personal embodiment of it. His conception of English history was a process, devoid of the extremes of struggle and bloodshed, which explicated the national characteristic of tolerance. A right-wing critic acutely observed that his historical sense was confused: 'Glamour to him is not in the movement of battle but in the stillness of memory.' (Green [1933]: 24). Baldwin himself declared 'a loyalty to the past – not always an historic past but . . . a past that lives and grows and has its being in the very essence of ourselves.' (Baldwin 1935: 191). Accordingly, it is hardly surprising to find Baldwin exploiting his own family genealogy to present himself as the authentic embodiment of the rounded national personality.

Speaking at a St David's Day dinner on 2 March 1925, he spoke as 'an Englishman' with historic Welsh roots and incorporated Wales within his imagined arcadian national community by denying that 'her industrial areas' were authentically representative of the country, whose true character resided in 'our rural civilisation.' (Baldwin 1926: 249–52). Again, and as befitted the historically more significant union of the former enemies – Scotland and England – Baldwin, speaking at the St Andrew's Day Festival of the Royal Scottish Corporation in November 1925, described himself as 'a typical Englishman', but one with ancestors who were Scottish Jacobites: 'the last time my ancestors wore the kilt was at Culloden.' Appropriately enough in this context, Baldwin took pains to praise Sir Walter Scott as a true Scottish patriot whose writings performed a vital role in consolidating the Anglo-Scottish Union. Indeed: 'had there been a Walter Scott for Ireland there would have been no Boundary Commission sitting today.' (ibid.: 237–43; also Baldwin 1935: 189–93). Baldwin could define Englishness within the narrow geographic boundaries of England, but usually it was presented within, and as being representative of, Britain as a whole (see Baldwin 1941: 437–62).

The specific purpose for which Baldwin projected himself and was promoted by his party, was as a peacemaker, 'to resolve harmoniously what he saw as specific national and moral crises. . . . Harmony in the nation and the constitution together formed his political thought.' (Schwarz 1984: 7). However, what is significant about Baldwin's presentation of the British national personality, for our purposes, is the deliberate ignoring of the Ulster dimension – despite the fact that he could claim historic family connections with the province. In fact, on the rare occasions that he mentioned Northern Ireland, as when he addressed a St Patrick's Day banquet in 1926 – shortly after the resolution of the controversy over the Boundary Commission – he defined it in an Irish context as 'a problem in the North'. Moreover, it was a problem – given the acceptance of the boundary settlement – that southern Nationalists recognized existed; and on this basis they could look on it as amenable to an eventual solution. This optimistic prospect, Baldwin suggested, was facilitated by the fact that 'in the North [Ireland] has a statesman [Craigavon], an Irishman and a man of deep wisdom' who, together with political leaders in the South, were dealing with Ireland's affairs with courage and honesty 'rare among statesmen. . . . We want the two Governments of Ireland to have fair play from the world.' (Baldwin 1926: 244–8).

There is, thus, an observable contrast between the political realities of the Tory position on the Ulster question – which was effectively tied to supporting Northern Ireland's place within the United Kingdom – and Baldwin's articulation of English/British identity which, in ignoring Ulster, effectively denied it membership of the British nation. In truth, however, it was not possible for Northern Ireland to be incorporated within that identity. Quite apart from the courting of controversy that any attempt to publicly do so would have entailed, the dominant image of Ulster was at variance with the characteristics identified as British.

National myths, as we have noted, are fundamentally constructions of stereotypes, or, as Barthes (1973) termed them, 'essences'. Such constructions do not allow for ambiguity, contradictions or complexities. Accordingly, the dominant public image of Ulster – largely industrial and with associations of bigotry, sectarianism and political extremism – could not easily be accommodated within the Baldwinite conception of British identity, emphasizing humour, tolerance, and compromise. Nor, given the controversy over partition, was it possible to fit Northern Ireland easily into any essential or 'authentic' conception of the national territory. The Baldwinite conception, focused on an ideal rural environment, could, so long as Wales and Scotland remained satisfied with their Unions with England, be promoted as a core myth for Britain despite the existence of large industrial areas incompatible with that myth. This, however, could not be done for Northern Ireland, despite the fact that visitors to the North in this period could be very impressed by its 'Englishness'. H.V. Morton (1930: 231), for instance, wrote thus of crossing the northern border from the Irish Free State and seeing war memorials, red pillar-boxes and Union Jacks: 'I seemed to be in England again.' It is also worth noting that Baldwin unequivocally rejected any attempt by Ulster Unionists to crystallize Northern Ireland's British identity. An attempt was made in 1927, when Craigavon sought to take advantage of a change in the royal title to have the North's official name changed from 'Northern Ireland' to 'Ulster'. Baldwin stymied the attempt by pointing out that this would involve changes to the Anglo-Irish treaty of 1921, and that any tampering with the Treaty could open up possibilities detrimental to Unionist interests (Baldwin to Craigavon, 15 February 1927: University of Cambridge, Baldwin papers, vol. 101). Thus, against this background and with recurrent anti-partitionist demands emanating from the Irish Free State, the observations of visitors such as Morton on the North's apparent 'Englishness' counted for little. Accordingly, when the Tory conception of the nation was made into a film for cinematic distribution – Soul of a Nation (1933) – the image of the British nation it presented was one which identified Ireland, north and south, as a place apart.

Focusing on the history of the nation since 1900, Soul of a Nation emphasized a historical tradition of peaceful change within a strongly monarchist perspective. In this context, the threatened civil war associated with Ulster and the third Home Rule crisis was presented as a solely Irish affair. In fact, the only specific mention of the UVF and the INV was in connection with their support for the British war effort. Thereafter, Ireland was ignored apart from the brief comment that by 1921 it was the only place in the Empire where shooting was still taking place. A brief reference to the Irish Civil War concluded with mention of the election of Liam Cosgrove as Irish Prime Minister, which event was seen as marking the end of the Irish troubles and, implicitly, the Irish question.[8]

Soul of a Nation reflected a concern in government that, in a period when Britain's economic power was diminishing and British overseas political and commercial interests appeared to be suffering from inadequate representation and explanation abroad, the favourable projection of British national identity world-wide had to be seriously promoted (Taylor 1981: 85). One of the central figures in the projection of British nationality was Sir Stephen Tallents, an experienced and talented diplomat who defined his task as the encouraging of sympathy with, interest in and admiration for, the British way of life (ibid.: 111). Tallents's opinion of what elements would be representative of that way of life included all the core ideas of British national character, culture and countryside: 'Parliament, the monarchy, Shakespeare, London life, English cathedrals and villages, law and order, coolness [of temperament] and fair play' (ibid.: 119–20). Tallents's view of the British way of life was unexceptional for the period, and especially so in its blindness to regional particularity. Thus, that Northern Ireland was not included in it is not, of itself, noteworthy. However, even if he had been concerned to take account of Britain's regional distinctiveness, it is still unlikely that Northern Ireland would have been included.

Tallents had been Lloyd George's representative in the North in 1922 – sent to investigate sectarian outrages in Belfast – and quickly formed a low opinion of the Ulster Government. The Special Constabulary he quickly recognized as openly sectarian. Yet he advised against a public inquiry into the Belfast events, largely because 'It would lead to a revival of propaganda about matters that are best forgotten.' (Tallents quoted in Canning 1985: 64). Tallents would, it seems reasonable to conclude, have been the last person to have cited Northern Ireland as representative of what was best in British life and culture. In this respect, it is worth noting that other organs of national propaganda also ignored Northern Ireland. The General Post Office (GPO) film, *Islanders*, was a presentation of British life that focused on the heartland island of Britain together with all the United Kingdom satellite islands *except* Northern Ireland (GPO Film Unit: 1937). Moreover, even an organization such as the British Broadcasting Corporation (BBC), which deliberately sought to act as an agency of national integration[9], reflective of the regional and national differences within the United Kingdom, had difficulties in this respect with the North.

The regional Ulster station could produce programmes on rural culture that resonated, on one level, with the wider arcadian British national myth; however, the fact that the Irish Free State was still a member of the Empire meant that the station had to reflect Irish culture in general (Cardiff and Scammell 1987: 164–5). And for a region whose Protestant population abounded in enthusiasm for the Empire,[10] the ironic and disturbing consequence was that this requirement often meant that Ulster was presented to the world in terms culturally indistinguishable from southern Ireland (see Cathcart 1984: Ch. 3). Relatedly, maps of the British Empire in this period could easily omit the constitutional distinction between Northern Ireland and the Irish Free State,[11] while it was not unusual for journals on world affairs to present the territory of the Irish Free State as encompassing the whole island of Ireland.[12]

Nevertheless, there were exceptions to the practice of marginalizing the Ulster dimension to British nationality. Arthur Bryant, a Nazi sympathizer and anti-Semite (see Roberts 1994: Ch. 6), as well as a major interpreter of English/British identity in the inter-war period, took a special interest in Northern Ireland. Later the author of a wide range of highly popular (and still read) historical studies celebrating British national character and achievements, he lectured at the Conservative Party 'political college' at Ashbridge and occasionally prepared speeches for Baldwin and Neville Chamberlain (Wiener 1987: 112–14; Street 1979: 100). Bryant sought to

identify the arcadian national image of Britain specifically with Conservatism – sometimes explicitly (Bryant 1929: 74–5; Wright 1985: 53) but
most frequently, implicitly – through his column, 'Our Notebook', which
he contributed for nearly forty years to the middle-brow *Illustrated
London News* (for a representative selection of his work, see Bryant 1969).

Like many British public figures with an interest in Ulster, Bryant had
family connections with Ireland:

> Several much loved kinsmen from the 'black North', large and shrewd Ulstermen
> of staunch Unionist convictions . . . my earliest impressions of the Irish question
> had a strong Orange tinge. Indeed, one of the proudest moments of my boyhood
> was an afternoon spent paddling Sir Edward Carson around the troutlake in my
> uncle's Wiltshire home, while the great orator occasionally regaled my revering
> ears with oracular words which, if possible, strengthened even further my
> conviction that Britain's Liberal rulers, in their lust for votes and power, were only
> awaiting the day when they would sell their country to Irish incendiaries and
> murderers!   (ibid.: 200)

Bryant would write that this impression of Ireland was, in time, much
modified by personal acquaintance with the island; nevertheless, his Ulster
connections, together with the fact that a much-loved uncle, an
administrator of the Congested Estates in Connaught, was assassinated
during the Irish Civil War (ibid.: 201–2), are sufficient to explain his
concern, whenever the occasion arose, to make better known in Britain the
fact that Northern Ireland was an integral portion of the United Kingdom.

Accordingly, on the occasion of the royal visit to Ulster of George VI in
July 1937, Bryant sought to counter the derogatory image of the North in
Britain, denying the validity of the Unionist reputation for fascistic bigotry
and violence. Instead, the Ulster Bryant described was 'the most democratic community I have ever visited', a model of law-abiding order,
reasoned social reform and genial good humour, even in its traditional
'defiance of wooden shoes and Popery'. Ulster people were proud of their
self-government, but such was the intensity of their loyalty to Great Britain
that 'they would surrender it at an hour's notice to the mother country
from which they derived it and whose children they are so proud to be'.
Yet, Bryant complained:

> the almost passionate devotion to the British link and the British past which is the
> Ulsterman's most distinguishing political attribute receives singularly little
> encouragement from the object of Ulster's devotion. Most people in this island
> [Britain] scarcely give her a thought. The great dominions and India figure far more
> often in our newspapers; so does . . . the Irish Free State. But of Ulster we hear
> little.   (*Illustrated London News*, 14 August 1937)

In his plea for a greater appreciation of Ulster in Britain, Bryant had
sought to counter the region's negative image by presenting it as an ideal
British community of his own imagining. Completely ignoring the presence
of the North's Catholic community and the recent controversies surrounding its treatment by the Stormont regime, Bryant argued that the

oppression by 'the men of Ulster' of 'men of different race and religion' was a 'tyranny of the past'; something that had occurred 'many generations' ago and had no bearing on the present (ibid.).

Bryant went further in his attempts to bring Ulster more firmly into British national life. When, in 1939, the Stormont government advertised for a publicity officer to represent Ulster interests in London, Bryant wrote to Craigavon pressing the case of Hugh Sellon, 'one of our most brilliant lecturers' at the Conservative Party's political college at Ashbridge, and who represented 'a whole-hearted Tory patriotism' (Bryant to Craigavon, 24 February 1939; PRONI, CAB9F/123/3). Despite Bryant's endorsement, however, Sellon's candidature was unsuccessful. But even if it had been it is unlikely that Bryant's objectives would have been attained. His references to Ulster were crowded out of the British public mind by greater questions such as India and pointed up an enduring truth about Anglo-Irish relations, namely: that Ireland only really impinged on British public opinion in times of crisis, and as an issue that Britain *had* to address. Ironically, in their concern to have their Britishness more fully recognized in Britain, Ulster Unionists faced exactly the same problem as had Irish Nationalists in the nineteenth century who wished to have their denial of it acknowledged. Moreover, and as Bryant must have realized, Britain's ongoing conflicts with the Irish Free State in the 1930s meant that when British attention was turned to Ireland, it was often in terms of an agenda set by de Valera and in which the constitutional status of Northern Ireland was vigorously contested. It was in these difficult circumstances that the Craigavon regime itself attempted to have the North accepted in Britain as an authentic part of the national territory and people.

IV

The adverse conditions in which the northern statelet was established, and the uncertainty over its status that prevailed until the resolution of the boundary issue in 1926, conditioned an anxious state of mind that characterized the Unionist regime, certainly until the outbreak of World War Two, and which fuelled its need constantly to work to make the British population appreciate the position of their fellow nationals in Ulster.

In the period 1922–25 the regime sponsored extensive propaganda to make the new Northern Ireland statelet better known 'at home and abroad'. Conducted mainly through the agency of the Ulster Association for Peace with Honour, a grouping of Ulster businessmen, the campaign included the establishment of offices in Belfast and London, the publication of an 'Ulster News Service' for every daily paper in Great Britain, and a weekly 'Ulster Letter' sent to between fifty and sixty weekly journals, while the Association also energetically sought to refute 'erroneous and unfriendly Ulster articles' in British newspapers. The effort the Association put into its work can be gauged by the fact that in the first year of its operations 60,000 columns were secured in the world's press while the Association's publicity committee distributed approximately 10,000 copies of each of several publications about Ulster (see 'Government Publicity: a Short Résumé Since 1922', 1 June 1943: PRONI CAB9F/123/3). While guiding the activities of this organization, the Government and especially Craig, exploited other avenues for asserting Ulster's British identity. The British Empire Exhibition of 1924 at Wembley, for example, was an ideal venue for this purpose and Craig made sure that his Government was well represented.[13] Again, Craig contributed a piece for the *Spectator* in February 1924 that sought to educate British opinion on the North and the threat to the regime from southern Ireland – a threat Craig used to excuse 'what is sometimes condemned as her [Ulster's] excessive patriotism.' (see *Tyrone Constitution*, 29 February 1924). This was only one of a number of articles Craig contributed to English journals in this period, all with the same purpose of presenting Northern Ireland as possessed of an uncomplicated British identity.

The settlement of the boundary issue in 1926 led to a winding down of this intense propaganda campaign, but the anti-partitionist rhetoric of southern politicians continued to stimulate what Craig euphemistically described as Ulster's 'excessive patriotism', and also the near-paranoid caste of mind that underlay it and which invested the vocabulary of 'Crown and Constitution' with almost occult properties. The liberal Unionist, W.S. Armour, wrote of its significance in Ulster politics thus:

the infallibility attached to the Crown, the Constitution, the Christian religion and the British Empire, gives to those under their aegis . . . mystic powers such as are not possessed in any part of the Empire known to me. . . . One singular notion that prevails in this Protestant area is that if you see anything wrong you must not say a word about it . . . for fear of disturbing the Crown, the Constitution, the Christian religion and the British Empire.   (Armour 1935: 189)

In this context, Armour argued, there could be no 'public opinion in the sense in which it is understood in England', only a 'herd instinct which could apparently be aroused over the whole area in a twinkling' (ibid.: 191–2, 196). Thus in Northern Ireland 'the only way of being loyal is to approve of every legislative and administrative act' (ibid.: 196). Armour wrote, however, not as an objective observer, but as a critic of the regime who had recently lost his post as editor of the *Northern Whig* as a result of a censure motion against him in the Stormont Parliament for breach of privilege, over his criticism of the siting of a new bridge in Derry (see Kennedy 1988: 15–16). Nevertheless, his argument has the ring of truth. The Government's use of the border issue in this period to enforce political discipline among the Unionist population provides telling examples of how patriotic myth can be employed to simplify, or 'purify', political debate in a context of virtually permanent constitutional crisis.

At the same time, however, as Armour's critique of Unionist politics indicates, it was one thing to produce regularly a majority for the Union with Britain, quite another to construct an image of Northern Ireland that could effectively register with British public opinion. This was an enduring problem for the regime in the inter-war period. It was succinctly expressed by Sir Robert Nugent in a memorandum advocating the appointment of a full-time publicity officer to represent the regime's interests in London:

we must decide what ideas and beliefs concerning Ulster we wish to implant in the British consciousness, satisfy ourselves that the ideas are of such a nature that it is psychologically possible to get them into the British mind and then see to it that all our publicity work . . . is consistent with the main objective.

(Sir Robert Nugent, 'Publicity', Confidential, 7 October 1938: PRONI, CAB9F/123/3)

That Nugent's recommendations were made in October 1938 reflects the limited success of previous efforts. The problem was not only the difficult one of registering the presence of Northern Ireland consistently in the 'British consciousness', but, more so, of the kind of image to be presented. A positive image was one which depended on the promotion of certain kinds of information and the suppression of others.

Craigavon might declare that he did not want the people of Northern Ireland to monotonously reproduce 'English ways' (Campbell 1941: 247), though his ministers repeatedly claimed that Northern Ireland was either part of Britain or England.[14] But the problem was, given the region's history of violence and sectarianism, how to construct an image of the North that was consistent with the British national myth of tolerance, compromise and peaceful evolutionary development. More exactly, the problem was that there were too many critics, both internally and externally, who were prepared to stymie any attempt to do so by publicizing the circumstances surrounding the creation of the statelet.

In May 1928 the Minister for Education, J.H. Robb, informed the northern House of Commons that, in an effort to remove the substantial 'misapprehension . . . among certain classes in England and Scotland' on the history and political status of Northern Ireland, he had contacted the English and Scottish Departments of Education together with 'publishers of textbooks in general use in the teaching of geography and history in public elementary and secondary schools across the Channel.' Accordingly, 'in every case our views have been met most cordially and promises made that in coming editions of those textbooks mistakes and omissions will be rectified, and the situation in Northern Ireland set forth in its proper light.' (Robb, N.I. Parliamentary Debates, vol. 9 (3 May 1928), cols 163–5).

But no sooner was this statement made than Joseph Devlin, the Nationalist leader, demanded to know exactly what was meant by it (ibid.: col. 317), while Samuel Kyle, a Labour MP, stated what he thought an understanding of Northern Ireland in 'the proper light' should entail:

I would like the Hon. Gentleman to let us see the primers that he intends to put into the hands of students on the other side. Will he tell them of the rebellious utterances of Lord Birkenhead, and of many of the rebellious activities of many of the hon. and right hon. gentlemen opposite in regard to the establishment of the Northern Parliament and the Northern Government? That will be very interesting to the pupils in Great Britain, and will show them the value of organised rebellion against the forces of the Crown.   (ibid.: col. 319)

The Government's concern to shape the thinking of northern school-children so that it would be consistent with opinion in Britain was reflected in the textbooks it sanctioned for use in schools. These had titles such as, *Physical and Economic Geography of the British Empire*, *The British Subject*, *The English Citizen Through the Ages*, *A History of Everyday Things in England* (see Cahir Healy, ibid.: cols 1330–31).

However, there was no prospect that the Government would be allowed to present unchallenged a version of Ulster history and politics shaped to fit easily into mainland British historical and political traditions. This was made clear when Joseph Devlin informed the house that he planned to send to all the educational authorities the Government had approached in Britain copies of his own speech criticizing the Government's plans, in order that these authorities be made aware 'that your propaganda should be well tested before it is made part of the textbooks either of Merrie England or Bonnie Scotland' – propaganda Devlin believed to consist of 'gross misrepresentations and historical inaccuracies' (ibid.: cols 1339–45). Not surprisingly, therefore, the Unionist regime became chary of how far explicitly political material should be used in presenting Ulster's case in Britain. An invitation to the Government in September 1936 by G.L. Marshall, controller of the BBC in Northern Ireland, to give a series of broadcast talks to explain what it stood for – to remove 'any miscon-ceptions in regard to it and its function' and the public confusion about Northern Ireland's political status – was refused. The Government wanted the talks restricted to trade and agriculture (Marshall to Sir Charles Blackmore, Cabinet Secretary, 29 September, 15 October 1936: PRONI, CAB9F/123/1).

In fact, in the area of trade and industry and the promotion of Ulster in this respect through the Empire Marketing Board, which the Government financed to a considerable extent, it was hoped that indirectly the political work of registering in Britain and abroad Ulster's British identity would be effectively conducted.[15] There were times, however, when direct action had to be taken, and this is especially evident in the effort the Government put into countering criticism of Northern Ireland in British newspapers.

Some British papers which had been long-standing supporters of Ulster Unionism, such as the *Scotsman*, could always be relied on to run the occasional paean of praise for the Stormont regime, but there were too few of these for the regime's purposes. Accordingly, in May 1932 the govern-ment wrote to 'all the leading newspapers of the United Kingdom inviting their co-operation in removing the misapprehension which exists in regard to the position of Northern Ireland' (W.D. Scott to Sir Charles Blackmore, 7 June 1932: PRONI, CAB9F/123/1). Again, it occasionally exerted influence discreetly with publishers to ensure that their coverage of Northern Ireland contained no 'anti-Ulster' bias (ibid.: 18 January 1934).

Influence was also exerted with organizations such as the National Service League to ensure that their publicity made due acknowledgement of Ulster's contribution to their efforts (E.P. Northland, Ulster Office, London to R. Gransden, 20 June 1939: PRONI, CAB9F/123/3). What tended to work best to facilitate the Government's propaganda efforts in the press, however, was when a press magnate could be persuaded actively to promote the interests of the regime – and this was precisely what the Northern Government succeeded in doing in the 1930s with Lord Rothermere.

As with most public figures who became interested in Ulster, family connections provided the basis for the interest. In Rothermere's case the connection was on his mother's side of the family – she came from County Down – and Craigavon was careful to cultivate his interest, encouraging a visit he planned making to the North in 1933 to visit locations associated with his family and also with the purpose of making preparations for a 'Come to Ulster' campaign (Craigavon to H. Malcolm McKee, 30 January 1933: PRONI, CAB9F/123/7). The owner of the influential *Daily Mail* and a number of regional newspapers, Rothermere pursued an independent line in right-wing politics, often highly critical of the Tory Party leadership (Seymour-Ure 1975: 249–55). Rothermere was keen to do what he could to assist the Stormont regime to gain the sympathy of British public opinion. Thus, in a period when authoritarian politics were in vogue and when Rothermere himself briefly put the *Daily Mail* behind Sir Oswald Mosley, so the case for Ulster was presented largely in terms of personality, with Craigavon presented as the embodiment of the northern character – brave, bluff, honest, dedicated, 'the man who occupies a position in Ulster similar to that of Hitler in Germany'; and with a personal biography shaped with a British readership in mind, one that ignored the UVF and the pre-war plans for rebellion in the North and focused instead on the Ulster Division's contribution to the war effort.[16]

Yet, however well disposed towards Ulster Rothermere was, and his newspapers consistently supported the Stormont regime, he did not have the power to create the permanent effect on British public opinion that the Stormont authorities desired. They still found it necessary to intervene extensively with newspaper editors when 'anti-Ulster' bias was detected. A complaint to the editor of the *Daily Mirror* about a report of sectarian violence in Belfast, when none apparently occurred, produced an apology and the information that the paper had cancelled its contract with the organization that had supplied the item: the Central News Agency (see Cecil Thomas, editor of the *Daily Mirror* to W.A. Magill, 27 July 1938: PRONI, CAB9F/123/1). The editor of the *Glasgow Daily Herald* proved less compliant when accused of publishing 'vicious and untruthful attacks' in an article on Northern Ireland (see E.P. Northland to H. Conacher, 16 June 1939: PRONI, CAB9F/123/1). He rejected the claims: 'I quite fail to see how, in a democratic country like Britain, anyone can object to the publication of such an article even though he may not agree with every sentence it contains.' Nevertheless, he did allow the Stormont authorities to reply in a series of articles on Northern Ireland, focusing on its constitutional position and especially its links with Scotland (for the first of these, see *Glasgow Herald*, 26 June 1939). There were, of course, incorrigible offenders, such as the *Manchester Guardian*, over whom it proved impossible to exert any significant influence, and with these all the authorities could do was refuse their co-operation when it was requested for coverage of Northern Ireland (W.D. Scott to Sir Charles Blackmore, 2, 6 July 1937: PRONI, CAB9F/123/1).

In addition to exercising pressure on the press, the northern government was also able, on specific occasions, to have its political message conveyed through the medium of film. For example, the occasion of the Ulster Grand Prix in 1931 was used to create an opportunity for British Movietone News, a newsreel company particularly close to the Tory Party (see Hollins 1981: 366–9), to make a film of Craigavon and his Cabinet speaking about Northern Ireland (R.J. Hulbert, British Movietone News, to Craigavon, 24 August 1931: PRONI, CAB9F/123/1). Moreover, while the London Government vetoed another attempt by the Stormont authorities to have the official title of the North changed from 'Northern Ireland' to 'Ulster', following de Valera's adoption of 'Eire' to replace 'Irish Free State' in 1936 (see government deliberations on the subject, 13–17 July 1937: PRO, HO45/202/2), the regime was more successful in exerting influence on the BBC in the North in this period. This was apparent in the way the Regional Director, George Marshall, reflected its outlook in his criticisms of a programme entitled, 'The Irish', broadcast on the BBC's Northern Region: 'There is no such thing today as an Irishman. One is either a citizen of the Irish Free State or a citizen of the United Kingdom of Great Britain and Northern Ireland.' (quoted in Cathcart 1984: 6).

But undoubtedly the major media coup of the period for the government came in 1938 when, to counter de Valera's anti-partitionist schemes, it called an election on the border question and was successful in having the newsreel organization of the Hollywood studio, RKO Pictures – *The March of Time* – cover it. Entitled 'Ulster versus Eire' and released in April 1938 – the only political item in a newsreel mainly given over to human interest stories – the report lasted approximately fifteen minutes and was explicitly pro-Unionist. Making a simplistic division between 'Protestant Ulster' and the twenty-six 'Catholic counties', it went on to praise Craigavon's shrewdness and leadership and the loyalty of the Ulstermen to Britain. Shown in cinemas throughout Britain and distributed abroad, it provided both the kind of message and the degree of exposition that the regime could be happy with.[17] To these efforts to shape British opinion on Northern Ireland can be added the influence Stormont exerted, over an extended period of time, on the activities of the Ulster Tourist Development Association.

That government promotion of tourism could both enhance the state's economic prospects and at the same time indirectly project a desired image of the nation abroad was, as we have noted, a view that was only taken seriously by the Westminster Government at the beginning of the 1930s.[18] Craigavon, however, driven by the urgency to secure Northern Ireland's constitutional position, had realized the utility of tourism for his purposes as early as the mid-1920s.

Inspired by a call from the Ulster Association in November 1923, the meeting inaugurating the Ulster Tourist Development Association (UTDA) took place in Belfast on 8 February 1924 (*Weekly Telegraph*, 9 February 1924). And although great play would be made about the non-political nature of the organization – to emphasize this point Craigavon referred to the fact that Joseph Devlin was a member of it *N.I. Parliamentary Debates*, vol. 8 (7 April 1927), cols 799–801) – indications were not wanting that the underlying agenda or the organization was distinctly political: to promote the concept of a British community in Ulster, completely distinct from the Irish Free State.[19]

The Association's earliest efforts in this regard, however, were counter-productive. One of its first brochures, distributed in the USA, had blatantly sectarian overtones, emphasizing Protestantism and detailing the supposed atrocities committed by the Catholic Irish during the 1641 Rebellion.[20] The controversy this brochure aroused forced the Association to employ more subtle methods. Indeed, it seems to have been aware already that such were needed for the British market. A poster commissioned by the UTDA from the distinguished Ulster artist, William Conor, was intended to register Northern Ireland in Britain, non-politically, as a quite separate entity from the south of Ireland. This concern was evident in Conor's introduction of the poster when it was displayed for reporters in January 1926. Entitled 'Come to Ulster: It's Jolly', the poster depicted two young girls playing in an Ulster glen. Conor explained his intentions thus:

My notion is to get as far away as possible from the conventional Irish poster of shawled peasant and whitewashed thatched cottage and brown melancholy bog. The tourist does not come to Ulster to weep over the sorrows of Dark Rosaleen; and besides, Dark Rosaleen in the North has dried her tears long ago, and has a smile on her face and very often silk stockings on her legs. Her house, or rather her father's house, is up to date.[21]

Conor's poster was given widespread distribution at railway stations throughout Britain and together with St John Ervine's guide to the North, entitled *Ulster* (UTDA, 1927), set the tone for the promotion of Northern Ireland as a holiday resort in the inter-war years. Apart from the titles of the UTDA guides, which emphasized 'Ulster' rather than 'Northern Ireland', and which carried a foreword, usually by Craigavon, stressing the North's status as a 'part of Great Britain' together with assurances to British visitors that 'in coming amongst us you will not have left your home country',[22] it was left to descriptions of Ulster's geographical and leisure attractions to create the desired impression on the British tourist.

Northern Ireland's British identity, moreover, could be expressed at a more subliminal level, as is evident in the posters British railway companies produced to advertise the two parts of Ireland. The posters advertising the Irish Free State were like those for Wales, invariably illustrating it as a wild untamed landscape evoking a Celtic 'timelessness'.

Those for Northern Ireland, however, were on the whole markedly different, being similar to posters for the north of England – for example, in the portrayal of shipyards – or, more often, like those for the south of England. Here the predominant imagery was of luxury hotels, leisure facilities such as golf and seaside resorts like Portrush.[23] The exact degree of influence exerted by the Government on the railway companies in regard to the production of posters advertising Northern Ireland is, of course, difficult to assess, but given the interest Stormont had in the promotion of the North's distinctive identity and the fact that the Government often worked closely with the railway companies on tourism, it is reasonable to assume that its views were influential.

As to the UTDA, generally, while the government's influence and direction was exerted discreetly, it was nevertheless real. Critics, for instance, noticed that only members of the Government were invited to take part in the UTDA's deliberations and to address its public meetings (Samuel Kyle, *N.I. Parliamentary Debates*, vol. 8 (7 April 1927), col. 796). Further, despite a public policy of friendship with its counterpart in the Irish Free State, when the latter made offers of co-operation to benefit Ireland as a whole, both the UTDA and Craigavon resolutely, if discreetly, refused, fearing such would damage their efforts to assert Northern Ireland's different identity from the South (see Robin Baillie to Craigavon, 15 August 1927; Sir Charles Blackmore, Memo., 4 April 1930: PRONI, CAB9F/114/1).

Yet, for all the Government's efforts in this respect, the results were hardly satisfactory. Despite the fact that the tourist traffic to Ulster from Britain increased significantly in the 1920s, it would seem that most visitors failed to take on board the political message of Ulster's membership of the United Kingdom; while any upsurge of anti-partitionist campaigning or Irish Republican Army activity could both nullify whatever limited success was made in this area and also have a catastrophic effect on the tourist trade. One organizer of tours from Britain to Ulster, who informed the UTDA in 1932 that political controversy in the South was badly affecting tourist trade to Northern Ireland, pointed up the seriousness of the problem by disclosing that 70 per cent of his own agents were not aware of the constitutional distinction between Northern Ireland and the Irish Free State (see Robert Maxwell to UTDA, 9 April 1932: PRONI, CAB9F/123/1). There was, however, one context which offered the opportunity to demonstrate unambiguously Northern Ireland's membership of the United Kingdom: the context created by royal visits; and in this period there were two visits of major significance.

V

The King may have been the supreme embodiment of British imperial identity across the globe, but as Allen Leeper perceptively remarked, he could be construed within the borders of separate political entities as *primarily* the monarch of that entity, i.e., Australia or South Africa.[24]

Certainly it was in this sense that the monarch was viewed by Unionists, as the King of the British nation and the national territory of the United Kingdom. In this they were facilitated both by the fact that the political climate in the Irish Free State made royal visits there unlikely and their own successful intervention in 1926 with the Baldwin Government – then considering a change in the royal title to take account of the position of the Irish Free State – in having Northern Ireland's constitutional position as a separate entity from the South clarified (*Londonderry Sentinel*, 25 November 1926).

The only royal visitors of any significance to come to the North in the 1920s were the Duke of York (later George VI) in 1924 and the King's daughter, Princess Mary, Viscountess Lascelles, in 1928. The first important visit was that of Edward, Prince of Wales, who came to open the new Stormont parliamentary buildings in November 1932.

The buildings were a present made to the new statelet by Westminster, planning for which began in 1921; and they were desired by Craig as an 'ocular demonstration that Ulster is ready and capable to maintain her own government, and can exist independently of Dublin'.[25] Several delays in fulfilling the building contract were experienced, however, and it was 1932 before the buildings were ready. That the Prince of Wales was to perform the opening ceremony was a guarantee of mass publicity in Britain and fitted well with Craig's opinion of their function in 1921. Certainly the Government was keen to exploit the occasion's publicity opportunities: fourteen articles, covering Northern Ireland's constitutional position as well as her industry and tourist facilities, were prepared for distribution to the vast number of British journalists expected to attend the opening (W.D. Scott to Sir Charles Blackmore, 12 November 1932: PRONI, CAB9F/123/7). For his part, Lord Rothermere eager to promote Northern Ireland, sought to 'impress the *Daily Mail* public with the immense imperial importance of the Prince of Wales's visit' (J. Ward Price to Craigavon, 14 November 1932: ibid.). And well before the event, the *Illustrated London News* – whose title suggested the importance of photo-journalism in its pages – signalled the event with extensive photographic coverage of the buildings, together with the information that Craigavon would invite the Prince to perform the opening ceremony.[26]

The royal visit, however, proved to be an uncomfortable experience for those who had awaited it so enthusiastically. Both nationalist and Unionist commentators noted that the Prince, on his drive through Belfast from the harbour, blatantly ignored the wildly enthusiastic crowds cheering his arrival. The *Derry Journal* (18 November 1932) remarked:

There was a noticeable lack of warmth about the entire proceedings. . . . Although the populace joined in the cheering all along the route to Stormont, the fact was commented upon that there appeared to be little sign of reciprocal enthusiasm shown from the official car leading the procession.

A similar impression was made on Lady Craigavon, who noted that despite the 'great ovation from the crowds . . . the Prince looked like thunder' (Craigavon diary, 16 November 1932: PRONI, D1415/B/38). Given the significance Unionists attached to royal visits it is, perhaps, not surprising that her speculations as to the reason for the Prince's coldness should focus on nationalist scheming to turn the Prince against the Ulster Protestant people:

we knew he never wanted to come over but the King said he must. He had . . . [heard] frightful tales about Ulster, the people, and the Government, put into him for some time by some of his entourage with southern sympathies, and had been given a completely wrong idea about everything. . . . It was hardly to be wondered at that he was cross. (ibid.)

However, it is highly doubtful that these speculations contained any truth. It is true that the Prince departed from his official itinerary to visit the Catholic Mater Hospital – something long remembered by the Catholic community. It is also true that when he delivered a personal message from his father to the Ulster people the Prince did not adhere to the official text which specified both his own pleasure in augurating the buildings and conveying His Majesty's wishes for the North's welfare and prosperity (see *Derry Journal*, 18 November 1932; *Northern Whig*, 16 November 1932).

The demeanour and actions of the Prince in Ulster, however, can be explained without reference to Northern Ireland. It has been pointed out, for example, that while he was capable of engendering mass affection, in this period he 'more often . . . gave demonstrations of an immature callousness and indifference to other people's feelings, and he troubled less and less to control the weariness and sadness with which he went about so much of his work.' (Donaldson 1974: 131). Edward's performance in Ulster, therefore, was more likely due to boredom, depression and immaturity. Indeed, in 1931 during a visit to Bermuda, he had acted very much as he was to do in Northern Ireland, causing an observer to record the Bermuda visit in terms almost identical to those in which Lady Craigavon recorded the Ulster visit (ibid.: 136).

But while the depression could lift, as it apparently did later, on the evening of his arrival, Edward's immaturity would remain. It was exhibited during an informal walk around Hillsborough village, where he was staying with the Governor of Northern Ireland. Apparently unaware of the significance of his actions, Edward, encouraged by the enthusiasm of the local populace, good-naturedly took the opportunity to have a go at playing a Lambeg drum.[27] It was the kind of apparently innocent gesture which in any other context would have been quickly forgotten. In Ulster, however, it was a major blunder, lowering the monarchy from its elevated position above politics and associating it directly with Orangeism, the most sectarian form of Unionism. The *Belfast News-Letter* (17 November 1932) was delighted with his performance, describing it as 'extraordinary': the Prince, 'seizing one of the big drums . . . beat it vigorously to the intense delight of the singing masses'; and having accepted the drumsticks as a gift, 'these, no doubt, he will value as a momento of what must have been one of the most extraordinary incidents in which he has ever figured.'

On leaving Northern Ireland Edward described the incident as 'a bit of fun' (*Northern Whig*, 19 November 1932), but a more perceptive comment on it was provided by the *Derry Journal* (18 November 1932), which posed the question: 'The Prince of Wales played the big drum with the Orangemen, but what is his real opinion of their loyalty?'

This was a question that would only admit of an answer as Edward gradually came to realize the significance of what he had done, and of the uses to which the Orangemen would put the incident. For his drum-beating was, it seems, photographed by the Orangemen and reproduced as postcards – something which irritated Ulster Catholics who, Edward was reliably informed, burned the postcards 'in indignation'. In the light of this information, he apparently came to interpret his 'bit of fun' in Hills-borough, less as a spontaneous occurrence, than as a plot hatched by the Unionists to make party use of his visit. Indeed, so embittered towards the Unionists did he become that when, as Edward VIII, he was planning his Coronation tours of the United Kingdom in 1936, he wished to avoid Ulster altogether; and while realizing that he would have to go sometime, he did 'not mean to go as part of the same tour with Scotland and Wales.' Edward, thus, wished to avoid according Northern Ireland any significance in 'connection with the Coronation'.[28] In this way, it would seem, he wished to convey that he did not regard them as standing on the same footing in terms of British identity as other regions of the United Kingdom. Had Edward retained his crown, therefore, it is possible that the demonstration of national identity based on the fulsome expression of homage and its acknowledgement between subjects and monarch, could have become problematic for Ulster Unionists.

In fact, although his alienation from Ulster Unionism did not become public, the impression of bad feeling between the King and his Ulster subjects was abroad. Compton McKenzie, in his impassioned defence of the former King written in the aftermath of the abdication crisis, accused the Ulster Unionists of agitating bitterly against the King from April 1936, when 'they got it into their heads' that he was too sympathetic to Popery and opposed to partition: 'nowhere was the propaganda against King Edward VIII fiercer or fouler than in Northern Ireland.' McKenzie was convinced that 'dark and secret elements' of the Belfast and London Governments were working together to produce this propaganda (McKenzie 1938: 155). However, McKenzie's work appears too emotive to be safely relied on. Certainly comment in the mainstream Unionist press was more restrained than a reading of McKenzie suggests. It was, in fact, a combination of respectful concern for the King and the nation's interests, though at street level incidents of protest against the monarch were recorded.

The *Belfast News-Letter* (3 December 1936) opined as the crisis erupted: 'We devoutly hope that . . . no problem has arisen which, on its solution, would affect in the slightest degree, the position which His Majesty enjoys in the regard of his people.' As the news of the King's abdication emerged, the *Londonderry Sentinel* (12 December 1936) neatly encapsulated the reaction of Unionist press opinion in an editorial, sombre and restrained, which praised Edward's personal qualities, deplored the circumstances surrounding his abdication and pledged support for the new King. In so far as it is possible to gauge popular Unionist opinion on the crisis, the action of Belfast cinema-goers in booing and walking out when Edward's picture was flashed on to screens during the playing of the national anthem may well have been representative (see *Derry Journal*, 9 December 1936), and may well have inspired McKenzie's diatribe against the Unionists. For its part, the Stormont Government's attitude to the crisis was consistent with its practice of following the policy of the London Government on great crises affecting the British nation as a whole. Summoned hurriedly to London to confer with the Prime Minister on the matter, Craigavon afterwards offered the succinct advice, 'Trust Baldwin' (*Londonderry Sentinel*, 8 December 1936).

The abdication crisis was quickly resolved and as George VI ascended the throne the attention of Ulster Unionists shifted accordingly. With their acute attention to any royal detail on which they could put significance, it was remarked that the Coronation visit to Northern Ireland of the new King and Queen – they arrived on 28 July 1938 – so soon after their Coronation (on 12 May), was 'a signal Royal honour to the Imperial race of this Imperial province.'[29] In this respect it would appear that the Ulster Unionists experienced in a more heightened form, conditioned by local circumstances, the effect of the Coronation in Britain in generating 'an increased feeling of security, of stability . . . [in] the permanence of the British Empire' (see Ziegler 1978: 46).

Reflecting the tendency of royal visits to crystallize for Ulster Unionists their British national identity in terms of myth, devoid of complexity, the Duke of Abercorn conveyed to the King 'the love and loyalty of *all* [my italics] the people of Northern Ireland.' However, when the Church of Ireland Primate, Archbishop Charles F. D'arcy, gave expression to this tendency by signing his address to the King, 'Charles F. Armagh', Baldwin, pointing out the possibility of Roman Catholic protests at his use of the title 'Armagh', advised him to 'sign himself as Charles F. D'arcy only'.[30]

That the commitment of Ulster loyalists to the monarch was more intense than in other parts of the United Kingdom is reflected in the observations of Sir Samuel Hoare (later Viscount Templewood), who as Home Secretary accompanied the royal party on the Northern Ireland visit. He recorded the reception they received as follows:

My main duty was to hand the King his various speeches and receive in return the formal addresses of welcome. For two whole days the King and Queen were in the midst of spontaneous and deafening demonstrations of loyalty. My head reeled with the cheers as we drove practically unescorted through the narrow streets of Belfast.   (Templewood 1954: 252)

In fact, the new King was already well disposed towards the Ulster Unionists. He had been 'astounded' by 'the wonderful enthusiasm of the people of Belfast' when, as Duke of York, he visited Northern Ireland in 1924 (Wheeler-Bennett 1958: 197). Accordingly, the warmth of their reception in 1937 encouraged a corresponding warmth on the part of the royal party. A message received by the Governor of Northern Ireland from the King on his return to London, thanking all those who had made the preparations for his visit, went beyond formal thanks to convey his appreciation of the depth of loyalty shown by Ulster Unionists: 'The Queen and I will always remember this day spent among our people of Northern Ireland. It was a moving experience for us to see their traditional loyalty manifested in the vast cheering crowds and the beautifully decorated streets' (see *Londonderry Sentinel*, 29 July 1937).

Nevertheless, while the relations of the new King with Ulster Unionists readily assumed a cordiality not evident with Edward VIII, it was not possible to divorce the context of what might be called 'national communion' between the King and his loyalist subjects from the ongoing Unionist-nationalist conflict over the status of Northern Ireland. The IRA used the occasion of the visit to mount a series of attacks on border posts and government installations, to drive home the point that Northern Ireland was not part of Britain and that a royal visit to the North was, of its nature, a political act. In fact, leaving aside George V's visit to the North to open its Parliament in the crisis circumstances of 1921, there had been nothing to compare with the level of disturbance during the King's visit since Edward VII visited Ireland as Prince of Wales during the height of the Parnellites agitation for Home Rule in 1885. Moreover the reaction of the British press to the bombings could only have had the effect the IRA intended.

While newspapers such as the *Daily Mail* (29 July 1937) and *The Times* (29 July 1937) could be relied on to emphasize the loyalty of Ulster Protestants to the crown, reports of bombs in Belfast and along the royal routes (*News Chronicle*, 29 July 1937; *Daily Express*, 29 July 1937) could only arouse concern in Britain about the safety of the monarch. Nor was the situation improved when politicians in Northern Ireland overreacted in their complaints about 'lying and scandalous statements reflecting on the good name of Belfast' in the mainland British press coverage of the visit (see *Yorkshire Post*, 4 August 1937; *Daily Mirror*, 4 August 1937; *Liverpool Post*, 4 August 1937). Moreover, the fact that boundary posts were targets for attack prompted some papers (see, for example, *Yorkshire Post*, 29 July 1937), to focus on the history of the boundary question.

The propaganda effect secured by the IRA through their series of attacks points up their achievement, and also that of de Valera, in the inter-war period. Although neither was successful in advancing significantly the cause of Irish unification, it is reasonable to conclude that they did succeed substantially in preventing the idea taking hold in Britain that Northern Ireland could be regarded as authentically British.

VI

It has recently been argued that the removal of the Irish question from British politics after 1921, especially in the effect this had in weakening the demands for Welsh and Scottish nationalism, led to the consolidation of British politics and the 'acknowledgement by British politicians that the "British" were one nation.' (Boyce 1988: 74). The British so defined, of course, were the people of Britain. Ulster Unionists may have secured their membership of the United Kingdom in 1921, and also made significant progress in financially integrating Northern Ireland more closely with Britain in this period (Canning 1985: 110), but the securing of an 'authentic' British identity was to prove much more problematic. The Irish question had not been removed from Ulster politics. And it could be argued that not only did this greatly complicate the identification of the North as British, but also helped to divert attention from the positive contribution that Northern Ireland could have made in the wider United Kingdom context.

In fact, the respected historian, Nicholas Mansergh, could give devolution in Northern Ireland a qualified recommendation for adoption in Britain to improve regional government: 'the principle of the Northern Ireland experiment might secure very serious consideration both in Scotland and Wales.' (Mansergh 1936: 313). A case could even be made for the one-party character of the northern statelet in the 1930s, when the formation of the National Government in Britain appeared to make the two-party system 'largely a thing of the past' (Shearman 1942: 171). However, there were other obstacles than Irish Republicanism in the path of establishing a secure British identity for the North. Probably the most serious difficulty lay in the fact that northern Unionists were addressing a constituency that existed only imperfectly. Keith Robbins's conclusion (1988: 182) that Britain was both a three-nation unit and a single unit in different contexts and for different purposes, is the key here. For while their anxiety about the nationalist threat made a consciousness of their British identity a permanent feature of the Ulster Unionist outlook, this was not the case in Britain, where a consciousness of national identity was only likely to emerge partially and temporarily. For British nationality to be experienced in a heightened sense by all the people in Britain simultaneously usually required a causal factor, such as a major war, and none emerged in this period. The nearest equivalent, as an agency of national consciousness, was the monarchy. Yet individual communities in Britain could experience national identity in relation to the monarch without necessarily feeling a common identity with other communities (see Ziegler 1978: 47). Certainly it would appear that royal occasions did not greatly enhance British popular perceptions of the recently created entity of Northern Ireland; and, as the IRA bombings during the royal visit of 1937 demonstrated, these occasions could be easily made to work against the interests of Ulster Unionism.

Finally, there is the contribution that Unionists themselves made to their own difficulties. They seem not to have appreciated that the efforts they put into promoting Northern Ireland as a member of the British national family could be undermined both by the sectarian statements made publicly by Craigavon and Brookeborough in this period, and by the regime's employment of the Special Powers Act. These, of course, were guaranteed to create scandal and controversy, and to ensure, only too often, that the publicity the Stormont Government received in Britain was such as to point up its departure from the standards of government associated with the British political tradition.[31] Even Unionist celebrations of British national character in general too easily exhibited a chauvinism that provided a target for criticism.[32]

Notes

1. See, for example, the correspondence between the Conservative MPs, Sir Malcolm McNaughton, Commander B. Eyres Monsell and D.D. Reid with Craigavon and Hugh Pollock in 1928–9, on the subject of Ulster Unionist parliamentary attendance (PRONI, CAB9J/6/1). A succinct assessment of Unionist representation at Westminster over the life of the Stormont regime is provided in Harbinson (1973: 97–106).

2. There were two significant groupings, the British Fascists and Mosley's Blackshirts, the former associated closely with Ulster loyalism and the latter unsympathetic to Orangeism. See Griffiths (1983: 90–93; Mosley (1968: Ch. 8 and p. 253).

3. These negotiations have been extensively covered, not only by McMahon (1984) but also by Bowman (1982) and Canning (1985 Ch. 11).

4. Inge's Outspoken Essays (1919), expressing anxiety about, among other things, social discontent and the future of the English race, went through seven impressions in two years.

5. Inge (1927: 27). First published in 1926 this work went through six impressions by 1938.

6. For Baldwin's repeated articulation of this national construction, see his enormously popular collections of papers and addresses, On England (1926); Our Inheritance (1928); The Torch of Freedom (1935).

7. See the insightful discussion in Schwarz (1984: 1–18).

8. Soul of a nation (1933). I am very grateful to Mr Toby Haggith of the Imperial War Museum for carrying out research on this film on my behalf. See also Hollins (1981: 359–69).

9. For example, Stanley Baldwin and that other important commentator on national identity in the inter-war period, Arthur Bryant, broadcast on this subject. See Baldwin, 'Our National Character' in Baldwin (1935: 15–22); Bryant, The National Character (1934). See also Street (1979: 100–101).

10. This was the impression made on Tyrone Guthrie (Forsyth 1976: 58). See also Briggs (1965: iii, 107–8, 324): Ulster ranked with 'the more outlying parts of the empire in its enthusiasm for programmes broadcast from Britain, especially London'.

11. See, for example, endpaper maps in Leacock (1940). Leacock, though he rejected the idea that the British military should be used to force Northern Ireland to unite with the south, yet held out the possibility that union might come about peacefully. See map of western Europe in Keesing's Contemporary Archives, No. 269 (17 August 1936), p. 22224a.

12. See Wiener (1987: 112–14); Street (1979: 100); Bryant (1929: 74–5); Wright (1985: 53).

13. See Belfast News-Letter (12 January 1924). On the significance of the Exhibition, generally, see McKenzie (1984: Ch. 4).

14. On this subject, of which many examples could be given, see *N.I. Parliamentary Debates*, vol. 10 (3 May 1928), cols 163–5.
15. See 'Government Publicity: Short Résumé Since 1922', 1 June 1943 (PRONI, CAB9F/123/3B); debate on parliamentary hospitality fund, especially criticism of government monopoly of it in the Unionist interest (*N.I. Parliamentary Debates*, vol. 12 (29 April 1930), cols 968–80).
16. See Geoffrey Harmsworth, 'Ulster's Great Leader' (*Daily Mail* 20 April 1934); Gareth Jones, 'Ulster More British Than Britain' (*Western Mail*, 10 March 1934); Lt. Col. L.C.R. Moore, 'We Must Stand By Ulster' (*Sunday Dispatch*, 22 April 1934); also series of articles on the Ulster Government and its British identity (*Western Morning News*, 8, 16, 22, 29 November, 6 December 1937).
17. See the correspondence on the *March of Time* Newsreel (Sir Charles Blackmore to W.D. Scott, 28 October 1937; Sir Wilson Hungerford to Craigavon, 27 April, 10 June 1938: PRONI, CAB9F/123/3A).
18. Following requests made by the UTDA in 1928, the British Travel Association was persuaded to include 'Northern Ireland' in its title, and Craigavon was invited to propose a northern Irish representative to the Association in 1929 (see H.V. Hacking to Craigavon, 10 April 1929: PRONI, CAB9F/114/1; UTDA 1984: 10).
19. See, for example, the speeches delivered at a meeting to honour the Ulster writer, St John Ervine, who agreed to write the first substantial tourist brochure for the organization (*Weekly Telegraph*, 13 February 1926).
20. See the criticisms of the brochure by P. O'Neill and Joseph Devlin (*N.I. Parliamentary Debates*, vol. 7 (6 May 1926), cols 1039, 1051–2).
21. *Belfast News-Letter* (26 January 1926). For the poster see Wilson (1981: 31).
22. See, for example, the UTDA guide, *Ulster* (1929: 13; 1939: 14).
23. For a comparison of some northern and southern Irish posters see Beverley Cole and Richard Durack (1992: 37, 49, 104, 116). I am very grateful to Beverley Cole, of the National Railway Museum at York, for providing me with photocopies of the range of Irish posters in the Museum's collection.
24. Allen Leeper (1937: 436). Leeper was the leading Foreign Office exponent of increased national propaganda and had an important influence on the formation of the British Council.
25. Vincent (ed.) (1984: 417). Craigavon joked that in the event of Irish unity the buildings could be used as a lunatic asylum.
26. *Illustrated London News* (20 February 1932). While Northern Ireland's image was not helped by sectarian rioting later in the year, this magazine's coverage of the events (22 October 1932) was pro-government.
27. The *Illustrated London News* (26 November 1932) carried a commentary on the incident together with a photograph of the drum and its owner.
28. See the memo. of the discussion on the proposed royal tours between the Home Secretary and the King (17 October 1936), sent for the attention of the Lord President of the Council, Ramsay MacDonald (PRO/30/69/8).
29. The Coronation was turned to economic advantage in the North. When the IRA warned southern cinema proprietors against showing films of the event, northern cinemas scheduled special showings for thousands of southern visitors (O'Sullivan 1940: 489).
30. See the substantial file of addresses to the King, July 1937 (PRO, HO45/20567/698952/12).

31. For a survey of British press reaction to the Council's report on the application of the Special Powers Act, see *Derry Journal* (25, 27 May, 1 June 1936).
32. See the criticism of the *Belfast News-Letter* for its opinion that 'types of the just man made perfect are rare outside the United Kingdom', in Fyfe (1940: 231).

6

WAR AND NATIONAL IDENTITY: ULSTER AND BRITAIN 1939–45

War, like exile . . . sharpens within everyday historical consciousness a sense of Absolute National Spirit. . . . Believing that they were 'making History' in harmony with the Absolute Spirit of 'England' (or 'Britain'), people tried to behave as that spirit seemed to dictate. Heroic mythology fused with everyday life to produce heroism. People 'made sense' of the fighting and chaotic actualities of wartime life in terms of heroic mythology, 'selecting out' phenomena which were incompatible with the mythology.   (Calder 1991: 10, 14)

Calder's exposition of how the popular experience of the blitz worked to integrate the usually separate spheres of national myth and everyday life is instructive. But, as he is aware, this did not apply by any means to all of London's citizens; and, as we shall see, the manner in which the spheres of everyday life and national myth were negotiated were often more complex than that presented here. Nevertheless, the war was a radicalizing experience – a people's war that had to take seriously the urban, industrial experience of the majority of the British people. Accordingly, while the ruralist image of the nation would persist – 'while cities could be blitzed and bombed, the countryside remained – eternal, timeless, self-renewing, indestructible: a fitting symbol for Britain at bay' (Richards 1988: 46) – the devaluing of urban experience that had been its pre-war concomitant greatly diminished. The war, moreover, was to produce a 'Churchillian' vocabulary and repertoire of national images for the future. In the context of these developments the war would also have important consequences for Ulster Unionists, allowing them to assert their British identity to a greater extent than had been the case since 1918. Yet, even in this favourable context, and as will become clear, the authenticity of that identity would continue to be contested, with the fortunes of war determining its importance for the Westminster government.

I

The first year of the war was a mixed one for Ulster Unionist interests. While the replacement of Neville Chamberlain as Prime Minister by

Churchill, a consistent supporter of the Stormont regime, was reassuring,[1] the failure to implement conscription in Northern Ireland (Canning 1985: 233, 237–8, 307–10) not only pointed up dramatically the limitations of British national sovereignty in Ulster, but also seriously diminished the region's ability to demonstrate whole-hearted commitment to the national struggle. Not that this was easy to decipher from the press reporting of Ulster's contribution to the war effort. A censored media made it easy to portray the area as vitally integrated into the British war machine, despite the absence of conscription. An extended *Times* report of 6 April 1940, for example, on 'Ulster in Wartime' exulted: 'On every front Northern Ireland is playing a full and worthy part in the struggle against Hitlerism.' The Ulstermen, Field Marshal Sir John Dill and Field Marshal Viscount Alanbrooke, were leading the British Expeditionary Force in France while, despite the absence of conscription in Ulster, 'there has been an impressive flow of volunteers into the Forces, so that more than once recruiting officers have had to close their doors to gain a temporary respite.' (ibid.).

The presentation of Northern Ireland as an integral and uncomplicated element in the national struggle was assisted further by the censorship code applied during the first year of the war. Among twenty-five lists of things the media could not refer to, was any mention of IRA activities in Northern Ireland (Pronay 1982: 93), while the Regional Controller of the BBC in Northern Ireland was to play a largely effective censorship role on radio output, ensuring that nothing offensive to the sensibilities of the Stormont authorities was broadcast (Cathcart 1984: Ch. 4). Again, the irrelevance of the pastoral myth of England/Britain to the prosecution of the war also implicitly worked to the Unionists' advantage. J.B. Priestley, an influential interpreter of urban industrial Britain, bluntly asserted its importance in the new conditions of wartime: 'Show . . . the real Britain in shirt-sleeves . . . the kind of castle-and-thatched-cottage-England that appears in British Council films could not have kept this war going for half a morning' (quoted in Ellwood 1982: 64).

The image of 'Deep England' would remain as an ideal of Englishness/Britishness but the demands of war necessitated a realistic acceptance of Britain's industrial character; and, in this context, Northern Ireland, with its long-established industrial identity, could more convincingly be established as authentically British.[2] Naturally the Stormont Government, assisted by the neutrality of the Irish Free State, took every opportunity to encourage that process (Craigavon, 'Ulster's Part in the War', *Listener* (2 February 1940), 266). Further, the fortunes of war could also assist in this regard. When, in 1941–2, Allied shipping losses were extremely severe, there was an attempt, albeit temporarily, to revive traditional British anti-Catholic and anti-Irish prejudice – something which chimed easily with Ulster Unionist sentiments. A news film on Ireland made by Paramount, and which gave the impression of preparing British popular opinion for an Allied invasion of Eire, made the case for British use of the Treaty ports with an argument that accused de Valera of dictatorship and appealed to Victorian stereotypes of Irish racial inferiority:

unlike the English they do not want more than they have. In many ways, the Irish peasants – sharing their cottages with pigs, living on potatoes – are freer than the English artisan. . . . By temperament he [the Irish peasant] is a born Roman Catholic – no country is more firmly attached to this religion. And as the Vatican seldom frowns on those who dislike Protestant England, the priest in Ireland is wholeheartedly behind de Valera.

This attack on the southern Irish, moreover, went together with extravagant praise of Ulster's contribution to the war effort and their virtues as a people: 'Because Ulstermen are wealthier than the Southern Irish, more enterprising, better businessmen, they refuse to be governed by Dublin.' (Paramount News, quoted in Fisk 1985: 393–5). This particular news item represented an extreme of anti-Irishness that did not surface again during the war. But it is a reasonable supposition that, had active preparations for a British invasion of Eire been seriously contemplated, such arguments would have been employed to encourage popular support in Britain for the enterprise.

That anti-Catholicism, if now largely a submerged element of British popular culture, could still be politically influential was acknowledged by D.W. Brogan in his *The English People* (1943: 69–70. 131–4). But since the kind of crisis that would have made anti-Catholicism politically useful never emerged, it was more usual for a common identity between Northern Ireland and Britain to be cited in terms of the extent to which the former shared the wartime experience of Britain. Moreover, involvement in the war effort allowed Ulster Unionists to exert pressure on the Westminster Government to have their constitutional position more widely publicized in Britain than had been the case in the inter-war period. Thus the attempt to get the Unionist view on this subject over to British schoolchildren – something Nationalists effectively thwarted in the 1920s – was now taken up more successfully when the regime persuaded the Ministry of Information (MOI) to distribute a pamphlet on Ulster in British schools (Cabinet Sub-Committee on Publicity, Memo., 16 December 1943; R. Gransden to Sir Ernest Cooper, 14 March 1944: PRONI, CAB9F/123/3B). It is also worth noting in this context that Ernest Barker's *Britain and the British People* (1942) was concerned to establish Northern Ireland's membership of the British nation: 'It is a British nation inhabiting the United Kingdom of Great Britain and Northern Ireland (only *Northern* for Southern and Western Ireland . . . is called Eire)'. Indeed, Barker, a highly respected scholar, was prepared to accord Northern Ireland the status of a 'nationality', one of four whose diversity was 'a source of national strength' (Barker 1942: 11).

Concerned to capitalize on the more secure relationship with Britain the war had brought about, the Stormont authorities produced a number of pamphlets explaining its part in the war effort. The most significant was *Ulster: the British Bridgehead* (1943), a publication explaining how vital that contribution was to 'the war strategy of the United Nations' and which pointed out, for example (p.9), that, 'It was from a coastal command station in Northern Ireland that the German battleship

Bismarck was sunk'. Moreover, what were, from the regime's point of view, misconceived newspaper articles, speculating on how Irish unity could be effected so as to bring all Ireland into the Allied war effort, could also be effectively countered. Nowhere is this more clear than in the way in which the highly popular *Picture Post*'s musings on this subject (20 January 1940), was followed (2 March 1940), after Stormont's intervention, by a vigorous rejection of the idea.

The rebuttal reflected Ulster's wartime importance, focusing less on the constitutional issue than on the region's identity, especially its industrial character. Entitled, 'Belfast', the article ran for nine pages of text and photographs – the latter portraying the industrial life of the city, together with the North's Orange Lodges. In fact, 'the Belfastman' was presented as an archetypal Ulsterman, and his virtues detailed in a way that directly challenged the long-established negative image of the Unionist population in Britain. Indeed the article claimed that the 'Belfastman' was never a 'bigot' as his enemies claimed; in fact, his ancestors included Huguenots who fled to northern Ireland to escape the bigotry of Romanism. But probably most important in terms of its propaganda value, the 'Belfastman' was presented as an archetypal Ulsterman to emphasize, invidiously, the difference between Northern Ireland and Eire:

a greater contrast between Belfast and Dublin could not be imagined, so little have they in common. The Belfastman is definite . . . and as his enemies contend, opinionated, by which, of course, they mean . . . he has his own opinions and is not prepared to accept theirs.   (ibid.)

And to drive the point home, it was declared that unlike the southern Irish 'the Ulstermen are adult; they do not behave like overgrown infants.' *Picture Post* had a circulation of over 2,000,000 copies at home and abroad (see J. Cooke-Collis to R. Gransden, 5 January 1940: PRONI, CAB9F/123/3A), and that Unionists should regard this article as an important piece of propaganda was understandable. Further, favourable propaganda in another medium was provided in a series of films describing the various dimensions of Ulster's wartime contribution by the Crown Film Unit for the MOI (see F.M. Adams, 'Films on Ulster Themes', 6 May 1946: ibid.).

Probably the best insight into the extent to which Northern Ireland shared the wartime experiences of Britain is provided by the Home Intelligence reports on civilian morale compiled by the MOI and based on the weekly reports of agents located all over the United Kingdom (see McLaine 1979). The reports of observers in Northern Ireland on civilian morale, on such subjects as the general course of the war, the effects of enemy bombing and attitudes to the enemy, did not differ significantly from those in other parts of the Kingdom, though the special political context of Northern Ireland was also reflected in the reports (see, for example, Home Intelligence Weekly Report, no. 12, 18–24 December 1940, section 6, Northern Ireland, in Addison (ed.) 1979: Reel One, p. 187). In this context, it is worth noting that when the Duke of Kent came to Derry as part of a visit to Northern Ireland in October 1940, he found a City Corporation which had drawn a parallel between the Seige of 1689 and the London blitz: it 'was now following with pride the history-making defence of its Mother City in the modern seige from the air' (*Londonderry Sentinel*, 26 October 1940).

This was the British national struggle seen through the lens of the Unionist political myth. Indeed, the Corporation was even making plans to re-enact the Seige of 1689: 'The Duke on arrival in the city drove through one of the ancient gates and saw what preparations had been made for its closing should the invader come again.' And much as the war brought its dangers, a certain relief is also noticeable when the North began to experience its effects, a relief that the enemy was acknowledging Ulster's British identity. When Belfast was blitzed in 1941 the *Londonderry Sentinel* (17 April 1941) declared:

Our Northern Ireland state is right in the front-line now. . . . When Great Britain entered the war the people of Ulster were prepared loyally to share the sacrifices which that decision involved, and, regardless of cost, they have never wavered in their attachment and devotion to Britain's cause. [Nazi attacks] in Britain . . . have failed to break the spirit of the common people. They will fail equally in Ulster.

German bombing of Belfast[3] and cities in Britain was also making its contribution to national unity. In this context, the work of documentary film makers such as Humphrey Jennings, whose film of the London Fire Service during the blitz, *Fires Were Started* (1943), conveyed the spirit of a British national community at war, resonated across the *whole* United Kingdom.[4] Newsreel scenes of firefighting in Belfast could have been included in Jennings's film without any sense of incongruity. Unionist satisfaction at sharing in the national struggle, however, did not please all northern Protestants. Denis Ireland, a Protestant Republican, disparagingly described the Unionist outlook as 'a form of what the Germans call *schadenfreude*, a delight in disaster. Here, at any rate, was final and irrefutable proof that there was no such thing as the Irish Sea' (Ireland 1947: 5). Yet, such comments could be safely ignored. Ulster's wartime importance was reinforced in 1942, when it became clear that de Valera would persist with his policy of neutrality and that the North – especially Derry – was playing a vital role in the war at sea. The significance of that role was illustrated in a BBC programme, 'Salute to Ulster' (*Londonderry Sentinel*, 23 June 1942). The Royal Air Force was to build seven new airfields in the North during the war; 140 warships would be constructed there, as would one-tenth of the entire merchant shipping fleet of the United Kingdom, together with guns, tanks, ammunition and aircraft, including 1500 heavy bombers (Fisk 1985: 280–81). The war served to align Northern Ireland more fully with Britain in other ways, with the acceptance by London of parity in benefits and social services between Ulster and Britain, while the regeneration of the North's economy during the war enabled the region to make a substantially increased imperial contribution (Harkness 1983: 94–6). Robert Fisk has described the significance – especially for Ulster Protestants – of Northern Ireland's place in the war effort at this time as follows:

By February of 1942, more than eighty naval escort vessels were moored in the Foyle, up which Captain Browning's *Mountjoy* had sailed in 1689 to relieve the besieged Protestants of the Maiden City. And in one sense, the Royal Navy's arrival in the Second World War represented an almost equally momentous delivery for the Protestants of Northern Ireland. Londonderry's strategic role meant that the six counties were now essential to the prosecution of the war and could no longer be used as a tempting bait for de Valera in return for the restricted use of the Treaty ports or the premature entry of British troops into Eire. De Valera's very refusal to hand back Eire's Atlantic harbours now served only to emphasise the loyalty of Northern Ireland's Unionist population whose six small and generally poor counties had become a defensive bridgehead to America. The province was not just a willing armourer, but a bastion in the Battle of the Atlantic. 'Here, by the Grace of God', Churchill later wrote, 'Ulster stood a faithful sentinel.'

(Fisk 1985: 281)

Churchill's comment on Ulster loyalty introduces another, and highly important, dimension to Northern Ireland's position within the British national community.

II

In a way that had few previous parallels, Churchill, in the conditions of Britain's isolation and defiance of Hitler after the fall of France in 1940, was seen to speak personally for Britain: 'The central and founding myth of World War II is of a nation *united* through idolatry for its totemic leader, Churchill. All other mythic aspects of the war are subordinated to this one, that had its genesis in May 1940,' (Dawson and West 1984: 11). In this context, the greatness of Churchill as a creator of national mythology was that the mythology was created while the events of 1940 – especially the defeat in France and the evacuation at Dunkirk – were taking place (Schwarz 1986: 180). At this time, according to the Gallup polling organization, public confidence in Churchill as a war leader who would deliver victory was in the high eighties, while, as one soldier later recalled: 'There is no doubt that the British were united, nor is there the least doubt that they found in Churchill an exact expression of their own obstinacy, courage and refusal to recognise the apparent logic of facts.' (Laurence Thompson, quoted in Calder 1991: 28–9). It is worth noting, in this context, that Home Intelligence reports on opinion in Northern Ireland reflected the mood in Britain. The report for 7 August 1940, for example, recorded 'no nervousness at invasion threats. . . . [The feeling was that] enemy troops may land, but Hitler will be sorry he sent them' (see Addison (ed.) 1979: Reel one, p. 187). Churchill's broadcasts were apparently appreciated no less in Northern Ireland than in Britain (Northern Ireland reports, 21 August, 5 September 1940: ibid.).

Here was a leader who had championed the Ulster cause since partition and might be relied on to facilitate the integration of Ulster Unionism with the wider British national family in the favourable conditions created by the war. Certainly Churchill's public statements on Ulster during the war appear to support this view. Seen as a whole from 1939–45, the image they present is of an Ulster community whose vital contribution to the war effort had established 'unbreakable bonds' with the mainland British population, whose gratitude would be expressed in support for Northern Ireland's position as an integral part of the national family. The northern Government's pamphlet, *Ulster: the British Bridgehead* (1943: 1), for example, quoted a typically hyperbolic statement by Churchill on the importance of Ulster to the Allied struggle:

But for the loyalty of Northern Ireland and its devotion to what has now become the cause of . . . thirty governments or nations we should have been confronted with slavery and the light which now shines so strongly throughout the world would have been quenched.

Again, it quoted Churchill's letter to J.M. Andrews of 9 May 1943 on the occasion of his resignation as Prime Minister of Northern Ireland, which referred to 'the bonds of affection' between Britain and the people of the North, bonds which had been 'tempered by fire' and were now 'unbreakable' (ibid.: 12). Churchill's praise of Ulster's wartime contribution culminated in his election message to Sir Basil Brooke in June 1945, following the end of the war in Europe, and which included the following:

The stand of the Government and people of Northern Ireland for the unity of the British Empire and Commonwealth and for the great cause of freedom for which we all risked our survival, will never be forgotten by Great Britain. . . .
   A strong loyal Ulster will always be vital to the security and well-being of the whole Empire and Commonwealth. Linked with us, Ulster must also share in the happier days to come, when the United Kingdom of Great Britain and Northern Ireland will renew its strength in peace and honour.
                                        (*Londonderry Sentinel*, 14 June 1945)

Churchill's message also repeated, in modified form, a passage in his victory speech on 13 May 1945, which stated blatantly that only Northern Ireland's 'loyalty and friendship' had prevented the British from being 'forced to come to close quarters with Mr de Valera or perish forever from the earth' – a statement widely regarded as a mistake as it allowed de Valera to make a statesmanlike reply on the theme of the vulnerability of small nations at the mercy of large aggressive neighbours with a tendency to equate their needs with the right to disregard the rights of other people (Fisk 1985: 538–40).
   Nevertheless, Churchill's message was widely appreciated among the Unionist community of the six counties. Speaking to Belfast Orangemen, Brooke described it as 'valuable', expressing how Ulstermen liked to be thought of in England. Ulster regarded England as the great bridgehead across which happiness and prosperity to Ulster would flow: 'We [Ulster and Britain] are one and indivisible and anyone who tries to break down

this bridgehead is doing a disservice . . . to every man and woman in the country.' (*Londonderry Sentinel*, 14 June 1945).

Churchill's public statements on Ulster are of a piece with his nationalist mythologizing in general during the war, in that the complexity of social and political realities was sacrificed to a vision of national resolve conceived in simplistic terms. Yet the national homogeneity that Churchill's Ulster statements gave expression to was far from doing justice to the actuality of Northern Ireland's relationship with Britain during the war years. In terms of how far the North could be regarded as 'authentically' integrated into the wider British national community there were problems, twofold in nature. First, there was the general problem of how far Churchill's national mythologizing informed and shaped the everyday experience of the British people. Second, there was the specific problem created by Anglo-Irish relations in the course of the war.

III

As Bill Schwarz has pointed out, while Churchill's nationalist speeches may have provided the most inspiring rhetoric for the British people, especially during the period 1940–41 when Britain stood alone, what is less obvious is *how* these sentiments mobilized people and to what ends: 'The discrepancies between a patriotism of greatness and empire, and one drawn from a common sense of the people pulling together in a time of crisis in order to create a better world could not have been more marked.' (Schwarz 1984: 180). Ultimately, the answer to this question emerged dramatically at the general election of 1945 when Churchill was decisively ousted from power. But indications of the limitations of the appeal of Churchill's brand of nationalism at the popular level were clear well before then. An attempt by H.V. Hodgson, Director of the Empire Division of the MOI, to engage public energies for the war effort through an 'Empire Crusade' in late 1940 – 'the scheme was meant to educate the public about the Empire and the Commonwealth, and in so doing, convince them of the superiority of the British way of life' – failed abysmally to enlist public interest (McLaine 1979: 223–4).

In fact, intelligence sources made clear that while the public appreciated governmental recognition of their resilience under attack, 'they resented too great an emphasis on the stereotyped image of the Britisher in adversity as a wise-cracking cockney. They were irritated by propaganda which represented their grim experience as a sort of particularly torrid rugby match.' (ibid.: 125). But, perhaps most significantly, not only was there resistance to governmental attempts to conceptualize the popular experience of war in terms of official nationalist ideologies, but also evidence to suggest that the 'popular mind' lacked any overall conceptual framework within which local experience was related to the war in general. Home Intelligence commented that the public appeared to 'see very little relation between the bomb "at the bottom of the street" and the war as a whole' (ibid.: 111). It would appear that although the Luftwaffe blitzkreig had invaded and devastated the local and private sphere of everyday life, the reaction was to deal with the problem at that level. In this context, it is worth noting that the lessons of the London blitz were lost on provincial cities even when officially communicated: 'each city and town had to experience a major attack before making adequate plans for the relief of the community.' (ibid.: 114).

For our purposes, however, this conclusion has important implications; it suggests that despite the propaganda emphasizing Northern Ireland's wartime contribution as a unifying experience with the people of Britain, and the fact that Unionists in Northern Ireland could similarly experience bombing such as that which occurred on the mainland, the widespread tendency for communities in Britain to localize their experience of the war indicates that, lacking the same imperatives that applied in the North, the feeling was not reciprocated. Certainly there is little evidence that a common experience of war led to a greater popular consciousness on the mainland of Northern Ireland as an inalienable part of the national territory.[5] There are several indicators of this. In the 1941–2 parliamentary session of the Northern Ireland House of Commons, for example, James Brown drew the Prime Minister's attention to the fact that a number of letters received by residents of County Down from relatives in the Services in England had contained an 'instruction from the Postal Censorship Department in England that "Picture Postcards addressed to this foreign country are stopped by the Censor"' (N.I. Parliamentary Debates, vol. 24 (22 July 1941), col. 1259). In 1944 the same concern was being voiced, though rather more seriously. The specific complaint was that 'a large number of members of the Forces . . . have no idea of Ulster's [constitutional] position.' (Hugh Minford, ibid., vol. 27 (13 May 1944), col. 1389). Patrick Riddell was to record his futile attempts during the latter stages of the war in Italy to convince a group of Allied servicemen that Northern Ireland was not a part of neutral and 'cowardly' Eire: 'Contemptuous hands brushed aside the author's attempted explanation of the different identity and outlook of Ulster.' (Riddell 1970: 101). Thus despite the efforts of the MOI and related government and propaganda agencies to register Northern Ireland with the population of Britain as a part of the national struggle, the results were less than successful. At the same time, however, it should be noted that government propaganda efforts on Ulster's behalf were not comprehensive, and some glaring weaknesses can be identified. Thus, for example, the British Council's major contribution to the promotion of British nationality, British Life and Thought (1941), gave merely three brief references to Northern Ireland in its 462 pages. A detailed discussion of the (patriotically loaded) landscape of the British Isles ignored Northern Ireland altogether, as did an exposition of the British national character, entitled 'The Englishman' and written by Stanley Baldwin. Moreover, an accompanying map of the British Empire made no distinction whatever between Northern Ireland and Eire. Likewise, Arthur Mee, a highly popular author who specialized in patriotic works for a youthful readership, also ignored Northern Ireland in his major propagandist work, The Book of the Flag (1941), a celebration of the British character and imperial achievements. This situation might have been redressed, at least to some extent, had Ulster's wartime contribution been represented in British feature films with a wartime theme, but this was not the case.

It has been persuasively argued that 'one of the most valuable tasks that the cinema could perform in wartime was to project an image of the national character and the national identity that would promote support for the war effort.' (Richards 1988: 43). This was a task that all the British studios took up enthusiastically, and especially the most famous and patriotic of them, Ealing Studios. Ealing promoted in its wartime productions an image of the British national family united in its commitment to the war effort (see Barr 1974: 98–104). This is graphically illustrated by comparing Ealing's *The Bells Go Down*, a feature film based on the work of the London Fire Service, with Humphrey Jennings's documentary work, *Fires Were Started*, dealing with the same subject.

Both films were released about the same time in 1943, but whereas the projection of British identity in Jennings's work is implicit, with the London Fire Service standing as a paradigm for the British people as a whole, in Ealing's film national identity is explicitly illustrated. The film opens by attempting to synthesize the pastoral idea of national identity with the reality of urban Britain by stating that London was really a collection of 'villages', and that the film's story would focus on the life of one of those 'villages' during the blitz. Thereafter, the induction of a group of firemen is followed through from enlistment to their baptism of fire during the blitz. The personnel of the group is intended to represent the various national groups of the United Kingdom. A no-nonsense Scot is controller of the group, which also includes a Welshman and various representatives of the English social classes, especially the 'wise-cracking cockney'. But most significantly for our purposes, the Irish were also represented, not as an integral member of the 'national' fire-fighting group, but in an important supporting role as the 'village' policeman, who does his best to uphold law and order in the midst of chaos. Yet, the Irish identity this character represents is not that of Northern Ireland, but that of the southern Irish Catholic. Nowhere in the film's representation of the British 'family' at war is there any acknowledgement of Unionist Ulster's contribution. Moreover, what was true of this film was true of Ealing's wartime output in general and also of the output of other British studios.

That Ulster was ignored in this way is, perhaps, not surprising. As we have noted, in so far as the province had a regional personality that was recognizable in Britain it was an unappealing one, associated with narrow sectarianism and violence. And while serious efforts were now being made to improve Ulster's image, that image (for those who were aware of it), together with the political controversy associated with the North, would have made it difficult to include Northern Ireland in a representation of the British nation dealing, as such representations did, in congenial mythic essences. Certainly, the negative evidence of British feature films – the most influential form of mass entertainment – in the wartime period can be seen as confirming the failure of Northern Ireland to register as an authentic part of the national community. Frustration with this state of affairs, moreover, occasionally found bitter expression in the Northern Ireland House of Commons.

For example, when the Canadian, Sir Ernest Cooper, was appointed Ulster Agent in London in 1944 in preference to Captain R.L. Henderson, an Ulsterman, the Labour MP, John Beattie, claimed that he had been informed by an MP in the Westminster Parliament that 'Ulstermen are not particularly popular across the water; that they are too narrow' – something which Beattie refused to accept (*N.I. Parliamentary Debates*, vol. 27 (1 March 1944), col. 381). Evidence of that narrowness was provided on another occasion by the Independent Unionist, J.W. Nixon, who was provoked by the way 'everyone' was telling Unionists 'how far we are behind England'. Nixon, however, took it as a matter of pride to be 'behind England' in some things, especially on the matter of education: 'There are no Anglo-Catholics in Northern Ireland that I ever heard of. We have our own religious education. . . . I would not change it for the Anglo-Catholic religion. . . . They can have it for themselves in England if they want to' (ibid. (21 March 1944), cols 773–4).

Nixon, no doubt, spoke for a majority of Ulster Protestants on this issue, irritated by British distaste for their religious fundamentalism and undoubtedly uneasy about what the implications of this situation could be. The unsympathetic Protestant Republican, Denis Ireland, cruelly but acutely described the relationship between Ulster Protestants and their English fellow-citizens as follows:

the sensation of landing in Belfast must be, for an Englishman, rather like arriving in a kind of political lunatic asylum where the walls are painted with panels depicting, in the most appalling taste, scenes from the most lurid and reprehensible portions of his own past, and . . . most embarrassing of all, the inmates insist on turning out with deplorably uncivilised fife and drum bands to welcome him as one of themselves.   (Ireland 1947: 20)

The sense of anxiety and isolation that often comes across in Unionist references to their relationship with Britain at this time is well reflected in the correspondence between E.P. Northwood, Northern Ireland's publicity agent in London, and F.M. Adams, a member of the Stormont Government's Cabinet sub-committee on publicity. Norwood, exhibiting slight paranoia, was concerned that official broadcasts on how to deal with incendiary bombs made no reference to Northern Ireland. This, he argued, only served to emphasize 'some sort of cleavage which . . . is very bad for our part of the United Kingdom.' When Northern Ireland 'is associated with Whitehall Ministry announcements there is the immediate reference that it is part of a family.' (Northwood to Adams, 16 December 1942, 7 January 1943: PRONI, CAB9F/123/3A).

Unionist frustration at their inability more effectively to register the North at the centre of British interests found expression in attacks on the BBC in Northern Ireland, which was accused of failing to accurately present the regional identity of the province (Cathcart 1984: 130–31). There was, however, a major problem for the BBC in dealing with the North, for the Corporation had a policy of avoiding the area's political issues and matters associated with them (ibid. 1984: 117). But with these matters excluded, the kind of British identity that Unionists would have been happy with would have been difficult to construct. The *Irish News* (19 October 1943), in a report on the controversy over the BBC's reporting of the province, came close to pointing out the nub of the problem for Unionists: 'Partition has given it [Northern Ireland] no literary standing; won for it no new culture, and supplied it with no new rights to establish a separate nationality [different from the heritage it shared with the rest of Ireland].' (quoted in Cathcart 1984: 131).

Of course, the Irish dimension to the Ulster question had quite specific and detrimental effects on the extent to which the North could participate in the British national struggle. The Nationalists' rejection of conscription in both 1939 and following the Belfast blitz of April 1941 (Bowman 1983: 203–4, 244–6; Fisk 1985: 91, 103, 509–22), led to a humiliating climb-down by the Churchill Government and, most importantly, indicated the limitations of British national sovereignty in the region. Indeed, while the Belfast blitz may have pointed up the North's membership of the United Kingdom, the appeal to Dublin for assistance to deal with it pointed up, no less, the region's separateness from the rest of the Kingdom. It was with these differences in mind that Denis Ireland mockingly described the 'Ulsterman' who had been told for years by 'the *Daily Blank* [Mail]' that he was truly British, only to find the war and the absence of conscription in the North throwing up the 'curtain' of division that separated him from his 'spiritual' home:

the more the 'Ulsterman' reads the *Daily Blank* the thicker the curtain becomes. He reads, for example, about a nation shaken out of ancient habits by experiences such as conscription which he has not shared; he reads about the rise of Socialism which he does not like. . . . Indeed the more intently the 'Ulsterman' studies the English press of today, the more his truncated province must appear to him as Six Counties in search of a nation.   (Ireland 1947: 6)

The failure to impose conscription in Northern Ireland may have been one of the most significant indicators of its failure to integrate wholly into the British war effort, but there were others, such as the ban on the ringing of church bells, which applied in Britain but not in the North; the sale of firearms, prohibited in Britain but not in Ulster; and the requisition of men and materials, more easily effected in Britain than in Northern Ireland (see Major A.F. Dobbs, *N.I. Parliamentary Debates*, vol. 23 (Senate), (25 June 1940), col. 226).

These differences, especially the lack of conscription in the North, had, argued one Northern Ireland Cabinet Minister, produced a situation in which the Stormont authorities became obsessed with local affairs to the detriment of wider imperial interests. Of a statement by the Prime Minister, J.M. Andrews, to the effect that Northern Ireland's interests were of paramount concern in the war, W.J. Warnock, on resigning from the Government, declared:

This is the only Parliament in the Commonwealth of Nations in which that statement could be made. The interests of the Empire, the interests of the country, as a whole, and not the interests of Northern Ireland are the test, the only test of any Government in time of war. . . . The supreme loyalty these days is not party loyalty; the supreme loyalty is loyalty to the Imperial cause.
(N.I. Parliamentary Debates, vol. 24 (20 January 1942), col. 2611)

Warnock's concern to place imperial interests above local interests in the war effort, however, should not be construed as a willingness to serve a concept of the national interest defined in London and which could easily envisage an end to partition as best serving that interest (see Fisk 1985: Chs 6, 16). In fact, it seems that he wanted to press for the extension of conscription to the North regardless of the difficulties it might cause for Westminster. Conscription was important fundamentally, 'not because of the actual numbers of men' it would provide for the war effort, but 'to bring unification with the British Commonwealth of Nations', against the time when 'the Constitutional problem becomes acute again' (N.I. Parliamentary Debates, vol. 24 (20 January 1942), col. 2011).

Certainly, Warnock was right to be concerned about the state of feeling in Northern Ireland on the war. Mass Observation reports detailed public apathy and annoyance with wartime restrictions – 'anyone who is keen on the war effort is liable to feel uncomfortable'. That the government was in large part responsible for the development of this situation was reflected in Wilfrid Spender's opinion that it had encouraged public complacency, leading the Unionist population to believe that they were making sacrifices greater than England and Scotland (Barton 1988: 210). Even Ulster's erstwhile defender, Churchill, concluded in 1941 that the North's contribution was not all that it should be (ibid.: 175). Despite the apparently impressive total contribution of the North to the production of wartime equipment (see p. 124), there was a persistent concern by Westminster throughout the war about the North's inadequate output, its poor record of contract completion in war industries, poor workmanship, resistance to the 'dilution' of restrictive practices in industry, high absenteeism among workers, strikes and strained labour relations; while despite the Government's enthusiasm for conscription, poor voluntary recruitment among the North's Protestant population suggested that it was less popular with its followers. Thus, while the relationship between Britain and Northern Ireland became closer during the war, this was due less to the region's contribution to wartime production than to

their shared experience of war and of Luftwaffe attack. . . . German control of much of western Europe, combined with Eire's neutrality, dramatically enhanced the significance of the North's geographical position. As a direct consequence, its role in Allied victory became a vital one.
(Barton 1988: 286, 281–5; see also Fisk 1985: 279–85)

However, while the record of Northern Ireland's wartime contribution and commitment to the British war effort may have been significantly at variance with Stormont propaganda, care needs to be taken in assessing whether the region's wartime experience demonstrates that it was less 'British' than other regions of the United Kingdom. In fact, while the region's geographical and political circumstances set it apart from the rest of the United Kingdom, its wartime difficulties tended to mirror those of Britain. In Britain, no less than Northern Ireland, 'dilution', absenteeism, strikes and strained labour relations could present serious problems for the authorities (see Calder 1971: 381–2, 448–9, 510–11, 299, 329, 456–60, 511–12). In one, no less than the other, the private sphere of everyday existence tended to have a primacy over the public sphere of national activity. Of course, it is true that the war years were different, in the extent to which the national context of the war effort impacted on everyday life in Britain. This was true also of Northern Ireland's wartime experience, if to a lesser extent, and should be remembered in the context of Robert Fisks's argument that that experience does provide evidence of the North's essentially non-British character.

Fisk focuses on the apparently differing attitudes to the war of Craigavon and Wilfrid Spender, the former concerned primarily with local Ulster interests, the latter with the wider imperial interest – 'the strategical importance of Northern Ireland to the British Empire'. He cites a number of examples to demonstrate Craigavon's localist outlook; for example, his lack of interest in the Treaty ports until Northern Ireland found advantage in de Valera's neutrality; his pressing for conscription, not because the Empire was in danger, 'but because Northern Ireland, to prove her right to equal citizenship within the United Kingdom, had to be seen to share an equal sacrifice' – an anxiety that also prompted his concern over the province's poor recruiting figures. Fisk also cites Craigavon's organizing of the North's Home Guard as a sectarian force controlled by the 'B' Specials, and his complaint of 'treachery' when the abolition of partition was proposed as an inducement to bring Eire into the war on Britain's side, 'as if *his* was the imperial government.' (Fisk 1985: 283–4). It is also worth noting that the essence of Fisks's argument was made during the war by D.W. Brogan: 'They [Ulster Unionists] refuse to sacrifice any of their real or alleged interests to English needs. Their first loyalty is to Ulster.' (1943: 77, n. 1).

The central weakness of this argument, however, is the assumption that to be considered truly British Ulster Unionists had to demonstrate that they were motivated by an altruistic or 'principled' commitment to a London-based conception of the national interest, one that was devoid of self-interest and which was assumed to have prevailed in Britain. But, as has been pointed out, neither in the British regions or Northern Ireland did this state of affairs apply. Indeed, as we have already noted (p. 127), when the MOI initiated a campaign to make the British public aware of the wider national and imperial interests at stake in the war, it found that the public was simply not interested. Accordingly, that Craigavon's perception of the national interest was conditioned by Northern Ireland's needs was neither un-British or unusual. What did separate the North from the British mainland significantly, was the different (and lesser) extent to which it was affected by the war effort, and the quite unique political circumstances created by the partition controversy. Moreover, that Craigavon should describe the proposal to abolish partition in order to serve London's conception of the national interest as 'treachery' was not evidence of un-Britishness, but the quite natural response of a political leader who desperately wanted to believe, and to have the idea accepted in Britain, that Northern Ireland was as authentic a part of the national territory as Yorkshire, a region which he quite rightly would have reasoned no London government would have considered ceding to another state under any conditions whatsoever. Nor is Fisk's comparison of Craigavon's supposedly narrow localism with Spender's wider imperial perspective of great significance. Spender was, after all, an Englishman.

The case, however, has been made for Sir Basil Brooke, Prime Minister of Northern Ireland in 1943 following the resignation of J.M. Andrews, that he would have been prepared, in a hypothetical moment of apocalyptic crisis, to accept Irish unity – if 'we were faced with the choice of losing our civilisation or accepting the unification of Ireland' – but only, it appears, if de Valera demonstrated 'pro-British' tendencies by first declaring war *before* any discussions on unification took place (Barton 1988: 161–2). These conditions, he would have known, would never have been acceptable to de Valera, and it is thus difficult to place any importance on Brooke's ideas on the ending of partition.

IV

While the specificity of Northern Ireland concerns did not disqualify it from membership of the British nation, the controversial nature of some of Stormont's activities were, as Fisk points out, identified as inconsistent with British values and the democratic aims for which the war was being fought. Thus, when Craigavon organized Ulster's Home Guard on the basis of the 'B' Specials and controlled by Stormont, a protest memorial to Churchill was raised by a group of prominent Irish and Anglo-Irishmen, a leading member of which was General Sir Hubert Gough, leader of the 'Curragh Mutiny' of 1914. The group complained of sectarianism and pointed to what it regarded as the Home Guard's anti-British nature by suggesting its likeness to fascist police forces:

Its [B Special] involvement has been largely governed by considerations of religion and politics which would be absent if it had been constructed on normal lines by the British War Office or under its direction. It has thus incurred the odium attaching to a political police force of a type familiar on the Continent of Europe rather than the general popularity and respect possessed in full measure by the Home Guard throughout the remainder of the United Kingdom.

(*The Times*, 15 October 1940)

Again, the fact that Northern Ireland had its own Parliament invited comparison between it, as a British parliamentary institution, and Westminster, in terms of how Stormont approximated to mainland British standards of conducting the war effort. In 1942, Arthur Greenwood, the Labour leader, in a debate on the extension of Parliament – the bill for which included Northern Ireland – pointed out how the national unity prevalent in Britain was absent in Northern Ireland: there was no coalition government and all 'the elements of political controversy are still alive today'. Accordingly, it was claimed that since Northern Ireland had neither a national government or conscription its inclusion in the bill was 'amazing': there was 'no parallel between Northern Ireland and this country' (see *Daily Mail*, 1 October 1941). But it was in its treatment of the Catholic minority that the failure of Stormont to abide by 'British standards' was most apparent.

Here the sins of the past came back to haunt the regime. In 1941, for example, Sean O'Faolain in *An Irish Journey* (1941: 243–6) rehearsed for a British readership the anti-Catholic statements of Craigavon, Brooke and Andrews in the 1930s, as did Rev. Dr John (later Cardinal) Heenan in the English *Catholic Herald* the same year (Heenan 1971: 243–6). But the most damaging condemnation came in October 1944, when Dr William Griffin, Roman Catholic Archbishop of Westminster, in a speech to a combined gathering of Christians and Jews condemning the Nazi persecution of religion, drew an analogy with Stormont's treatment of Catholics in the North: 'I need hardly mention the persecution that is going on even at the present day in Northern Ireland.' Widely reported in the London papers, Griffin's comments caused great concern at Stormont with demands that the authorities take action to limit their possibly harmful effects in Britain (see Hugh Minford, *N.I. Parliamentary Debates*, vol. 27 (8 November 1944), cols 2190, 2240). Considered individually, criticisms of the Stormont regime such as the above may have been of no great import, but when frequently stated and reported they pointed up the difficulties that stood in the way of Northern Ireland being fully integrated into the British national community, especially in a period when the British national myth of unsullied liberal democratic values represented the standards for which the war was being fought. Certainly, Northern Unionists were never confident that their membership of the British national family was wholly secure. As late as April 1944, Home Intelligence reported that in Northern Ireland the speeches of even that most consistent friend of the Unionists, Churchill, were being carefully scrutinized for any clause or sentence which indicated a hint of Ulster's 'betrayal' (Home Intelligence, Weekly Report no. 186 in Addison (ed.) (1979): Reel Two, 27 April 1944, p. 242).

In this respect, Unionist instincts may have been right. Friendly as Churchill was to the northern regime, he was subject to volatile changes of mood; and, on at least one occasion in 1943, a hasty consideration of Anglo-Irish relations led him to forget his commitments to the Stormont regime and to decide abruptly on a 'solution' to the Irish problem. Only a firm collective refusal to support him by the Cabinet deterred Churchill from pursuing it (see Leo Amery, diary entry, 22 September 1943, in Barnes and Nicholson (eds) 1988: 942–3).

Northern Ireland did make some important and lasting friendships as a result of her wartime experience. Perhaps the most surprising was Herbert Morrison, the Labour Party Home Secretary, who was initially hostile to Ulster Unionism but gradually became a firm supporter of their interests (see Donoghue and Jones 1973: 10, 307–8, 386). Unionist MPs at Westminster were careful to cultivate his goodwill (see Savory 1957a: 139–40). Such conversions to the Unionist cause, however, were never plentiful enough to provide loyalists with the kind of constitutional reassurance they desired. Moreover, wartime conditions, paradoxically, appear to have diminished to some extent the ability of the monarchy to affirm, in an uncomplicated way, their membership of the British nation.

V

From the published images of the monarchy in wartime there is little indication that their importance for the British public might have changed. That the royal family stayed in London despite aerial attacks on Buckingham Palace was widely appreciated as an act of solidarity between crown and people. As the *Londonderry Sentinel* (24 April 1941) put it in the wake of the Belfast blitz of April 1941, despite the bombing of the Palace the King was still in town, 'along with Mr Smith and Mr Brown, typical of the ordinary, everyday folk of Britain who are sticking to their posts and carrying on despite Hitler's Huns of the Air. They are not "Blitz-Quitters".' Accordingly, this newspaper regarded it as only natural that when Belfast was bombed the Duke and Duchess of Gloucester should visit Ulster 'to convey in person Royal sympathy to the people . . . in their time of trial'; and, of course, by so doing acknowledge Ulster's membership of the British national family.

These bonds of identity were further strengthened when King George VI and Queen Mary made a three-day visit to Northern Ireland in June 1942 (*Londonderry Sentinel*, 27 June 1942); a visit, which, according to Home Intelligence reports, had a similar morale-boosting effect on the people as one to Scotland not long before, especially 'among the many thousands of war workers in the Belfast factories' (Home Intelligence, Weekly Report no. 91 in Addison (ed.) (1979): Reel Two, p. 462). The next visit by their Majesties to Ulster came in July 1945. This visit, which included Princess Elizabeth, was noteworthy for the fulsome praise expressed by the monarch for the North's contribution to the war effort in an address to both Houses of the Northern Ireland Parliament. In this respect the King's speech served to obliterate both the difficulties surrounding the North's constitutional position during the previous five years and also his own expressed dissatisfaction with the regime's war output in the early 1940s.[6] Naturally enough, given the Unionist tendency to comprehend the significance of the monarchy through their own perspective on the British national myth, when the royal party visited Derry it was pointed out that the royal launch was following the historic course taken by the *Mountjoy* 'when it broke the Boom' (*Londonderry Sentinel*, 20 July 1945). Thus was the celebration of the delivery from Nazi aggression assimilated to the loyalist liberation myth of 1689.

Yet for all that the monarchy could function as a means of national representation at the popular level, it has been argued that it was less important in this respect in wartime than in peacetime. For example, Mass Observation reports during the first year of the war, especially in blitzed areas, found that people regarded the monarchy as irrelevant to their everyday conditions of existence. As already noted, just as people faced with the invasion of their private sphere of existence by war were prepared to fight *despite* the exhortations of official nationalistic propaganda, so it would seem, they likewise found it difficult to relate the elevated national status of the monarchy to their own personal struggles – the gap appeared to be too wide (Ziegler 1978: 72; Harrisson 1990: 162). Indeed, as the strains of war began to take effect, indifference could turn to outright resentment when personal destitution was compared to royal opulence (Ziegler 1978: 72–3). There was, however, more to it than that, for the war had produced abnormal conditions and also, in Churchill, a leader skilled in the arts of nationalist rhetoric, who shaped the myth of the nation in the worst days of the war. In this context, the King's traditional role of supreme national symbol became somewhat diminished, especially so as the King personally lacked the propagandist skills and exuberant personality of Churchill. Accordingly, the public reception of Churchill could be more enthusiastic than that for the monarch. But if the King's role as the supreme embodiment of the nation was not quite what it was in peacetime, evidence exists to suggest, nevertheless, that his earnest efforts to share the struggles of his people were widely appreciated, especially so when Buckingham Palace was bombed (Wheeler-Bennett 1958: 469–70).

As for Northern Ireland, the special political circumstances of this part of the United Kingdom determined a quite different response to the monarchy. For example, there was, it seems, no popular diminishing – as an embodiment of the nation – of the status of the King as compared with Churchill. Here the identification of Churchill as the supreme embodiment of the national will was mitigated by an appreciation of him as a politician whose fidelity on the question of Northern Ireland's constitutional status had always to be carefully watched – something that did not apply to the King. Moreover, while Belfast was severely bombed, its duration was brief and royal visits few, so the development of indifference or resentment by the public had much less opportunity to develop. In any event, it seems unlikely that it would have, given the Unionist anxiety about national identity and their desire for any opportunity that would serve to demonstrate their membership of the British national family.

The only complication, such as it was, that the monarchy as a symbol of British national identity seems to have presented for Northern Ireland, was very minor and wholly local in nature. Unlike peacetime, when the role of the monarchy as an agency of national integration was simple and uncomplicated, in wartime, when many northern Catholics enrolled in the

Civil Defence service, royal visits could cause them embarrassment (Oliver 1978: 68). In this context, it is also worth noting that such visits could touch directly on the national question. During their visit in 1942, for example, the royal visitors called on the widow and family of Catholic RUC Constable, Patrick Murphy, who had been killed in an IRA ambush. The dead policeman's widow was presented with the King's Police Medal (*Londonderry Sentinel*, 27 June 1942).

In the main, though, it could be argued that Northern Unionists gained considerable long-term political advantage from the wartime connection with the monarchy. It was, it appears, during this period that Princess Elizabeth formed the deep affection for the Unionist population that she, as Queen, has maintained to the present day. This period had been a formative experience for her and she was keen to get involved in war work (see Lacey 1977: Ch. 9). It was in this context that she formed a keen appreciation of Ulster Unionist loyalty. Some months before the royal visit of July 1945, she took the initiative in making known directly to the Stormont authorities that she wished to visit the North.[7]

Notes

1. For a detailed discussion of this issue, especially Chamberlain's deliberations on partition, see Fisk (1985: Ch. 6).
2. See, for example, the enthusiastic report on Ulster's industrially-based war production in *The Times* (8 April 1940).
3. The most exhaustive account of the Belfast blitz is provided in Barton (1989).
4. For some insightful comment on the film see Stead (1988: 71–2).
5. It should be noted that the unflattering comparisons made by Stormont ministers between the population of Belfast and that of other British cities under blitz conditions (Barton 1988: 198) were unfair. The panic-stricken reaction of the Belfast population was not in fact unique, but similar to that of towns and cities in Britain which abruptly experienced heavy raids without previous conditioning (on the latter, see McLaine 1979: 113). Nor was the practice of 'trekking' – leaving the city in anticipation of air-raids – which was widespread in Northern Ireland (Barton 1989: 236–41), unique to the province. It was also common in Britain (McLaine 1979: 120, 210).
6. The King had questioned J.M. Andrews on whether the Stormont authorities were working amicably with the military, when Andrews paid a formal visit to Buckingham Palace shortly after Craigavon's death (Fisk 1985: 455), and complained directly to Stormont ministers about their inadequate contribution to the war effort when he visited the North in 1942 (Taylor, Television documentary, 1991).
7. See Minute to the file on the royal visit to Northern Ireland by 'R.H.', 12 March 1945 (PRO, HO 45/20434/529400/1).

7

ULSTER, LABOUR AND NATIONAL IDENTITY
1945–51

I

While the weakness of the Churchillian national myth of heroic imperialism was graphically demonstrated by the Tory electoral defeat of 1945, that myth continued to exist and was to provide a vocabulary and imagery that would inform the interpretation of national crises in the future (Dawson and West 1984: 9). Churchill, moreover, was not only the major subject of that mythology but also its active promoter. Just as he had sought, after World War One, to shape the British interpretation of the wartime experience through his multi-volume, *The World Crisis*, so after 1945, and in much more favourable circumstances, he sought to shape British understanding with his *History of the Second World War* (6 vols, 1948–54) – a work that earned him the Nobel Prize for Literature and which has been described as a great work of myth in which the unifying perspective was not so much 'the British people' as 'Britain' itself: '"The People" are not substantially present in any recognisable form, but appear as a mythicised heroic unity which endures, struggles, "does its bit" in the common national cause'. Moreover, Churchill's history was World War Two made known from his *personal* viewpoint (Dawson 1984: 6–7). As such, and given its immense popularity, Churchill's ability to impose his construction on the popular conception of the war must be considered as highly impressive.

For our purposes, however, it is important to note that while Churchill's presentation of the British people in general was abstract, Ulster's wartime role merited a specific acknowledgement; for just as he had, in his wartime speeches, made reference to Ulster's contribution, so too, in his history of the war was this the case, as the tribute to the North in volume two (1949: 529) makes clear: 'by the grace of God Ulster stood a faithful sentinel.'[1] Moreover, Churchill would repeatedly refer to Northern Ireland and the constitutional debt owed by the rest of the United Kingdom to it in his post-war speeches. Thus, during a general attack on Labour Government policies in Parliament on 28 October 1948, the only credit he gave the Government was for a resolution rejecting any attempt to coerce Ulster –

'without whose loyalty we could not have maintained our lifeline into the Mersey and the Clyde during the war' – out of her allegiance to the crown and membership of the Empire (James (ed.) 1974: vol. vii, 7720–21). In November 1948, when the Irish Government made clear its intention to leave the Commonwealth, Churchill argued that it made 'the maintenance of the position of Northern Ireland . . . all the more obligatory upon us. It is evident that a gulf has been opened, a ditch has been dug, between Northern Ireland and Southern Ireland which invests partition with greater permanency and reality than it ever had before.' (ibid.: 7747).

Churchill's speeches reflected the greater constitutional security that had been the reward for Northern Ireland's contribution to the British war effort and the Stormont regime was keen to exploit this situation. Accordingly, it established, in late 1945, a propaganda magazine, *Ulster Commentary*, aimed at refuting attacks on the regime from critics in Eire and Britain.[2] By early 1947, 20,000 copies had been circulated, mainly in Britain (Major J.M. Sinclair, *N.I. Parliamentary Debates*, vol. 31 (8 May 1947), col. 283). The attempt was also made to explain the characteristics of the 'Ulsterman' in terms consistent with traditional notions of British national character. The Ulsterman was

naturally empirical, preferring to rely on experience rather than untried theory. This trait has been a powerful factor in determining public policy and individual action in many a situation where a false step would have been calamitous and irretrievable. . . . It is against this background that Ulster life and ideals must be understood.[3]

Ulster Commentary was also the means for disseminating the regime's view of Ulster's place in the wider imperial setting; a view which, if Brooke's contribution to a mass meeting organized by the Empire Trades Association and British Empire League was representative, preferred to ignore the implications of Indian independence and to present the Empire in terms more appropriate to the late nineteenth century: 'We in Ulster see in the British Empire the nucleus of a still wider community of nations, banded together against aggression and working in unison for the peaceful and ordered progress of the race.' ('Keystone of British Empire Unity', *Ulster Commentary*: June 1949). Given Eire's departure from the Commonwealth and the subsequent reinforcement of partition embodied in the Ireland Act (1949), which guaranteed Northern Ireland's membership of the United Kingdom so long as this was the wish of the Stormont Parliament, such sentiments as those expressed by Brooke are understandable. Brooke's speech, moreover, has to be seen against the background of important social and economic agreements between Belfast and London that would be enacted in the period 1946–51, establishing parity of services and taxation between Northern Ireland and Britain (Buckland 1981: 86–7). Brooke's speech also followed a general election held in February 1949 which produced the expected solid majority for the Union, and which provided the material for a Unionist Party publication intended to refute the anti-partitionist propaganda of Eirean politicians and 'the very small nationalist minority in Northern Ireland.' (Ulster Unionist Council 1949: 1). Furthermore, in this publication and others produced by the Unionist Party in this period (see Savory 1947), the North's wartime record was relentlessly exploited to combat the nationalist threat.

Perhaps most indicative of the fund of goodwill in British government circles that Unionists could rely on at this time was the readiness of Westminster to accept Stormont's response to the complaints of discrimination and maladministration emanating from British Labour no less than Irish nationalist sources. The Labour critique came in particular from Geoffrey Bing, an MP with a County Down background and a leading member of the loose grouping of Labour members termed the 'Friends of Ireland' group. Bing framed his attack on the Stormont regime in terms, not of opposition to partition, but of the failure of Stormont to apply British standards of democracy in Northern Ireland.[4] When Bing raised the question of Westminster's power to intervene in the North following the banning of a nationalist meeting in County Londonderry, the pro-Unionist Home Secretary, Herbert Morrison, resorted to the by now standard explanation in cases such as these, namely, that he had no authority to interfere with powers conferred on Northern Ireland by the Government of Ireland Act of 1920: the regime was 'acting indisputably within their powers.'[5] On allegations of maladministration against the Stormont Government, the approach was to marginalize their significance. Discrimination in public employment was something the regime had 'a genuine desire' to eliminate while that in employment controlled by local authorities was dismissed with the explanation, 'there is no official information about this.' As for the Special Powers Act, this was regarded as drastic only 'formally', in practice it was administered with 'great moderation'. As for the issue of the manipulation of ward boundaries, central to the controversy over the Unionist minority in Derry having control of the city Corporation, Lord Craigavon's defence that Catholics had made no submission to the independent commission when ward boundaries were redrawn in the early 1920s, together with a submission by the Stormont authorities that section fifteen of the Town Improvement (Ireland) Act of 1854 bound them to give valuation equal consideration with numbers, was apparently accepted (see Adrian Robinson to C.G. Markbreiter, 28 October 1948; W.S. Murrie to A. Johnston, 28 January 1950: PRO, HO45/25053/815509/170). It is also noteworthy that the British Council, which in its wartime publication, British Life and Thought, made scant acknowledgement of Northern Ireland, in this period promoted Ulster through a well-produced and substantial booklet entitled, The Ulstermen and their Country (1947), written by the pro-Unionist Ulster poet, Revd W.R. Rodgers. The booklet constituted the Northern Ireland section of a series under the title, 'The British People: How They Live and Work'.

Given the British Council's imprimatur on this publication as an expression of the British way of life, its contents are worth close examination. What is initially noteworthy about Rodgers's work is his attempt to establish a regional or 'national' personality: 'the Ulsterman', a being 'of strong will and stubborn independence', characteristics that 'mark him off from the other people of Ireland'. The 'strong, active and enterprising' Ulstermen had their own government and territory, with its 'own deliberate frontier fencing it from the South of Ireland'. Nor was Ulster's distinctive identity a recent development: 'you may yet see the remains of the Black Pig's Dyke, a great wall built by Ulstermen in the 3rd century A.D. to keep out the Southerners.' (Rodgers 1947: 1). Thus unlike traditional Unionist mythology, which located the defining experience of the Protestant community in the Ulster plantation of the early seventeenth century, Rodgers sought to establish an authenticity of identity based on age-old historical residence. In this context, the Ulster 'personality' that developed was one that could not be reduced to the planter's mentality of early modern history, though there was in the Ulsterman 'a strain of the colonist who came to this corner of Ireland only three centuries ago.' (ibid.: 3).

The theme of identity based on antiquity is also evident in Rodgers's treatment of the industrial character of the North. Ulstermen may have been proud of the growth of Belfast over the previous one hundred years, but Rodgers was concerned to stress the *newness* of this development, presenting it as a somewhat artificial imposition on a more authentic rural society. Concerned to emphasize the value of organic community as against 'that of the rootless industrial cities' (ibid.: 13–14), Rodgers employed the pastoral imagery so popular in the discourse on national identity in Britain, and especially with the British Council (see Ch. 6, p. 121), to claim that Ulster society had 'always been a rural one and the people a peasant people. . . . The peasant's craft is the root of all the skilful growths of civilisation. And the source and sap of culture is agriculture.' (ibid.: 4–6). Rodgers's ruralist argument, however, was taken to the point of absurdity when he claimed, 'you may find that the peat fire which glows in the farm kitchen you visit has not been allowed to go out for two or three hundred years.' (ibid.: 13).

That Rodgers should present Ulster in this way is, perhaps, not surprising in a publication intended to emphasize the Britishness of Northern Ireland. Moreover, by denying the significance of industrial urbanization to the identity of the region, he prepared the ground for the marginalization of that other associated and negative aspect of the region's identity – its reputation for bigotry and political fanaticism. In fact, Rodgers sought to neutralize the latter by arguing that while the Ulsterman was preoccupied with politics, his interest was not negatively aggressive but benign:

He will try to lure you into the arena of political argument. But do not take his combativeness too seriously. Remember that politics is the chief recreation of the Ulsterman. He likes it because he passionately likes the company of people, even if it is only to disagree with them. . . . there is no more sociable nature than the Ulsterman's.   (ibid.: 11)

Rodgers's experience as a Presbyterian minister in Loughgall, County Armagh, makes it impossible to accept that he actually believed this. It only makes sense as an attempt to accommodate Ulster politics to popular mythic notions of British political tolerance. This is also evident in his account of religious division in the province.

Rodgers acknowledged that religious conflict, long dead in Europe, was still alive in Ulster and ran through society from top to bottom. Further, he argued that it corresponded to a historic racial division. Employing late-Victorian ideas on the racial characteristics of Celt and Saxon, Rodgers described Catholics as voluble, glib, emotional, though at the same time, charming, courteous and eloquent in speech. Protestants, on the other hand, were 'cautious, logical and far-seeing in speech and action.' The Protestant distrusted eloquence: 'His virtue is that of stability.' (ibid.: 15). Rodgers's accounts of community differences in the North have their source in the racial arguments used by Matthew Arnold in the nineteenth century (see Ch. 2, p. 24; Chapman 1978: 93–5). Moreover, just as Arnold sought to argue that the qualities of Celt and Saxon came together to make one composite British personality, so too did Rodgers seek to neutralize the implications of communal division in Northern Ireland by arguing for the existence of an underlying homogeneity in Ulster life:

These characters, Protestant and Catholic, are complementary. They make the two halves of life. One takes a long view of life, the other a short and roundabout one. One is thoughtful individual, the other is emotional and communal. One tends to a democratic and progressive way of life, the other to a hieratic and static way. It is this diversity and interplay of opposites that makes Ulster life such a rich and fascinating spectacle.

It is quite obvious which of these 'characters' Rodgers thought the more valuable; nevertheless, he claimed that they shaded into one another – each 'lend-leases itself to the other' (ibid.: 16–18) – and on this basis sought to minimize the extent of sectarianism in Ulster. The political passions associated with the religious divide were confined to the two dates of 12 July and 15 August, after which, 'the occasion over, he [the Ulsterman] goes quietly back to the orderly uneventful round of life.' (ibid.: 23).

Like all myths, Rodgers's construction of 'Ulster', emphasizing organic wholeness in environment and community, is as significant for what it excludes as for what it includes, but it represented perhaps the only way in which the region could have been portrayed as representative of the 'British way of life'. Certainly the political realities of the North were most undesirable as subjects for the British Council to promote for this purpose. It is worth noting that when Ulster Unionists suggested replying to the anti-partitionist campaign being waged by Nationalists in this period by sending a deputation of Orangemen to make the Unionist case among American Protestants with a supposed Scots-Irish background, the prospect was viewed in London and in the British embassy in Washington with horror, and steps were quietly taken to quash the proposal. Northern Ireland's interests outside the province, it was emphasized, were best dealt with by Westminster departments.[6]

II

The idea suggested by Rodgers, that 'Ulster' was an 'organic' national entity within the United Kingdom, became more developed in the post-war period. There were, for example, demands in the Northern Ireland House of Commons that the government produce an 'authentic' history of Ulster for use in the region's schools. This development, it is important to note, was distinct from the practice in operation since 1922 of teaching only British history in the North's state schools (see Magee 1970: 4–7). Although not stated explicitly, the purpose behind these demands was clear enough – to produce, not so much a history, as a national myth for Northern Ireland on the basis of which the identity of the region and the Unionist population as a distinct 'national' grouping within the United Kingdom could be promoted.

The Ulster history proposal arose out of a resolution passed at the Ulster Unionist Annual Conference and was taken up in Stormont on 14 March 1949 by Francis Hanna, Nationalist MP for Central Belfast. Hanna was concerned that, 'coming from the source which it does it makes one suspicious that what is being sought is the introduction into schools of a political propaganda masquerading as history', and demanded that any such history be written from 'purified sources' (*N.I. Parliamentary Debates*, vol. 33 (14 March 1949), col. 244). Unionists, however, pressed the Minister for Education, Lieut. Col. Hall-Thompson, 'to make the study of an approved Ulster history an obligatory subject in all primary, intermediate and grammar schools which are in receipt of any grant from public funds.' (William May, Revd J.G. Macmanaway, ibid. (5 April 1949), col. 556). There were, however, problems in the realization of such a project: first, in producing a *single* such history that could be suitable for all school levels, from primary to grammar; second, in finding 'a suitable person who could write a totally reliable history of Ulster.' (Hall-Thompson, ibid.). The demands nevertheless persisted, but to no avail. Hall-Thompson expressed sympathy for the objectives of Unionist MPs on this issue,[7] but regretted that he could be of little assistance. He hoped that such a history could be written, but 'obviously it is better that books of this kind should be written independently and not be commissioned by a Government department.' As for the compulsory teaching of such a history, he had to have regard to sound educational practice: 'Compulsion is not the British way of educating our young people.' (ibid. (6 July 1949), col. 1326).

However, to the reasons Hall-Thompson gave for the failure to move on this issue can be added the fact that no such politically inspired history could be written and achieve credibility. Nationalists made it clear that any such history would come under fierce scrutiny to ensure that the truth was told. Moreover, as Harry Diamond informed Parliament, he would be concerned to ensure that 'a special tribute be paid to the founders of the prosperity of this city who also enunciated Republican principles – I refer to the United Irishmen'. Nationalists were also concerned that any Ulster history should include the whole nine counties of the province (ibid.; also

J.F. Stewart, ibid., vol. 34 (7 March 1950), col. 85). Thus, despite a claim from the Unionist MP, A.F. Wilson, that 'the people of Northern Ireland have a historical destiny and that it is necessary to start at an early age to show the children how they can get the facts and defend themselves against other ideas' (ibid., col. 85) – Wilson had earlier called for the name of 'this small nation' to be changed to 'British Ireland' (ibid. 5, vol. 32 (1 December 1948), col. 3714 – the Government felt there was little it could do to meet this demand. In fact, the Government had already gone as far as it could in this direction with the production of a short booklet, written by Hugh Shearman, entitled *Northern Ireland: its History, Resources and People* (1946).

Having obtained, during the war, permission from the London Government to produce a booklet on Northern Ireland for distribution in British schools, Shearman's work was intended to fulfil this purpose. The booklet was divided into four parts: physical geography, history, constitution and 'Northern Ireland Today'. In each of these areas the distinctiveness of Northern Ireland from southern Ireland was stressed. Thus, on geography, 'the province forms, by its internal physical structure, a distinct unit and a natural home for a distinctive local economy and culture'; added to which 'strong external frontiers of rocky sea coasts, lakes, hills and rivers' made an effective barrier between north and south and further tended 'to make Ulster a separate unit and to favour the development of its historical and political individuality' (Shearman 1946: 60). From this basis history was used, as Rodgers was to do the following year, to argue that, long before the plantation of the early seventeenth century, Ulster was a separate region from the South – with which it was also frequently at war (ibid.: 7).

As might have been expected, Shearman's treatment of Ulster history was carefully presented to serve Unionist interests. For example, the 'grim experiences' of the seventeenth century – especially the 1641 Rebellion – were described as having given 'a stubborn strength and cohesion to the Ulster community' Those 'years of peril and isolation' had produced that 'sober, disillusioned, practical outlook, the individualistic and self-reliant piety and the strong sense of communal solidarity which distinguishes their descendants to the present day.' (ibid.: 11–12). Shearman did acknowledge the existence of a Catholic community in Ulster and provided an insightful account of why united political action between the two religious communities had always been difficult to effect (ibid.: 12), but his designation, 'the Ulster community', was reserved for the Ulster Protestants.

With American distribution of the booklet in mind, a brief section was devoted to Ulster's contribution to the making of the USA, a section followed by a more substantial account of the North's opposition to Home Rule in the period 1885–1914 and its contribution to the British war effort in the two World Wars (ibid.: 13–14). Shearman's account of contemporary Ulster was more frank than that provided by Rodgers, especially in his advice to the visitor to 'avoid any hasty indulgence in political argument'; however, and no doubt with the negative image of the 'Ulsterman' in Britain in mind, the visitor was also advised to 'refrain from too hastily classifying the people he meets by the views they express.'

(ibid.: 14–20). Shearman's booklet concluded with a discussion of the 'Ulster character': 'For the most part the Ulster genius tends to be concrete, practical, administrative or scientific'; attributes which, while they tended to discourage 'superficial attractions or accomplishments', could yet produce striking results. As with Rodgers, the characteristics of the Ulsterman Shearman identified belonged firmly within the dominant conception of British 'national character' – one that defined it as empirical and anti-intellectual – and Shearman amplified this point by providing the familiar list of Ulster generals who had served in the British Army during the war, together with other prominent Ulstermen who had made distinguished careers in British science, politics and the arts (ibid.: 31–2).

The publication of Shearman's *Northern Ireland* in 1946 was an important event. Although not an official history of the kind Unionists would have preferred, it represented the closest the regime would come to providing a state view of the North as a distinctive region of the United Kingdom. It would remain in print, suitably amended by Shearman as required, until the prorogation of Stormont in 1972. But the account of Ulster it presented, while it included no deliberate misstatements, was yet cleansed, as far as possible, of any material deemed inconsistent with Unionist mythology. Thus, it excluded any mention of the United Irishmen and – though there was external pressure applied here – the rejection of Parliament's authority that the rebellion against the imposition of the third Home Rule Bill entailed. Exclusion, of course, had its limits. Ideally, the regime would have preferred to present the North as inhabited by a wholly loyal people but the Catholic population could not be ignored; however, the presentation of them in Shearman's work reflected fairly clearly the attitude to them of the Stormont regime: citizens of the state but not authentic members of the Ulster community.[8]

It should be noted that there was another hand in the shaping of Shearman's booklet. The chief reason for producing it had been the desire to make the people of Britain more aware of Northern Ireland and its membership of the United Kingdom. The corollary of that permission, however, was that the Department of Education in London insisted on vetting the work before publication (see R.S. Bramwell to W.N. McWilliams, 8 March 1947: PRONI, CAB9F/123/114). It seems that the London authorities were concerned that nothing a mainland British audience might find objectionable should be included. It is possible that this accounts for the fact that, despite its central importance to Unionist life, the booklet made no mention whatever of the Orange Order, an organization whose image was indelibly associated with sectarianism. Accordingly, although the work carried photographs of most aspects of life in Northern Ireland – photographs produced by the British Council (G.S. Robertson to J. Knipe, 10 October 1944: PRONI, CAB9F/123/114) – none depicted the Orange Order.

The most significant example of London censorship, however, was the excision of a substantial passage on the period 1912–14, describing in detail the Ulster resistance to Home Rule, especially the Covenant, the raising of the UVF and the activities of Carson and Craig. The result was that the original edition of 1946 carried no mention of the Unionist leaders.[9] It is difficult to be precise about why this section of the work was censored, but it was possibly because any detailed account of Unionist activities during the third Home Rule crisis was bound to entail some discussion of Tory complicity in the Ulster rebellion, and, as such, could hardly have been seen either as consistent with British notions of political tolerance and constitutional legality or an encouragement to good citizenship for British schoolchildren.

It is impossible, of course, to know how far – if at all – Shearman's booklet contributed to a greater popular consciousness of Northern Ireland in Britain, but it is clear that the Stormont authorities believed it would have beneficial effects. Copies of the first edition were sent to fifty-one newspapers in the United Kingdom (note to file on Shearman's booklet, 24 June 1946: PRONI, CAB9F/123/114), while in the period 1946–50 it went through three editions. At the same time, efforts were made to expand the activities of the Ulster Office in London and also to employ the many Ulster Associations in Britain to promote knowledge of Northern Ireland as an area for industrial expansion (Major Sinclair, *N.I. Parliamentary Debates*, vol. 30 (26 November 1946), col. 2856; Brian Faulkner, ibid., vol. 34 (4 May 1950), cols 779–94).

At this point, it is worth mentioning that the Unionist Party did not have a complete monopoly of discussion within the Protestant community on Ulster's identity. John Hewitt explored the subject in 1945, and in a wider context. Concerned mainly with the development of a distinctive cultural identity in the North, Hewitt pointed out that 'our most troublesome and deeply fissured problem has been . . . the lack of integration of Ulster's peoples' (Hewitt 1987: 119). Returning to the subject in 1947, he made the case for regionalism in terms which, from the orthodox Unionist perspective, could only have been seen as politically unsound:

Ulster, considered as a region and not as a symbol of any political creed, can, I believe, command the loyalty of every one of its inhabitants. For regional identity does not preclude, rather it requires membership of a larger association. And whether that association be, as I hope, of a federated British Isles, or a federal Ireland, out of that loyalty to our own place, rooted in honest history, in familiar folkways and knowledge, phrased in our own dialect, there should emerge a culture and an attitude individual and distinctive, a fine contribution to the European inheritance and no mere echo of the thought and imagination of another people or another land.   (ibid.: 125)

Hewitt's ideas were imaginative, but had little prospect of gathering support in the context of the times, when the anti-partition campaign was at its height and with Unionism more confident and secure than it had been for some time past. Hewitt spoke, if for anyone, for a very small body of liberal Protestant opinion, and would pay with blighted career prospects soon afterwards for his independence of mind.[10]

Circumstances did occasionally arise in this period, however, which caused the Stormont regime concern about their image in Britain. In 1946, the movie director Carol Reed came to Belfast to make a film of F.L. Green's novel, *Odd Man Out*; a story about an IRA payroll raid on a Belfast factory which goes wrong when the gang's leader is wounded and separated from his followers. His wanderings around the city's industrial landscape culminating in his shooting by the police form the substance of the story. The film's focus was human interest rather than political and it could not be regarded as pro-republican (for an insightful commentary, see Rockett *et al.* 1987: 157–60). Nevertheless, it starred one of Britain's leading actors, James Mason; it was intended for widespread British distribution; and it carried a prologue identifying Northern Ireland as a place of 'political unrest'. Further, it did not provide support either for republicanism or the Stormont regime, opting instead for a neutral stance, declaring that the film was 'not concerned with the struggle between the law and an illegal organisation' (Two Cities Films, *Odd Man Out*, 1946). While the northern government could do nothing to stop the film being made, it refused to co-operate in its making, having decided that the film was, from its standpoint, definitely not good propaganda.[11]

Odd Man Out was the only feature film of the immediate post-war period to which the Stormont authorities took serious exception; and against whatever negative effects they imagined it would have on British audiences must be set the regime's own film propaganda, embodied in *The Voice of Ulster*, a film released in 1948 and taken for a six month run in its theatres by Metro-Goldwyn-Mayer (F.M. Adams to E.P. Northwood, 27 August 1948: PRONI, CAB9F/123/81).[12] The confidence Unionists felt about their constitutional position at this time was reflected in the comments of one of the regime's most enthusiastic academic supporters, F.H. Newark, Professor of Jurisprudence at Queens University, Belfast who, in reviewing the first twenty-five years of the northern statelet, hoped that 'the next twenty-five years will see Northern Ireland return to that more complete Union which existed before 1920.' (Newark 1948: 66). Indeed, Unionists had every reason to be pleased in this period, especially about the way in which Eire's precipitate declaration of a Republic allowed them to have Northern Ireland's constitutional position reinforced in the Ireland Act of 1949. At the same time, however, it is important to note the limits to which that position could be secured.

There was never, for example, any prospect of the 'more complete Union' Newark desired. The next twenty-five years would indeed see the ending of Stormont rule and the return of direct rule from Westminster, but the circumstances under which Stormont was prorogued in 1972 were hardly what Newark had had in mind. And while the Attlee Government was generally sympathetic to Stormont and established a good working relationship with it, the fact was that it did not see the status quo as a solution to the Northern problem, being apparently still favourable to Irish unity (Barton 1992: 5–6). Thus, even under the most favourable circumstances, Northern Ireland was not accepted as an integral part of the national territory.

It should be noted, however, that some Unionists were prepared to accept, enthusiastically, this reality. Opposed to the 'rampant' socialistic legislation enacted by the Labour Government, distrustful of its perceived nationalist sympathies, and influenced by a mistaken idea of the North's financial viability based on the inflated *gross* imperial contribution the region made in the war years and immediately afterwards, some Unionists – the most vocal being W.F. McCoy, MP for South Tyrone – made the case for dominion status.[13] The demand was most vocal in 1948, and while the Northern authorities had already decided against this option, they still hoped for an extension of their powers (Barton 1992: 5, 8). Several factors, however, militated against any change in the existing constitutional position. Apart from the fact that the Labour Government had shown itself to be reliable on the constitutional question, dominion status would re-open the Irish question in general at a time when the anti-partition campaign was at its height; it went against all that the Unionist Party was supposed to stand for, and could very well alienate the goodwill Northern Ireland had established in Britain. Again, there was a fear that the issue would split Unionism, leading to a socialist-nationalist alliance coming to power in Ulster and that the independence that dominion status apparently offered would, in fact, be illusory given the North's geographic and economic dependence on Britain. But the two most important reasons undoubtedly were (a) analysis of the financial question showed that in an independent Northern Ireland the standard of living, given the loss of imperial subsidies, would drop dramatically; and (b) that 'the proposal is *impracticable*'; moreover, even if it was feasible, 'no British Government would consider the grant of complete independence' to Northern Ireland (Cabinet Paper, 'Dominion Status', n.d. [1947]: PRONI, CAB9F/6/2; Barton 1992: 8–9). Nevertheless, it is still worth considering that had it been possible, some Unionists, at least, would have been prepared to break the constitutional link with Westminster and the form of British identity that it entailed. Such an eventuality, it is reasonable to assume, would have encouraged the intensification of Ulster's local brand of Britishness while only the crown – representing national identity at an abstract level and which the subject invested with his own particular national meanings – remained to represent unity with Britain. As it was, however, the crown came to take on an enhanced significance for Ulster Unionists in the post-war period.

III

That the crown should be invested with a greater significance was inevitable once the Government of Eire decided that the state should become a republic. Sir Basil Brooke quickly took advantage of the occasion when, in a Stormont debate on Northern Ireland's constitutional position, he argued that the crucial question was that of their allegiance to the crown, 'our sentimental side' – allegiance to an institution that in Northern Ireland symbolized freedom, whereas in the South and for Ulster

Nationalists who wanted an Irish republic, it was supposed to symbolize aggression: 'That surely should describe our position . . . better than anything else.' (*N.I. Parliamentary Debates*, vol. 32 (30 November 1948), col. 3668). Certainly the royal dimension to Northern Ireland's relationship with Britain was one that prospered in the post-war period and, to a significant extent, on the basis of the North's wartime contribution. In the years 1946–50 there were five visits to Northern Ireland by leading members of the royal family, and of these, two were by Princess Elizabeth and one by the Queen (*Ulster Year Book* 1953: xvi). And while political capital could not be directly made out of these visits, the Stormont regime used them indirectly, and as far as possible, to enhance the North's constitutional position.[14] This was especially the case with Princess Elizabeth's visit to Northern Ireland in May 1949.

Given the political tensions surrounding the Irish Free State's departure from the Commonwealth and in the context of the anti-partition campaign which saw reunification as the next step, there had been 'unofficial' suggestions that the visit might be postponed – a suggestion, however, that the royal party rejected: 'Neither of them [Prince Philip accompanied the Princess] was in the least bit likely to be deterred' from visiting Ulster (see Nickolls 1949: 66). It is against this background that the significance of the speeches the Princess made in Northern Ireland have to be assessed. The major event of the visit was the conferring of the freedom of Belfast on the heir to the throne. And she took advantage of the occasion to emphasize, not just the region's constitutional membership of the United Kingdom, but also – though she did not mention the word 'Unionist' – the Northern Ireland people's membership of the British nation; interestingly, doing so in terms which defined Belfast's industrial character as representatively British:

Crossing the sea, even in an aeroplane, usually makes people feel that they are far from home, but when Belfast is at the end of the journey, that feeling is only an illusion. The warmth of an Irish welcome, the loyalty which the very name of Ulster recalls, the sight of your great factories and shipyards – all these, in different ways, remove any thought of separation, and make us feel as much at home in your midst as in any other part of the United Kingdom.   (ibid.)

This was a statement the significance of which could only be read against the immediate background of Anglo-Irish relations. As one commentator who accompanied the royal tours of 1949 put it: 'It was a delicate tribute, particularly at this moment.' (ibid.), while the speech, in general, he described as 'one of the most outstanding I have heard the Princess make.' (ibid.: 66–7). It was clearly, as Nickolls's comments suggest, one that came straight from the heart, as was natural given the affection the Princess had developed for the Unionist community. Certainly the major theme of the speech spoke directly to Unionist concerns, especially in its references to the crown – 'the focus of unity, comradeship and moral standards' – and the British nation. The United Kingdom, she declared, though small in territory, had a great history:

The exploits of its people, English, Scottish, Irish and Welsh – *so different in origin and so well blended on the whole* [my italics] – have left their stamp on the world, even deeper than that of the Roman Empire.

Our strength, founded on our unity *and fostered by the industry of great towns such as this* [my italics], is neither aggressive nor exclusive. We have never yielded to force, but our aim is to maintain our influence through goodwill among the nations.   (ibid.: 67)

This passage is significant for two reasons. First, it affirmed what Ulster Unionists wished to believe, namely, the existence of a homogeneous British nationality based on great historical achievements, having great international prestige, and of which they were an integral part. But perhaps just as significant, was the fact that the Princess chose to identify the urban, industrial character of Belfast as the defining characteristic of Northern Ireland's Britishness. Of course, this choice was natural given the setting. Nevertheless, it can also be seen as reflecting changing perceptions of Britishness itself in the post-war period.

The source of this change lay in the war experience and how it had exposed the weakness of the arcadian conception of Britain for a nation fighting a modern war. This was bound to entail a re-evaluation of urban, industrial society. The reaction against the pastoral conception of the nation was reflected in the post-war writing of Thomas Burke, a popular 'authority' on English social history, who vigorously rejected the rural/authentic vs urban/rootless dichotomy that was at the centre of debate on the nature of national identity in the prewar period. Burke, arguing that urban life was as authentically national as rural life (1946: 1–2), drew heavily on the war experience:

Yes; whatever criticisms the countryman and back-to-the-lander have made in the past about the townsman have, in the last five or six years, received their refutation; a refutation not of argument and logic, but of spirit and act. . . . Never has town life been so exhilarating. Never have they and people been so markedly one . . . both have lived through a spiritual ordeal. The cities have thrown up against the common peril the strength of the ages, the heritage left by generations of proud and resolute citizens.   (ibid.: 140–41)

Burke's defence of the cities is a good example of writing conditioned by the myth of the blitz, and points up how the place of the urban environment in imagining the nation had changed since the inter-war period. In this context, and for a royal personage for whom the war had been a formative experience, the citation of Belfast's industrial character as indicative of the North's British identity had an authority that was only really possible in this period.

It is also worth noting that the war had brought home to Ulster Unionists directly the inappropriateness of the pastoral conception of the nation to their conditions of existence. Hugh Shearman was to write irritably in 1949: 'All over wartime Ulster we have encountered that bewildered English face peering out of an army truck and saying, "But where is the village?"'. Such people had to be told, 'they don't arrange things that way in Ulster'. Shearman went on to make sharp criticisms of the supposed opposition between rural 'naturalness' and urban 'artificiality' that were very much in tune with the post-war mood: 'is not this loose thinking, and may not much of the beauty of the countryside be said to arise from its artificial and man-made character?' (Shearman 1949: 240–42).

The circumstances, then, in which Princess Elizabeth affirmed the British identity of Ulster Unionists were, for them, highly favourable, and their reaction to her speech was an intensification of the great Unionist enthusiasm that usually greeted royal visitors to the North. The whole experience encouraged the tendency to ignore the deep national divisions in the region, a tendency also evident in the telegram sent by the Governor of Northern Ireland to the King on the conclusion of the visit, which gave the impression that the whole population of the North were loyal citizens: 'They charmed everyone and were received everywhere by all classes with unbounded enthusiasm and loyalty.' (quoted in Nickolls 1949: 66). Such sentiments, of course, expressed exactly how Unionists wished the North to be seen; however, it can also be argued that they were a silent encouragement of the Unionist view that their interests should take primacy over all others. A further tribute to the loyalty of Ulster was forthcoming in 1950, when the Queen arrived for a short visit. Reports of the visit, together with articles defending the regime against charges of religious discrimination, abuses of the Special Powers Act and economic dependency on Britain, appeared in *Ulster Commentary* (August 1950: 3, 8), the regime's propaganda organ produced largely with the purpose of persuading the British public that the North was representative of the 'British way of life'. The Stormont authorities, however, were able to do this to much greater effect the following year through its involvement in the Festival of Britain.

IV

Ostensibly, the purpose of the Festival of Britain was to commemorate the Great Exhibition of 1851, but this was little more than a pretext. Originally conceived as an ambitious international exhibition to which other nations would be invited to contribute, considerations of expense and labour availability reduced this ambitious intention to a purely national affair, which only took on concrete form when the Home Secretary, Herbert Morrison, took control (Hillier 1976: 12–13). Indeed, it was not just national but fiercely nationalistic, and yet different from the nationalism of the imperial exhibitions of the past; for this exhibition had upon it the imprimatur of the Labour Government and was both a celebration of its achievements and a representation of its anti-imperialistic patriotism:

The visitors were all made to pursue a pilgrim's way unfolding 'the tale of the continuous impact that this particular land had upon this particular people, and of the achievements that this people has continued to derive from its relationship with this land.' . . . Its view of history was patriotic, evolutionary and non-expansionist. . . . British supremacy over the reconstituted Commonwealth of Nations rested no longer on power but on 'common ideas and ideals'. The vision was of harmony, of men and women heroically one, though descended from different stock . . . of a land teeming with natural resources to be tapped by valiant workers in field and factory, where traditional crafts were to be cherished, where industry and commerce were about to boom and bring a hitherto unknown universal prosperity; above all, the past, present and future were seen to be moulded by the British, a 'mixed and venerable folk', whose character combined 'on the one hand, realism and strength, on the other fantasy, independence and imagination'.

(Strong 1976: 8)

As Strong's exposition indicates, the Festival of Britain was primarily about the reforging of British national identity as a result of the experience of war and immediate post-war changes, which pointed the way to Britain's future non-imperial world role. Hence the emphasis placed by the Festival's President, Princess Elizabeth, in her speech inaugurating the Festival, on the virtue in troubled times of dwelling on the arts of peace and Britain's leading contribution to the store of human happiness and knowledge. It was in the areas of the arts, science and industry that Britain's leadership in the world would have now to be forged and hence the greater significance these things should have in the 'national life'. As a recent commentator has remarked, the Festival was to provide a new 'persona' for the British people (Ebong, thesis, 1986: 60–66).

However, despite the concern to present a non-party-political national exhibition and the endorsement of the Festival's 'national character' through the patronage of the royal family, the initial reaction of the Tory Party and its press supporters was to condemn the enterprise. Only when his friend, General Ishmay, was appointed Chairman of the Festival of Britain Council and when it became clear that the Festival was going ahead, did Churchill and his supporters reluctantly accept it (ibid.: 13–14; see also The Times, 3 May 1951).

The Festival ran from 5 May to the end of September 1951, and its success has been much debated (see essays in Banham and Hillier (eds) 1976). The public reaction was, on the whole, favourable. A Gallup Poll taken in the summer of 1951 on public impressions of the main South Bank exhibition centre revealed that 58 per cent were favourably impressed, with only 15 per cent unfavourable. Moreover, nearly 8,500,000 people visited the South Bank Centre during the Festival. So while not as significant a national occasion as the Great Exhibition of 1851 – seen by 6,000,000 people, a third of the population of Britain – which inspired it, overall, it was still a public success and was widely accepted as having provided a welcome relief to the drabness of the period (Frayn 1986: 324–5). More solid achievements are harder to identify; nevertheless, there is widespread agreement that it was a formative stylistic influence on the British nation. Enshrined in the memory, the Festival represented 'the popularly accepted idea of "modern" for a whole generation.'[15] Paul Addison has described its impact thus:

The Festival helped to popularise a new style of living. The television pavilion, or the Home and Garden Exhibition, the piazzas and brightly decorated restaurants, the accent on youth and fashion . . . foretold the consumer boom of the late 1950s.

(Addison 1985: 210)

In the broad context of British national identity since the war, if the latter was to provide new 'Churchillian' forms of national expression, the Festival of Britain, which can be seen as marking the end of the wartime period, provided a new national imagery – forward-looking and dynamic. But while, for the rest of the United Kingdom, the major impact of the Festival was in its social, cultural and aesthetic dimensions, there was for Ulster Unionists an added significance, given the anti-partitionist campaign of the period.

Certainly, the political advantages the Stormont regime would gain from participation in the Festival were quickly appreciated. The Armagh Unionist MP, Dinah McNabb, placed Northern Ireland's involvement in the context of the region's contribution to the war effort and emphasized how its 'native' and 'traditional' culture would contribute to 'a Festival which will demonstrate to the world the undaunting courage and patriotism of the British people.' (N.I. Parliamentary Debates, vol. 34 (28 February 1950), cols 13–14). It was quickly settled on, by the Northern Ireland Festival Committee under the chairmanship of Sir Robert Nugent, that the specific form of Northern Ireland's contribution to the Festival would be a 'farm-and-factory exhibition' that would demonstrate the industrial and agricultural achievements of the North and the part it had played 'in the overall progress of the United Kingdom in these spheres.' It was also noted that, in addition to these advantages, the Festival should prove a boost to the local tourist industry (William McCleery, ibid. (11 May 1950), cols 888–9).

The significance the Stormont authorities placed on participation in the Festival is indicated by the fact that the North's exhibition at Castlereagh was, with Glasgow's Industrial Power exhibition, one of only two major Festival sites outside the London metropolitan centre. As such, it allowed Northern Ireland to be represented at the heart of a Festival devoted to illustrating the British way of life; and all the more so given that the Festival presentation of Britishness was modernistic and largely focused on industry and technology. Northern Ireland's exhibition, designed by Willy de Majo, a Yugoslav émigré with naturalized British citizenship – according to de Majo, his appointment provoked calls in Ulster for an 'English Englishman' rather than a 'Yugoslav Englishman' to be appointed – was itself highly modernistic and of a piece with the exhibits in the main centre in London (Mary Banham, interview with de Majo in Banham and Hillier (eds) 1976: 156–8).[16] The North's exhibition was also filmed as part of 'a record of activities' by the Festival of Britain Office for the MOI (Dinah McNabb, Major Sinclair, N.I. Parliamentary Debates, vol. 35 (20 March 1951), cols 488–9). Further, a special Festival film, Family Portrait, depicting the British nation and its 'national character' was made by the distinguished documentary film maker,

Humphrey Jennings, and which also acknowledged Northern Ireland's British national membership (Jennings 1951).

Jennings's film combined historical imagery and reference with a depiction of the modes of life encompassed within the term 'British'. As such, his depiction of Northern Ireland, though brief – it focused on shipbuilding – nevertheless registered the North as naturally interwoven with the fabric of British national life. Later commentators would criticize *Family Portrait* as the 'cultural equivalent of "Land of Hope and Glory"', and especially Jennings's use of such sweeping terms as 'imaginative' and 'practical' to describe different aspects of the 'national character' as 'sentimental guff' (Addison 1985: 209). However, Jennings's treatment of British nationality was conditioned by the purpose of the film, which was intended as an undemanding statement of nationality for public consumption. As such, it employed a popular vocabulary of nationality, which, while its mythic characteristics are obvious now, was less so at the time – and not in Northern Ireland.[17]

Here the concern was to integrate the region's Festival activities as closely as possible with Britain's. Indeed, one anonymous contribution to Northern Ireland's Official Souvenir Handbook of the Festival went so far as to suggest that, while the Festival would commemorate the Great Exhibition of 1851, *that* exhibition was inspired by a linen trade exhibition in Belfast that Prince Albert and Queen Victoria had visited in 1849 and were greatly impressed by (*Festival of Britain in Northern Ireland* 1951: 10). Again, the introductory panel to the Ulster Farm and Factory Exhibition declared: 'Britain – great in the past – is still Great Britain. We, the men and women of Northern Ireland, have played and are playing still our part in that endeavour.' (ibid.: 4). It was a theme Sir Basil Brooke elaborated on during a speech delivered at the opening of a Festival exhibition of local manufactures entitled 'Derry on Show': 'if we Britishers have kept the spirit of unconquerableness that we are so proud to remember in our ancestors, the future of this country as a leader of the world may be even greater than its past.' (See *Derry Journal*, 28 May 1951).

To complement the integration of Northern Ireland with the rest of the United Kingdom that involvement in the Festival entailed, the attempt to identify the North as an authentic historic and national entity within the United Kingdom continued. In the Stormont Parliament, the Unionist MP, Brian Maginess, defended the regime's right to use the term 'Ulster' to describe the North by claiming that, historically, the boundaries of the province had expanded and contracted according to the fortunes of war. In this context, nine-county Ulster had only been a fairly recent creation of the English conquest. But whatever the historical dimensions of Ulster's territory

The people of the north-east counties in Gaelic times, Norman times, Saxon times, or any other times stood on their own feet and were proud, just as the people of today are standing on their own feet. . . . there was always something in the free soil of Ulster that bred a free race of men who would neither accept dictation from Strongbow in Wexford or de Valera in Dublin.

Rather more surprisingly, Maginess went on to claim that 'present conditions in Ulster' were such that

the people . . . in every section and every religion are gradually coming to glory in the name of Ulster, and in the name of Ulstermen, and are coming to take a pride in our free institutions . . . in the prosperity we are building up, and in the heritage which we are creating at the present time and which other people both in the South and elsewhere are envying.

(*N.I. Parliamentary Debates*, vol. 35 (6 June 1951), cols 1502–06)

Maginess's comments are partly explicable by the heat of argument, but they were not isolated. Rather they were part of a consistent strand of Unionist opinion that emerged against the political background of the time, especially greater constitutional security and the anti-partition campaign. Yet it should also be noted that this strand of opinion extended beyond the narrow frame of Unionist Party politics.

Denis O'D. Hanna's book, *The Face of Ulster*, written in 1951 as part of the Batsford 'Face of Britain' series, sought to make 'a special attempt to capture that illusive quality called nationality' (Hanna 1952: v). 'Northern Ireland', he continued,

is a land insignificant in area but possessing a territorial identity as ancient as any in Europe. From the moment its estuaries embrace the steamer that carries the visitor across the Channel, the quality of ancientness strikes him and clings about him perpetually. It is a land of tradition and bardic lore, whose tales can take their place beside Greek mythology or the Norse sagas without losing face.   (ibid.: 2)

Hanna's book, unlike those produced by Shearman (1949) and Richard Hayward (1950) in this period, expressed a Unionism that was almost subliminal, being gently conveyed to the British reader it was intended to attract to Northern Ireland.

Much the most substantial attempt at establishing an 'authentic' cultural identity for the North at this time, however, was the volume, *The Arts in Ulster* (1951). Edited by Sam Hanna Bell, Nesca Robb and John Hewitt for the Northern Ireland Committee of the Festival of Britain, its purpose was to demonstrate the 'not unimportant contribution made by the Province to the culture of Great Britain', and focused on the development of poetry, prose, drama, architecture, music and painting, especially in the 'past decade, which has produced work of national and European importance' (Bell *et al.* 1951: jacket notes).

This was a pioneering work on its subject and certainly could not be dismissed as narrow political propaganda. Nevertheless, the purpose for which it was written inevitably imposed parameters which limited its analytical perspective. Thus, although Bell could admit the existence of the deep religious and political divisions in the province, and even criticize Ulster writers for failing to deal with them in their work – they 'start off boldly enough, lose their nerve, and plunge up to their oxters in sentimentality' (Bell *et al.* 1951: 14–17) – he, no less than the unnamed writers he criticized, also shied away from dealing with the problem of national and religious divisions in the North, and resorted to whimsical quotations from W.R. Rodgers's *The Ulstermen and Their Country* on the Protestant and Catholic 'characters' in the North being 'complementary', making 'two halves of Life' (ibid.: 14–15). Again, as with other Unionist writers in this period, Bell looked back on the decade from 1940 as a crucial one for the development of a new regional and cultural identity in the North. Against this background the 'problem' in Ulster was merely 'one of the growing-pains of an alive and energetic people' (ibid.: 19–20).

The argument made here also found expression in the official Festival handbook for Northern Ireland. Patrick Riddell enthused about the Ulster 'personality' and 'character', finding in a 'mixing of Irish and Scottish blood' a development 'for the good of Ulster' (Riddell 1951: 14–15). Jack Loudon, writing on the 'Festival of the Arts', borrowed freely from *The Arts in Ulster* to explain the existence of an 'Ulster mind' in culture (Loudon 1951: 49–56). The regional identity of Ulster was also explained in the publication, *Northern Ireland*, one of the 'About Britain' series published by Collins for the Festival of Britain Office and written by E. Estyn Evans. Evans also pointed out the significance of Ulster's wartime experience in consolidating the bond between Northern Ireland and Britain (Evans 1951: 7); however, apart from a tendency to reserve the term 'Ulsterman' for the Protestant community, his treatment was evenhanded. Evans did not attempt to minimize the community divisions in the North and avoided glib remarks as to how they could be resolved. All too often the tendency in the writings of Unionists and commentators sympathetic to the Stormont regime was to wish those divisions away. A striking example of this tendency was Sir Basil Brooke's reply to nationalist objections that a royal visit to Northern Ireland, to be undertaken as part of the Festival celebrations, would be an endorsement of partition. Brooke was confident that when their Majesties came, not only Unionists, but Nationalists, would give them 'a thoroughly good Northern Ireland welcome' (*N.I. Parliamentary Debates*, vol. 35 (20 February 1951), cols 34–5).

The most important aspect of the Festival for Unionists was that it gave concrete expression to the idea of the United Kingdom as an imagined community, and especially in the way that Festival activities integrated the sphere of private and local interests with the public domain of national ideology. At the opening ceremony of the Festival, an opening performed by the King, the Stormont Government was represented by Sir Basil Brooke and Dame Dehra Parker along with several other government ministers. Brooke and Parker expressed pride in the Ulster people and their contribution to the British nation and Empire (*Belfast News-Letter*, 3 May 1951; *Londonderry Sentinel*, 5 May 1951). Certainly the Unionist population responded enthusiastically to the Festival. Fifty-one local centres held their own celebrations, with twenty-nine Festival or civic weeks, eight Festival days and fourteen other special occasions, some of which marked the inauguration of permanent fixtures, such as new municipal headquarters at Bangor and the Rose Garden at Coleraine. In general:

The typical local programme in Northern Ireland combined Protestant religious services, processions, exhibitions of industry and handiwork, plays, dances, fancy-dress parades, firemen's demonstrations, sports and children's competitions and treats. The local agricultural show, usually one of the highlights of the Northern Ireland year, was frequently the centre-piece of local celebrations around which a Festival Week was created. Aside from these events, the local authorities encouraged a great deal of decoration, repainting, tree-planting and tidying up, as well as giving impetus to the acquiring of new civic amenities such as town halls and civic centres.   (Ebong, thesis, 1986: 420–21)

One index of the Unionist population's response to the Festival was the numbers attending the Farm and Factory Exhibition at Castlereagh. Over the eighty days that it was open 156,760 people visited it – an average of 1,960 per day – a figure, the organizers stated in their final report, that was 50 per cent higher than expected (ibid.: 446). There was, thus, some plausibility to the claim that the Festival had done a great deal to 'stir feelings of local patriotism in Ulster as [it had] in Great Britain.' (*Belfast News-Letter*, 5 May 1951).

The supreme embodiment and focus of patriotism in Northern Ireland during the Festival was, of course, the royal visit. It had been expected that it would be undertaken by the King, George VI, who would 'find ample evidence of how thoroughly the people of Ulster have entered into the Festival, for they are proud of their British heritage.' (*Londonderry Sentinel*, 5 May 1951). As it turned out, the King was too ill to make the visit and it was undertaken by the Queen and Princess Margaret. Unionists were much encouraged, however, by the nature of the visit, for it almost seems to have been designed as an indirect retort to nationalist critics of the Festival. As with all royal visits, no party political statements were made, but this visit was clearly an exception to those of the recent past, for the programme included – 'despite a formidable list of engagements immediately after their arrival on Friday June 2nd' – an extensive tour of towns and villages in Counties Armagh and Down and also a tour of the Dundrod race circuit (*Belfast News-Letter*, 4, 31 May 1951). The visit, covering over seventy miles, was described as having 'made history' (ibid.: 4 June 1951). And while the Stormont authorities avoided an explicit politicization of the event, the arrangements made for it – arrests of prominent Republicans amidst great publicity, overwhelming demonstrations of force along processional routes[18] – constituted a clever situational statement that made the visit's political significance evident. It would be tempting to cite the Festival celebrations in the North as a useful counterpoint to Labour criticisms of Stormont, made in Westminster at this time; but, in fact, even here the Unionist cause was being well served.

V

The Festival of Britain took place during the short parliament which sat from the general election of February 1950 to October 1951. The 1950 result, which returned Labour to power with a majority of only five seats, consequently increased the importance of Ulster Unionist MPs to the Conservative Party. Accordingly, when a by-election arose in Londonderry in 1951 following Sir Ronald Ross's resignation to take up the post of Ulster Agent in London, Winston Churchill was quick to write expressing his appreciation of the efforts of the 'Ulster Unionist team in this close run Parliament', and to give his assurance that the Conservative and Unionist party would 'never waver in their determination to support Northern Ireland in her avowal and resolve to remain within the United Kingdom.' (see *Belfast News-Letter* 12 June 1951). The satisfaction which this communication gave to Brooke and the Londonderry Unionists was enhanced by the fact that it came shortly after the first significant debate in Westminster on the working of the Government of Ireland Act of 1920 and which focused on the practices of the Stormont regime.

A motion criticizing the Northern Government had been moved by the Welsh Labour MP, George Thomas. Thomas was concerned not to make the case for Irish unity but, like his supporter, Geoffrey Bing, to highlight cases of gerrymandering and religious discrimination which indicated that 'British' standards of democracy did not apply in the North.[19] The signs, however, were discouraging from the start. The debate itself was untimely, taking place on the day that the royal visitors began their Ulster tour – visitors, the *Daily Telegraph* (2 June 1951) pointed out, who represented 'the personal embodiment of the unbreakable bonds which attach them [Ulster Unionists] to Great Britain.' Moreover, Thomas himself was hardly the best qualified to speak on Northern Ireland, having visited the six counties only once, for a rugby match, and the case he made was abstract and lacking in authority. Indeed, he seemed mainly concerned to use the debate to condemn the Tory idea of democracy (*Hansard 5*, vol. 488 (1 June 1951), col. 600). Further, the case was made to a badly depleted House – only fifty of over six hundred members were present, and no leading politicians from either major party except Chuter Ede, the Home Secretary, whose duty it was to be there to respond to Thomas (see 'The British fiasco and after', *Derry Journal*, 4 June 1951). What made the debate a 'fiasco' was not the rebuttal of Thomas's complaints by Tory and Unionist MPs, which was generally inept and unconvincing (see *Daily Telegraph*, 2 June 1951; Lord Winterton, *Hansard 5*, vol. 488 (1 June 1951), cols 594–601; Sir Hugh O'Neill, ibid., cols 573–81); it was a fiasco because Labour MPs signally failed to support Thomas's motion. In fact, one Labour MP, John Haire (a native of the North), claimed that 'bigotry and bias have been gradually disappearing from Northern Ireland' (ibid.: col. 614). But, most importantly, it was clear when the Home Secretary rose to speak that his sympathies were with the Stormont regime.

Ede began by establishing a formally neutral position, referring to the 'difficulties of all Irish debates' in exciting 'the maximum of animosity. That goes for both sides of the question.' He went on to emphasize that he was not there to defend Stormont (ibid.: cols 623–5). That said, however, his sympathies became clear, especially on the issue of religious discrimination. Declaring how difficult it was for 'a mere Englishman' to enter into the mind set of those who were motivated by sectarian bigotry in Ulster, Ede welcomed Sir Hugh O'Neill's disclaimer that this existed to any great extent, and then, surprisingly, in effect went on to argue that it was still a part of the way of life in Britain, by citing examples from his own experience of it among Nonconformists (ibid.: 626). Pointing out the responsibilities Westminster had conferred on Stormont, he declared that the Northern Government would 'have to justify what they have done to their own constituents' (ibid.). But while this statement made perfect sense in a mainland British context, it was wholly ineffectual as a warning against discrimination in the very different political environment of Northern Ireland. Furthermore, to make it clear that he would not be taking any action against the Stormont authorities, Ede cited Ulster's wartime activities and the threat from the IRA to excuse the regime's policies:

The government of Northern Ireland have to live, not on an island as we do, but on a smaller part of an island with an open border. They have to deal in legislation with the problems that situation creates.   (ibid.: cols 627–9)

Ede ended by appealing for reconciliation in Northern Ireland and urged, successfully, the proposers of the motion not to proceed to a division on it (ibid.: cols 630–31).

For a motion from which many Labour MPs and many more Nationalists expected much, the only gainers were the Unionists (see editorials in *Belfast News-Letter*, 2 June 1951; *Londonderry Sentinel*, 5 June 1951). Perhaps its real significance lies in its indication of the extent to which Stormont's perspective on the Ulster problem had become accepted by both major British political parties. It is true that Churchill did not speak against the motion, but as the *Derry Journal* (4 June 1951) put it: 'There was no need for Churchill to intervene when a Socialist was there to give Stormont a clean bill of health in the matters of bigotry, bias and discrimination.' For good measure, *The Times* sent a 'Special Correspondent' to investigate conditions in the province at the end of June. The result was a report that echoed Ede's speech in the Commons (*The Times*, report on Northern Ireland, quoted in *Londonderry Sentinel*, 30 June 1951), as did a 'Message to Ulster' penned by Churchill during the October 1951 general election campaign. The familiar tribute to Ulster's wartime contribution preceded a pledge of undying Conservative fidelity to the Union between Great Britain and Northern Ireland:

we reaffirm our determination that the present relationship of Ulster to the United Kingdom and the Empire shall never in the slightest degree be altered without the consent of the Parliament of Northern Ireland . . . your destiny is forever bound up with Britain and the British Commonwealth.
(See James (ed.) 1974: vol. viii, 8261–2)

Yet despite the security of Northern Ireland's membership of the United Kingdom in this period, Unionists never lost their anxiety about their constitutional status. History had shown that changing circumstances could put it at risk. As for the promotion of a 'national' identity for the North, the wishful thinking behind this idea was exposed even before the Festival of Britain was over.

In 1951 the Northern Ireland Government had to decide on the reorganization of the BBC as it affected the region. Lord Beveridge had produced a report in January which recommended that Scotland, Wales and Northern Ireland should have their own broadcasting commissions, with powers to 'secure regard for the distinctive national cultures of the three countries'. However, fear that such a commission, which would have to be representative of both communities, would be controversial in Northern Ireland and the source of public scandal, played a large part in moving the Government to reject the proposal (Cathcart 1984: 164–7). The *Belfast News-Letter* (17 July 1951) also came to the same conclusion:

In Northern Ireland . . . the fact has to be faced that the question of what is our 'distinctive national culture' is itself a matter of political controversy. It would be easy, indeed, to start an interminable wrangle on whether Northern Ireland has, or is even entitled to say that she has, a national culture that is distinctive.

Given the 'delicate political conditions' existing in Northern Ireland, this editorial concluded, it was best to let the BBC pursue the 'careful course through our political shoals' that it had so successfully done to date. Only in this way, by avoiding the reality of the region's internal divisions, could the myth of 'nationality' and that of an uncomplicated membership of the British nation be pursued.

Notes

1. Churchill (1949) vol. ii, 529; ibid. 1954: vol. vi, 667).
2. See, for example, *Ulster Commentary* (12 December 1945; 5 January 1946). These issues attempted to refute claims by Professor Harold Laski that the Ulster regime was wholly dependent on British subsidies; that it had been an encouragement to the invasion of Britain by Hitler due to anti-British Eire's neutrality; and that its wartime contribution was overrated.
3. *Ulster Commentary* (May 1946). Early in 1946 this publication, originally typewritten, began to be professionally produced and appeared monthly instead of weekly.
4. On the 'Friends of Ireland' and Bing in particular, see Bob Purdie (1983: 81–94).
5. On this subject, see G. Bing to H. Morrison, 6 March 1948; Sir D. Stephens to A. Maxwell, 19 March 1948; Maxwell to Stephens, 11 March 1948; Morrison to Bing, 16 March 1948 (PRO, HO45/22028/919703/1).
6. On this question, see, for example, the following correspondence: Visc. Addison to J. Chuter Ede, 17 January 1946; Sir Francis Evans to Neville Dick, 22 June 1946; 'Chancery', British Embassy, Washington to 'Dear Dept.', 23 September 1946 (PRO, HO45/25053/815509/57/62). For the wider political context see Bowman (1983: Ch. 6).

7. It is worth noting in this respect that when W. Scott was asked whether Saint Patrick or King William III should be used in the presentation of Northern Ireland at an exhibition in Toronto, he preferred 'the Red [Hugh] O'Neill, especially if he could be depicted in the act of securing his territory.' (Scott to R. Gransden, 14 June 1948: PRONI, CAB9F/123/3B). Even nationalist heroes, it seems, could be employed in Unionist 'national' myth-making.

8. Shearman's *Ulster* (1949), his contribution to the British 'County' series of books produced by the publisher, Robert Hale, elaborated on his Northern Ireland booklet, and was more explicitly Unionist. The North was described as 'this living organism' (p. v); its wartime activities cited as marking it off from the South (134–5); and an attempt made to establish a more civilized image for the 'Ulsterman' (Chs xix–xxi).

9. See Henry Maxwell to Sir Basil Brooke, 4 March 1947 (PRONI, CAB9F/123/114). Permission was given, however, to include the names of Carson and Craig in the second edition (F.M. Adams to J. Mortimer, 23 July 1948: ibid.).

10. Hewitt claimed that his prospects of succession to the directorship of the Belfast Museum and Art Gallery in 1952, were thwarted by 'McCarthyite' smears of being pro-Communist and 'pro-Catholic' (Hewitt 1987: 151).

11. On this issue, see Cabinet Committee on Publicity discussion of *Odd Man Out*, 2 October 1945; R. Gransden to H.C. Montgomery, 20 February 1946; Montgomery to Gransden, 26 February 1946; F.M. Adams, 'Films on Ulster Themes', 6 May 1946 (PRONI CAB9F/123/81).

12. The *Scotsman* (21–4 May 1948), for example, ran a three-issue pro-government report on Northern Ireland. See also *The Leader*, 12 February 1949.

13. For a fair discussion of this issue, focusing on its financial aspects, see O'Nuallain (1952: 188–93).

14. When Princess Elizabeth visited the North in 1946, the government propaganda organ, *Ulster Commentary* (May 1946: 2), keen to exploit any connection between the royal family and Ulster's wartime contribution, reported the visit with special reference to Caledon, where 'she was quick to notice a banner with the words: "This is Caledon, Field Marshal Alexander's home town."'

15. William Feaver, 'Festival Star' (Banham and Hillier (eds) 1976: 54). See also Addison (1985: 209–10); Marwick (1991: 8).

16. See the detailed account of the Castlereagh exhibition, complete with photographs in *Architects' Journal* (1951, 114, No. 2943: 103–12).

17. For insightful comment on the collapse of national mythologies and the shaping of popular opinion in an age of 'cynical intelligence', see Billig (1992).

18. For nationalist criticisms of the security arrangements as an attempt to 'curry favour' with the royal family, see *Derry Journal* (4 June 1951).

19. See 'Ulster Critic Explains' (*Belfast News-Letter*, 31 May 1951); *Hansard 5*, vol. 488 (1 June 1951), col. 588.

8

NATIONALITY, MODERNITY AND POLITICAL CRISIS 1952–72

I

In words that could have been penned by, and were undoubtedly inspired by, Walter Bagehot, *The Times* editorial on the day of Queen Elizabeth II's Coronation (2 June 1953) described the monarchy's role in representing national identity:

In her is incarnate on her Coronation day the whole of society of which the State is no more than the political manifestation. She represents the life of her people in their fullness as men and women, and not in their limited capacity as Lords and Commons and electors. It is the glory of the social monarchy that it sets the human above the institutional.

This was a succinct statement of the ability of the monarch to transcend and unify in an expression of national identity the public and private spheres of British life. This, of course, had been true of all British monarchs since Queen Victoria. This Coronation, however, was believed to have a significance far greater than any of the period covered by this study.

The country was coming out of the austerity associated with the war years; there was the Queen's youth which chimed well with the sense that a new age was being inaugurated – a new Elizabethan age which the Queen's name recalled, an age of prosperity and expansion: 'Drake, Raleigh, the Tilbury speech, the Armada . . . all were potent symbols in the popular imagination, signifying the birth of national greatness.' (Ziegler 1978: 97). The Coronation was, therefore, to be a rebirth; the new Elizabethans would march united into a brave new world.[1] At this time it was still possible to believe that while the Empire was crumbling, the Commonwealth would be a worthy successor; that it was, in fact, a national and progressive evolution from imperialism, and would be a suitable vehicle for Britain to maintain its status as a world power in the new age that the new Queen appeared to inaugurate. Moreover, when the news arrived on the morning of the Coronation that a British mountaineering team led by Colonel John Hunt had scaled Mount Everest, it seemed an auspicious start to the new Elizabethan age. The account of the feat in *The Times* (2 June 1953) conveyed effectively the historicist frame of reference within which the Coronation was contextualized: 'Seldom since Francis Drake brought the Golden Hind to anchor in Plymouth Sound has a British explorer offered to his Sovereign such a tribute of glory as Colonel John Hunt and his men are able to lay at the feet of Queen Elizabeth for her Coronation day.' Further, the sense of historical occasion was enhanced enormously by the role of television (Ziegler 1978: 125). Television made the process of imagining the Coronation as a great British national event much more immediate and meaningful, and this was as true for Northern Unionists as it was for the population of Britain.

Given the traditional Unionist enthusiasm for the crown, it was only to be expected that the Coronation would be an occasion of special significance. Unlike Britain, where the months leading up to the Coronation had seen a 'national debate' about the event – an opinion poll in February, for example, had shown that only 44 per cent of the population intended to participate in the occasion (ibid.: 98) – no such hesitation was evident in the North. Indeed, the Unionist MP, R.N. Wilson, made, shortly after the death of George VI, what must have been one of the first projections of the greatness of the forthcoming 'Elizabethan Age' from a reading of the 'evidence' of the state of the English nation in Elizabeth I's time (*N.I. Parliamentary Debates*, vol. 36 (21 February 1952), col. 87). Again, in an open letter accompanying presentation copies of William Le Hardy's *Coronation Book* (1953), the chairman of Londonderry County Education Committee, D. Hall Christie, encouraged schoolchildren to remember the 'Golden Age' of Elizabeth I, as an indication of what could be expected in the reign of Elizabeth II (copy in the author's possession). In fact, Unionists had a special reason to be enthusiastic about this, the most portentous Coronation of the century, for there was a substantial Ulster involvement in the Coronation ceremony.

As if to confirm, at the most exalted level of national identity, the security of Northern Ireland's constitutional position that had been the reward for her contribution to the war effort, those very generals who most prominently represented that contribution – Field Marshal Lord Alanbrooke, Viscount Montgomery of Alamein and Earl Alexander of Tunis – were to perform central Coronation functions. Alanbrooke would command the 30,000 troops taking part in the procession and lining the route, and would also take part in the Grand Procession in Westminster Abbey in his capacity as Lord High Constable of England. Viscount Montgomery would carry the Royal Standard, while Earl Alexander would bear 'the Orb, the Golden globe surmounted by a cross, which is the symbol of the Sovereignty of Christ.' Also, Lady Moyra Hamilton, daughter of the Duke of Hamilton, 'will be one of the six Maids of Honour who will bear the Queen's train when she walks within the Abbey.' To those Ulster personages at the centre of the Coronation ceremony can be added others. Brooke, for example, ennobled as Lord Brookeborough when Elizabeth acceded to the Throne on her father's death in 1952, attended along with a contingent of Commonwealth Prime Ministers, as did Lord Wakehurst and a number of lesser civic figures. Reviewing the complete list for a readership actively concerned with its status as British nationals, the *Northern Whig* (Coronation Souvenir Edition, 1 June 1953) could, without exaggeration, claim that while it would be inaccurate to describe the Coronation as an 'Ulster' occasion, 'it is true that in proportion to their numbers no section of the Queen's subjects will take a more active part in her crowning than the people of Northern Ireland.' Also, as if to cap that involvement, great satisfaction was taken in the fact that, as a result of Eire's withdrawal from the Commonwealth and the change in the royal title this had entailed, this would be the first Coronation at which 'Northern Ireland' would be specifically cited as part of the title of the realm over which the Queen would reign (*Londonderry Sentinel*, 2 July 1953).

The North's Coronation celebrations took place as part of those within the United Kingdom as a whole, but naturally great significance was attached to any specific acknowledgement the monarch made of Northern Ireland, such as the two swans she donated to the people of Portadown and which were named 'Charles and Anne' (Lisburn Camera Club 1991). Further, as a local dimension of the practice of invoking the Elizabethan period to contextualize the Coronation's significance, a bell rung in St Patrick's Cathedral, Dublin, to mark the Coronation of the first Elizabeth, was brought to St Bartholomew's Church in Belfast and rung again for the Coronation of the second (ibid.). Again, it undoubtedly enhanced the significance of the Coronation as an expression of national identity for loyalists that Nationalists in Ulster and the South objected to the celebrations (see E.V. McCullough, *N.I. Parliamentary Debates*, vol. 36 (21 October 1952), col. 1453). In Dublin, for example, a garden party hosted by the British, Canadian and Australian Ambassadors was boycotted by both government and opposition; the Union Jack was burned in the streets and threats of violence were made against cinema managers who dared to exhibit Coronation films or newsreels (*Londonderry Sentinel*, 6 June 1953). In the North, against a background of IRA bombs, nationalist protests and disputes with Unionists about the celebrations (Moloney and Pollock 1986: 63–4), the Roman Catholic Primate, Cardinal D'alton, expressed the wish that the new monarch's reign would 'see our country restored to its natural unity' (*The Times*, 3 June 1953). Even in London the Irish protests were echoed when, a week after the Coronation, a bottle filled with 'corrosive fluid' was thrown through the window of the Ulster Office in an unsuccessful attempt to destroy a portrait of the Queen (*The Times*, 9 June 1953). Nationalist anger, moreover, could only have been intensified by the tendency in much of the British reporting of the Coronation celebrations in Ulster to ignore the fact the Catholic community did not participate. The reporter who covered the celebrations in Dunmurray, outside Belfast, for example, went on to generalize, 'Dunmurray was typical of all Northern Ireland.' (*Time and Tide*, 6 June 1953; see also *The Times*, 3 June 1953). Nor were Nationalists and Republicans very successful in rectifying this situation when the Queen made her Coronation visit to Northern Ireland a month later. A clamp-down on protests against the visit was rigidly enforced by the RUC to maintain the appearance of a community united in its allegiance to the monarch, and was justified in Stormont on the grounds that objections by nationalist MPs to the royal visit were inconsistent with their oath of allegiance to the Queen, taken on entering Parliament (see Harry Diamond, *N.I. Parliamentary Debates*, vol. 37 (20 May 1953), col. 1270; ibid. (7 July 1953), cols 1308–10; A.F. Wilson, ibid., cols 1325–6).

The preparations made for the Queen's Coronation visit helped enor-mously to invest the occasion with the combination of threat and reassurance that is characteristic of national myth in general and of Unionist myth in particular. The preparations were based on the premise of a republican threat to the life of the monarch. The railway lines along which the royal train would travel from Lisburn to Lisahally in County Londonderry were patrolled by police throughout the night before the journey, while the royal train itself was preceded by a 'pilot train' intended to take the blast of any explosive device that might have been planted. Against the background of nationalist protests, occasion was also taken to stress the legitimacy of the Queen's rule in the North. When the train stopped at Ballymoney, the local Anglican Rector, Canon Armstrong, presented the Queen with an illustrated book detailing her putative descent from the ancient Irish and Scottish Kings of Dalriada (Lisburn Camera Club 1991). Moreover, it was indicative of the way in which the North was regarded as unproblematically British by Unionist supporters in Britain that *The Times* (1 July 1953) could describe the population as 'inflexibly loyal'; a people 'whose contribution to the British way of life is historic and abiding.' (see also *Londonderry Sentinel*, 2 July 1953). And taking the opportunity to again emphasize the North's membership of the United Kingdom, the Stormont authorities produced yet another publi-cation, *This is Ulster*, which rehearsed the now familiar litany of Ulster's wartime contribution, her importance in the cold war period to Western defences, together with an attempt to neutralize the negative image of the region in Britain by references to the 'pulsating life of a people with a twentieth-century outlook.'

What, however, was missing from Unionist reactions to the Coronation in Ulster, but which was first noticed as a significant factor in English celebrations in 1953 and which investigations into popular attitudes to the monarchy have since identified as a pronounced element, is the belief that Britain's monarchy made other nations – especially Americans – envious (Ziegler 1978: 100; Billig 1992: 52–3). As one of Michael Billig's interviewees expressed it: it 'puts us *above* America because they've got none' (ibid.: 52). Such expressions, Billig convincingly argues:

might be said to express an ideology of national decline. . . . World power may have been conceded to the Americans, but monarchy is a prized consolation. It is a reassuring thought. Increasingly, one eye is kept upon the royal pageant itself whilst the other looks towards the foreign audience, whose imagined gaze of jealousy is part of the occasion. . . . The Americans are richer and more powerful than 'us'. They can buy anything they want ten times over. But they cannot buy that which they are imagined to desire above all else. They cannot buy 'our' monarchy, 'our' history, 'our' nation.   (Billig 1992: 53)

Thus as British power declined, the significance of the monarchy as a *nationalist* institution became enhanced. That Unionist attitudes to the monarchy did not indicate such a development is noteworthy, but it can readily be explained. First, the meaning of the crown for Ulster loyalists was always defined primarily in a local context, and in the 1950s they were most reluctant to accept that Britain's status as a world power was being reduced. This was indicated in May 1954 during a parliamentary debate on a royal tour of the Commonwealth. Unionists saw the royal tour as expressing 'the family life of Great Britain at its best', something they could now appreciate more fully through the television broadcasts of the tour (Norman Porter, Dr Robert Nixon, *N.I. Parliamentary Debates*, vol. 38 (13 May 1954), cols 2042–3). Lord Brookeborough, in congratulating the Queen, declared: 'I feel sure that by her presence she has shown the world that [British] leadership and British prestige stands higher than they have ever stood before.' (ibid.: col. 2041). Nationalist claims that the tour symbolized colonial oppression in the face of rising nationalist movements and reflected Britain's evident decline as a world power (Diamond, Murtagh Morgan, ibid.: cols 2044–7), brought a chorus of Unionist dissent. Bessie Maconachie expressed what was probably a widespread opinion among Unionists as to what specifically Britain's world role was when she declared:

I believe that at no time has the British Commonwealth of Nations shown such unity or held so much power. I believe that Her Majesty's visit has greatly strengthened this unity, and I believe that in the years to come the British Commonwealth of Nations will have a tremendous role to play in holding the balance of power between two great nations, Russia and the United States. . . . At one time Great Britain held the balance of power in Europe. I feel that the balance of power throughout the Commonwealth of Nations is being used in a greater and wider way.   (ibid.: cols 2047–50)

Maconachie found no Unionists to dissent from her view. For them, the realization that Britain was losing its great power status had yet to occur. Thus, in the more circumscribed context in which the monarchy had its primary significance for Unionists, the Coronation and its aftermath had appeared to demonstrate the crown's greater importance as an embodiment of their British nationality. There would be, in the decade from the Coronation visit to the North in 1953 until the resignation of Brookeborough as Prime Minister of Northern Ireland in March 1963, a further eighteen visits by members of the royal family to Northern Ireland to offer reassurance to Unionists about their status as British nationals. The second factor that militated against a Unionist attitude to the USA such as that which developed in England at this time was the pride they took in their Presbyterian ancestors who had made an important contribution to the foundation and building of the United States.

II

Given the greater security Unionists felt about their constitutional position in the 1950s, many were encouraged, despite government refusal, to continue the campaign for a history of Ulster that could be used to inculcate a foundation myth among Protestant schoolchildren to underpin their British nationality. Alex Hunter explained exactly what they had in mind:

there is [an] urgent necessity for a history book so that instead of one child in 500 knowing about King William's progress in Northern Ireland (sic) and possibly one child in 10,000 knowing about Lord Carson and Lord Craigavon we will have educated children in our schools in Ulster.
                              (*N.I. Parliamentary Debates*, vol. 41 (30 May 1957), col. 1348)

Despite the oft-repeated government explanation that, while it sympathized with this sentiment, it did not have the power to commission such a book and have it imposed on history teachers in Ulster schools, the demands persisted. The extreme loyalist, Norman Porter, returned to the issue a fortnight after Hunter. He rejected government explanations and used the practice of history teaching in the rest of the United Kingdom as a precedent for the Stormont Government to follow:

I am reliably informed that if one entered a school in Scotland he would have no difficulty in finding . . . a history book dealing with the background of that country. . . . the children are told of the great men of the past, and the story of Scotland's progress from a religious point of view. . . . This is taught to the Protestant children. I cannot for the life of me see why that cannot be done in so far as Protestant children [in Northern Ireland] are concerned.
                                              (ibid. (12 June 1957), col. 1601)

In June 1958 J.W. Morgan made the nationality concerns of Unionists explicit when he claimed that we 'have an ancient civilisation of which we are very proud. . . . There is one weak link, that is the teaching of history in the schools.' Morgan then cited a list of historical authorities, all of whom 'agree that Northern Ireland (sic) was the ancient nation of Scotia.' Claiming the centrality of history to citizenship, Morgan argued that if a 'people's' history was not taught, young people would be 'brought up without a knowledge of who they are, what they are, and what their mission is . . . like a ship without a rudder or a chartless sea.' (ibid., vol. 42 (5 June 1958), cols 1266–7). Such pleas would continue to be made, without success, until the early 1960s (see J.E. Warnock, D. McNabb, William May, ibid., vol. 48 (27 April 1961), cols 1557–9).

The attempt to create an historical myth for promotion in state schools, however, was not the only means by which an Ulster nationality was promoted. This concern is also evident in the decision to establish a Folk Museum for Northern Ireland, as the Report in March 1954 of the Folk Museum Committee, chaired by Sir Roland Nugent, makes clear. The

Report noted that in Scandinavia, Wales and the Irish Republic such museums were either already constructed or in the process of being built. But it was clearly the Folk Museum in the Irish Republic that stimulated action. The Committee declared:

We feel it our duty to point out that the establishment of a Folk Museum in the Irish Republic would tend to accelerate the process by which objects of great interest *to all who value the past of Ulster* [my italics] pass into the ownership of people and institutions outside Northern Ireland.

(Folk Museum Committee, Government of Northern Ireland 1954: 3)

It is easy to read in this statement the ubiquitous Unionist anxiety about southern expansionism; in this case, the belief that the Republic was engaged in a form of cultural imperialism designed to obliterate everything that made Ulster distinctive from the rest of Ireland. Accordingly, the Committee warned that it would 'be a tragedy not to preserve now, while there is still time, surviving examples of the Ulster way of life as it has developed through the years.' A Folk Museum for the North to effect this purpose would 'stimulate in present and future generations of Ulster people an interest and pride in the life and works of their forebears.' (ibid.: 4). Given the context in which it was used, it is clear that the expression 'Ulster people' referred to the Unionist population.

At an academic level, the most significant endorsement of the North's distinctive identity was provided in *Ulster Under Home Rule* (1955), a collection of essays edited by Tom Wilson, the propagandist value of which was not in the least diminished by occasional and tentative criticisms of the Stormont regime. It was, however, at a popular level, and chiefly visitors to the North from Britain, that the regime hoped to impress in this respect. Thus, in the early 1950s, in the joint handbook of the Ulster Tourist Development Association and the Northern Ireland Tourist Board (NITB) – a body set up in 1948 to capitalize on the North's increasing attractions for the British holidaymaker (UTDA 1984: 15) and which would soon supersede the former as the major tourist body in the region – the constitutional position of Northern Ireland was spelled out, together with a photograph of the Stormont Parliament, in a Foreword welcoming the British visitor written by Sir Basil Brooke (see, for example, UTDA/NITB 1950: 5–7). As the 1950s wore on, the tourist handbooks for Northern Ireland changed significantly, becoming less ponderous and detailed in their descriptions of the people, towns and countryside of the six counties, while the Prime Minister's Foreword was dropped altogether. Instead, the emphasis centred more and more on entertainment and sports, with a brief introduction informing the British visitor that here was 'a small province of one and a quarter million people working hand-in-hand with their brothers and sisters in England, Scotland and Wales.' (NITB 1954: Introduction). It is difficult to account exactly for the change, but it may have reflected the greater constitutional security Unionists felt in the 1950s and also the realization, made clear in studies of northern tourism for the period since 1969 (see Wilson 1993: 140), that once tourists are persuaded to come to Northern Ireland they are far less concerned about the border than those living on either side of it.

But if the specific political message of the regime became muted in the 1950s, the concern to portray the North as having a distinctive cultural and national identity remained. As the reference to the population of Northern Ireland in the 1954 handbook demonstrates, no indication of the national division in the region was given: the nationalist community was completely submerged as part of a total population loyally working 'hand-in-hand' with Britain. Moreover, a map of Northern Ireland was provided with the Republic of Ireland blacked out, while the cover illustration of the handbook depicted 'Finn MacCoul', legendary builder of the Giant's Causeway, standing with arms outstretched to welcome visitors from Britain. Other individual works of this period intended primarily for a British readership also served this purpose.

For example, this was true of Richard Hayward's last major work of Ulster travelogue-cum-propaganda, *Border Foray* (1957). As with his previous works,[2] this book was designed to appear at a moment of political crisis – the IRA's border campaign began the previous year – and to serve Unionist interests. It made a pro-Unionist argument in a text denying political purpose, and, among other things, focused on the distinctive character of 'Ulster'. Hayward posed and answered the question, 'is there any real difference between the folk of Ulster and the folk of the rest of Ireland?' thus:

All my reading, all my study . . . and all my heartwarming contacts with the Irish people of the whole country . . . tell me there is. All Irish history and pre-history, tells me the same story, so that it is not only to those forcibly-planted English and Scottish planters of Elizabethan and Jacobean times, potent as those plantations have been in the moulding of the unmistakable Ulster character, that we have to look for an explanation of this undoubted differentiation [between North and South].   (Hayward 1957: 140)

Hayward denied that the basis of that difference was religious, arguing that in both Catholic and Protestant communities in Ulster there was an 'ineradicable northern bias' (ibid.: 15). Instead, he claimed that Ulster's regional difference can be traced back to the legends of Cuchulainn. In this context, the Ulster plantation, 'the ruthless supplanting of the native people by strangers', was merely 'the amplification of the spirit and feeling of the people of Ulster as a different kind of Irish from their fellow-countrymen' (ibid.: 21). As to the deep community divisions that the plantation gave rise to, like other Unionists enamoured of the idea of a distinctive Ulster identity, Hayward's attempt to explain this away was the product of sheer wishful thinking:

By various ways and devious means the old inhabitants of Ulster crept back into part of their stolen lands . . . and the Ulsterman of today is a product of this vitalising mixture of the blood of the Scots and English adventurers with that of the sturdy and independently minded old stock.   (ibid.: 21–2)

Ridiculous as it may seem now, Hayward's views on Ulster's identity were attractive to many Unionists at a time when their membership of the United Kingdom appeared to be unassailable. As Brian Faulkner was to recall, the constitutional guarantee of 1949 'gave Unionists a sense of belonging which lasted for over twenty years' (Faulkner 1978: 20). Hayward's arguments were to be reproduced, in essence, in the regime's propaganda magazine, *Ulster Illustrated* ('Ulster Through the Ages', February 1959: 14–15), for more effective dissemination among the British public.

Ulster Illustrated and *Ulster Commentary*, together with a team of lecturers organized by Stormont to present the regime's view of Ulster and operating through the Ulster Office in London and in the regions through 'Ulster Associations' – bodies of Northern Ireland men and women residing in Britain – represented a forceful campaign for the ideological integration of Northern Ireland as an authentic member of the British national family, reflecting the 'British Way of Life' in common with the other national communities of the United Kingdom.[3] It was probably as a reflection of a widely-held view among Unionists then, that John Cole, in contributing to a special Ulster number of the *Spectator*, argued that Northern Ireland remained a 'community, comprehensible and identifiable in a way which few English regions do. Englishmen who shudder at the thought of the deep religious division rarely understand the compensating homogeneousness' (*Spectator*, 'Offshore Counties': 28 April 1961). Moreover, the ideological campaign waged by the Stormont regime was underpinned by a close political relationship with the Conservative Party.

III

The Unionist representation at Westminster during the fifty years of Stormont rule is usually held to have been of little account. As John Cole described it in this period, totally subservient to the Conservative Party: 'None has ever risen above PPS level, and the general image of the group at Westminster is a faceless one indeed' (ibid.). However, while the Unionist impact on Westminster in general may have been minimal, it could be argued that there was more to their role of serving Stormont's interests in Britain; and in this respect some Unionist MPs, at least, pursued those interests vigorously. In particular, Professor Douglas Savory, MP for South Antrim, relentlessly exploited Ulster's wartime activities in a series of publications that made the case for partition.[4] Again, friendships made between Ulster Unionist MPs with Tory Party members could, at least, neutralize possible sources of criticism,[5] while the IRA's bombing campaign in 1956 saw the Tory Party enthusiastic in its support of the Stormont regime. Brian Faulkner's memoirs authentically catch the mood of cordiality that characterized Unionist-Tory relations at this time:

The strong sense of patriotism which was such an important factor in Ulster was also seen as finding expression through the Conservatives. That the party of those days also looked favourably on the Ulster link was made clear. Colonel Glover, then Vice-Chairman of the National Union of Conservative and Unionist Associations, said in Belfast that Ulster must remain 'one of the brightest jewels in the Queen's crown'. . . . The relationship between Stormont and Westminster at this time makes an interesting contrast with the one that developed later. As Minister of Home Affairs I was in charge of the counter-terrorist measures. Westminster was helpful and co-operative at all times, providing troops when they were needed for a particular operation, and making various representations to Dublin.   (Faulkner 1978: 23–4)

Indeed, in this period politicians who would later disapprove of the regime for its unfair practices, then seemed to fully support it. Faulkner's account of a visit by the Conservative chief whip, Edward Heath, to Ulster in the mid-1950s, exhibits an understandable note of resentment at the later turn of events: 'He gave me no reason to believe that he was anything but sympathetic to the Unionist point of view.' (ibid.: 22). In this respect, moreover, Heath merely reflected the opinion of the Prime Minister, Harold Macmillan. Faulkner recalled: 'I heard him on two occasions in Belfast . . . and on each occasion he was given a deservedly rapturous reception.' (ibid.: 23).

Certainly Macmillan gave the Stormont regime unstinting support throughout the period of the IRA's 1956–62 campaign and emphasized the integrity of Northern Ireland's membership of the United Kingdom (see Brookeborough, *N.I. Parliamentary Debates*, vol. 40 (18 December 1956), col. 3209; *Derry Standard*, 19 December 1958). As Rab Butler put it in a message to Queen's University Unionist Association: 'Your territory is our territory, and your honour, our honour' (ibid.). Unionist influence with Macmillan, moreover, could only have been enhanced when the extreme Orangeman, Knox Cunningham, was appointed his Personal Private Secretary. Unlike Anthony Eden, who never consulted his private secretaries, Macmillan relied considerably on their advice; and in Cunningham's case, according to Macmillan's biographer, he was often badly advised (Horne 1989: ii, 161, 493). Macmillan, however, formed a very favourable impression of Cunningham: 'an upright and sincere man and . . . very painstaking' (see Bryans 1992: 52–3). It is difficult to be precise about the extent of Cunningham's influence with Macmillan, but it is at least likely that he encouraged both the fulsome praise Macmillan expressed for the RUC and the 'B' Specials in their fight against the IRA and the public attacks he made on de Valera when on a visit to Northern Ireland in the election year of 1959 (*Derry Standard*, 10 March 1959; *Londonderry Sentinel*, 11 March 1959). And here, yet again, Macmillan made a ringing endorsement of his fidelity to the Union between Northern Ireland and Britain: 'My party will never abandon or betray Northern Ireland and no Government over which I have the honour to preside will ever think of it.' (ibid.). It is difficult to conceive of how the security of Northern Ireland as part of the United Kingdom could have been more fully expressed. Moreover, the campaign against the IRA allowed the considerable coercion of the Catholic community that took place in the North in the

1950s either to go unnoticed or to be seen as excusable in Britain (see Farrell 1976: Ch. 9). Yet Unionist anxieties remained.

The problem was that the kind of union desired by Ulster loyalists was one conceived in terms that were mythically 'pure'; in which a total homogeneity existed between the public sphere of politics and the local sphere of everyday interests; or, more exactly, in which the kind of constitutional reassurance given publicly by Macmillan was reflected at the local level of everyday existence in Britain by a consciousness of the republican threat to Northern Ireland and active support for the Unionist cause. This, however, was not the case, and evidence to this effect was easy to come by and could be very disconcerting – as when it was found that, while the struggle against the IRA was going on in the North, it was legal to collect money for the IRA in Britain. As the Labour MP, David Bleakley, put it: 'all responsible citizens in Northern Ireland are shocked by the news that money can be collected in one part of the United Kingdom to do damage to life and property in another part.' (*N.I. Parliamentary Debates*, vol. 43 (1 May 1958), col. 459).[6] The worry was that such incidents suggested that the population of Britain did not accept Northern Ireland as really a part of the national territory, that in Britain it was not imagined as part of the nation.

In fact, the shocking news about IRA collections in Britain was merely the latest in a number of disturbing disclosures about mainland British ignorance of, and uninterest in, Northern Ireland. The most serious recent disclosure had been the result of a 'commercial survey conducted by an Ulster firm to determine how well Ulster was known to the average Englishman'. The results were not encouraging:

45 per cent of the people interviewed did not know what Ulster was!
48 per cent did not know that the Six Counties took part in the last war.
56 per cent did not know that Ulster had its own Government. Many thought that Ulster was part of 'Eire'; part of Scotland (!); a British colony; an independent State.

To the findings of this survey, James McFadden, the reporter who brought it to public notice in 'Around and About Britain' (*Ulster Illustrated*, Spring 1957: 21), added his own anecdotal evidence: of the 'leading manufacturing concern' at a London trade exhibition which advertised its products as being sold in 'the United Kingdom *and* Northern Ireland'; of people who, intending to send parcels to Ulster, had applied to the Post Office for customs forms; and of the first Home International football match between Northern Ireland and England in 1956, when the flying of the Tricolour in honour of the Ulster team was prevented only at the last minute.

Thus, despite the favourable relationship the Stormont regime had with the British political establishment in the 1950s, the sense of threat and isolation that came from fighting a war on two fronts – the 'military' struggle with the IRA and the struggle against ignorance of, and indifference to, Northern Ireland in Britain – was an ever-present reality. In this context, loyalist attitudes about how Northern Ireland was presented in Britain verged on the paranoid, especially so as they were aware that the endemic sectarianism of the region could be easily demonstrated to be inconsistent with modern conceptions of 'the British way of life'. The virulently anti-Catholic loyalist, Norman Porter, could rightly claim that Ulster Unionist principles 'are laid down in the British way of life' (*N.I. Parliamentary Debates*, vol. 40 (10 October 1956), col. 2366); however, the Unionist manner of giving expression to those principles was something that in Britain had been consigned to history. This was the reality that loyalists had to deal with; and a reality that was all the more difficult to accept given the increasing secularism and materialism that were replacing the values that united the North and Britain in the nineteenth century. Thus when the BBC, reflecting opinion in Britain, broadcast discussions on whether or not the National Anthem should be sung after 'public' performances, and took an objective approach to religious issues, the Unionist reaction was to accuse the Corporation of promoting 'anti-British' and 'alien' propaganda, rather than accept what these broadcasts implied about 'the British way of life' in Britain.[7] However, it was when the BBC presented Northern Ireland to the population of Britain in a way that highlighted, negatively, its differences from the mainland that Unionist reaction was most hysterical.

A case in point was the *Tonight* programme in January 1959, which dealt with Northern Ireland and was hosted by Alan Whicker. Whicker's programme was not untruthful, it merely highlighted aspects of northern Irish life that lay outside the mythic image of the region presented by the Stormont regime in Britain, namely: the fact that all policemen carried revolvers; that despite its loyalty to Britain conscription did not apply to the North; that public houses were open from morning to night; that betting shops were legal; and gable-wall evidence of the sectarian and political divisions in the North (Cathcart 1984: 190–91). The Unionist response to the programme was furious. That Whicker had erred grievously in presenting Northern Ireland in terms outside the narrow framework of idealized Britishness that was characteristic of government propaganda was made plain when a resident of the Derry hotel with whom he watched the programme being broadcast declared, that despite its truthfulness, 'You just can't say that sort of thing' (Whicker 1982: 113–14). The intensity of the Unionist reaction from all classes was such that the BBC made no further programmes of an investigative kind on Northern Ireland for several years:

The consequence was that Northern Ireland did not feature on the television network except in news bulletins. Effectively there was a Westminster rule in the BBC as there was in politics. Questions were not asked because they were the concern of another place. So the greater British public knew little of what was going on in its own backyard.   (Cathcart 1984: 193)

It was against this background that Terence O'Neill began his period of office in 1963 and sought to consolidate Northern Ireland's membership of the United Kingdom by inculcating Northern Unionism with modern British values.

IV

The major inducements and stimuli for O'Neill's campaign of liberalization have been clearly established. Economically, there was the pressing need to address the persistent problem of unemployment, which, since the war, had run at four times the United Kingdom average – due partly to the decline of traditional industries, movement from the land, and a continually high birth rate. The proposed solution to this problem was provided by the Wilson Report of 1964, which recommended a development plan designed to create 30,000 jobs in manufacturing industry (O'Leary 1979: 158–9). Job creation on this scale – deemed necessary also to defuse a rising threat to the Unionist Party from Labour – could only be achieved by attracting outside investment, and this was an added inducement to create conditions of democratic normalcy. Moreover, the political environment in 1963 appeared conducive to liberalization. The IRA campaign of 1956–62 failed, largely due to lack of Catholic support. Northern Catholics, whose quality of life was improved by the welfare state, were showing indications in the late 1950s of accepting the existence of the Northern statelet (ibid.: 158).

Furthermore, there were indications of liberalization in the South, where Sean Lemass succeeded de Valera as Taoiseach and expressed his *de facto* recognition of Northern Ireland. The much-publicized meetings between Lemass and O'Neill in 1965 were the logical development of this mood of liberalization (Darby 1983: 24, 31). Again, within Catholicism there was, following the lead of Pope John XXIII and the Ecumenical Council of 1962, a turning away from antagonism towards Protestantism in favour of reconciliation (Harkness 1983: 139). Further, the impression of a modernization of mentalities taking place in the North was enhanced by a domestic media, especially television, which marginalized political extremism in its concern with moderation, and which in so doing was to underestimate the forces opposed to O'Neill (Cathcart 1984: 201–2). But in the immediate term, all these factors seemed conducive to O'Neill's political project.

Throughout his period of office, the standard against which O'Neill judged developments in Ulster – negative and positive – was a conception of British identity and behaviour, of which secularism, materialism and tolerance were the defining characteristics and which were translated directly from developments in Britain. Harold Wilson came to power nine months after O'Neill, promoting an urban, industrial and 'technological' conception of the British nation: a 'modern' conception that O'Neill, anxious to advance the commercial and industrial development of the North, easily identified with, and saw in it the means for securing the effective integration of Northern Ireland with the rest of the United Kingdom.

The development of O'Neill's Britishness was based on a threefold process of persuasion: persuasion of the Protestant community that it was in their interest to modernize their religious and political mentalities; persuasion of the politicians and people of Britain that Northern Ireland was authentically British in the 'modern' sense; but, probably most importantly, by the promise of equality of treatment and greatly improved living standards, to persuade Ulster Catholics to accept a British identity. O'Neill believed that, given his ancestry, he was especially well fitted to accomplish this task:

Although I was descended from Sir Arthur Chichester, the founder of Belfast . . . I was also descended from the O'Neills through the female line. Because of my name and my attitude to the minority they could accept me and identify with my aspirations. In a country where you can tell whether a person is a 'Gael' or a 'planter' by his name, this was important.   (O'Neill 1973: 129)

Nevertheless, other personal characteristics of O'Neill would militate against a successful outcome to his campaign. As a reading of his autobiography indicates, he was sensitive, aloof, vain and lacking the iron will that is usually associated with the 'man of destiny' – an opinion he clearly had of himself. Moreover, O'Neill's Britishness, while in tune with the materialist values of 1960s Britain, was still, essentially, the Britishness of a paternalistic Tory gentleman, a cast of mind that inhibited radical interventionism. Thus, as a man and as a politician, he was constitutionally predisposed towards the campaign of political modernization that he undertook – one that might best be described as *educational* and *generational*, terms which suggest gradual change over many years and which rapidly became inadequate when the expectations of the Catholic community rose significantly from the mid-1960s.

O'Neill did have some initial successes. He did succeed in selling Northern Ireland both in Britain and America as a desirable place for industrial investment. As regards the latter, he put that success down substantially to a form of ethnic disposition: 'a southern Englishman has far less in common with an Ulster Presbyterian than an American has. This partly explains our incredible success in attracting American industry to Northern Ireland' (ibid.: xii). And of the regime's success in attracting inward investment during the O'Neill years there is little doubt. From 1964–9 sixty new factories were set up, including a complex of six synthetic fibre factories, the greatest of its kind in the world (O'Leary 1979: 160). It was in selling 'Ulster' in Britain, however, that O'Neill – who was inclined at times to regard himself as English (see Longford 1974: 99) – appears at his most enthusiastic and effective, as even his arch-rival, Brian Faulkner, admitted (Faulkner 1978: 53). O'Neill's commitment was evidenced especially in the 'Ulster Weeks' that ran over the period 1964–9, and which consisted of promoting Northern Ireland and its goods in a number of major British cities (O'Neill 1973: 64–6, 84–5, 94, 102). Faulkner, who as Minister of Finance was actively engaged in selling the province, delivered a speech during the Ulster Week in Leeds in 1966 that succinctly illustrates the intention of the campaign:

We want you to learn that here is a community proud to be British and leading a busy, productive life. Our farms and factories are as much a part of the economic muscle of the country as the mills of Yorkshire. We export linen and whisky, ships and missiles, optical lenses and oil drills, playing a full part in the economic struggle for prosperity which is vital to every citizen in Britain.

(quoted in Faulkner 1978: 37)

O'Neill, moreover, sought to shape the perception of Ulster in Britain in other ways. Thus, just as pro-regime writers such as Hugh Shearman and Richard Hayward tended to reflect Stormont's political outlook under Brookeborough, so under O'Neill, but in a rather different way, was this the case.

The major popular work on Ulster in the O'Neill years was Robin Bryans's, *Ulster: a Journey Through the Six Counties* (1964), a work intended to describe what 'Northern Ireland is like today' (dustjacket note). As the title – which, significantly, embodied both the most common Unionist and nationalist descriptions of Northern Ireland – suggests, this work intended to get away from the narrow Unionist outlook of the 1950s and to present a region whose way of life was modernizing rapidly. Bryans, for instance, described his impression on returning to the province after a long absence, thus: 'To my special joy, I found that the old bitternesses are waning and that the beauty of Ulster is no longer scarred by old terrors.' (Bryans 1964: 16). This was a major and recurring theme, the dissolving of religious antagonism under the impact of modernization. Moreover, Bryans identified in the Orange Order a major victim of the modernization process, something no previous Unionist writer would have dared to suggest (ibid.: 18–19, 21, 42, 88–9). Indeed, he could even lament the fact that while the demise of the Orange Order entailed 'the gradual decline of bitterness and hatred', at the same time, 'a form of folk-art is disappearing as a result' (ibid.: 115).

Bryans's was not a coincidental work that just happened to express views in line with O'Neillite thinking. It was, in fact, commissioned as a work – according to Bryans O'Neill was personally responsible for having him commissioned to write it (Bryans 1992: 63) – that was intended to convey the regime's desired representation of Northern Ireland, chiefly for British readers. When he came to Ulster to research it, the Government 'was most anxious that I see as much as possible of Senator Lennon, the Catholic leader', who was then engaged in discussions with Orange leaders designed to eliminate religious bigotry (ibid.: 72). And when the book was completed, the Government placed its imprimatur on it with high profile reception launches at the office of the Ulster Agent in London and also in Belfast, which both Nationalists and Unionists attended (ibid.: 62–3, 244). The *Belfast Telegraph*, moreover, serialized the book and sent reporters 'to the Catholic and Protestant places and people I had written about but not illustrated' (ibid.: 244–5).

Ultimately, O'Neill wished to see a united Northern Ireland forming one element in a form of regional federation of Parliaments in the British Isles, that would include England, Wales, Scotland and the Irish Republic (O'Neill 1973: 138; Longford 1974: 99). It is perhaps a measure of O'Neill's success in promoting Ulster as a modernizing region of the United Kingdom up to 1968, that in discussions of devolution within the United Kingdom the North could be cited as a model for regions in Britain. The respected academic and Labour MP, John MacKintosh, argued that Northern Ireland demonstrated that devolution need not imply complete independence. More exactly, Stormont showed that economically poor regions would wish to retain the high levels of social services that close constitutional links with the centre allowed: 'So whether Stormont was controlled by the Unionists or not, the pressure for a high degree of uniformity and co-operation would remain.' Again, Stormont showed that devolved government allowed for a more efficient attention to local needs than central government, and had 'real vigour and receives strong support from the community'. Furthermore, 'the speed of decision and personal attention the Northern Irish ministries can offer is a positive asset in attracting industrialists.' (MacKintosh 1968: 180–82; see also *Illustrated London News*, 22 February 1969). As a self-governing region of the United Kingdom, Northern Ireland was much more problematic than it appeared here, as events over the following year would show. But as a statement which expressed how the O'Neill Government wished Northern Ireland to be seen in Britain, it could hardly have been improved upon if O'Neill had written it himself.

V

It is ironical that many of the political difficulties O'Neill faced within Northern Ireland over the period 1964–9, derived substantially from the same strategy that had been successfully employed to sell Ulster in Britain and abroad as an area for industrial investment. A central plank of that strategy was publicity and image building, and this was also true of his policy of promoting reconciliation in the North. Again, like his industrial strategy, it was a policy conceived without a specific time limit; it was intended to be ongoing, long term.

Bringing an essentially cross-channel British perspective to the North's problems, O'Neill adapted the ideas and vocabulary of 1960s Britain to Ulster's problems, especially the notion of the 'generation gap' – the idea that 'youth' was wholly out of harmony with the obsolete ideas of its parents. Giving a speech to the Queen's University Unionist Association on 13 February 1964, for instance, O'Neill, in a lecture designed to inculcate a greater consciousness and appreciation of British nationality in a United Kingdom context, spoke as he would have done to students in Britain: 'I know well your generation has a deep antipathy to the idea of war – that you have no sympathy with anything that smacks of militarism' (O'Neill 1969: 47). At Ballymena in January 1967, he asked: 'What do the people of England today – what, indeed, do our own young people – know or care of Ulster's courageous and colourful past? We will be judged in Ulster, we will be judged elsewhere by what we are and what we hope to become.' (ibid.: 55). Again, in Belfast and Nottingham in January and March 1967, O'Neill avowed that he had never shared 'the disapproving opinion which some people seem to hold about our younger generation', which he regarded as 'full of energy and idealism', embodying a rich source of 'community spirit', and which it was the purpose of his 'Policy to Enlist the People' to capitalize on (ibid.: 152–4). But most significantly, O'Neill's strategy was indicated on 15 October 1968 in his reaction to a National Opinion Poll conducted among the 17–24 age group in Northern Ireland. O'Neill exultantly informed the Stormont Commons that, when asked what the government's priority should be, they desired more industry and houses: 'such things as alleged discrimination and the franchise, which form the political catch-cries of politics, come far behind.' (ibid.: 134).

This generational theme, identifying a younger generation as a homogeneous, non-sectarian, cross-community social strata on which his conciliationist hopes for Northern Ireland rested went together with the economic prosperity that would make 'increasing numbers from every background' realize 'the benefits of the British connection' (speech to Unionist Party Conference, 29 April 1966, ibid.: 53). In this context, O'Neill hoped that, as his policies took effect, the monarchy could play a part in consolidating the British identity of the region. He hoped, in particular, that the Queen could be persuaded to establish a permanent royal residence in the North, and was to claim that this proposal was under 'embryonic discussion' when the civil rights agitation arose and 'successfully killed the project' (O'Neill 1973: 4). It is difficult to know, in fact, what importance to put on this statement in the absence of corroborating evidence, yet O'Neill's claim that the Queen personally supported his policies (ibid.: 82) is reasonable, and it is a fact that when the politics of the North moved towards street conflict from mid-1968, royal visits ceased altogether. There would be none from that time until February 1977 when the Duke of Gloucester, followed by Princess Anne the following month, prepared the way for the Queen's Silver Jubilee visit to the North in 1977.

Her only visit to the province in the 1960s was in 1966, an occasion which served to defuse an intra-Unionist dispute over the naming of the new Lagan Bridge – the 'Somme' and 'Carson' were being vigorously proposed by different groups – when a decision was made to honour the monarch by naming the bridge 'Queen's Bridge' (ibid.). It also was read as an index of increasing liberalization in the North that a protest by a Catholic youth who dropped a piece of concrete on the Queen's car during its procession along Royal Avenue failed to provoke any significant Protestant unrest (see Irish News, 5 July 1966; Belfast News-Letter, 5 July 1966; O'Neill 1973: 82). It is also worth pointing out in this respect that the monarchy in general, and the Queen's visit in particular, could be seen as marking one of the limits of Paisleyite protest. At a time when Ian

Paisley was building his role as a loyalist leader, largely through vociferous attacks on the Unionist establishment, he moved quickly to deny rumours that he would make the Queen's visit a focus of loyalist protest: 'We are not the Queen's enemies. We support the Union Jack.' (*Belfast News-Letter*, 4 July 1966). Of course, while the monarchy could provide an interpretative focus for political developments in the North, it could make little contribution on its own initiative to further the cause of reconciliation, especially given the long-term nature of O'Neill's project.

Although O'Neill's political rhetoric marked a radical departure from that of his predecessors, it is important to remember that it was intended to attain a goal of which they would have approved: the acceptance of Northern Ireland as an integral part of the British national territory by the people of Britain. Accordingly, that population was to be the judge of how far the North had proved itself worthy of British citizenship:

the ordinary decent Englishman, Welshman or Scot has an innate sense of fair play. He will judge us on our merits. If we can show him we are pulling our full weight in the economic struggles of Britain; if we demonstrate that behind all the talk about 'discrimination' is a warm and genuine community spirit; if we can demonstrate that we seek the advantages of British citizenship only because we bear the same burdens – then the voices of criticism will fall increasingly upon deaf ears.

O'Neill claimed that he did not want to change the nature of Ulster, but rather to show again its best face to the world – 'the face of decent, hard-working, self-reliant people, playing a part in modern Britain of which they and their fellow-citizens "across the water" can be equally proud.' (speech to Mid-Armagh Unionist Association, 19 November 1966, in O'Neill 1969: 54–5).

The ideas expressed here are of a piece with the 'generation gap' theme evident in O'Neill's speeches to Young Unionists. In both, the concern is with attitudinal change rather than fundamental reform; and it is here that the analogy between O'Neill's industrial and conciliationist strategies breaks down, for together with the industrial salesmanship went tangible financial inducements to attract outside investment. For too long, and until pressed by Westminster, there was little substance to his conciliation project. Indeed, what is revealing about this speech, is its indication of how close O'Neill's outlook was to that strand of Unionism which emerged in the post-war years and which found expression in the writings of W.R. Rodgers and Richard Hayward – a strand which sought to marginalize fundamental community divisions by claiming the existence of an underlying and 'genuine community spirit' which talk of 'discrimination' disguised.

Again, as this speech also indicates, like his predecessors O'Neill liked to indulge in the belief that the population of Britain was as concerned about, and as conscious of, British national identity as Ulster Unionists, and took an interest in their affairs: a view for which there was little evidence, but which O'Neill may have been inclined to by a conception of the Union between the north of Ireland and Britain which, he liked to point out, dated from the period of the Napoleonic Wars. Thus, 'the Union is not a thing of any decade or generation, but an enduring part of British history' (speech to the Ulster Unionist Council, 30 April 1965, in O'Neill 1969: 50). Where O'Neill differed from his predecessors was that whereas they saw the Union as securing a distinctive Ulster Unionist way of life within the United Kingdom, he saw it as providing standards of 'Britishness' which Unionists would have to adopt, and on the adoption of which the prosperity of the North and its constitutional security ultimately depended.

It was fundamental to the success of this ambition that the Catholic community be reconciled to the Union, but even more so was it vital to keep the Unionist community united. It was this consideration which fed O'Neill's ideological and personal disposition to prefer attitudinal change rather than fundamental reform. In this context, moreover, it can be argued that, despite his pose as the objective arbiter of fair treatment between the two communities, O'Neill's concern with British nationality limited seriously his ability to recognize and deal with Catholic rights and grievances. This is indicated by a speech O'Neill made at a joint Protestant-Catholic conference at Corrymeela on Good Friday, 8 April 1966:

it would be all too easy at a gathering such as this to speak soft words on this subject [the existence of the N.I. statelet], and to give you the impression that all that is needed to overcome every difficulty is goodwill. But that would be less than honest. I must say clearly that the constitutional position of Northern Ireland is not a matter on which there can be any compromise, now or in the future, and I must say, too, that I believe we have a right to call upon all our citizens to support the Constitution. The whole concept of constitutional government would be debased if the State were not to expect of its citizens at any rate the minimum duty of allegiance. (O'Neill 1969: 114)

Given this conceptual framework, O'Neill was incapable of taking an objective approach to the two political traditions in the North. Thus, he described the organizers of the Easter Rising celebrations in Belfast in 1966 as 'extreme republicans who sought to flaunt before *our people* [my italics] the emblems of a cause which a majority of us abhor.' (speech in Stormont Commons, 13 December 1966, in O'Neill 1969: 123). Similarly, while he condemned the Paisleyite harassment of delegates and guests at the Presbyterian General Assembly in 1966, O'Neill argued that it played into the hands of 'the permanent enemies of public order, the IRA', and gave them 'the opportunity to create communal discord' (*N.I. Parliamentary Debates*, vol. 64 (15 June 1966), cols 308–9). While one can see what O'Neill's purpose was here, it was nevertheless irresponsible to raise the spectre of IRA violence at a time when the movement had clearly given up armed struggle in favour of socialist propaganda. But, most importantly, for a politician who wanted to persuade the Catholic community to accept British nationality, it was hardly a sensible policy to insult their political traditions; and it was all the more unwise given the failure of O'Neill to accompany his conciliationist propaganda with substantive reform. Thus, at a time when all that O'Neill was effectively prepared to offer the Catholic community was liberal gestures, he was demanding what should have been expected only as the result of fundamental reforms – their acceptance of British nationality. Moreover, at least one commentator effectively cast doubt on O'Neill's nationality project when she claimed that even if Catholics did 'adopt the national flag and support the Queen', those Unionists who challenged them to do so would be 'the first people to condemn them for insincerity'. It was much better, she continued, to accept the reality of national divisions in the North and to rest the constitutional security of the province on the fact that it could not be changed while a majority for the status quo existed (Sheelagh Murnaghan, Liberal MP for Queen's University, *N.I. Parliamentary Debates*, vol. 70 (29 January 1969), col. 482). Certainly, O'Neillite rhetoric notwithstanding, there is little evidence to suggest an intercommunal ideological rapprochement. The only significant occasion on which the issue of a shared identity between Protestants and Catholics arose in Stormont was indirectly – on the question of whether Saint Patrick's day should be made an official holiday. This proposal, raised by the nationalist MP Edward Richardson, was not taken up, though there was substantial sympathy for the idea among government and opposition. But this was only because Saint Patrick was a mythical figure that both communities had long interpreted separately and for their own purposes. (for the debate, see ibid.: cols 1655–70).

The problem of identity arose in other areas. While the O'Neill-Lemass meetings of 1965 resulted in an agreement between the tourist boards of north and south to promote Ireland as a *whole* – something that could be seen, at one level, as involving the acceptance of a common identity, and which was certainly a radical departure from the way in which tourism in Northern Ireland had been promoted in the 1950s – the project was slow in materializing, partly, it seems, because 'they cannot even agree on a brochure that depicts the island of Ireland' (G. Fitt, ibid., vol. 64 (14 December 1966), col. 130). It is also clear, that while O'Neill expected Ulster Catholics to accept British nationality, this was not to be associated with any attempt by the regime to construct a new community identity that Catholics could readily accept. O'Neill could urge both Unionists and Nationalists to 'mute their historical trumpet calls' (speech to the Irish Association, 19 February 1968, in O'Neill 1969: 129), but as government literature describing the 'character' of the Ulster people over the period 1964–72 demonstrates, the type described is the Ulster Protestant loyalist, distinct from both Ulster Catholics and the population of the South.[8]

O'Neill could, on occasion, declare that his government was Irish – 'My colleagues and I are Irishmen too' – but these expressions tended to occur in reaction to southern calls for an end to partition, and to be associated with vehement assertions of Ulster's British identity: 'We were British people before the nationhood of most members of the United Nations had been thought of' (speech to the Commonwealth Parliamentary Association, Westminster, 4 November 1968, in O'Neill 1969: 171). Similarly, when members of O'Neill's Government were questioned about the relevance of Irishness to their conception of national identity, they gave ambiguous answers that indicated its marginality, especially when associated with their definite assertions of Britishness.[9] Further light is thrown on the interpretation Unionists placed on the term 'Irish' as a label of national identity in Richard Rose's Governing Without Consensus (1971), the research for which was undertaken in 1968.

Of the Protestants questioned on their national identity, 20 per cent described themselves as Irish; 39 per cent as British; while 32 per cent adopted the label 'Ulster'. Of those who chose the term 'Irish', 60 per cent supported the existing constitution, and Rose described the choice of this term as reflecting the historical view of Ireland as an integral portion of the United Kingdom. Moreover, he argued that this choice, and the label 'Ulster', for the overwhelming majority of those who chose them, simply followed as a consequence of having been born and bred in Northern Ireland; in contradistinction to those who adopted the label 'British' and who believed that that identity followed as a result of constitutional arrangements – a foundation that was fundamentally less secure psychologically than custom and upbringing, especially in Northern Ireland. Significantly, Rose also made a correlation between 'Britishness' and respect for legality, whereas the 'Ulster' identity, based on the naturalness of birth and upbringing, reinforced the readiness to resort to arms against legal but 'unnatural' political measures (Rose 1971: 208–9).

As for O'Neill's hopes of persuading Catholics to accept British nationality, Rose's poll evidence suggests that this was not going to be successful, even if the crisis associated with the Civil Rights Movement and the Unionist reaction to it had not developed. Only 15 per cent of Catholics in 1968 were prepared to regard themselves as 'British', and of these, only fifty-five per cent accepted Northern Ireland's existing constitutional arrangements (ibid.: 208). On the issue of 'minimal identification', contradictory signals were registered. While Protestants and Catholics regarded each other as being most like themselves compared to other national groups in the British Isles, Protestants regarded religion as central to their identity and saw 'Irishness' as strongly associated with Catholicism; and while a majority desired better relations with Catholics, there was also majority support for more government attention to the views of 'strong loyalists', discrimination in jobs and housing against Catholics, stronger measures to defend the border, and no change in the existing relations between the two communities (ibid.: 214–16).

But even in the area in which O'Neillism was most successful, economic regeneration, this did little for the cause of reconciliation, as most of the new industries attracted to the province – fifty of fifty-eight – were located in the Protestant east of the province rather than the Catholic west where unemployment was highest. To the sense of discrimination this development fuelled was added the apparent confirmation provided by the siting of the new city of Craigavon in County Armagh, linking the towns of Lurgan and Portadown. But most seriously in this context, there was the decision to site a new university for the province in the Protestant town of Coleraine rather than in Derry, which already had Magee University College on which to build (O'Leary 1979: 161). However, nowhere was the vacuity of O'Neillite conciliationism in the mid-1960s more apparent than in O'Neill's reaction to a report in *The Times* on the position of the Catholic community, 'Ulster's Second-Class Citizens'. When nationalist MPs used the report to highlight the divergence in Northern Ireland from the values and practices associated with 'the British way of life' and to urge immediate reforms (see H. Diamond, E. McAteer, A. Currie, *N.I. Parliamentary Debates*, vol. 65 (25 April 1967), cols 625–32), O'Neill's reaction was to ignore *The Times*'s criticisms and nationalist demands, and to produce a report from the *Yorkshire Post* which praised him as a great leader, 'A Man of Vision' (ibid.: cols 630–32).

Ultimately, the stimulus for substantive reform would come, not from O'Neill, but from the pressure of events and from a London Government anxious to keep O'Neill in power so as to maintain its distance from the province's affairs (Bew *et al.* 1979: 180–81; O'Neill 1973: 112–13). In this context it is worth noting that despite the fact that the one-hundred-strong Campaign for Democracy in Ulster group existed within the Parliamentary Labour Party to press for reforms in the North, its influence was not as significant as its numbers might suggest – apparently, at least in part, because many MPs were afraid of raising 'religious controversies' in their own constituencies (Bell 1982: 104). Yet the external pressure for reforms was also bound to stimulate the opposition within the Unionist community to O'Neill's policies, opposition led by Ian Paisley.

To a significant extent the conflict within Unionism between Paisley and O'Neill is analogous, at an abstract level, to the tension we noted (Introduction, pp. 2–3) between 'authentic' understanding and 'true' knowledge in everyday life, with the former likely to be preferred over the latter. In this context, Paisley and O'Neill can be seen as representing, respectively, particularist/local and universal – in the wider British sense – forms of national identity; the subscribers to which Rose effectively identified when he made the distinction between those in Northern Ireland who, in his questionnaire on national identity, chose the label 'Ulster' and those who chose 'British'. Moreover, unlike the conditions of wartime, there existed no external threats or pressures acting to integrate these spheres of identity; and in the context of the crisis that developed in Northern Ireland in the course of 1968, it was the Ulster identity, deeply embedded in the subjectivity of everyday experience and validated by Unionist mythology, that was bound to predominate. O'Neill's appeal to abstract notions of British tolerance and compromise, with all the uncertainty associated with its effective rejection of indigenous political traditions and practices – even if O'Neill's own political practice failed to quite make the break with the past that his rhetoric demanded – could not compete with the comfort and certitude associated with an uncompromising defence of the traditional Ulster Protestant way of life.

Yet, while Paisley was the most enthusiastic defender of traditional Ulster Protestant values, Richard Rose's claim (1971: 216) that he identified 'with Protestantism rather than nationality' is unsatisfactory. In the sense in which the term 'nationality' is used predominantly today – implying identity with an imagined community – Paisley, no less than O'Neill, thought in terms of a United Kingdom nationality. Where they differed was in their fundamentally distinct points of reference. For O'Neill, it was the secular, modernistic, technological society that Britain appeared to be developing in the 1960s which provided the model for Ulster to emulate and assimilate to, one making the sectarian preoccupations of the past obsolete. For Paisley, the fundamental point of reference in his conception of Britishness was the Glorious Revolution of 1688 and the Protestant values it embodied – values that, in the 1960s, appeared to be under threat from a treacherous and pro-nationalist Labour Government in league with the 'media' to subvert those values through 'destroying the identity of Ulster'. This policy would 'be disastrous. . . . Britain 's vital ocean flank would be fully exposed in time of war to an implacable enemy scheming to destroy this realm and liquidate the last bastion of Protestant and evangelical truth in the world.' (see C.D. Alexander, 'The Great Sell-Out: Ulster Today – Britain Tomorrow', *Protestant Telegraph*, 5 November 1966; for a similar argument by Paisley against Margaret Thatcher, see Bruce 1986: 269–70).[10] For both O'Neillites and Paisleyites, however, the ultimate test of the extent to which the Britain of their imagining identified with the outlying region of Northern Ireland would come in the aftermath of the outbreak of civil strife in 1969.

VI

In what was undoubtedly a truthful statement and one which would be repeated many times over in the years that followed, the Stormont propaganda organ, *Ulster Commentary* (November 1969: 2–3), pointed out that the numbers engaged in the August riots were a tiny minority of the population and that the vast majority of the people lived in conditions of normalcy. Yet, and despite the Hunt Committee's strictures on the distorted picture of Northern Ireland the media presented in Britain (ibid.: 2), the fact was that the image of Northern Ireland was already established as a volatile 'Irish' one; one characterized by political and religious extremism and quite at odds with mythic standards of British tolerance, fair play and compromise. Unfortunately for Unionists, while 1969 was to see Northern Ireland impact on the consciousness of the population of Britain in a more significant way than had been the case for many years, the impression made was both the reverse of what they desired and also failed to elicit any significant sympathy for the region's people – Protestant or Catholic. As one commentator remarked: 'Neither the cause of

Catholics demanding civil rights nor the cry of the Union Jack flying over Stormont aroused any enthusiasm.' For most people the Irish sea 'seemed to provide sufficient insulation from any real sense of involvement.' (David Walder, 'Lucky Old Pope', *Spectator*, 16 September 1969). In other words, for most British people, the Irish Sea separated the national territory of Britain from Ulster, the 'alien other'. And this was also largely true for the two main political parties.

James Callaghan found, on taking up the responsibility for dealing with the Northern Ireland crisis in 1969, that he had the full support of the Tory opposition (Callaghan 1973: 64); support that was all the more noteworthy given that the shadow Home Secretary was Quintin Hogg, who had strong family and personal links with the Unionist community in the North. Moreover, as the conflict proceeded, the British people's detachment from the conflict only became more clear. And it was noted with some surprise that this applied even to the Roman Catholic community in Britain: 'There has been no closing of the ranks [in support of Ulster Catholics] as there often has been over issues such as abortion, divorce or . . . Biafra.' (Hugh Macpherson, 'Political Commentary', *Spectator*, 11 December 1971). Again, the passage of time had failed to register the development of any substantial body of support for Unionists in the Conservative Party. Accordingly: 'The days when the Irish Question was argued on such esoteric terms as the "unity of the nation" seem to have gone'. (ibid.).

For one Tory commentator, Patrick Cosgrove, the reason for the alienation between the people of Ulster and the British population lay in the fact that, for the latter,

the highest political imperatives – like the fate of the nation – were intimately bound up with a day to day pattern of Government, administration and political argument, whereas the highest political imperatives in Ireland . . . nationalism and the union, had become completely separated from daily life and were held to with all the more passion because they were so separated.   (Cosgrove 1969: 326)

The truth, however, was rather different. *Britain*'s 'borders' were secure, so the question of national determination or survival was not an issue in politics, leaving the interest and 'fate' of the nation to be defined and debated in social, economic and party political terms. In the North, however, the national question was a burning issue – all the more burning, not because it was separated from daily life but because, as we have noted, the national and local spheres of existence in the North were so inextricably integrated.

Nevertheless, while the people of Britain as a whole may have regarded the Ulster problem as Irish rather than British in nature, the Unionists did have significant and consistent support in the Conservative press, especially from the *Daily Express, Daily Mail* and, in particular, the *Daily Telegraph*, which James Callaghan described as having no other interest than to 'voice the views of the Ulster Unionists' (Callaghan 1973: 22). These were all papers with well-established readerships which their editors attempted to infuse with their own perspective on the Ulster problem, but largely without success. Their readerships proved resilient to their Unionist message; and this is understandable, certainly in regard to the *Daily Telegraph*. Its analysis of the Ulster problem largely reproduced the paranoid perspective of Ulster Unionism, which saw in the crisis an international Communist-Anarchist-Irish Republican plot (see for example, T.E. Utley, 'Britain's Role in Ulster', *Daily Telegraph*, 15 July 1970). The marginality of the extreme Right's view of the Ulster problem in this period is perhaps best illustrated by comparison with the mainstream Tory *The Times*, which reacted to the events of August 1969 by calling for consultations with Dublin in the process of finding a solution (Sayers 1969: 404).

In fact, it was not simply the case that Ulster Unionism provided the inspiration for right-wing interpretations in Britain, but, in a rather circular fashion, Unionists also found confirmation of their views in those interpretations (see, for example, the quotations from the *Daily Express* and *Daily Telegraph* in the Unionist Party publication, *Ulster: The Facts* 1969). Increasingly, as the crisis of 1969 developed, Ulster Unionist opinion gravitated towards the conspiracy theory of its nature, that 'Ulster' was being threatened by a co-ordinated attack from enemies within and without,[11] conspiracy long warned of by Ian Paisley, and whose political influence grew as a result (Nelson 1984: 59). At the same time, as the media onslaught on Northern Ireland developed from late 1968 and as the Unionist reputation in the outside world deteriorated accordingly, their attitudes became more extreme (ibid.: 74), and thus the possibility of their developing a constituency in Britain sympathetic to their position more remote. Nevertheless, despite their growing alienation from the British political establishment in this period, no substantial movement representing Ulster nationalism and independence developed. It was usual to blame the Labour Government for their troubles and to hope that when their natural allies, the Conservatives, were returned to power they would behave differently and 'put things right' (ibid.: 96–7).

In fact, the British media perspective on the Unionist movement did change with British intervention, which reshaped perceptions of the problem in terms of British impartiality versus extremes on both sides; and was reshaped again when the development of the Provisional IRA campaign worked to identify republican violence as the chief evil. Nevertheless, throughout these developments Ulster Protestant behaviour and attitudes appeared to British commentators as un-British and antediluvian (Butler 1991: 109–15). Further, while those attitudes continued to alienate British opinion, they also prevented Unionists from taking any effective action to redress the situation. One suggestion floated in London in August 1969, was that the troubles could only be effectively dealt with by a coalition government in the North. As Keith Kyle put it:

the proposal would test the intentions of the opposition even more than the Establishment. If prominent Catholics and Civil Righters took office – and under the law the choice of ministers is not confined to members of Stormont – they would be accepting the existence of the border *and the British character of Ulster in a most decisive way* [my italics].

(Kyle, 'Ulster', the *Listener*, 21 August 1969: 238)

This suggestion, however, was psychologically unacceptable to a Unionist Party increasingly convinced that the minority was engaged in a conspiracy to destroy Ulster.

With the 'British' solution of political compromise having been rejected, the only way in which the North's identity could be reforged in a mainland sense was if the initiative came from Westminster. Some suggestions were made: for example, better communications between the North and Britain; the promotion by publishing and broadcasting organizations of articles of a non-crisis nature, written by Ulster journalists, 'of broad concern to the UK at large' and which would help reduce the sense in which 'Ulster life and manners' were regarded as alien to mainstream British life; the siting of British government offices in Northern Ireland to 'help stress the administrative unity of Ulster and Great Britain'; according Westminster Cabinet status to an Ulster politician as 'Ulster Secretary' to emphasize the value Britain placed on the Ulster connection; changing the titles of Northern Ireland ministers, especially that of 'Prime Minister', to emphasize the North's constitutional subordination to Westminster and its membership of the United Kingdom (see Dr Ian Bellamy to Editor, *Spectator*, 27 November 1971: 788). But as the author of these suggestions recognized, their feasibility presupposed the willingness of British governments to integrate the North with the rest of the United Kingdom, and of this there was little evidence.

And yet, ironically, while unwilling to regard Northern Ireland as truly British, Westminster politicians sought to deal with the problem on the basis of assumptions drawn from the political experience of mainland Britain. In an incisive, if politically biased, analysis of the British approach to the Ulster problem, T.E. Utley characterized what he regarded as the wrongheaded, but dominant, characteristics of the British approach, namely: a belief in negotiation; that all problems have accessible solutions; and, most importantly, the concept of 'the centre' – 'This is deemed to consist of the vast majority of mankind whose specific characteristics are held to be silence, moderation and a taste for compromise.' (Utley 1975: 13). And where, as in Ulster, such a 'centre' has been difficult to find, British politicians seek to summon it into existence:

The method has been simply to induce certain Ulster politicians, cast in the mould of their fellow-countrymen, to assume the demeanour and language which are favoured by moderate-minded men at Westminster. In the process of course these politicians have totally lost the support which they originally enjoyed in Ulster and have been rendered incapable of discharging the service for which they were employed – to deliver the Protestant majority.   (ibid.)

Certainly Ulster Unionists found, despite expectations to the contrary, that when the Tories succeeded Labour in 1970 their expectations of how Stormont politicians should behave was, in substance, no different from their predecessors'. Reginald Maudling's tenure as Home Secretary differed from that of Callaghan only in that Maudling was less keen to exercise government guidance of Ulster's affairs, thus leaving more space for the Stormont regime to exercise its own initiative, especially on security (Callaghan 1973: 146). However, when the internment policy of Brian Faulkner failed, Westminster's demands for it to be phased out and the conflict that ensued with Westminster over security policy – leading to the resignation of the Faulkner Government and the imposition of direct rule – pointed up the different interests that underlay the supposed bond of patriotism that Unionists liked to believe was the basis of a common political outlook.

Notes

1. For a typical comparison of England in the two periods, which argued from the 'evidence' of the first Elizabeth that another age of greatness would follow under the second, see the *Listener* (28 May 1953: 863–4).
2. Hayward's previous substantial works coincided with the Treaty Ports dispute (*In Praise of Ulster*, 1938) and the anti-partition campaign (*Ulster and the City of Belfast*, 1950). For a vehement declaration of Hayward's Unionism and how his works were intended to serve the Unionist cause, see Hayward to Sir Wilson Hungerford, 26 February 1940 (PRONI, CAB9F/123/3A).
3. For debate on the work of the Ulster Office and Ulster Associations in Britain, see David Bleakley (*N.I. Parliamentary Debates*, vol. 43 (23 October 1958), cols 113–14). On the arrangements for disseminating *Ulster Commentary*, see Bleakley, T. O'Neill (ibid., vol. 44 (9 June 1959), cols 1704–11).
4. Savory's output of Unionist propaganda was impressive, and included, for example, in 1958, four separate articles in the *Contemporary Review* alone. See bibliography.
5. See, for example, Norman Tebbit on his friendship with Robin Chicester-Clark (Tebbit 1989: 137, 154–5, 166–7).
6. On Unionist reaction to British press and BBC reporting of the IRA campaign, see Captain Henderson, Norman Porter and Brian Faulkner (*N.I. Parliamentary Debates*, vol. 40 (18 December 1956), cols 203–7).
7. See J.W. Morgan, Brookeborough (*N.I. Parliamentary Debates*, vol. 41 (3 December 1957), 2721–2, 2726). It should be noted that Nationalists as well as Unionists could be offended by the increasing materialism of British life as broadcast by the BBC. See James McSparran, Francis Hanna (ibid., cols 2718–20, 2722–5).
8. See, for example, Northern Ireland Information Service, *Notes On Northern Ireland* (February 1964: 3); 'The New Ulster' (*Ulster Annual 1969*), 1969: 10–12); 'The Ulsterman' (*Ulster Annual 1972*, 1972: 60–61). See also Shearman (1968: 67).
9. See discussions on national identity with Sir James Chicester-Clark, Dr Robert Simpson and Brian Faulkner (Rose 1971: 206–7).
10. For attempts to bring these values to the fore in Britain in the 1960s, see the following articles in the *Protestant Telegraph*: 'Ramsey's Romeward Run' (18

June 1966); 'Protestants Awake: the Fight is on in England' (30 July 1966); 'Cardinal Heenan: Britain's Mini-Pope' (17 December 1966); 'The Pope's Puppets – Made in Scotland' (8 July 1967); 'Romanising Britain' (14 October 1967).

11. See, for example, Clifford Smyth, *Ulster Assailed* (1970); The Ulster Group, *Recent Events in Northern Ireland: the Northern Ireland Troubles in Perspective* (1971).

9

DIRECT RULE AND BRITISH IDENTITY IN
ULSTER 1972–85

I

The imposition of direct rule gave a boost to support for the Vanguard movement, a loose coalition of right-wing Unionists, chiefly former members of the Official Unionist Party led by William Craig and loyalist paramilitary organizations such as the Ulster Defence Association, the Loyalist Association of Workers and the Orange Volunteers. Vanguard reacted to the implementation of direct rule with a two-day work stoppage on 27–8 March 1972 which involved 190,000 people and brought Northern Ireland to a virtual standstill. (Harbinson 1973: 174).

As a movement, Vanguard largely reflected the Unionist community's increasing alienation from Westminster administrations and its frustration at the lack of viable constitutional alternatives. Thus while its policy statements could give expression to an Ulster nationalism voiced in demands for a unilateral declaration of independence as the best means of preserving Ulster's British heritage, at the same time, because of the doubtful viability of this option, Vanguard was reluctant to give it the status of official policy. Probably the most developed statement of Vanguard's outlook on Unionist identity following the prorogation of Stormont was contained in *Betrayal in Ulster: the Technique of Conservative Betrayal* (1972), a document apparently produced for distribution among delegates at the Conservative Party Conference in October 1972, and which focused on the relationship between the Party and Ulster Unionism.

The document was concerned to make the Ulster Unionist case within a context that Conservative MPs with purely mainland interests could relate to. Thus it located the source of the errors in the Conservative approach to Ulster generally in post-war consensus politics, something it argued that had 'petrified' political debate in Britain since Macmillan's time, and was evident in the party's approach to immigration, law and order, industrial relations and state intervention. In this context, the party's approach to Ulster only 'proves the charge conclusively' (Ulster Vanguard 1972: 2–3). Moreover, during the gestation period of the present crisis in the 1960s, when the Republican Clubs and the 'so-called' Civil Rights Movement were preparing to overthrow the state, Unionists were disadvantaged by their 'obstinate adherence to the traditional British virtues of respect for authority and belief in order and discipline, qualities which, to say the least, are hardly fashionable in cross-channel society.' (ibid.: 4). Accordingly, a deliberate plot, involving staged demonstrations and nationalist influence on the Wilson Government, produced the 'denouement' of 1969 and the discrediting of the Stormont regime.

Vanguard regarded Westminster's failure to fight the IRA 'to the finish' as inevitably entailing a process leading to a united Ireland, something that would not happen abruptly but rather as the result of 'the evolution of a series of Constitutional perversions which must render the Union finally untenable.' (ibid.: 12). The ultimate consequence of Government policies for Northern Ireland was that, by marginalizing the Unionist community and its interests, loyalists now risk 'losing their nationality'. The real issue in Ulster was sovereignty, and doubt on this score together with 'concommitent confusion as to identity and nationality' was a certain recipe for 'chronic instability in any state'. Nevertheless, the document both warned that despite Westminster's treachery 'Ulster is determined to survive as a British entity within or without the Union' and claimed that Ulster's loss would imperil British nationality in the rest of the United Kingdom: 'if Ulster is forced to a secession situation it will mean that Britain has failed the final test of nationhood – the ability to defend its own territory and its own people in its own country'. Accordingly, the loss of Ulster 'could well be followed by the secession of Scotland and Wales and the balkanisation of the British Isles.' (ibid.: 16–17).

While the audience for which this document was constructed largely accounts for its mainland focus, nevertheless, this should not diminish our appreciation of the extent to which anxiety about loss of British identity and nationality permeated the Vanguard movement following the implementation of direct rule. Its publications produced primarily for a domestic Ulster readership likewise pitched their argument in terms of British political values and practice. Vanguard could accept that the problem of their relationship with Britain lay in the fact that their respective values had diverged greatly – 'Both in terms of "permissiveness" and in attitudes to religion, urbanised society in Great Britain is far out of step with Ulster' (Ulster Vanguard, *Ulster – a Nation*, 1972: 10) – but, nevertheless, insisted that the culture and identity of Ulster loyalism was no less 'British' for that and made the case for a renegotiation of Ulster's place within the United Kingdom based on an acceptance in Britain of the validity of Ulster loyalist values (ibid.: 10–15). Moreover, as the following critique of direct rule by the Newtownards Branch of Vanguard demonstrates, the movement was keen to employ the foundation myth of British nationality to legitimize its case:

Long ago English Protestantism lodged its protest against the exercise of arbitrary power as an abuse and violation of law itself. It is Englishmen that have provided Ulstermen with the precedent of their Glorious Revolution against what Ulster now

protests. . . . To uphold that Bill of Rights Ulstermen fought at the siege of Derry
and at the battle of the Boyne. That Bill is part of our constitutional inheritance,
older than and underlying the Government of Ireland Act of 1920.

(Ulster Vanguard (Newtownards Branch) 1972: 1–2)

This was a forceful statement of the Ulster Unionist case claiming
legitimacy based on the Glorious Revolution. However, the identification
of the existing Westminster government with the 'arbitrary power' of 1688
was the point at which Ulster Unionist perspectives would have parted
company with those in Britain. Further, to employ the principles of the
Glorious Revolution to assert the primacy of Ulster regional opinion over
the authority of Westminster was to claim a relationship between centre
and periphery that was not likely to register in the rest of the United
Kingdom.

One of the most worrying and annoying aspects of direct rule for
Unionists was the clear evidence they perceived of Westminster's
'neutrality' between the contending forces in Northern Ireland: a neutrality
which, though of course it was not expressed as such, effectively denied
Ulster Unionists the authentic belonging indicative of true membership of
the British nation. It is against this background that the desire –
impractical but reflecting accurately enough the mindset of many Unionists
– to declare independence from Westminster and establish Northern
Ireland as an independent state owing allegiance only to the crown
(Vanguard (Newtownards Branch) 1972: 2–3) has to be seen. Stormont
had, since 1921, been the institutional means through which their British
identity had been expressed. Its abolition and Unionist exposure to the
depth of mainland British indifference and even hostility to their situation
was bound to bring an anxious reassessment of their national identity in
its wake. Unionist isolation was indicated during the parliamentary
passage of the bill establishing direct rule (Northern Ireland (Temporary
Provisions) Bill). Only eight British Conservative MPs, the most influential
of whom was Enoch Powell, voted against it, together with nine Ulster
Unionists and Bernadette Devlin (Schoen 1977: 107).[1]

Indeed, British public opinion, even before direct rule, had clearly
registered its alienation from the North and its problems. A National
Opinion Poll, taken in Britain in September 1971, for example, showed
that only 42 per cent of respondents wanted to keep Northern Ireland
within the United Kingdom, while 32 per cent wanted it to unite with the
Irish Republic. Moreover, Northern Ireland was considered only the *fourth*
most important national problem, coming after the cost of living,
unemployment and the Common Market. The conclusion of one
commentator that 'public opinion as a whole was shocked by the ferocity
of events in Northern Ireland and receptive to any solution which
promised to rid Britain of a nagging problem which, in the last analysis,
had little to do with life on the British mainland' (ibid.: 106), would seem
to have been representative of British opinion generally. In fact, the
imposition of direct rule, while at one level drawing the North politically
closer to Britain, yet at the same time seemed to increase the percentage of

British opinion wishing Ulster to be united with the South (see ibid.: 107). Perhaps the most effective way to appreciate the shock to the Unionist system that direct rule entailed is to note how it revealed the apparently comprehensive nature of British alienation from Northern Ireland, running right through the sphere of national politics to that of everyday life. Nor, at this time, was there much comfort for Unionists to be had from that traditionally most reassuring symbol of their British nationality, the monarchy. Direct rule was implemented in the middle of the period of British royalty's absence from Northern Ireland, which lasted from 1968 to 1977.

Some idea of the angst experienced by extreme loyalists at this time was conveyed in a statement given by the UDA to the Dublin newspaper, *Sunday World* in June 1973:

We are a hybrid race descended from men who colonised Scotland from Ireland in the fifth century and who then colonised Northern Ireland from Scotland in the seventeenth century. . . . For 400 years we have known nothing but uprising, murder, destruction and repression. We ourselves have repeatedly come to the support of the British Crown only to be betrayed within another twenty years or so by a fresh government of that Crown. What is happening now mirrors similar events in the seventeenth, eighteenth and nineteenth centuries. . . .

Traditionally the English politicians let us down – betrayal we call it. The Catholics try to overwhelm us so we are caught in between the two lines of fire. Second-class Englishmen, half-caste Irishmen. . . . We do not have large funds from over-indulgent sentimentally sick Irishmen in America who send the funds of capitalism to sow the seeds of communism here. We do not have the tacit support of the Government of Southern Ireland and we do not have the support or interest of the British people. . . .

We are a nuisance to our so-called allies and have no friends anywhere. Once more in the history of our people we have our backs to the wall, facing extinction by one way or another.   (quoted in Dillon and Lehane 1973: 281–2)

It was this understanding of the Unionist position that informed Vanguard politics; nevertheless, Vanguard did not reflect a wholly unified ideological response among the various Unionist groups that crystallized following the imposition of direct rule. Besides Vanguard's coalition of paramilitaries and extreme loyalist politicians inclined to independence, there were the Faulknerite Unionists, opposed to any form of independence and keen to restore Stormont within the Union. Again, there were O'Neillite Unionists who had largely joined the pro-Union Alliance Party (Harbison 1973: 174–7); and Paisleyite Unionists, whose leader at this time saw in direct rule the prospects for total integration with Britain (see *Spectator*, 15 April 1972). The divisions between these groups crystallized when the Heath Government produced its White Paper, *Northern Ireland: Constitutional Proposals* (March 1973), which proposed a power-sharing assembly that would have control over the North's internal affairs, apart from law and order issues.

In so far as it affected the question of national identity, the division within Ulster Unionism was between those, like the Faulknerites, whose participation in the power-sharing executive of 1974 with its proposed Council of Ireland showed that they were prepared to accept some form of extra-territorial Irishness as a part of their British identity, and those, mainly lower middle-class and working-class Unionists, who saw Stormont as an expression of their Protestantism – defined in opposition, not only to southern Irishmen and Ulster Catholics, but also to modern secular Britain. It was this conception of identity that informed much of the sentiment for Ulster independence in the 1970s, an issue, which, despite its economic impracticality, continued to be seriously debated. However, the more it was debated the more unlikely did it become as a solution to the Ulster problem.

For example, the notion of Ulster as an independent Protestant home-land was only feasible if Catholics could be expelled from it, and of this there was never any possibility. Indeed, recognizing the enormity of this problem, William Craig suggested that an accommodation might be reached with Catholics and short-lived discussions followed with the Social Democratic and Labour Party (SDLP). The prospects for success, though, were poor and the fact that they were taking place at all provoked division within Vanguard ranks. The fundamental problem, however, lay in how to construct a national myth which both Protestants and Catholics could identify with. As Sarah Nelson acutely observes:

The problem was to decide just what did they share as a basis for this identity? Good will alone could not solve this question. One side's victories were the other's defeats, and the idealised Protestant image they [Vanguard] had themselves proclaimed was supposedly the antithesis of Catholic character. As their pamphlets on a federated British Isles . . . showed, Vanguard members were certainly more willing than other Protestants to contemplate new constitutional forms and relationships but none of the pamphlets really offered any basis for a shared Ulster identity.   (Nelson 1984: 112; see also pp. 108–11)

In other words, the creation of a new Ulster identity designed to meet the psychological needs of both communities would have meant the effective abandonment of the existing Unionist identity; but it was the intensely felt nature of that identity and its value for Unionists that moved them to consider the extreme option of independence in the first place. Moreover, Vanguard, whatever its stated willingness to consider a constitutional break with Westminster, could never quite make the break psychologically. Thus William Craig could participate in a rally at which an effigy of William Whitelaw was burned, on one day, yet urge his followers not to vent their anger against crown forces on another. Likewise the UDA could 'engage in furious battles with the army one day and declare themselves staunch supporters of the army the next' (ibid.: 109).

The period from 1972–4 created conditions of severe shock and alienation of Ulster Unionists from Westminster. If an Ulster independence movement was ever likely to develop substantially within the Unionist community, it should have developed then. However, not only did the Unionist conception of Britishness militate against such a development, but, as has already been noted, unlike the Scots, Welsh and English, the Unionists lacked an authentic myth of ethnic nationality as the basis on which an Ulster nationalism could develop. The realities that this period clarified for the Unionist community were those of rationalizing their relationship with a mainland British population that did not regard them as authentically British, and ensuring that the Union was maintained.

II

Unionists were perplexed by the failure of the population of Britain to sympathize with or understand their position; however, they wished to believe that the strength of their commitment to the Union would remedy this situation and assist them to re-establish the old Stormont system (ibid.: 114). The problem with this view, though, was that the constituency Unionists wished to exist – a mainland population interested in the North and inclined to accept their view of the Ulster problem – did not do so. Those in Britain who were sympathetic to Unionism and whose consciousness of their British national identity was as sharp as theirs were only to be found on the political extremes.

The National Front (NF), for example, actively supported the Vanguard movement from the beginning. It helped to organize Vanguard's major protest in London against direct rule in April 1972, with the NF chairman, John Tyndall, sharing the platform with William Craig (see *Listener*, 28 December 1972; Walker 1977: 159). The NF newspaper, *Spearhead*, ran a special Ulster issue in which Tyndall sought to integrate the Front's particular interests with those of Ulster loyalism as follows:

Ulster Protestants and indeed loyal Ulstermen of all creeds would do well to come to grips with the meaning of the New Papacy. Its capital is not Rome and its purposes are not Christian, but it is today the most important contender for a world monopoly of power. Its financial centre is New York; its forum is the United Nations; it is strangely friendly to the Soviet bloc; its enemy is the survival of national sovereignty, and most of all British national sovereignty. That is why it is attacking Ulster.   (quoted in Walker 1977: 159)

But while Ulster loyalists and the NF might have separate interests, what they had in common was a conspiracy theory outlook, in which the complexity of political issues was simplified to a dichotomy between authentic patriotism (and patriots) and external 'alien' interests. Nigel Fielding has described the mindset of the NF in this respect – and by extension that of northern loyalism – thus:

those who do not subscribe to the belief system, who are outside the conjunctive community, are victims of a false consciousness. . . . all reasonable men must see the truth as we do, and if all men do not see that truth, then they must be obstructed and manipulated. . . . The assumption that the vast bulk of one's fellows are ignorant of . . . reality . . . involves a conscious decision to reject ordinary proof and to dismiss all conflicting data. It is basically an anti-rational stance. The base for an assumption of false consciousness is the assumption of one's own infallibility, an assumption that nothing is what it seems. It is an attitude disturbingly similar to the blind faith of the religious cult member.

(Fielding 1981: 121–2)

The loyalist parallel to the conspiracy theory about the threat to Britain as outlined by Tyndall lay in the readiness of Ulster Unionists to lump together Westminster politicians, the Foreign Office, the Roman Catholic Church and the Irish Government as engaged in a conspiracy to push Ulster out of the United Kingdom. Accordingly, in the 1970s loyalists proved receptive to the NF's propaganda. Indeed, one NF representative was elected unopposed to Castlereagh Council, and while this should not be given undue importance, nevertheless, compared to the rest of the United Kingdom – where the unopposed election of a member of the Front would have been virtually unthinkable – it was significant. That they were not more successful in the North was explained by the Front's spokesmen as being due to the existence of loyalist organizations which drew off possible supporters, just as the Scottish Nationalists were blamed for the failure of the Front to prosper in Scotland, and the fact that Ulster loyalists did not understand the 'immigration problem' (ibid.: 41–2).

At the same time, however, NF support for the gamut of loyalist demands – the restoration of Stormont, the rearming of the RUC, the revival of the 'B' Specials, the death penalty for those convicted of terrorist offences – together with a common and rather archaic, neo-imperialistic perception of Britain's world role (see ibid.: 69–81), allowed them to establish political contacts at a level that would have been unlikely in Britain, contacts including not only Craig's loyalist paramilitaries but Official Unionist MPs such as Rev. Robert Bradford (ibid.: 181–3). And yet, while the NF represented the most enthusiastic supporters of Unionism in Britain at this time, even within this organization there was evidence of the mainland British reluctance to regard the North as a truly authentic part of the national territory. It would seem that concern for Ulster's membership of the British nation existed chiefly among NF activists. Ordinary members exhibited a low level of politization in general and on Ulster – 'the Irish thing' – in particular (ibid.: 154).

III

To a significant extent the nature of the mainland British response to the Ulster problem in the 1970s was determined by the ways in which the media reported the issue. For example, with direct rule, as the British Government became more involved in the routine affairs of the province, the interests of the British press waned to the extent that it was almost on a par with foreign news: 'With the reduction of the Northern Ireland story to quasi-foreign news, Ulster has become another of those far-off countries about which we know little and care less' (Elliott 1978: 146). This, Elliott argues, was inevitable given the British need to have stories which register in the 'public mind'. In Ulster's case, the initial stage of the troubles was one in which considerable mileage could be made from colourful local personalities – Paisley, Bernadette Devlin, Faulkner, etc. – and in which a solution appeared possible. However, as a solution failed to emerge and especially after the British took control, British interest waned to the point where the troubles only registered in Britain if they had a mainland dimension – as in 1974, when, in a three-week period, twelve people were killed in the North and five in the Guildford pub bombings. Two-thirds of the British press's coverage of Ulster-related trouble focused on the violence that happened in England. On the mainland, each incident was likely to lead from the initial disaster to a successful outcome for the forces of law and order, whereas this was not likely in Ulster: it was 'just one damn thing after another' (ibid.: 146).

What was true of the press was also true of the broadcast media. Increasing British involvement in Northern Ireland was accompanied by an ever-decreasing analytic content in British mainland reports. Moreover, the imposition of direct rule removed the institutional bias in broadcast journalism in favour of the 'reformed' Unionist position and, from the London perspective, placed Protestants and Catholics in the same footing. Increasingly, it became easy to define the problem in highly simplistic terms – as consisting of the activities of republican and loyalist extremists – something which encouraged the idea, popular in government circles, that if they could negotiate a 'reasonable' settlement between the region's political parties 'the good sense of the vast majority would prevail, isolating the tiny minority of malcontents'. This was the purpose behind the Sunningdale Agreement of 1974, with its power-sharing executive and Council of Ireland arrangements. The general election of February 1974 and the subsequent Ulster Workers Council (UWC) strike, however, demonstrated that no such silent majority existed(Butler 1991: 111–12). Moreover, the UWC strike, in proving that this was so, also demonstrated that mainland British conceptions of Britishness, emphasizing tolerance, reason and the willingness to compromise, did not apply to Northern Ireland. It was something that did not apparently occur to loyalists but which registered deeply in British political circles. Merlyn Rees would rationalize his inaction during the strike by claiming that he was faced with the emergence of an 'Ulster nationalism' and sought to base his policies as Secretary of State for Northern Ireland on the premise that 'the British could not solve the Irish problem'. This could only be achieved by Ulstermen themselves and they should be encouraged to develop 'a new Ulster identity to include the republicans' rather than continue to foster separate aspirations in both Dublin and London (Rees 1985: 91–3).

Rees was rightly criticized by Edward Heath for using the term 'Ulster nationalism' to describe the identity of Ulster Protestants. Such ideas, as we have seen, did not strike deep roots in the Unionist community. Yet Rees may have been encouraged in this direction by widespread feeling in Britain in the aftermath of the loyalist strike that the time was coming when Britain should disengage from Ulster, a view expressed even by Reginald Maudling (ibid.: 92, 94–5; also Fisk 1975: 225–36). British sentiment in this respect was probably best expressed by Lord Hailsham, who reacted to the strike's success by condemning the loyalists as traitors to the British state (ibid.: 223). And he wrote, as the news of the Executive's collapse emerged:

I hoped that Ulster would develop into a normal democracy, with both communities participating in Government from time to time, the Unionists tending to become a Conservative party based on a prosperous and public-spirited middle-class, and their opponents, based on the interests of the wage-earner, tending to recruit a number of Protestant working-class leaders, and to break the stranglehold on communal hatred and substitute normal and healthy political conflict.

(Hailsham 1975: 242)

The Unionist sense of alienation from British politics in the period 1972–4, however, increased the attractiveness of the idea that regional particularity was the essence of 'Britishness'; that the term need not imply a uniformity of religious, political, cultural and social values across the United Kingdom: 'we're only as different [from the mainland British] as a Geordie is from a Londoner. We're still British' (Nelson 1984: 116). There was much in this. As we have noted, that 'British' be read as implying diversity rather than uniformity has been pointed out by Keith Robbins (1988) with reference to the nineteenth century. However, Robbins's work was confined to the British mainland and regional diversity there existed within the context of a widely-held popular belief that Britain was one authentic national territory and people; a view that did not extend, certainly since the late nineteenth century to any great extent, to Ulster or Ireland generally. Nor was there much comfort forthcoming for loyalists following direct rule from the supreme embodiment of British nationality, the monarchy. Not only were there no royal visits to Ulster in this period, but on the rare occasions when the Queen referred to Northern Ireland the notion of the North as a different region from the rest of the United Kingdom, something that was significant given the traditional function of royal language and ritual in conveying the impression of national homogeneity across the United Kingdom, was clearly conveyed. Certainly the Queen's most significant statement on Northern Ireland, given in her Christmas message of 1972, could only be read as an index of the gulf that existed between the North and the rest of the United Kingdom.

Not only did the political neutrality characteristic of royal speeches fail to convey the impression of a united British nation at war with an alien foe, but so too did the content of her references to the North: 'In the United Kingdom we have our own particular sorrows in Northern Ireland, and I want to send a message of sympathy to all those men, women and children who have suffered and endured so much.' Further, the Queen's praise for the forces of law and order continuing 'their thankless task with the utmost fortitude' could not, given the sectarian atrocities of loyalist paramilitaries in 1972, be seen as a simple endorsement of the Unionist position (see Listener, 28 December 1972).

IV

The period 1974–84 can be seen as one which bridges two phases of extreme turbulence in Ulster's relationship with Britain – the period of violent upheaval, British engagement and constitutional experimentation from 1969–74, and the no less unsettling period since the signing of the Anglo-Irish Agreement in November 1985 to the IRA and loyalist ceasefires of September and October 1994. Yet it was not without significance. Indeed, for our purposes it is highly significant in that it was a time when policies based on the recognition that Northern Ireland was not British in the mainland sense of the term were pursued. It has been argued, in fact, that one reason why the action of the BBC in carrying strike bulletins during the UWC strike was allowed when no such activity was permitted during the General Strike of 1926, was because the 'integrity' of the state was not regarded as being at stake in 1974 (Butler 1991: 112). Moreover, the actions of the main Unionist Parties after the strike, in triumphantly calling for the return of the old Stormont system with majority Protestant rule, emphasized that difference as did the Prevention of Terrorism Act of 1974, with its provisions that effectively made Northern Ireland a place of internal exile for terrorist suspects. This period also saw the intensification of the mode of media representation of Northern Ireland in Britain which presented both sides to the conflict as morally equivalent, with the British security forces neutral between the two and trying to maintain order. In so doing, and by 'counterposing the hellishness of NI to the comparative serenity of British politics and society' (ibid.: 195), both negative (Irish) and positive (British) national stereotypes were reaffirmed; especially so as black propaganda and the effective censorship of potentially damaging media reports on the conflict were also being pursued (see Curtis 1984). But while Nationalists expected nothing less from the British media, this representation was deeply unsettling to Unionists. It brought home to them that, viewed

from Britain, the Protestants of Ulster defy understanding. Their behaviour and attitudes seem antediluvian. Their outlook, in spite of noisesome claims to the contrary, is rudely un-British. Yet they reject Irishness. They are, in other words, hard to make sense of, and therefore difficult to sympathise with or assimilate to the British way of life.   (Butler 1991: 195)

Nor were Unionists particularly well served by the small band of British MPs – especially Enoch Powell – who wholly supported their case.

Powell was drawn to the Unionist cause by a shared conception of the population of the United Kingdom as an imagined national community. He brought to the Unionist cause the same clarity of thought that characterized his politics as a whole. Powell was elected Official Unionist MP for South Down at the general election of October 1974 on the retirement of L.P.S. Orr. He pitched his argument to the constituency's electorate in a rhetoric combining historicist British nationalism with an Ulster focus (see *New Society*, 5 February 1976). Powell was a great catch for the Ulster Unionists following the imposition of direct rule and the alienation from Westminster that it had induced. Under his influence the Unionists' small voting power would be used to maximum effect in a deadlocked House of Commons (ibid.: 22 July 1976) Certainly Powell was regarded as a valuable ally by Ulster Unionists at a time when Edward Heath had refused the Tory whip to loyalist MPs. James Molyneaux's opinion was that Powell was one of the few men capable of stopping Heath in what Molyneaux believes was his intention of destroying Ulster Unionism (Purdy 1989: 28, 82). Jim Prior, however, credited Powell with misleading Molyneaux with the wrongheaded belief that the complete integration of Northern Ireland with the rest of the United Kingdom was possible and that Irish Nationalists and the government of the Irish Republic would simply go away (ibid.: 82–3).

In fact, Powell was not an unmixed blessing for Unionism. His belief in integration was based on the primacy of the will of the Westminster Parliament, something which infuriated many Unionists now highly distrustful of British parties and seeing Powell's stance as being 'in total contradiction to Ulster history'. Indeed, Powell regarded Ulster history as providing a legacy of 'ambiguities inherited from a dead past, which are Ulster's chief peril' and acted on by Ian Paisley whom Powell regarded with particular venom (ibid.: 87–9). Further, Powell's alienation from the leadership of the Tory Party was largely responsible for preventing a rapprochement between it and the Ulster Unionists (New Society, 22 July 1976). Even the most important achievement of the Unionist integrationist project in this period – the concession of increased parliamentary seats for Northern Ireland, from twelve to seventeen – could only be truly seen as advancing integration if the will for it had existed at Westminster, and this was not the case. In fact, by the time the Labour Government had conceded the extra seats it had also implemented its 'Ulsterization' policy of placing the police and the Ulster Defence Regiment at the forefront of the campaign against the Provisional IRA and had put the onus of finding a solution to the Ulster problem on the shoulders of local politicians.

Indeed, 'Ulsterization' was even reflected in British media coverage of Northern Ireland. Local media outlets could reflect the complexity of the problem while British audiences were treated to the reinforcement of the national stereotypes noted above (Butler 1991: 114–15). But not only did the British failure to explore the complexity of the problem reinforce stereotypes, when the PIRA took its bombing campaign to Britain in 1974 the effect was to solidify and mobilize mainland opinion against the 'external' Irish threat (New Society, 25 November 1976. There were, of course, elements in mainland British society that supported one side or another in the Ulster conflict, especially loyalists in Scotland. But Scotland had never constituted a major element in the popular conception of British national identity, which was overwhelmingly English-centred, and Scottish loyalists had no desire to extend the Ulster conflict to Scotland. Again, the PIRA did not embark on a bombing campaign in Scotland, but confined their activities to England (see Bruce 1985: 170–81). In England there was, as we have noted, support for Ulster loyalism from the NF but that movement's political weakness made its support of doubtful value. In any event, the largest loyalist group the UDA, was, in the post-1974 period, in the process of radically re-thinking the whole question of Ulster's identity.

V

This reassessment of Ulster's identity was based on the realization, and acceptance of the fact, that Ulster Unionists were not regarded as authentic members of the British national community, the belief that Ulster Catholics were, as regards the South, in a similar position, and that the different conditions attached by the two communities to the re-establishment of devolved government in Ulster made political progress on that basis almost impossible. The solution, put forward initially as the personal view of Glen Barr, a leading UDA member involved in the UWC strike, lay in the forging of an Ulster identity that would include both Catholics and Protestants and would entail the abandonment of the traditional aspirations of Unionism and Nationalism: 'Ulstermen would not be second class Englishmen or second class Irishmen, as they have been until now. They would be first class Ulstermen'. Barr accepted that his ideas would be difficult to sell to both communities, but thought it possible if support was forthcoming from Westminster, Dublin and, not least, the European Economic Community (EEC). Support from the last would be essential to secure the economic viability of the new Ulster state ('Glen Barr's Ulster', *Fortnight*, 12 September 1975). This was an idea, however, that the Scottish Nationalists would employ to better effect than the UDA.

Barr's ideas were part of a general discussion on options facing Ulster at a time when devolution for Scotland and Wales was being widely debated, together with their identities and those of the various English regions (see *Fortnight*, 19 November 1976); and when it seemed that Britain would get out of Ulster as soon as it decently could (ibid.: 12 September 1975). But while Barr's discussion of Ulster independence was more considered than that of Vanguard, it failed to address the fundamental problem of how to invent an identity which both communities could willingly embrace, a problem which Sarah Nelson succinctly described (see p. 195). Moreover, the independence proposal now came under more sustained criticism. Tom Hadden, for example, argued that an Ulster identity was essentially negative: 'To be an Ulsterman is to be specifically non-Irish' (ibid.: 26 September 1975). Other commentators focused on the close similarity between the loyalist mentality and that of the NF: both needed scapegoats to blame for the problems they faced, and just as the Jews and the black community in Britain performed this role for the NF, the Catholic community performed it for extreme loyalists in Ulster (see Bell 1976: Ch. 4). Indeed, the mutilation that Catholic victims of loyalist murder squads were subjected to suggest that Catholics were regarded as *untermenschen*: 'The tortures, the terrible abuse of the victims, sprang from a desire to degrade and humiliate that is typical of racist attitudes to an "inferior" group. As is common, this desire is strongest among the poorer elements of the dominant group.' (Holland 1981: 107–8).

At the same time, circumstances can arise when extreme loyalist attitudes permeate the Protestant community as a whole. Patrick Shea, for example, records the extent of middle- and upper-class support for the UWC strike: 'it was astonishing that so many apparently intelligent, educated people could, in the presence of open anarchy, feel anything but fearful concern for the future of their community.' In this context, Shea recognized 'that centuries of privileged treatment created in Ireland a governing class of which . . . the Northern Ireland Unionists remain the residue; a possessive, unbending remnant of a powerful ruling class.' (Shea 1981: 200–201). Similarly, Padraig O'Malley's assessment of Official Unionism was that anti-Catholicism was such a prominent element of it that it both constituted an effective bar to Unionists regarding Catholics as equals and 'acknowledging any dimension of the [Ulster] problem but their own.' (O'Malley 1983: 144–5). Thus one of the most fundamental conditions for the invention and promotion of a common national identity in Northern Ireland did not exist – the belief that all the people of the region constituted one 'horizontal' community with fundamental interests in common that overrode their differences. Indeed, it is worth noting that there is nothing in UDA discussions of Ulster independence in this period to suggest that Catholics would have been accepted as equal partners in government.

But as important in deterring the development of Ulster nationalism was the reluctance of Unionists to accept that their membership of the United Kingdom was under serious and immediate threat. Unionists could not but be aware of the lack of interest in Northern Ireland on the part of the population of Britain, but denied that its verdict should be the basis on which their membership of the British state be judged. When James Molyneaux was asked this question he replied that the English would not be sufficiently interested to vote: 'if you have a referendum you can depend on it that the three, four or five million people in England of Irish descent are going to come out and vote while the ordinary Englishman is not going to come out and vote on the future of what he sees as an obscure province of the U.K. . . . So it is bound to go against us.' (ibid.: 143). Molyneaux much preferred to blame what demand there was for reunification in Britain on Foreign Office intrigue that misled the Prime Minister and Northern Ireland Secretaries of State on the Ulster problem (ibid.: 159–65). Even Harold McCusker, who willingly accepted that 'the British want out', and, significantly, based his view on a recognition that the Ulster Unionists were seen in Britain as not conforming to the British national stereotype and way of life based on reasonableness, moderation and a willingness to compromise (ibid.: 152), yet preferred to believe that Ulster's membership was presently safe because 'it served British interests', while 'expulsion' might prove more troublesome than the present position (ibid.: 157–8). The only Unionist leader to occasionally call for a referendum in Britain on the North's membership of the Kingdom and to accept an independent Ulster as the result of a negative decision, was Ian

Paisley (ibid.: 143). These calls, however, were very occasional, which left the UDA as the only significant loyalist organization consistently promoting Ulster nationalism and independence; and an attempt was made to address the major problem at the heart of the project, the promotion of an 'authentic' Ulster identity. In particular, an attempt was made to create a historical basis for this in the works of Ian Adamson.[2]

Adamson argued that the 'Cruithin', the ancient inhabitants of Ireland, were driven north by invading Gaels and their last foothold was in present-day Down and Antrim. Many, however, fled to Scotland, strengthening the link between the Scottish and Irish populations; and seen in this context, the Ulster plantation of the seventeenth century represents, not the alien status of a people lacking authentic roots, but a homecoming (see McAulay 1991: 55–6). At the centre of this loyalist vision of Ulster ethnicity was the legend of Cuchullain and the mythic events of the Tain, in which an invasion of Ulster by the King and Queen of Connaught was resisted single-handedly by Cuchullain. For Adamson, the republican monopoly of Cuchullain is a reflection of the Gaelic domination in Irish language and culture; a domination which has disguised 'the long cruel extermination of the population and culture of the ancient kindred of the Ulster people' (Adamson, *The Cruithin*, p. 15, quoted in ibid.: 56)

The recourse to ancient Ulster history by Unionists was, as we have seen (Ch. 7), nothing new: Cuchullain was the logo of Northern Ireland Tourist Board literature in the 1950s. However, the difference between the 1950s and the 1970s was that whereas in the former period Unionists sought to establish an Ulster ethnic identity to *build on* the security of their constitutional position within the United Kingdom – to establish their Britishness on a basis similar to that of Scotland and Wales – in the 1970s the UDA's objective was to build an identity that could be the basis for an Ulster national group *outside* the Kingdom. Nevertheless, little success attended UDA efforts. While an instinctual Ulster identity, shaped by family and communal experience, permeated working-class loyalism it was unlikely that this constituency would make the sustained effort necessary to develop a new national identity. As we have noted in the course of this study, the primary function of myth is to explain and give meaning to the existing circumstances within which the Unionist community exists and the realities it has to contend with. The intention of the UDA, in creating a new myth as the basis for the development of other, unfamiliar and problematic political circumstances to that which currently existed, was to invert the relationship that usually existed between myth and circumstance – and was thus highly unlikely to be successful. Moreover, there existed, in the Orange Order, an organization deeply embedded in the working-class Protestant community whose role was to inculcate the community with the traditional plantation myth and an imperialistic form of Britishness, and which constituted a virtually insuperable obstacle for the UDA to overcome. To this it can be added that, however strong loyalist paramilitary organizations were in working-class communities, those same communities proved very reluctant to vote for paramilitaries when they entered the orthodox political arena. All this of course assumes that the

UDA was united in support of the Ulster nationalist project outlined by Glen Barr. In fact, this was hardly the case (see Bruce 1994: 101–7).

The most obvious weakness in the UDA's approach to Ulster nationalism lay in the contradiction between ideology and practice. It was essential to the success of the Ulster nationalist project that the Catholic community be persuaded to accept it. However, at the same time as it was appealing to Catholics on this score it was also waging a sectarian murder campaign against Catholics. Thus, by 1977, three years after independence was first seriously mooted, it was clear that it would not attract any significant support from either the Protestant or Catholic communities, though the UDA would continue to promote it.

However, one important question, it was noted, that was not widely discussed in reference to independence was whether the new independent Ulster would be a monarchy or a republic: 'There was no problem over a bill of rights which would guarantee everyone's right to argue for whatever constitutional system they liked. Whether some form of connection with the British monarchy could be so easily disposed of was apparently more doubtful.' (*Fortnight*, 12 September 1975). There was much point to this comment. The monarchy, as the supreme embodiment of British national identity, was deeply embedded in the Unionist consciousness. In fact, this realization appears to have persuaded the UDA to opt for independence within 'the EEC and the Commonwealth' (see O'Malley 1983: 332–3). But of more import for the UDA's independence hopes, the Queen's Silver Jubilee visit to Northern Ireland in August 1977 was seen as marking the end of a period when it was widely believed that Westminster had been seriously considering withdrawal from the province:

The real reason for the visit . . . was to emphasise that the exercise in British disengagement from Northern Ireland which Whitehall toyed with from 1972 to 1975 was over. The Queen had to come to complete the process of persuading the Provisionals that there is no point in fighting on.

('Why the Queen had to Come', *Fortnight*, August 1977)

VI

Given that eleven years had elapsed since the last visit of the Queen to Ulster, it was inevitable that this visit – coming between the annual commemoration of internment and the Apprentice Boys march in Derry, and involving 32,000 police and troops in 'Operation Monarch' – would carry enormous political import. As expected, it was greeted with a bombing reception by the Provisionals – one, indeed, planted at the New University of Ulster at Coleraine where the Queen was to make her only important speech of the visit and which was deeply embarrassing given the strict security surrounding the campus. Moreover, the Social Democratic and Labour Party boycotted the visit while Nationalists in the North organized protest marches and counter-celebrations (*The Times*, 8–10 August 1977).

Yet Unionists no less than Nationalists were keen to make political capital out of the visit. Nationalist opposition to the visit, for example, was read as indicating the unworkability of any power-sharing arrangement. Under minority rule, it was argued, there would be no royal visits to the North: 'The hostility by a section of the minority has indicated to the United Kingdom as a whole just what the future attitude would be under power-sharing.' (*Londonderry Sentinel*, 10 August 1977). William Ross, the Westminster MP for South Londonderry, declared that the Queen's morale-boosting visit was the personal action of a sovereign who recognized the need for her presence in Ulster, and had given back to the loyal people of the province the sense of being part of the United Kingdom (ibid.: 17 August 1977).

Certainly it would seem that indications were sent out by the Queen of her support for the Unionist people. Nationalists detected a 'particular emphasis' on 'Northern Ireland' in the claim to sovereignty made by the Queen during the ritual opening of Parliament (*Derry Journal*, 12 August 1977). And during her speech at the New University of Ulster she invoked the idea of a world community concerned about Ulster's troubles, and especially the British population on the mainland:

The sufferings here have invoked sympathy and concern throughout the world, and *nowhere more than in the rest of the United Kingdom. To see such a conflict taking place within our own country* [my italics] emphasises the clear and continuing responsibility for us all to bring back peace and stability to this community.   (*The Times*, 12 August 1977)

This speech was noteworthy. It expressed the most pro-Unionist sentiments the Queen had uttered in many years. In particular, the monarch's assurance that the rest of the United Kingdom was actively concerned about the plight of the Unionist community would have been especially welcome, expressing, as it did, what Unionists wished to believe, though opinion poll evidence suggested otherwise. Indeed, it would seem that the major concern of the British people during the visit was the safety of the Queen rather than the plight of the Ulster Unionists. As the Labour MP, Maureen Colquohoun warned the Prime Minister, James Callaghan: 'the British people would never forgive you if anything happened to her' (*The Times*, 9 August 1977). Moreover, the point of the visit – demonstrating that Northern Ireland was an integral part of the United Kingdom – was undermined by the precautions it was found necessary to take during the visit. For instance, the great difference between the Ulster tour and the rest of the Queen's 'extensive jubilee programme' was illustrated by Stormont Castle's advice that 'members of the public not invited to the official functions [should] keep well away from the venues' (ibid.: 9 August 1977). Relatedly, it was noted that parts of the province appeared 'to be virtually under martial law' (ibid.: 11 August 1977). Thus there was much truth in the claim that 'the presence of the Queen, which has done so much to emphasise unity during jubilee celebrations in every other part of Britain, has shown up the divisions in Northern Ireland society.' (ibid.).

Ulster Unionists, however, while undoubtedly aware that this was so, would have preferred to ignore it and focus instead on the sentiments expressed by the Queen; sentiments, indeed, that the Queen was to express even more explicitly in references to the Ulster visit made during her Christmas broadcast some months later. Her opinion that *'people of goodwill in Northern Ireland* [my italics] were greatly heartened by the chance they had to share the celebrations with the rest of the nation and Commonwealth' (*Voices Out of the Air: the Royal Christmas Broadcasts 1932–1981*, intro. Tom Fleming 1981: 145) was exactly how Unionists viewed the Jubilee visit. By the same token, however, her effective identification of 'people of goodwill' with the Unionist community reflected a striking inability to understand the viewpoint, or respect the traditions of, Ulster Nationalists. But the Queen's outlook on Ulster was also like that of the Unionists in the evident desire to ignore the fact that this outlook was not shared by the population of Britain, which tended to see the Ulster problem as an 'Irish' problem. It is worth noting in this respect that two of the most significant royal books prompted by the Jubilee (Lacey 1977; Ziegler 1978) made no mention of the Queen's connection with, or visit to, Northern Ireland. Yet the Jubilee visit to the North had an importance that transcended the occasion itself. Preceded by the visits of the Duke of Gloucester and Princess Anne in February and March 1977, it re-established the practice of royal visits to the province after an absence of nine years. There would be twenty further visits to the North by members of the royal family between 1977 and 1985 (information supplied by the Northern Ireland Office, Information Service, 16 September 1993); and, significantly, they would not be deterred by the killing of Lord Mountbatten in 1979. Further, with the revitalizing of the royal connection with the North under way in the late 1970s there was also, at the more specifically political level, the election to office of Margaret Thatcher, a Prime Minister with more sharply defined British nationalist instincts than any since Bonar Law.

VII

On the face of it, Margaret Thatcher's election was an unalloyed joy for Ulster Unionists. She shared with them a conception of British identity located in the imperial glories of the past and also Protestantism 'of a type which scarcely comprehended Catholicism'. Accordingly, she had no 'natural sympathy for a Catholic minority living in an otherwise oppressively Catholic island' (Young 1990: 464–5). Indeed, when, in 1980, Thatcher formed and chaired a small Cabinet committee to consider the implications of Prince Charles marrying a Catholic, something that then seemed possible, Thatcher gave vent to an 'extreme anti-Catholicism' (ibid.: note 22: 570). Relatedly, Thatcher was 'instructed in the Orange perspective' by influential friends and mentors such as Airey Neave – murdered in 1979 by the Irish National Liberation Army – and Enoch

Powell (ibid.: 465). Certainly, Thatcher acknowledged a close similarity in outlook between herself and the Unionist community.

> My own instincts are profoundly Unionist. . . . I knew that these people shared many of my own attitudes, derived from my own staunchly Methodist background. Their warmth was as genuine as it was usually undemonstrative. Their patriotism was real and fervent, even if too narrow. . . . From my visits to Northern Ireland, often after terrible tragedies, I came to have the greatest admiration in particular for the way in which the little rural Protestant communities would come together, looking after one another, after some terrible loss. But, then, any Conservative should in his bones be a Unionist too.   (Thatcher 1993: 385)

There were other similarities. A self-proclaimed 'conviction' politician, Thatcher's often abrasive political style – quite at odds with the traditional political etiquette of compromise in British politics – resonated well with Ulster Unionist politicians, as did her Union Jack waving patriotism and anti-permissive moralizing (Gaffikin and Morrissey 1990: 35–6). Indeed, it is worth noting that Thatcher's national chauvinism enabled the Tories to capture the race and immigration issues from the NF at the general election of 1979 (see *New Statesman*, 11 May 1979).

In the early years of her premiership Thatcher appeared to be acting very much as Unionists would have wished. While the killing of Airey Neave led to the collapse of a plan apparently agreed by Neave, Thatcher and Molyneaux to pursue the latter's integrationist agenda with administrative devolution for the North on a regional council model; and while Molyneaux boycotted Humphrey Atkins's conference on the government of Northern Ireland (Purdy 1989: 75–7), Thatcher's inflexible stand during the hunger strikes of 1980–81 – during which she declared that Northern Ireland was 'as British as Finchley' – (O'Leary and McGarry 1993: 284) – and her opposition to Jim Prior's 'rolling devolution' scheme in 1982 (Young 1990: 465–8), were encouraging to Unionists. And they were further encouraged by Thatcher's alienation from Charles Haughey and the Irish Republic following Haughey's refusal to support European Community sanctions against Argentina on the outbreak of the Falklands War (ibid.: 468). Indeed, what was to make the shock of Unionists at the signing of the Anglo-Irish Agreement in November 1985 so intense was the evidence of Thatcher's concern to defend British sovereignty during the Falklands War, and which they read as an indicator of her attitude to Northern Ireland. Ulster Unionist reactions to the Falklands conflict, David Trimble affirms, were at one with the people of Britain (interview with author, 19 July 1993).

Patriotism, or chauvinistic nationalism, pervaded the Labour Party no less than the Tories. Both, Anthony Barnett argues, were motivated by anxieties about British 'standing' in the world (Barnett 1982: 20–21). Moreover, if there was any danger of the Falklands crisis having only an implied and understated relevance to the Ulster problem, this danger was averted by Enoch Powell, who performed the role envisioned for him by Ulster Unionists by explicitly spelling out its lessons for the Government's policy on the North – especially the folly of Prior's devolution proposal – which Powell argued was designed as part of a long-term conspiracy to put Northern Ireland into an all-Ireland state (ibid.: 35–6). Barnett describes the connection between Powell's Ulster statements and the Falklands as follows:

Powell feared that London was beginning to consider the abandonment of Ulster. There too, a majority of the population wishes to remain 'British'. As every politician or journalist who has listened to Ian Paisley knows, those who follow his Orangeman's pipe and drum are Irish. Yet the Protestant Irish say they are British, and they fly the Union Jack with a fervid passion that can only be found in such places as Gibraltar and . . . the Falklands. . . . a central aspect of British politics is associated with the 'right' of the Falklanders to stay governed by the Crown. They do not seek self-determination and their land is claimed by another state – Argentina – just as the Irish Republic claims the North. Give way in the South Atlantic, and the position of Ulstermen becomes more precarious. The integrity of the nation itself – the United Kingdom of Great Britain and Northern Ireland – might be threatened. Thus on the British side the Falklands War had an Orange pigmentation that the rest of the world largely failed to perceive.   (ibid.: 36)

Barnett, moreover, notes how, for Thatcher, the war invested the idea of the United Kingdom with an 'expansionist assertion of nationalism, revealed by her claim that she had put the "'Great' back in Britain"' (ibid.: 87). Further, he effectively identifies the ability of chauvinistic nationalism to obliterate the distinctions between the Falklanders and United Kingdom nationals: 'The islanders are pressed into the opportunity to "replenish" the "national will" . . . the islanders themselves are us and *ours*: part of our "Island Race"' (ibid.: 97–8) – a development that could only be reassuring to Ulster Unionists given the insecurity associated with their own geographical detachment from the British mainland.

There was, however, a characteristic of the Falklands that was important in explaining the ease with which they could be regarded in Britain as authentically British: pastoralism. Drawing on Martin Wiener's *English Culture and the Decline of the Industrial Spirit 1850–1980* (1987), Barnett notes the 'immensely powerful cultural force' of the ideal of 'the countryside' in Britain:

This reflection might seen of slight relevance to an analysis of the Falklands Crisis; in fact, it helps explain the strange social empathy with such a distant part of the world. The joining together of support for the [Falklands] Armada from distinct, and even antagonistic, sectors of the population was partially shaped by shared, historic attitudes of nostalgia towards an 'empty' countryside. . . . By contrast, had the population of the islands been engaged in a company mineworks, the evidently industrial nature of their settlement might not have been so accommodating to mythologization . . . it was the very blighted quality of the rural setting that made the Falklands seem so 'organic' and 'noble'. . . . The solitary life of the . . . [Falklands] seemed to have . . . a kind of ultimate authenticity.

Moreover, 'Falklands Pastoralism' gained enhanced resonance in Britain, argues Barnett, due to an established tradition, drawn from the experience of the First World War, which combined 'the intense ruralism of English culture' with military conflict (Barnett 1982: 102–3).

It was at this point, however, that the relevance of the Falklands conflict as an indicator of British attitudes to Northern Ireland broke down. At the level of cultural identity, for example, it was not easy to identify pastoralism as a common bond between the North and Britain. Despite the fact that Northern Ireland was predominantly rural, the dominant image of the area is an industrial one centred on Belfast. But more importantly, the population of the Falklands, while small, was yet ethnically British and homogeneous, unlike the North with its national divisions, conflict over which since 1969 had indelibly imprinted on British opinion the perception of the problem as an 'Irish' one. Again, the Falklands conflict arose over a specific act of aggression – the invasion of the islands by a military dictatorship. Accordingly, the parameters of right and wrong were – especially if the history of British colonization of the islands was ignored – easily drawn and maintained. By contrast, the nature of the Ulster problem denied any such simple explanation. The Dublin and London governments agreed on facilitating a solution to the problem; and, as the Anglo-Irish Agreement (AIA) would recognize, the existence of the nationalist minority – some 40–42 per cent of the population – gave the Irish Republic some claim to influence on the administration of the province. Thus, while London governments maintain that Northern Ireland will retain its membership of the United Kingdom so long as *a* majority of its people wish it, they have usually declined to employ the language of British patriotism – e.g., defence of 'national sovereignty' and 'the British way of life' – in describing their role in the province.

It is noteworthy that even Thatcher, despite her 'Finchley' statement and for all her Unionism, made the distinction between Northern Ireland and the 'authentic' national territory. For example, while, in the course of her first lecture to commemorate Airey Neave, killed by the INLA, on 3 March 1980, she acknowledged 'the endurance of Ulster men and women, in the face of danger', she nevertheless made the distinction between Ulster and 'the homeland of Britain', where the IRA 'have met a united response from a nation which has shown . . . that, when faced by a clearly identifiable menace, it can respond with wisdom and fortitude' (Thatcher 1986: 61). Thus for Margaret Thatcher, no less than her predecessors, Northern Ireland was a place apart from the authentic national homeland of Britain. This point was elaborated in Thatcher's memoirs when she wrote: 'what *British* [my italics] politician will ever fully understand Northern Ireland? I suspect that even the most passionate English supporters of Ulster do so less than they imagine.' (Thatcher 1993: 385). And the point is further clarified by the fact that in 1981 she considered 'redrawing the existing border' (ibid.: 398) – in effect, ceding some strongly republican areas in the west and south of Northern Ireland to the Irish Republic.

Such speculations, of course, were private and did not enter the public domain to disturb Ulster Unionists highly impressed by her uncompromising stance on the hunger strikes and her defence of the Falklands. For a community whose experience of the troubles since 1969 had enhanced their sense of Britishness (see Moxon-Browne 1991: 25), Thatcher seemed a reliable guarantor of their constitutional position. The need for certainty on this score, it can be argued, increased in the 1980s as a result of disquieting population trends in Northern Ireland. Evidence drawn from the 1981 census, for example, showed that Protestants were emigrating from the North in higher numbers than Roman Catholics ('The Biggest Irish Exodus Since the Famine', *Listener*, 25 November 1982). Further, beginning in 1981 and reaffirmed periodically throughout the 1980s, was opinion poll evidence showing that most people on the mainland wanted Britain out of Northern Ireland (see *Guardian*, 12 August 1989). Again, and at the party political level, there was the disturbing change in the Labour Party's Northern Ireland policy, which broke with the bi-partisanship hitherto pursued and opted for unity by consent – a policy change resulting from the hunger strikes controversy (see Bell 1982: 147). To these developments can be added others which highlighted the apparently ever-increasing divergence of interest between the Ulster Unionist community and the population of Britain. One such was the Pope's visit to Britain in 1982. The success of the visit, coming at a time when Britain was at war with a Catholic power, served to illustrate the marginality of popular Protestantism in British life (for informed coverage see *The Times*, 15 May–6 June 1982). A protest of 300 funda-mentalists led by Dr Ian Paisley was easily contained by police when the Pope visited Liverpool, while protests against the visit in Wales were peaceful (ibid.: 31 May 1982). But the crucial test came in Scotland, where extreme Protestants had prophesied great disturbances if the visit went ahead; and here the Protestant dog failed to bark in any effective way (see Bruce 1985: Ch. 9). Indeed, it is indicative of the marginality of sectarianism in Scottish life at this time that anti-Catholic views expressed by the President of the Scottish National Party, William Wolfe, effectively ended his political career (ibid.: 8 May 1982).

In a context in which so many developments had occurred that Ulster Unionists could only regard with disquiet, Thatcher appeared as a pillar of strength in the Unionist interest. And yet, it was because of their confi-dence in Thatcher's Unionist credentials, together with a misplaced reliance on important mediators of the Unionist interest with the Conservative Party such as Enoch Powell, that the Anglo-Irish Agreement came as such a shock to Unionists.

Notes

1. It was indicative of the historically-based suspicions of Westminster entertained by Unionists that significance was placed on the fact that John Redmond, a Tory MP and descendant of the Irish Home Rule leader, congratulated William Whitelaw on his work in Northern Ireland and expressed his interest in Irish nationalism (Ulster Vanguard (Newtownards Branch), *Government Without Right* 1972: 2).
2. The most significant of these are *The Cruithin* (1974); *The Identity of Ulster* (1982).

10

A QUESTION OF NATIONAL INTEGRITY: ULSTER AND BRITISH IDENTITY 1985–94

The period from November 1985 to September 1994 was, for Ulster Unionists, largely one of perceived maximum threat to their constitutional position and national identity; a threat reflected, especially among loyalist paramilitaries, in a rejection of 'Irishness' and the identification of a 'pan-nationalist alliance' to justify a murder campaign against the Catholic community in general. The ending of the IRA's 'military operations', however, was to provide some indication of how changing political circumstances could modify attitudes to identity.

I

The sense of betrayal felt by Unionists at the signing of the Anglo-Irish Agreement (AIA) was probably most intensely felt by the Ulster Unionist Party Leader, James Molyneaux, who was old enough to have fought for the United Kingdom during World War Two:

There was a great feeling of bitterness on my part because even though I tried to divorce myself from what small sacrifices I might have made during war-time, I could not help but remember dozens of close friends who had been killed. . . . You said to yourself, 'Well, this is the reward isn't it?' (Purdy 1989: 14)

However, for both Molyneaux and the Ulster Unionist Party leadership generally, their sense of betrayal was all the more acute because of assurances given them by trusted English supporters such as Enoch Powell and Norman Tebbitt (David Trimble, interview with author, 17 July 1993), and undoubtedly others among the twenty-one Tory MPs who voted with them against it, that the AIA would make no change in the Unionist position. For the wider Unionist community that lacked these contacts, the abruptness of the AIA's emergence, together with the extent of British 'treachery', proved scarcely less unsettling. As seen by Unionists, the constitutional guarantee for the majority community in Ulster contained in clause one of the Agreement was substantially nullified by the determination expressed in clause two, that 'all efforts' would be made to find agreement between the London and Dublin governments on the administration of the North. Moreover, the crisis in Unionist relations with Westminster that followed the AIA only served to intensify their angst and isolation.

The policy of refusing to negotiate until the Agreement was got rid of, combined with intimidatory strikes and attacks on Catholics and the RUC, only reinforced British perceptions of northern Protestants as alien and un-British. Just how little impact their protests made in Britain was reflected both in the performance of Boyd Black, who stood as a Unionist candidate in the Fulham by-election of April 1986 and who secured fewer votes than 'Lord Sutch' of the Monster Raving Loony Party, and in the abysmal failure of the proposed 'mass meetings' in Britain to oppose the Agreement – the first in Liverpool attracted under 100 people (O'Leary and McGarry 1993: 253).[1] Relatedly, the Friends of the Union group of Tory MPs, set up by some leading Conservatives to direct the opposition campaign in Britain, have had little influence either on élite or popular opinion (ibid.). The indifference of British public opinion to the Ulster problem in general was reflected in a number of opinion poll findings which, over the period 1986–93, indicated increasing distance and alienation.[2] Further, and most seriously for Unionists in this respect, their traditional Tory support was greatly diminished: only 23 per cent of Tory supporters favoured retaining Northern Ireland (Guardian, 11 November 1993). This development was reflected even more clearly within the Tory Party in Parliament. In the twenty years since the abolition of Stormont the more squirearchial members from Northern Ireland who had served in Tory administrations had been replaced – with the exception of Enoch Powell – by MPs with deep roots in local Unionist politics. Further, of the twenty-one Tories who opposed the AIA in a Commons vote in 1985, only eleven were still in Parliament in November 1993; and of them one was a whip, another Deputy Speaker, leaving only nine, of whom the most prominent is Nicholas Budgeon (The Times, 24 November 1993). The comment that if the IRA thought that by killing Ian Gow they were striking a blow at British Unionism their intention was misguided, as the animal was already dead ('Heart of the Union', New Statesman and Society, 3 August 1990), exaggerated only slightly. Accordingly, as the band of leading British Tory Unionists diminished, only a relatively small number of rank-and-file activists, together with the Neofascist Right, remained to give unqualified support for Ulster's membership of the British nation. The latter's view that the reason why 'British public opinion . . . has no heart for the maintenance of the Union' is because it is 'hopelessly misdirected and confused' due to a reliance on a media controlled by 'people who do not want Britain to survive as a nation.' (Tyndall 1988: 441), was one that many Unionists heartily agreed with.[3]

The emergence of Conservative Associations in Northern Ireland in 1988–9 and the decision of the Conservative Party to support this development at its Party Conference of 1989 (Conservative Political Centre (Discussion Programme), Ulster: Politics and Security, July/August 1990), was very much an activist rather than a leadership initiated development. That the most prominent spokesman of the Ulster Conservatives, Dr Laurence Kennedy, resigned his seat on North Down Council in July 1993 disillusioned at a lack of support from the Northern Ireland office and the Prime Minister, John Major (*News Letter*, 28 July 1993), is not surprising. Shock at the Shankill bombing of October 1993 could move Sir Patrick Mayhew to declare of Northern Ireland: 'this is not the Gaza Strip, but a part of our democracy, a part of *our own country* [my italics]' (BBC, Radio Ulster News, 23 October 1993). However, the real sentiment of the Conservative leadership on Ulster's membership of the British nation was reflected by the decision taken at the Party Conference of October 1993 not to debate the integration issue, despite the fact that thirty-one pro-integration motions were presented (*News Letter*, 4 October 1993). Moreover, despite the political compact agreed between the Tory and Ulster Unionist Parties, the extent of the substantive concessions to Unionists this has entailed is a Select Committee for Northern Ireland Affairs (*Belfast Telegraph*, 27 July 1993; *Guardian*, 21 July 1993). Despite his standing 'four square for the Union', Major went no further in securing Northern Ireland's place within it than affirming the traditional position of British Parties that the Union is secure only so long as there is a majority for it in the province.

However, for most Unionists the AIA stood, and stands, as a blatant contradiction of such assurances. Such was the fury of their initial reaction to it that they even considered that an existence for Northern Ireland outside the United Kingdom might be preferable to life under it. When the 'Task Force', consisting of Harold McCusker, Peter Robinson and Frank Miller, and intended to produce ideas on alternatives to the Agreement, made its report – based on consultations with all sections of Unionist opinion – along with specific proposals went the warning that any failure of negotiations 'would leave the Unionist leadership no alternative but to seek an entirely new base for Northern Ireland outside the present constitutional framework.' But the team 'offered no promise or definite suggestion as to what the alternative might be.' (Purdy 1989: 158–9).

The threat to seek an existence for Northern Ireland outside the United Kingdom can be put down to pique and seen as an ill-thought-out attempt to pressurize Westminster (see the sharp criticism of this suggestion in Aughey 1989: 177–81). Certainly the failure to articulate what an existence outside the United Kingdom would entail would suggest, rhetoric apart, a private acceptance that this was simply not a realistic option. There is simply no other option for Unionists than to make the best of their present constitutional position; and this can involve some rationaliz-ation. For example, while Unionist leaders acknowledge the findings of recent opinion polls in Britain which demonstrate increasing alienation from the North, they nevertheless display a desire to undermine their validity, by suggesting that many people interviewed by pollsters in Britain are, like Kevin MacNamara, from the Irish Republic and have retained their Irishness. Further, the British media is blamed for disinforming the

British people about Ulster, many of whom are 'very much with us'; something, indeed, that was enhanced by the IRA campaign, which led more people to become informed about the nature of the problem than would otherwise have been the case (interview, David Trimble, 19 July 1993; Rev. Martin Smyth, 9 August 1993. Dr Paisley expressed a similar view, 31 August 1993).

There is also the belief that Ulster Unionists share an everyday culture with the people of Britain; that in the sense of a nation in Benedict Anderson's term as an 'imagined community', Unionists share a common fund of values and outlook with people in Britain, faulted only on the British side by a desire on the part of 'the dominant element in London' to sacrifice Ulster in what they see as their interests (Paisley, ibid.). Significantly, Dr Paisley, while accepting that the people of Britain no longer appear to subscribe to Protestantism as an element of British identity in the way that they once did, nevertheless takes the view that this, in itself, is not of great significance, as under the surface of everyday life there is a common bond of fundamental Protestant values that unite Ulster Protestants and people on the mainland; and that if, for example, the Williamite Settlement was tampered with those values would be given expression explicitly in Britain (Paisley interview, 31 August 1993).

It is also worth pointing out in this context that the Unionist reaction to their predicament since 1969 is not regarded as exceptional; that any other population group in the United Kingdom, especially the Scots, would react in exactly the same way that they have if placed in the same position. Accordingly, and with reference to the idea of 'conditional loyalty' – something that is usually only discussed in relation to Ulster Unionism – the point is made that its applicability to Ulster is not unique: it was 'representative of the entire institutions of the state and the relationship of people to them' – a point illustrated by reference to the fact that William III was only offered the crown on condition that he accepted the Bill of Rights: conditional loyalty was thus 'the bedrock of the British constitution' (ibid.). Moreover, the desire to emphasize the community of interest with the rest of the United Kingdom can, ironically, even extend to the very politicians usually accused of wanting to betray Ulster. Thus the reluctance of the Tory leadership to support the foundation of Conservative Associations in the province is explained as being due to their desire 'to reforge links with Unionism'. Even Thatcher's signing of the AIA can be explained away as the 'Whitehall establishment' having misled the Prime Minister: 'she simply didn't understand what she did: she was outmanoeuvred' (Trimble interview, 19 July 1993; see also Molyneaux in Purdy 1989; 12–14) – an opinion that is given plausibility in Thatcher's memoirs, which register her disappointment with the results of the AIA (Thatcher 1993: 413–15). Thus, co-existing with their distrust of the British political establishment there is, in Ulster Unionist Party thinking at least, the desire to identify signs that point to rapprochement. This characteristic of Unionist thinking has been evident in a number of areas and, while its roots go back to before 1985, it is likely that it has intensified since the signing of the AIA.

II

One dimension of Unionist identity that seems clearly to have been undergoing a process of change since 1986, however, has been the idea of Ulster nationality. In the period 1974–86 the literature on this subject was largely produced to serve the UDA's Ulster independence project; however, the publications of the Ulster Society, established in 1986, effectively exist to counter that project. While they accept the existence of a distinct Ulster identity, they define it as an 'Ulster British culture and heritage' (McAuley 1991: 57); something which emphasizes the compatibility of an Ulster identity with British nationality in much the same way that post-war Unionists sought to promote Ulster ethnicity firmly within a British context. It is also reflective of the thinking of present Unionist leaders who, like the Revd Martin Smyth, are wary of Ulster nationalism as a threat to their British nationality, and who argue, not entirely unreasonably, that Merlyn Rees's promotion of it in the mid-1970s was motivated by a desire to 'shunt' the Unionist community out of the United Kingdom in obedience to the Foreign Office and the Northern Ireland Office (Smyth interview, 9 August 1993). In this context, David Trimble's rejection of separate Ulster nationhood – Unionists had 'only asserted a "two-nations" theory in the context of a crisis and then only as a reactive thing' – is an accurate statement given special point by the political context in which it was uttered (Trimble interview, 19 July 1993). Similarly, Ian Paisley has declared: 'I don't believe Ulster was a nation and I don't believe in nationalism in that sense, but I believe in the process that brought about modern Ulster. There is a clear identity of being a British Ulsterman.' (Paisley interview, 31 August 1993).

In this context, it is worth bearing in mind that the distinction described by Jennifer Todd, between Unionists for whom 'Ulster' is their primary identity and those for whom their primary identity is British (Todd 1987: 3), is one that can be difficult to maintain in a political context that places the former at a discount. Certainly opinion polls on national identity in Ulster since direct rule was imposed in 1972, and especially since 1986, reflect the preference of Unionist leaders for the label 'British' rather than 'Ulster' (see Moxon-Browne 1991: 29). Moxon-Browne's conclusion that this may be due to a 'perception that the Ulster identity was linked to a "weak" political unit and that Britain, although constituting an untrustworthy custodian of Ulster's political future was the stronger of the two contenders for control over Northern Ireland', is certainly plausible (ibid.). At the same time, however, it would be wrong to place too much significance on the distinction between these two identities. As the findings of the Opsahl Commission suggest, underlying them and the quite separate political values associated with each – i.e. British tolerance and compromise/Ulster fundamentalism – is an underlying homogeneity based on a deeply embedded Protestant faith and fear of the Catholic Church (Pollack (ed.) 1992: 96). As Marianne Elliott, a Commission member, concluded: 'This fear of Catholicism, not simply as a religion but as a powerful political system, exists at every level of the Protestant community . . . it is the main defining element of their Britishness and the perceived link with a Protestant power' (Elliott in *Belfast Telegraph*, 16 August 1993).

The Unionist concern, in a perplexing and uncertain political climate, to marginalize any aspect of their identity that confused the perception of an uncomplicated Britishness was a recognition of the simplified popular understanding of the Ulster conflict in Britain and the need to address perceptions there in their own terms. As the Revd Martin Smyth put it, the term 'Ulster people' is 'not really recognised', while 'Northern Ireland' gave the impression that Ulster Protestants were part of the Irish nationalist community (Smyth interview, 9 August 1993). Indeed, since the signing of the AIA, the percentage of Protestants willing to describe themselves as Irish has dropped to only 3 per cent: the figure on the eve of the troubles in 1968 was 20 per cent, dropping to 8 per cent in 1978 (Moxon-Browne 1991: 25). Some commentators have identified its use as an apparently national label since the 1880s (Boyce 1991: 405–6; Hennessy 1993: 35; Todd 1993: 196). However, this is relatively easy to do on the basis of a few sources. As to whether this term was adopted as a community-wide label requires more extensive research. It is the finding of this work, drawing on previous research (Loughlin 1986: 153–71, 295–6) and an extensive examination of loyalist speeches and press comment, that 'Irish' was a term employed by Unionists very tentatively, and especially in the context of a resurgent Irish nationalism. It is the same today. Protestant testimony to the Opsahl Commission expressed the belief that Irish history and language had been appropriated by Nationalists as political weapons. Accordingly, for Protestants the term 'Irish' was used only in a geographical sense (Pollack (ed.) 1992: 97–9), or, as Unionist political leaders put it, in a non-political sense (for Sammy Wilson and Ken Magennis on this issue, see *Belfast Telegraph*, 16 August 1993). Ian Paisley, while also taking this position, gave a typically forthright account of the Irish element in his own character:

I was born in the island of Ireland. I have Irish traits in me – we don't all have the traits of what came from Scotland, there is the Celtic factor . . . and I am an Irishman because you cannot be an Ulsterman without being an Irishman.

Nevertheless, even though he was careful to define his Irishness in a non-political context as having no essential place in, or implications for, his concept of nationality, Paisley's admission of his Irish identity during the Brooke talks provoked criticism from his Democratic Unionist Party (DUP) colleagues (Paisley interview, 31 August 1993). Relatedly, those Unionists who, despite criticism from within their own community have taken an interest in learning the Irish language, have been concerned to separate it from the politics of nationality (Chris M'Gimpsey, Aodan MacPoilin, *Sunday Times*, 9 May 1993). Thus it is unsatisfactory to identify the label 'Irish' as one of a number of 'national' labels used by Unionists. Its significance for Unionists needs to be evaluated. Certainly it lacks the importance and emotional force for them of the terms 'Ulster' and

'British'. At the same time, however, the new political context created by the IRA ceasefire has produced some signs that Unionists, while concerned to limit the parameters of a solution to the Ulster problem to an internal settlement, have yet seen in 'Irishness' a point of common identity with Nationalists.

Perhaps most surprisingly, given the UVF's perception of the problem as one of Ulster against 'the Irish', is Gusty Spence's admission that while he would always be British he 'loved the Irishness which he felt' (*News Letter*, 7 October 1994). Irishness as an identity everyone in Northern Ireland can share also has academic support (see Simon Lee, *Belfast Telegraph*, 30 September 1994). Moreover, the newly appointed Controller for BBC Northern Ireland, Pat Loughrey, has said that following the practice of 'BBC Wales and Scotland [,] we have a particular role in providing an indigenous language output' and that, accordingly, Irish language broadcasts would be expanded. In fact, the language was essential to an understanding of the North: 'There is a fascination with how family names, townlands and town names arose. The Irish language is key to that. It does not belong exclusively to any one community' (*Belfast Telegraph*, 10 October 1994).

Dennis Kennedy, a member of the Unionist Cadogan Group, has expanded on Irishness as a shared identity by defining it in traditions of art, learning, arms, song, sport and science. This concept of Irishness transcended – indeed, was superior to – political division and allied to 'practical, mundane co-operation' should, he argued, be given specific form in a North-South Council or a Council of Ireland, 'with a mandate to promote co-operation in all manner of economic, social and cultural co-operation' (*Belfast Telegraph*, 13 October 1994). For some Unionists, however, it is not identity that is the primary key to a solution of the Ulster problem but 'rights'; and the AIA stimulated a project – the Campaign for Equal Citizenship (CEC) – to secure the rights of northern Unionists through the integration of Northern Ireland with the rest of the United Kingdom.

III

Led by the liberal Unionist lawyer, Robert McCartney, the CEC was inspired by the Civil Rights Movement of the 1960s. It argued that Northern Ireland's exclusion from the British system of party competition condemned the region to sectarianism, and sought to provide for the people of the North the right to vote for the government of the United Kingdom (Aughey 1989: 146). However, McCartney's energetic challenging of the Ulster Unionist Party leadership on equal citizenship effectively posed a threat to Unionist unity, ironically on an issue on which the Party leader, Jim Molyneaux, agreed with McCartney but was not prepared to push regardless of the consequences for the wider Unionist movement. Accordingly, when, in the run-up to the general election of 1987 McCartney defied the 'no contest' agreement arranged by Unionist leaders

– that all sitting Unionist MPs should be unopposed – by standing in North Down, he and his North Down Constituency Association were expelled from the Party (ibid.: 161–5). In this situation the logical path for the North Down Unionists to take was to join one of the major British parties, and given their politics the Conservative Party was the natural choice. In keeping with the fundamental tenets of the CEC campaign, the policy of the North Down Conservatives has been to focus on the rights of citizenship rather than nationality as the basis of their appeal to the people of Northern Ireland.

Their most prominent spokesman, Dr Laurence Kennedy, when asked if the Ulster Conservatives sought to promote a more authentic form of Britishness than that represented by the Unionist Parties, made the distinction between the 'burning British nationalism' of Enoch Powell, a former Ulster Unionist MP, and from which he distanced himself and his Party, and the moderate patriotism associated with mainstream Toryism. Nationality for Kennedy was civic, concerned less fundamentally with emotion and belonging than with a rational concern for political rights. Northern Ireland was a 'geographical' slice of the United Kingdom denied effective participation in its politics. Accordingly, he defined his own national identity as 'an Ulsterman', but also part of 'the British social, political and cultural ethic'. Nor did he accept that the people of Northern Ireland suffered from a 'cultural identity crisis' any more than did the Scots, Welsh or English (Kennedy interview, 19 July 1993).

Kennedy was concerned to explain that he included Ulster Catholics in his conception of the Ulster people. Catholics may not define themselves as 'British' but would 'not necessarily find identification with the British ethic any more difficult than [with] an Irish ethic'. This is a plausible argument given the increase in the number of Catholics describing their identity as 'Northern Irish'. E. Moxon-Browne explains this phenomenon as being due to the fact that for Catholics this label can be adopted without implying any diminishing of their Irish nationalist identity (Moxon-Browne 1991: 28). Yet while this is a reasonable case, it can also be argued that this development is related to the growing numbers of the Catholic middle class whose economic well-being is tied up with the maintenance of the existing status quo, and for whom Britishness in the 'civic' sense – requiring merely observance of the law and the requirements of citizenship without having to endorse a form of British nationalist myth – is increasingly acceptable (for interesting comment bearing on this issue, see Boyle 1991: 72; O'Connor 1993: 38–43, 349–54).

But while it is clear that this is essentially what Kennedy means when he refers to the 'British ethic', it is also clear that his own concept of Britishness is more developed. Like mainstream Unionists, for example, he endorses the myth of a fundamental division between North and South going back long before plantation times. Again, he is opposed to membership of the European Community (EC), though on grounds closer to the British Tory Right than to the DUP. Whereas the latter see it as a largely Roman Catholic organization with interests inimical to the United Kingdom as a sovereign Protestant State (Paisley interview, 31 August

1993; DUP, *The Surrender of Maastricht: What It Means for Ulster* (Belfast: DUP, 1993)), Kennedy's opposition is based on the 'rational' ground that it could become overly centralized and bureaucratic, embodying a form of incompetent government such as was exhibited by the old Soviet Union (Kennedy interview, 19 July 1993). But perhaps the most significant aspect of Ulster Conservatism, as expressed by Kennedy, is the belief, shared with the Unionists, that the AIA was promoted by the Foreign Office as a means of forcing Northern Ireland into a united Ireland.

Accordingly, Kennedy expresses the Ulster Tory concern at the failure of John Major to fight for the Union in Ulster with the same enthusiasm as he does in Scotland. But when it is pointed out that the reason why this is so is because of the deep national divisions in the region, he avoids this issue and resorts to the argument that the real reason was fear of offending the Irish Government and the State Department of the USA, and that British political involvement in Ulster would have the effect of removing religious and sectarian division. At the same time, however, Kennedy accepts the proposition that the British left Ulster in 1921 because they did not regard Northern Ireland as an authentic part of the national territory, and reflection on this subject moves him, as it does occasionally with Unionists, to declare exasperatedly that if this is so the British should say so 'and get out'. And yet this is only a momentary consideration. For Kennedy, as for the Ulster Tories generally, the central task is to compel Westminster to treat Northern Ireland as a full member of the United Kingdom. A major problem facing the Ulster Tories in furthering this project, however, is that of expanding their support base and the brand of Britishness they represent among the wider Unionist community.

Certainly both DUP and Ulster Unionist supporters are most unlikely to endorse a concept of Britishness that did not have Protestantism at its centre (David Trimble, for example, could not envisage it: Trimble interview, 19 July 1993); and yet this, arguably, is essential both to integrating Northern Ireland with the wider British community and to consolidating that integration by attracting the support of Ulster Catholics. The central problem here is not just that the rejection of Protestantism would entail the rejection of that which gives historical meaning to the Ulster Protestant experience, but also that it would largely divest the idea of Britishness – or at least their membership of the United Kingdom – of any imaginative dimension for Protestants. Indeed this is recognized by supporters of the CEC and its academic advocates have made a virtue of it. Arthur Aughey, for instance, argues: 'The identity of Unionism has little to do with the idea of the nation and everything to do with the idea of state'. Authority for this proposition is found in the work of Bikhu Parekh, who claims that the modern state 'does not depend on, and in fact has nothing to do with, a sense of nationality' (quoted in Aughey 1989: 18). Aughey elaborates this argument in the United Kingdom context thus:

the modern state has transcended its dependence on extrinsic legitimations such as race, nation or religion, and is grounded in the political universals of right and the rule of law. In so far as those within the state accept the rule of law (justice being the impartiality of law designed for the general welfare), then there can be the fullest expression of ethnic, religious and social diversity. . . . The United Kingdom is a state which, being multi-national and multi-ethnic, can be understood in terms of citizenship and not substantive identity. . . . And it is significant that the character of the British state has always been associated with the idea of law, common and statute.   (ibid.: 18–19)

This is a plausible argument, though not beyond question. As Linda Colley suggests (see p. 229), the demise of popular Protestantism has had serious implications for the integrity of the state. Moreover, the idea that the British state can be divorced from a conception of nationality – described here as 'primitive simplicity' – is suspect. Certainly the experience of the Falklands War demonstrated that a concept of national identity – indeed, of a distinctly imperialistic kind – with all the emotional reassurance it embodied in the heady days when the South Atlantic Task Force was being assembled, was very much at the heart of the idea of the United Kingdom state, still often described as a 'nation state'. While the idea of the 'rule of law' was certainly a part of the rhetoric justifying the South Atlantic Campaign, it was never enough, on its own, to arouse and maintain popular support. It was inextricably linked with national aggression, identity, power and prestige as motivating factors (see Aulich (ed.) 1992). The Falklands War is only the most recent example to illustrate this point. The much more nationally crucial struggles of the First and Second World Wars could also be cited in this respect.

Thus the notion that the state can be conceptualized in terms of the political universals of 'right and the rule of law', abstracted from the emotions of nationalism, is not very convincing. Indeed, while Aughey notes that Robert McCartney employed the Union Jack in his campaign literature at the general election of June 1987, 'against his better judgement' (ibid.: 164), its use in this context is instructive. It is impossible to dissociate the national flag from notions of national identity and it is impossible to imagine the state without also imagining the national flag. Moreover, McCartney's impassioned rejection of the peace process following the IRA ceasefire which, he argues, will endanger the British identity, no less than the British citizenship, of the people of Northern Ireland (see, for example, McCartney in Belfast Telegraph, 5 September, 3 October 1994), has raised concerns that a rejection of Irishness, no less than a safeguarding of constitutional rights, motivates him (see 'Irishness vital to Unionism', Belfast Telegraph, 10 October 1994). Rights of citizenship and equality under the law are undoubtedly important to state stability and, in Northern Ireland, to reconciling Ulster Catholics to the constitutional status quo, but they have never been, and certainly it is unlikely that for Ulster Unionists they can ever be, dissociated from particular forms of British national myth.

Further, it can be argued that the stability of the United Kingdom state has been dependent, less on 'the principle of right and equality before the law' than on its ability to provide economic well-being for its constituent parts, especially Scotland. The recent growth of Scottish nationalism in the context of the European Community, together with the application of 'law' in the service of English-based Thatcherism, at least raises the possibility that its continuation in its present form is far from secure. This possibility is all the more worthy of consideration given that the most important institution symbolizing the unity of the United Kingdom, the crown – and which, surprisingly, Aughey considers only in passing – is itself under attack.

IV

Tom Nairn's argument that the crown 'binds the State together' (Nairn 1988: 89), has a special relevance in the Ulster Unionist case. Unionist leaders very much define the place of their community within the United Kingdom and, indeed, their conception of the state in general, in terms of the Williamite Settlement and the constitutional role it established for the monarchy; a Protestant settlement, moreover, established in no small measure through the Ulster Protestant sacrifices at Derry, Aughrim and the Boyne. With the demise of popular Protestantism in Britain, the monarchy, the Protestant character of which is constitutionally safeguarded, has enhanced its importance as an embodiment of British identity for Ulster Unionists. Thus it is hardly surprising that the crown, unsullied by the treachery of Westminster politicians, should have been regarded as the major safeguard of their constitutional position and national identity in the wake of the AIA – a role, moreover, that can only have been enhanced by the ability of monarchy to register identity at the level of the familial and the everyday (ibid.: 104, 136; Billig 1992: 87). Accordingly, in the post-1985 period Unionists looked, even more earnestly than hitherto, to the monarch for reassurance.

In fact, there is circumstantial evidence that the government itself used the monarchy in this period to calm Unionist fears of betrayal. Whereas twenty-one royal visits to Northern Ireland took place between the Silver Jubilee of 1977 and the signing of the AIA, from November 1985 to 16 September 1993 sixty-one took place (Northern Ireland Office, Information Service, 16 September 1993). The suspicion of Westminster political manipulation of the royal family in this respect, to bolster 'rotten policies' (Paisley interviewed on 'House of Windsor or House of Cards?', *Counterpoint*, Ulster Television, 1993), can cause great resentment. At the same time, however, it would seem that this is a case where government intentions coincided with royal sentiment. The Queen's long-held sympathy with Ulster Unionism was clearly to the fore in this period. Lady Kernohan, wife of the former Lord Lieutenant for Belfast, Sir Robert Kernohan, testified to her 'very great love of Ulster. She always goes out of her way to talk to anybody she hears comes from Ulster.' (ibid.). This affection for the most loyal subjects in the Kingdom is all the more understandable given the rise of Welsh and Scottish nationalism in recent decades. Indeed, in the early 1970s she feared her Kingdom would disintegrate, and later, in May 1977, made a dramatic intervention in the devolution debate by insisting on a firm statement in her speech opening Parliament declaring that, while she recognized the desire for devolution, she could not forget that she was crowned Queen of the whole United Kingdom (Tomlinson 1994: 289–91).

The most significant recent instance of the Queen's sympathy with Ulster Unionism came on 29 June 1991 when she made her first visit to the North since the Jubilee of 1977 for the purpose of presenting colours to four of the nine battalions of the Ulster Defence Regiment (UDR). Her speech on this occasion was a ringing endorsement of the UDR and its role in the present conflict: 'The UDR stands for those who are not prepared to stand by and let evil prosper. It provides for everyone in Northern Ireland – regardless of faith or background – the opportunity to make a contribution to the defeat of terrorism.' (*The Times*, 30 June 1991). This simple, indeed mythic, description of the UDR, ignoring its controversial character, especially its 'bad apples', its links with loyalist terrorism and, in the wider context, the conflict of national identity that lies at the heart of the Ulster problem and which makes Catholic enlistment in state forces much more complicated than the Queen acknowledged, reflected exactly the Ulster Unionist mentality.

In her personal commitment to Northern Ireland the Queen compensates for the inability and unwillingness of the British political class to integrate it as an integral part of the British national family, certainly as compared with other parts of the United Kingdom. And since November 1985 Unionists, having little success in having their anxieties addressed in the party political sphere, have turned to the monarch. Thus, when it was clear that their campaign of protests against the AIA was not going to yield significant results Unionists raised a petition to the Queen that included 500,000 signatures. For Ian Paisley the petition was a means of asserting the authenticity of the British identity of Ulster Unionists and at the same time successfully releasing tensions that came perilously close to provoking a civil war in Northern Ireland (Paisley interviewed on *The Monarchy*, London Weekend Television, 1992; Paisley interview, 31 August 1993). In this context, it is a reasonable assumption that Buckingham Palace's recent decision – quickly reversed – to bar leaders of Britain's large Irish community from royal garden parties on the ground that as they have not taken out British citizenship they must be regarded as foreign nationals (see *The Times*, 12 June 1994; 'Queen Lifts Irish Ban', 23 June 1994), was regarded by Unionists as a welcome clarification of national membership.

There are, however, limits to which the crown can be divorced from the party political sphere and still perform the function of authenticating British identity. The suggestion that, in the context of joint authority over Northern Ireland by Dublin and London the monarchy could still perform the essential function of authenticating the British nationality of Ulster Unionists, was emphatically rejected by all the Unionist leaders consulted for this study. As Dr Paisley put it, in that context the monarchy could not provide an 'anchorage' for Unionists (Paisley interview, 31 August 1993). There is, moreover, a related question here that bears on this issue, and which concerns the changing status of the monarchy in Britain as the pre-eminent symbol of national identity. For example, there are serious concerns about the cost of the monarchy and the limitations of Prince Charles as a future monarch, concerns which, it should be noted, are also expressed in Northern Ireland ('House of Windsor or House of Cards?', *Counterpoint*, Ulster Television, 1993). But arguably most important for Ulster Unionists are the calls that have been made for the monarchy to be more truly representative of the British nation by breaking the consti-tutional link with the Church of England, and especially, by allowing the monarch to marry a Roman Catholic. A Market and Opinion Research International (MORI) poll for the *Sunday Times* (21 January 1990), found that 47 per cent of respondents held this view, while 62 per cent thought that members of the royal family should not be required to seek the Queen's permission to marry a Roman Catholic.

Given the centrality of the Protestant settlement to the historical myth of Ulster Unionism, this is an issue of some importance, and, indeed, of some immediate import given the highly publicized conversion to Catholicism of the Duchess of Kent and Prince Charles's apparent questioning of the link between the crown and the Church of England (see *The Times*, 12–15 January, 26 June 1994). On this issue there might be a difference between the two main strands within the Unionist movement. Revd Martin Smyth, for example, accepts, theoretically, that a Catholic monarch who did not seek to impose his/her religion in affairs of state might be acceptable to Ulster Unionists; though he thought that there would be 'a hard core of Ulster Protestants' who would see this as a great crisis. This crisis, however, would not result in an attempt to break the connection with Britain. Rather it would invest loyalists with 'a mission to call the nation back to the true path' (Smyth interview, 9 August 1993).[4] Not sur-prisingly, for Dr Paisley it would be impossible for the monarchy to embody British national identity for Ulster Unionists if the personal link with Protestantism was broken. Indeed he sees the Catholic Church as being actively engaged in the recent scandals surrounding the royal family with the intention of undermining it (Paisley interview, 31 August 1993).

For the Ulster Conservatives, at least as far as their views were represented by Dr Laurence Kennedy, the monarchy was not essential to their 'sense of belonging to the United Kingdom', which was tied more closely to 'enlightened liberal democracy' (Kennedy interview, 19 July 1993). Yet if this view was representative of Ulster Tories generally, it would set them apart, not only from mainstream Ulster Unionism, but also, presumably, from many mainland Tories who identify not only with 'citizenship rights' but also with the national past and the historically infused nationality which the British monarchy embodies.

Notes

1. For a more sympathetic account of Boyd Black's defeat, see Aughey (1989: 161).

2. The Prudential MORI assessment of British opinions on national issues in 1991, for example, showed that when asked to identify four or five issues that concerned them most, interviewees ignored Northern Ireland. It came joint sixteenth with nuclear power, selected by 9 per cent of those questioned (Jacobs and Worcester 1991: 107). Nor did the upsurge of sectarian violence in Ulster in the autumn of 1993 reverse this state of affairs. A MORI poll in late November 1993, following intense media coverage of sectarian killings and the peace initiative promoted by the Prime Minister, showed that Ulster was rated as the most important national issue by only 3 per cent of respondents (*The Times*, 26 November 1993). Indeed, at the same time as John Major was giving Unionists a guarantee that joint authority would not be considered as a solution to the Ulster problem, an ICM poll showed that only 18 per cent of British voters believed that Northern Ireland should remain a part of the United Kingdom (*Guardian*, 11 March 1993).
3. For an account of Loyalist-Neofascist links in the aftermath of the signing of the AIA, see *Fortnight* (7 July 1986).
4. Smith, however, appears to make a distinction between a case where the monarch is *personally* no longer a Protestant and that in which the *constitutional* link between Church and State is broken, a prospect which he would vehemently oppose. See 'Allegiance put to the Test' (*Belfast Telegraph*, 11 July 1994).

CONCLUSION

Since its emergence as a specifically political issue in the 1880s, the nature and context of the Ulster problem has remained remarkably consistent. Fundamentally, it has been a problem of national identity set within the framework of the problematic relationship between the British state and the British nation. Yet if the nature of the problem has remained substantially intact, its proportions have changed significantly over this period. For example, the terms of debate on British nationality were transformed by World War One. The war destroyed the deep division between the major British Parties that had existed from the 1880s to 1914 on the question of national identity and the national interest, leaving Northern Ireland as an expendable part of the United Kingdom. After the war there was no longer a Tory Party willing to risk civil war to secure Ulster's British national membership and constitutional position. From then Ulster Unionists became, and as Richard Rose argues (1982: 129), are today, the only community in the state committed to defend – through membership of legal military and illegal paramilitary organizations – its present borders.

The seeds of Ulster's alienation from the mainland are to be found in the late nineteenth century, especially in the demise of popular Protestantism. At the same time, the core idea of the English/British nation changed from an industrial to an arcadian one, and while this was not absolutely crucial to Ulster's British identity, it nevertheless set a standard of mythical national authenticity which made it all the easier to regard 'industrial' Ulster and its sectarianism as alien to the British 'way of life'; a tendency that was enhanced further by the gradual demise of Empire which began with Irish independence in 1921. Thus, from a position at the beginning of this period, when the Ulster Protestant community's membership of the British nation was strongly underpinned in the three areas identified in this study as important to an understanding of the issue – national imagery, party politics and monarchy – by 1921 its British national membership had been seriously undermined in the first two of these areas.

The fundamental problem facing Ulster Unionists in securing their constitutional position has been the fact that, in a state without a written constitution, what is deemed to be constitutional or unconstitutional, and what is or is not national and in the national interest, has been determined in London by politicians representing a population with chiefly a mainland conception of the British nation and its national territory. And at no time in the recent past have the dangers inherent in this state of affairs been more apparent for Unionists than in the period since November 1985. This period, beginning with the signing of the AIA and the initiation of southern influence in the government of Northern Ireland, and with progressively larger percentages of British public opinion polls favouring withdrawal from Northern Ireland, is seen by Unionists as more threatening than any since the outbreak of the present troubles in 1969; and they have been in a quandary as to how they can effectively cope with it.

A major difficulty lies in the nature of the Unionist myth – the role of which, historically, has been to defend a privileged 'way of life' and to resist any change that seems to threaten it. As one commentator puts it, compared to the Irish nationalist myth – a mobilizing myth – it 'has had to perform fewer functions and is necessarily simpler.' (Brown 1985: 8). A recent television inquiry dealing with the Unionist dilemma, and which consulted a number of media specialists, contained the recommendation that they market their cause specifically with a mainland audience in mind ('Protestants and the Media', *Counterpoint*, Ulster Television: 1994). Yet, however sensible the media experts' advice at first seems, there is a serious problem facing its adoption: the problem of reshaping and modernizing ideas and beliefs deeply embedded in the local, everyday life of the Unionist, especially the working-class loyalist community, so that they conform to what the community regards as an alien norm. Indeed, as G.J. Watson's reminiscences illustrate (1989: 147–59), such a patriotic norm – English/British, and suffused with the values of moderation and tolerance – had been disseminated in Northern Ireland by the BBC for many years. However, it failed to make any impression on the loyalist mentality. It was those like Watson, a Catholic with an ambivalent attitude to nationalism and who had never been socialized into the Unionist myth, who were more likely to be attracted by it. In the same context, it can be argued that the centrality of the Unionist myth in giving meaning to the loyalist way of life will defeat the efforts of those who argue for the rejection of nationalist myths in favour of a common Ulster identity binding both communities and grounded in a common environmental culture of traditions and modes of living (for statements of this viewpoint, see Evans 1970, 1985). And while it is the case that the IRA ceasefire has produced some indications of a loyalist softening of attitude towards 'Irishness', it is, as yet, far too early to judge whether this will be the beginning of a developing common identity between Protestants and Catholics in the North. Fundamentally, it is not to their relationship with Ulster Catholics that loyalists look for a definition of their nationality, but to the British mainland; and despite the differences between Ulster loyalism and mainland patriotism, they do share certain, albeit largely negative, characteristics.

For example, it has been argued that loyalism is like mainland nationalism above all in 'its imperial memory of being masters once, and thus in its inability to conceive, let alone accept, becoming a minority in someone else's nation.' Again, like the people of Britain, they 'see the nation embodied, not in the people, but in the Crown' and are thus unable to translate their sense of grievance 'into a genuine democratic nationalism' (Ignatieff 1993: 184). Loyalists, however, would be less likely than other groups to embrace 'democratic nationalism' embodied in the people. This would almost certainly be 'mainland' focused and thus less likely than monarchy to offer the Unionists constitutional reassurance. The relationship with monarchy offers them an ideal embodiment of British nationality – the only nationality they desire.

Nevertheless, while there is both in Ulster and Britain a common allegiance to the Queen, that allegiance, being directed vertically, does not necessitate or necessarily encourage – certainly in Britain – a horizontal bond of common national identity across the whole Kingdom. And while their relationship with the monarch constitutes for Unionists an ideal standard of national identity it has proved, frustratingly, impossible to replicate in the more crucial sphere of Westminster party politics.

Status provides another area in which a similarity exists between Ulster loyalism and mainland patriotism, especially in how the Unionist anxiety about their constitutional status is mirrored in the mainland, chiefly Tory, anxiety about the status of the Anglo-American 'special relationship' – itself inspired by late nineteenth-century race-nationalist theorizing on the unity of the 'Anglo-Saxon family'. As with the Unionist perspective on the Union, this relationship also tends to be subject to near-paranoid speculation on the British side when anything occurs, however slight, that appears to endanger it.

However, negative similarities such as these offer no solution to the Unionist difficulty in securing their membership of the United Kingdom. Moreover, not only is it virtually impossible to modernize Unionism for a mainland audience but it is also difficult effectively to construct a positive propaganda image of Unionism to market in Britain. To do so would require the kind of conditions that existed in the inter-war years, when the Stormont regime and influential media supporters in Britain such as Lord Rothermere could substantially shape how the North was presented there. In the era of mass media, with few restrictions on reporting, it is difficult to see how such a propaganda exercise could be managed, assuming – and it is a large assumption given that a British national consciousness does not exist in the same way that a loyalist consciousness exists – that the intended audience can be effectively addressed. In this context, while the paramilitary ceasefires may have allowed loyalist extremists to adopt a more conciliatory political stance, even to the extent of appearing to marginalize Ian Paisley and the DUP (see, for example, Liam Clarke, *Sunday Times*, 16 October 1994), the fact remains that Paisley is, for the British population, the most easily recognizable representative of Ulster Unionism, and he has enhanced his reputation for political extremism by a virulent opposition to the current peace process (see Paisley in *Belfast Telegraph*, 13 September 1994). Another complication, however, resides in the fact that the nature of British nationality itself is now a subject of contentious debate.

Michael Portillo's recent opportunistic attempt to play the British nationalist card by lamenting the decline of national identity and blaming an 'alien' establishment for public contempt towards great national institutions such as the church, Parliament and the crown, provoked debate which, if not always coherent, at least revealed the seriousness of the issue (see, for example, *The Times*, 15, 18, 20 January, 12 February 1994). One of the most penetrating replies to Portillo came from Linda Colley ('Britain 1994: Nation in Search of an Identity', *The Times*, 31 January 1994). Colley identified both short- and long-term causes for the crisis of British identity; and among the former she cited fifteen years of one-party government. But the more fundamental causes were long term and were to be found in the demise of empire and the need for reconciliation with a Europe that many in England still distrust. Colley, however, placed most importance on the demise of popular belief in Protestantism:

The decline of Protestant zeal has meant that the majority of Britons, including John Major, have become reconciled to Ulster's absorption in a united, predominantly Catholic Ireland. By the same token, the erosion since the 1950s of Scotland's once fiercely Protestant working class is an important cause of the Conservative-Unionists' fading appeal north of the border.

Colley's comments usefully point out that Ulster Unionists are not the only group to be adversely affected by the demise of Protestant belief. But there can be little consolation for Unionists in this state of affairs, which could, given the rise of Scottish nationalism, result in the dismantling of the United Kingdom. David Trimble's speculation, that in the event of breakup Ulster would have difficulty in deciding whether to ally with Scotland or England (*Irish News*, 8 May 1991), may well reflect general Unionist thinking on the subject. However, it is unlikely, in the event, that an independent Scotland would be prepared to take on Northern Ireland – or, as would be more likely, a much reduced Protestant homeland obtained by the efforts of loyalist paramilitaries.[1] At a more general level, the crisis of British identity on the mainland is one that exists chiefly in the sphere of public debate: it is unlikely to invade the private sphere of personal, everyday life; and this, of course, is much less true of Northern Ireland where the distinction between the public and the private, so far as the issue of national identity is concerned, is not always easy to define.

British identity, as assessed in this study, is not explicable in terms of one simple idea. Rather it has been shown to be, historically, a complex, multi-faceted and dynamic phenomenon, the specific manifestation of which, at any one time, has been determined by the circumstances in which the questions of national identity and the 'national interest' have arisen.

The present phase of the Ulster conflict is, for many Unionists, one in which London and Dublin appear allied in a conspiracy to drive Ulster into the Irish Republic and this has made particularly problematic the accommodating of Britishness as an overall shared identity with the rest of the United Kingdom, with Britishness in the diverse sense of regional and ethnic particularity. As we have noted, Britishness in the latter sense accords more with the reality of national existence across the Kingdom. As one English Tory commented with reference to the Ulster Unionists in this context: 'The crucial point is that Britishness is not merely [English] . . . and so it is irrelevant whether Ulstermen are "like us". They prove their Britishness in blood and allegiance again and again.' (Charles Moore, 'Why does Everyone Hate the Unionists so?', *Spectator*, 27 November 1993). Accordingly, while Steve Bruce is right to identify the Ulster Protestants as an ethnic group, his view that their British identity is firmly subordinated to their Ulster identity and that the former 'is fundamentally threatened by British actions and attitudes' (Bruce 1986: 253, 258–9), is to suggest a distinction between the two that not all Unionists would find easy to make. Further, the simple lack of constitutional alternatives for Ulster loyalists – other than Irish unity – is likely to ensure that Ulster ethnicity and Britishness remain symbiotic states of being for the great majority of the Unionist community.

Notes

1. For a penetrating account of the differences between Ulster and Scotland in the period 1886–1914, a period when an enthusiastic commitment to Empire was common to both, see Walker (1994: 97–115).

BIBLIOGRAPHY

Manuscript Sources

British Library
Arthur James Balfour papers
Walter Long diaries

House of Lords Records Office
Willoughby de Broke papers
Bonar Law papers

Public Records Office (Kew)
Cabinet papers
Home Office papers
Ramsay MacDonald papers

Cambridge University
Stanley Baldwin papers

Birmingham University
Joseph Chamberlain papers
Austen Chamberlain papers

Public Records Office of Northern Ireland
Cabinet minutes and papers
Edward Carson papers
Lady Craigavon diary
Adam Duffin papers
William Johnson diary
Papers of Theresa, Lady Londonderry
Papers of the Ulster Tourist Development Association

Printed Sources

Addison, P. ed. (1979), *Home Intelligence Reports on Opinion and Morale 1940–1944*, Four Reels, Brighton, Harvester Press Microfilm Publications Ltd.

Amery, L. (1980), *The Leo Amery Diaries, Vol. 1: 1869–1940*, eds J. Barnes and D. Nicholson, London, Hutchinson.

——, (1988), *The Empire at Bay: The Leo Amery Diaries, Vol. 2*, ibid.

Boyce, D.G. ed. (1987), *The Crisis of British Unionism: the Domestic Political Papers of the Second Earl of Selborne, 1885–1922*, London, The Historian's Press.

Brock, M. and Brock, E. eds (1982), *H.H. Asquith: Letters to Venetia Stanley*, Oxford, Oxford University Press.

Buckland, P. ed. (1973), *Irish Unionism 1885–1923: a Documentary History*, Belfast, HMSO.

Buckle, G.E. ed. (1931), *The Letters of Queen Victoria: a Selection from Her Majesty's Correspondence and Journals 1886–1901*, 3 vols, London, John Murray.

Cooke, A.B. ed. (1975), 'A Conservative Leader in Ulster: Sir Stafford Northcote's Visit to the Province, October 1883', *Proceedings of the Royal Irish Academy*, lxxv, sect. C, No. 4: 61–84.

Fitzroy, A. (1925), *Memories*, 2 vols, London, Hutchinson. Fitzroy's diaries.

Gilbert, M. ed. (1979), *Winston S. Churchill: Companion Vol. V: the Exchequer Years 1922–1929*, London, Heinemann.

Haultain, A. ed. (1913), *Goldwin Smith's Correspondence*, London, T. Werner Laurie.

James, R.R. ed. (1974), *W.S. Churchill: His Complete Speeches 1897–1963*, 9 vols, London, Chelsea House Publishers.

Marx, K. and Engels, F. (1971), *Ireland and the Irish Question*, Moscow, Progress Publishers.

Middlemass, K. (1971), *Thomas Jones: Whitehall Diary: Vol III: 1918–25*, London, Oxford University Press.

Pinney, T. ed. (1981), *The Letters of Thomas Babington Macaulay*, vol. 5, Cambridge, Cambridge University Press.

Pollack ed. (1992), *A Citizen's Inquiry: the Opsahl Report on Northern Ireland*, Dublin, Lilliput Press.

Ramsden, J. ed. (1984), *Real Old Tory Politics: the Political Diaries of Sir Robert Sandars, Lord Bayard 1910–1935*, London, The Historian's Press.

Riddell, Lord (1934), *More Pages From My Diary 1908–1914*, London, Country Life.

Vincent, J. ed. (1984), *The Crawford Papers: the Journals of David Lindsey, 27th Earl of Crawford and 10th Earl of Balcarres 1871–1940*, Manchester, Manchester University Press.

Williams, R.H. ed. (1988), *Salisbury-Balfour Correspondence: Letters exchanged Between the Third Marquess of Salisbury and His Nephew Arthur James Balfour*, Hertfordshire, Hertfordshire Record Office.

Williamson, W. ed. (1988), *The Modernisation of Conservative politics: the Diaries and Letters of William Bridgeman 1904–1935*, London, The Historian's Press.

Audio Visual Sources

Northern Ireland Office
Information Service

Interviews
David Trimble

Dr Laurence Kennedy
Dr Ian Paisley
Revd Martin Smyth

Cinema (Documentary)
GPO Film Unit (1937), *Islanders*, London, GPO.
Jennings, H. (1943), *Fires Were Started*, London, Crown Film Unit.
——, (1951), *Family Portrait*, Festival of Britain Office.
Williams, J.B. (1933), *The Soul of a Nation*, London, Associated British Film
    Producers (film sponsored by the Conservative Party).

Cinema (Fiction)
Ealing Studios (1943), *The Bells Go Down*, London, Ealing Studios.
Two Cities Films (1946), *Odd Man Out*, London, Two Cities Films.

Television
Lisburn Camera Club (1991), *A Royal Occasion: the Story of how the People of
    Ulster Celebrated Coronation Day 2 June 1953 and later Welcomed their New
    Queen, Elizabeth II*, Belfast, BBC Northern Ireland.
London Weekend Television (1992), *The Monarchy*, London, London Weekend
    Television.
Taylor, P. (1991), *Atlantic Bridgehead*, Belfast, BBC Northern Ireland, Brian
    Waddell Productions.
Ulster Television (1993), 'House of Windsor or House of Cards?', *Counterpoint*,
    Belfast, Ulster Television.
——, (1994), 'Protestants and the Media', ibid.

Works of Reference

Annual Register
Hansard's Parliamentary Debates
Keesing's Contemporary Archives

Northern Ireland Government Publications

Reference
Northern Ireland Parliamentary Debates
Ulster Year Book
Ulster Annual

Magazines
Ulster Commentary

Inquiry
Report of the Folk Museum Committee, 5 March 1954, Cmd 326

Promotional
Notes on Northern Ireland (1964).

Shearman, H. (1946–72), *Northern Ireland: its History, Resources and People*.
   This booklet was republished on several occasions between 1946 and 1972.
   Issues cited in the text:
——, (1946), *Northern Ireland: its History, Resources and People*, Belfast, HMSO.
——, (1950), *Northern Ireland: its History, Resources and People*, Belfast, HMSO.
——, (1968), *Northern Ireland: its History, Resources and People*, Belfast, HMSO.
This is Ulster (1953).
Ulster: the British Bridgehead (1943).

Promotional (Government related)
Festival of Britain in Northern Ireland: Official Souvenir Handbook (1951)
Loudon, J. (1951), 'The Festival of the Arts', ibid.: 49–79.
Riddell, P. (1951), 'Ulster Farm and Factory', ibid.: 13–47.
UTDA (1926–51), *Ulster Guide*. (Published in association with the Northern
   Ireland Tourist Board from 1949–53, and from then by NITB. Issues cited in
   text:
——, (1927), *Ulster*, Belfast, UTDA.
UTDA/NITB (1949), *The Ulster Guide*, Belfast, UTDA/NITB.
NITB (1954), *The Ulster Guide*, Belfast, NITB
Ulster Unionist Council (1949), *Ulster is British*.
Ulster Unionist Party (1969), *Ulster: the Facts*.

Magazines and Newspapers

Magazines
Architects Journal
Blarney; a Loyal Comic Journal
Chamber of Commerce Journal (London)
English Life
Fortnight
Illustrated London News
Leader
Listener
New Society
New Statesman and Society
Picture Post
Protestant Telegraph
Spectator
Time and Tide
Ulster Illustrated

Newspapers (Northern Ireland)
Ballymena Observer
Banbridge Chronicle
Belfast News-Letter (later *News Letter*)
Belfast Telegraph
Coleraine Chronicle
Cookstown News
Derry Journal
Down Recorder

Fermanagh Times
Impartial Reporter
Irish News
Larne Times
Lisburn Herald
Lisburn Standard
Londonderry Sentinel
Londonderry Standard (later *Derry Standard*)
Newry Telegraph
Newtownards Chronicle
Northern Whig
Portadown News
Strabane Chronicle
Tyrone Constitution
Tyrone Courier
Ulster Gazette
Weekly Northern Whig
Weekly Telegraph

Newspapers (Southern Ireland)
Sunday World
United Ireland

Newspapers (Britain)
Birmingham Post
Daily Express
Daily Mail
Daily Mirror
Daily Telegraph
Evening News
Glasgow Herald
Liverpool Post
Manchester Despatch
Manchester Guardian (later *Guardian*)
News Chronicle
Sunday Dispatch
Sunday Times
Times
Western Mail
Western Morning News
Yorkshire Post

Theses

Baker, P.S. (1978), 'The Sociological and Ideological Role of the Monarchy in Late
    Victorian Britain', M.A. Thesis, University of Lancaster.
Callan, P. (1984), 'Voluntary Recruiting for the British Army in Ireland During the
    First World War', Ph.D Thesis, University College, Dublin.
Ebong, I.I.I. (1986), 'The Origins and Significance of the Festival of Britain 1951',
    Ph.D Thesis, University of Edinburgh.
Foy, M.T. (1986, 'The Ulster Volunteer Force: its Domestic Development and

Political Importance in the Period 1913–1920', Ph.D Thesis, Queen's University, Belfast.

Jones, G.A. (1965), 'National and Local Issues in politics: a Study of East Sussex and the Lancashire Cotton Towns 1906–1910', Ph.D Thesis, University of Sussex.

McEwan, J.M. (1959), 'Unionist and Conservative Members of Parliament 1914–1939', Ph.D Thesis, University of London.

Meehan, C. (1992), 'Ulster Unionism and British Identity 1886–1902', M.A. Diss., University of Ulster.

Moon, H.R. (1968), 'The Invasion of the United Kingdom: Public Controversy and Official Planning 1888–1918', Ph.D Thesis, University of London.

Smith, S.R.B. (1985), 'British Nationalism, Imperialism and the City of London 1880–1900', Ph.D Thesis, University of London.

Works published in the period to 1922

Arnold, M. (1882/1891), *Irish Essays and Others*, London, Smith Elder.

Bagehot, W. (1867/1976), *The English Constitution*, intro. R.H.S. Crossman, London, Collins/Fontana.

Balfour, A.J. (1914), *Nationality and Home Rule*, London, Macmillan.

Beddoe, J. (1885/1971), *The Races of Britain: a Contribution to the Anthropology of Western Europe*, London, Hutchinson.

Boutmy, E. (1904), *The English People*, London, T. Fisher Unwin.

Burke, E. (1790/1868), *Reflections on the Revolution in France*, London, Rivingtons.

Cecil, H. (1912), *Conservatism*, London, Thornton Butterworth.

Citizens Committee (1919/1991), *The Great War 1914–1918*, Belfast, Pretani Press.

Cornford, L.C. (1912), 'Home Rule and Civil War', *National Review*, 59: 436–43.

Dicey, A.V. (1885/1914), *An Introduction to the Study of the Law of the Constitution*, London, Macmillan.

——, (1888), 'New Jacobinism and Old Morality', *Contemporary Review*, liii: 475–502.

——, (1905/1952), *Lectures on the Relation Between Law and Public Opinion in England in the Nineteenth Century*, London, Macmillan.

——, (1912), 'The Parliament Act 1911 and the Destruction of all Constitutional Safeguards' in *Rights of Citizenship*, London, Frederick Warne: 81–107.

——, (1913), *A Fools Paradise*, London, Macmillan.

Dickson, J.M. (1896–1900), 'Notes on Irish Ethnology', *Ulster Journal of Archaeology*, 2nd series, II, No. 3: 156–60; IV, No. 1: 12–17; V, No. 4: 232–6; VI, No. 4: 205–9.

Dilke, C. (1869), *Greater Britain*, London, Macmillan.

Doyle, L. [Leslie A. Montgomery] (1921), *An Ulster Childhood*, Dublin, Maunsel.

Fleure, H.J. (1914), 'Distribution of Races and Languages' in A.S. Herbertson and O.J.R. Howarth (eds), *The Oxford Survey of the British Empire: the British Isles and Mediterranean Possessions*, Oxford, Clarendon Press: 298–316.

Freeman, E.A. (1872/1906), *The Growth of the English Constitution*, London, Macmillan.

Gardiner, S.R. *et al.* (1878), 'England', *Encyclopaedia Britannica*, 9th ed., viii: 247–344.

Good, J.W. (1919), *Ulster and Ireland*, Dublin, Maunsel.

Grousset, P. (1888/1986), *Ireland's Disease: The English in Ireland 1887*, London/
  Belfast, Routledge and Blackstaff Press.
Harrison, J. (1888), *The Scot in Ulster: a Sketch of the History of the Scottish
  Population of Ulster*, Edinburgh and London, Blackwood.
Hume, A. (1852), 'Origins and Characteristics of the Population in the Counties of
  Down and Antrim', *Ulster Journal of Archaeology*, i: 9–16, 120–29, 246–54.
Inge, W.R. (1919), *Outspoken Essays*, London, Longmans Green.
Lee, S. (1904), *Queen Victoria: A Biography*, London, Smith Elder.
McCarthy, M.J.F. (1901), *Five Years in Ireland 1895–1900*, Dublin, Sampson
  Low.
Macaulay, T.B. (1848–61/1907), *The History of England From the Accession of
  James II*, ed. T.F. Henderson, London and New York, George Routledge.
McKnight, T. (1896), *Ulster As It Is: or Twenty-Eight Years Experience as an Irish
  Editor*, 2 vols, London, Macmillan.
Moneypenny, W.F. (1913), *The Two Irish Nations: An Essay on Home Rule*,
  London, John Murray.
Moore, F.F. (1914), *The Truth About Ulster*, London, Naish.
Morrison, H.S. (1920), *Modern Ulster: Its Character, Customs, Politics and
  Industries*, Edinburgh and London, Blackwood.
National Union (1891), *National Union Pamphlets 1887–1890*, London, National
  Union.
O'Brien, R.B. (1880), *The Land Question and English Public Opinion*, London,
  Cameron and Ferguson.
Paton, J. (1892), *British History and Papal Claims From the Norman Conquest to
  the Present Day*, 2 vols, London, Hodder and Stoughton.
Peel, G. (1914), *The Reign of Edward Carson*, London, P.S. King and Son.
Pollard, A.F. (1920), *The Evolution of Parliament*, London, Longmans Green.
Rights of Citizenship: a Survey of Safeguards for the People (1912), London,
  Frederick Warne.
Rosenbaum, S. ed. (1912), *Against Home Rule: the Case for the Union*, London,
  Frederick Warne.
Sale, M.O. (1913), 'The Problem of Wales', *National Review*, 62: 507–18.
Salisbury, Lord (1865–1883/1972), *Salisbury on Politics* ed. P. Smith, Cambridge,
  Cambridge University Press. A collection of Salisbury's essays.
Salmon, G. (1890), *The Infallibility of the Church: a Course of Lectures Delivered
  in the Divinity School of the University of Dublin*, London, John Murray.
Seeley, J.R. (1883/1920), *The Expansion of England*, London, Macmillan.
Selborne, Earl of (1912), 'The Referendum' in *Rights of Citizenship*, London,
  Frederick Warne: 198–232.
Smith, F.E. (1912), 'The Parliament Act Considered in Relation to the Rights of the
  People' in *Rights of Citizenship*, London, Frederick Warne.
Smith, G. (1894), *Essays on Questions of the Day*, New York, Macmillan.
Wallas, G. (1908), *Human Nature in Politics*, London, Constable.
Willoughby de Broke, Lord (1912a), 'National Toryism', *National Review*, 59:
  413–27.
——, (1912b), 'The Constitution and the Individual' in *Rights of Citizenship*,
  London, Frederick Warne: 44–80.
——, (1914), 'The Unionist Party and the General Election', *National Review*, 63:
  775–86.
Young, F. (1907), *Ireland at the Crossroads*, London, Grant Richards.

Works published since 1922

Adamson, I. (1974), *The Cruithin*, Belfast, Pretani.
——, (1982), *The Identity of Ulster*, Belfast, Pretani.
Addison, P. (1985), *Now the War is Over: a Social History of Britain 1945–51*, London, BBC.
Amery, L. (1953–55), *My Political Life*, 3 vols, London, Hutchinson.
Anderson, B. (1983), *Imagined Communities: Reflections on the Origins and Spread of Nationalism*, London, Verso.
Armour, W.S. (1935), *Facing the Irish Question*, London, Duckworth.
Aughey, A. (1989), *Under Siege: Ulster Unionism and the Anglo-Irish Agreement*, Belfast, Blackstaff Press.
Aulich, J. ed. (1992), *Framing the Falklands War: Nationhood, Culture and Identity*, Milton Keynes, Open University Press.
Baldwin, S. (1926), *On England*, London, Philip Allen and Co.
——, (1928), *Our Inheritance*, London, Hodder and Stoughton.
——, (1935), *This Torch of Freedom*, London, Hodder and Stoughton.
——, (1941), 'The Englishman' in *British Life and Thought*, London, Longmans Green for the British Council.
Banham, M. and Hillier, B. eds (1976), *A Tonic for the Nation: the Festival of Britain 1951*, London, Thames and Hudson.
Barker, E. (1942), *Britain and the British People*, London, Oxford University Press.
Barnett, A. (1982), *Iron Britannia*, London, Allison and Busby.
Barr, C. (1974), 'Projecting Britain and the British Character: Ealing Studios', *Screen*, 15: 98–114.
Barthes, R. (1973), *Mythologies*, London, Paladin.
Barton, B. (1988), *Brookeborough: the Making of a Prime Minister*, Belfast, QUB, Institute of Irish Studies.
——, (1989), *The Belfast Blitz*, Belfast, Blackstaff Press.
——, (1992), 'Westminster-Stormont Relations During the Attlee Administration', *Irish Political Studies*, 7: 1–20.
Bebbington, D.W. (1982), 'Religion and National Feeling in Nineteenth Century Wales and Scotland' in S. Mews (ed.), *Religion and National Identity*, Oxford, Basil Blackwell: 489–503.
Bedarida, F. (1979), *A Social History of England*, London, Methuen.
Bell, G. (1976), *The Protestants of Ulster*, London, Pluto Press.
——, (1982), *Troublesome Business: the Labour Party and the Irish Question*, London, Pluto Press.
Bell, G.K.A. (1935/1952), *Randall Davidson: Archbishop of Canterbury*, London, Oxford University Press.
Bell, S.H., Robb, N. and Hewitt, J. (1951), *The Arts in Ulster*, London, Harrap.
Best, G.F.A. (1967), 'Popular Protestantism in Victorian Britain' in R. Robson (ed.), *Ideas and Institutions of Victorian Britain*, London, Bell: 115–41.
Bew, P., Patterson, H. and Gibbon, P. (1979), *The State and Social Classes in Northern Ireland*, Manchester, Manchester University Press.
Billig, M. (1992), *Talking of the Royal Family*, London and New York, Routledge.
Birch, A.H. (1989), *Nationalism and National Integration*, London, Unwin Hyman.
Biron, C. (1936), *Without Prejudice; Impressions of Life and Law*, London, Faber and Faber.
Blake, R. (1955), *The Unknown Prime Minister: the Life and Times of Andrew Bonar Law*, London, Eyre and Spottiswode.

Blondel, J. (1963), *Voters, Parties and Leaders: the Social Fabric of British Politics*, Harmondsworth, Penguin.

Bolt, C. (1984, 'Race and the Victorians' in C.C. Eldridge (ed.), *British Imperialism in the Nineteenth Century*, Basingstoke, Macmillan: 126–47.

Bowman, J. (1983), *De Valera and the Ulster Question 1917–1973*, Oxford, Clarendon Press.

Boyce, D.G. (1972), *Englishmen and Irish Troubles: British Public Opinion and the Making of Irish Policy 1918–1922*, Cambridge Mass., MIT Press.

——, (1986), 'The Marginal Britons: the Irish' in R. Colls and P. Dodd (eds), *Englishness: Politics and Culture 1880–1920*: 230–53.

——, (1988), *The Irish Question and British Politics 1868–1986*, Basingstoke, Macmillan.

——, (1989), 'Edward Carson (1854–1935) and Irish Unionism' in C. Brady (ed.), *Worsted in the Game; Losers in Irish History*, Dublin, Lilliput Press: 145–57.

——, (1991), *Nationalism in Ireland*, 2nd ed., London and New York, Routledge. First published 1982, London, Croom Helm.

Boyle, K. (1991), 'Northern Ireland: Allegiances and Identities' in B. Crick (ed.), *National Identity: the Constitution of the United Kingdom*, Oxford, Blackwell: 68–78.

Brand, S. (1978, *The National Movement in Scotland*, London, Routledge and Kegan Paul.

Briggs, A. (1965), *The History of Broadcasting in the United Kingdom: Volume III: the Golden Age of Wireless*, London, Oxford University Press.

British Council (1941), *British Life and Character*, London, Longmans Green.

Brogan, D.W. (1943), *The English People: Impressions and Observations*, London, Hamish Hamilton.

Bromage, M. (1964), *Churchill and Ireland*, Notre Dame, Ind., University of Indiana Press.

Brown, T. (1985), *The Whole Protestant Community: the Making of a Historical Myth*, Derry, Field Day Theatre Company.

Bruce, S. (1985), *No Pope of Rome: Anti-Catholicism in Modern Scotland*, Edinburgh, Mainstream.

——, (1986), *God Save Ulster! the Religion and Politics of Paisleyism*, Oxford, Clarendon Press.

——, (1992), *The Red Hand: Protestant Paramilitaries in Northern Ireland*, Oxford, Oxford University Press.

——, (1994), *The Edge of the Union: the Loyalist political Vision*, Oxford, Oxford University Press.

Bryans, R. (1964, *Ulster: a Journey Through the Six Counties*, London, Faber and Faber.

——, (1992), *The Dust Has Never Settled*, London, The Honeyford Press.

Bryant, A. (1929), *The Spirit of Conservatism*, London, Hutchinson.

——, (1934), *The National Character*, London, Longmans Green.

——, (1969), *The Lion and the Unicorn: a Historian's Testament*, London, Collins.

Buckland, P. (1973), *Irish Unionism 2: Ulster Unionism and the Origins of Northern Ireland*, Dublin, Gill and Macmillan.

——, (1979), *The Factory of Grievances: Devolved Government in Northern Ireland 1921–39*, Dublin, Gill and Macmillan.

——, (1981), *A History of Northern Ireland*, Dublin, Gill and Macmillan.

Bullock, S.F. [1931] *After Sixty Years*, London, Sampson Low, Marston and Co.

Burke, T. (1946), *The English Townsman*, London, Batsford.

Butler, D. (1991), 'Ulster Unionism and British Broadcasting Journalism 1924–89' in B. Rolston (ed.), *The Media and Northern Ireland: Covering the Troubles*, Basingstoke, Macmillan: 99–121.

Calder, A. (1971), *The People's War: Britain 1939–1945*, London, Panther.

——, (1991), *The Myth of the Blitz*, London, Jonathan Cape.

Callaghan, J. (1973), *A House Divided*, London, Collins.

Campbell, J.J. (1941), *Fifty Years of Ulster*, Belfast, Irish News.

Cannadine, D. (1983), 'The Context, Performance and Meaning of Ritual: the British Monarchy and the "Invention of Tradition", c. 1820–1977' in E. Hobsbawn and T. Ranger (eds), *The Invention of Tradition*, Cambridge, Cambridge University Press: 101–64.

——, (1990), *The Decline and Fall of the British Aristocracy*, New Haven and London, Yale University Press.

Canning, P. (1985), *British Policy Towards Ireland 1921–1941*, Oxford, Clarendon Press.

Cardiff, D. and Scamell, P. (1987), 'Broadcasting and National Unity' in J. Curran *et al.* (eds), *Impacts and Influences: Essays on Media Power in the Twentieth Century*, London, Methuen: 157–73.

Cathcart, R. (1984), *The Most Contrary Region: the BBC in Northern Ireland 1924–1984*, Belfast, Blackstaff Press.

Cesarani, D. (1989), 'The Anti-Jewish Career of Sir William Joynson-Hicks, Cabinet Minister', *Journal of Contemporary History*, 24, No. 3: 461–82.

Chadwick, O. (1970), *The Victorian Church: Part II: 1860–1901*, London, A. and C. Black.

Chamberlain, A. (1936), *Politics From Inside: an Epistolary Chronicle 1906–1914*, London, Cassell.

Chancellor, V. (1970), *History for Their Masters: Opinion in the English History Textbook 1800–1914*, Bath, Adams and Dart.

Chapman, M. (1978), *The Gaelic Vision in Scottish Culture*, London and Montreal, Croom Helm and McGill-Queen's University Press.

Churchill, W.S. (1929), *The World Crisis: the Aftermath*, London, Thornton Butterworth.

——, (1948–54), *History of the Second World War*, 6 vols, London, Cassell.

Coetzee, F. (1991), *For Party or for Country: the Dilemma of Popular Conservatism in Edwardian England*, Oxford, Oxford University Press.

Cole, B. and Durack, R. (1992), *Railway Posters 1923–1947*, London, Laurence King Publishing.

Colley, L. (1992a), *Britons: Forging the Nation 1707–1837*, New Haven and London, Yale University Press.

——, (1992b), 'Britishness and Otherness: an Argument', *Journal of British Studies*, 31: 309–29.

Collini, S. (1985), 'The Idea of "Character" in Victorian Thought', *Transactions of the Royal Historical Society*, 5th series, xxxv: 29–50.

Colls, R. and Dodd, P. eds (1986), *Englishness, Politics and Culture 1880–1920*, London, Croom Helm.

Colvin, I. (1934, 1936), *The Life of Lord Carson*, vols 2 and 3, London, Gollancz. Vol. 1 by E. Marjoribanks (1932).

Cosgrove, P. (1969), 'The Insoluble Problem of Ulster', *Round Table*, 59, No. 233: 319–26.

Cosgrove, R. (1980), *The Rule of Law; Albert Venn Dicey, Victorian Jurist*, London, Macmillan.

Cunningham, H. (1989), 'The Language of Patriotism' in R. Samuel (ed.),

Patriotism: the Making and Unmaking of British National Identity: Volume I: History and Politics, London, Routledge: 57–89.

Curtis, L. (1984), *Ireland: the Propaganda War: the Media and the 'Battle for Hearts and Minds'*, London, Pluto.

Curtis Jr, L.P. (1968), *Anglo-Saxons and Celts: a Study of Anti-Irish Prejudice in Victorian England*, Bridgeport, Conn., Conference on British Studies.

——, (1973), *Apes and Angels: the Irishman in Victorian Caricature*, Newton Abbot, David and Charles.

Dakers, C. (1987), *The Countryside at War 1914–1918*, London, Constable.

Dangerfield, G. (1935/1961), *The Strange Death of Liberal England*, New York, George Putnam's Sons.

Darby, J. (1983), 'The Historical Background' in J. Darby (ed.), *Northern Ireland: the Background to the Conflict*, Belfast and Syracuse, Appletree and Syracuse University Press: 13–31.

Davey, J.J. (1940), *1840–1940: the Story of a Hundred Years: an Account of the Irish Presbyterian Church From the Foundation of the General Assembly to the Present Time*, Belfast, Baird.

Dawson, G. (1984), 'History-Writing on World War Two' in G. Hurd (ed.), *National Fictions: World War Two in British Films and Television*, London, BFI Publishing: 1–7.

Dawson, G. and West, B. (1984), '"Our Finest Hour"? the Popular Memory of World War II and the Struggle over National Identity', ibid.: 8–13.

Democratic Unionist Party (1993), *The Surrender of Maastricht: What it Means for Ulster*, Belfast, DUP.

Dillon, M. and Lehane, D. (1973), *Political Murder in Northern Ireland*, Harmondsworth, Penguin.

Donaghue, B. and Jones, G.W. (1973), *Herbert Morrison: Portrait of a Politician*, London, Weidenfeld and Nicolson.

Donaldson, F. (1974), *Edward VIII*, London, Weidenfeld and Nicolson.

Doyle, L. (1935), *The Spirit of Ireland*, London, Batsford.

Elliott, P. (1978), 'All the World's a Stage, or What's Wrong with the National Press' in J. Curran (ed.), *The British Press: a Manifesto*, London, Macmillan.

Ellwood, D.W. (1982), '"Showing the World What it Owed to Britain": Foreign Policy on "Cultural Propaganda"' in N. Pronay and D.W. Spring (eds), *Propaganda, Politics and Film 1918–1945*, London, Macmillan: 50–76.

Ensor, R.C.K. (1936), *England 1870–1914*, Oxford, Clarendon Press.

Evans, E.E. (1951), *Northern Ireland*, London, Collins.

——, (1970), 'The Personality of Ulster', *Transactions*, No. 51 (November): 1–20.

——, (1985), *Ulster: the Common Ground*, Dublin, Lilliput Press.

Fair, J.D. (1971), 'The King, the Constitution and Ulster: the Interparty Negotiations of 1913 and 1914', *Eire-Ireland*, VI, No. 1: 35–52.

Fair, J.D. and Hutcheson Jr, J.A. (1987), 'British Conservatism in the 20th Century: an Emerging Ideological tradition', *Albion*, 19, No. 4: 549–78.

Falls, C. (1922), *The History of the 36th (Ulster) Division*, Belfast, McCaw, Stevenson and Orr Ltd.

Farrell, M. (1976), *Northern Ireland; the Orange State*, London, Pluto Press.

Faulkner, B. (1978), *Memoirs of a Statesman*, London, Weidenfeld and Nicolson.

Feaver, G. (1969), *From Status to Contract: a Biography of Sir Henry Maine*, London, Longmans Green.

Fest, W. (1981), 'Jingoism and Xenophobia in the Electioneering Strategies of British Ruling Elites before 1914' in Kennedy and Nicholls (eds), *Nationalist and*

Racialist Movements in Britain and Germany Before 1914, Basingstoke, Macmillan: 171–89.

Fielding, N. (1981), *The National Front*, London, Routledge and Kegan Paul.

Finley, M.I. (1975), *The Use and Abuse of History*, London, Chatto and Windus.

Firth, R. (1975), *Symbols: Public and Private*, London, George Allen and Unwin.

Fisk, R. (1975), *The Point of No Return: the Strike that Broke the British in Ulster*, London, Andre Deutsch.

——, (1985), *In Time of War: Ireland, Ulster and the Price of Neutrality 1939–45*, London, Paladin.

Forsyth, L.J. (1976), *Tyrone Guthrie: a Biography*, London, Hamish Hamilton.

Frayn, M. (1986), 'Festival' in M. Sissons and P. French (eds), *The Age of Austerity*, Oxford, Oxford University Press.

Fuller, J.G. (1990), *Troop Morale and Popular Culture in the British Dominion Armies 1914–1918*, Oxford, Clarendon Press.

Fyfe, H. (1940), *The Illusion of National Character*, London, Watts and Co.

Gaffikin, F. and Morrisey, M. (1990), *Northern Ireland: the Thatcher Years*, London, Zed Books.

Gailey, A. (1987), *Ireland and the Death of Kindness: the Experience of Constructive Unionism*, Cork, Cork University Press.

Garvin, J.L. (1932–3), *The Life of Joseph Chamberlain*, 2 vols, London, Macmillan. (completed in 6 vols in 1969).

Gilbert, M. (1971), *Winston S. Churchill: Volume III: 1914–16*, London, Heinemann.

——, (1979), *Winston S. Churchill: Volume V: 1922–39*, London, Heinemann.

Glendenning, F.A. (1973), 'School History Textbooks and Social Attitudes 1804–1911', *Journal of Educational Administration and History*, v: 33–43.

Goffman, E. (1971), *The Presentation of the Self in Everyday Life*, Harmondsworth, Penguin.

Gollin, A.M. (1964), *Proconsul in Politics*, London, Macmillan.

Grainger, J.H. (1986), *Patriotisms: Britain 1900–1939*, London, Routledge and Kegan Paul.

Green, J. [1933] *Mr Baldwin: a Study in Post-War Conservatism*, London, Sampson Low, Marston and Co.

Gribbon, S. (1987), 'An Irish City: Belfast 1911' in D. Harkness and M. O'Dowd (eds), *The Town in Ireland: Historical Studies XIII*, Belfast, Appletree Press: 203–20.

Griffiths, R. (1983), *Fellow Travellers of the Right: British Enthusiasts for Nazi Germany 1933–1939*, Oxford, Oxford University Press.

Gwynn, D. (1932), *The Life of John Redmond*, London, Harrap.

Hailsham, Lord (1975), *The Door Wherein I Went*, London, Collins.

——, (1978), *The Dilemma of Democracy; Diagnosis and Prescription*, London, Hodder and Stoughton.

Hanna, D. O'D. (1952), *The Face of Ulster*, London, Batsford.

Harbinson, J.F. (1973), *The Ulster Unionist Party: its Organisation and Development*, Belfast, Blackstaff Press.

Harbinson, R. [Robin Bryans] (1964/1987), *No Surrender*, Belfast, Blackstaff Press.

Hardie, F. (1970), *The Political Influence of the British Monarchy 1868–1952*, London, Batsford.

Hardy, W. Le (1953), *The Coronation Book*, London, Staples Press.

Harkness, D. (1983), *Northern Ireland Since 1920*, Dublin, Helicon.

Harris, R. (1972), *Prejudice and Tolerance in Ulster*, Manchester, Manchester University Press.

Harrisson, T. (1990), *Living Through the Blitz*, Harmondsworth, Penguin.

Hayes, C. (1960), *Nationalism: a Religion*, New York, Macmillan.

Hayward, R. (1938), *In Praise of Ulster*, Belfast, Mullan and Son.

——, (1950), *This is Ireland: Ulster and the City of Belfast*, London, Arthur Barker.

——, (1957), *Border Foray*, London, Arthur Barker.

Heenan, J.C. (1971), *Not the Whole Truth: an Autobiography*, London, Hodder and Stoughton.

Heller, A. (1975), *A Theory of History*, London, Routledge and Kegan Paul.

Hempton, D. (1990), '"For God and Ulster": Evangelical Protestantism and the Home Rule Crisis of 1886' in K. Robbins (ed.), *Protestant Evangelicalism: Britain, Ireland, Germany and America c. 1750–c. 1950*, Oxford, Blackwell: 225–54.

Hempton, D. and Hill, M. (1992), *Evangelical Protestantism and Ulster Society 1740–1890*, London and New York, Routledge.

Hennessy, T. (1993), 'Ulster Unionist Territorial and National Identities 1886–1893: Province, Island, Kingdom and Empire', *Irish Political Studies*, 8: 21–36.

Hertz, F. (1951), *Nationality in History and Politics: a Psychology and Sociology of National Sentiment and Nationalism*, London, Routledge and Kegan Paul.

Hewins, W.A.S. (1929), *The Apologia of an Imperialist: Forty Years of Empire policy*, 2 vols, London, Constable.

Hewitt, J. (1987), *Ancestral Voices: the Selected Prose of John Hewitt* ed. T. Clyde, Belfast, Blackstaff Press.

Hillier, B. (1976), 'Introduction' in Banham and Hillier (eds), *A Tonic for the Nation: the Festival of Britain 1951*, London, Thames and Hudson: 10–17.

Hobsbawm, E. (1969), *Industry and Empire*, Harmondsworth, Penguin.

Holland, J. (1981), *Too Long a Sacrifice: Life and Death in Northern Ireland*, New York, Dodd, Mead and Co.

Hollins, T.J. (1981), 'The Conservative Party and Film Propaganda Between the Wars', *Historical Journal*, 46: 359–69.

Holloway, J. (1959), 'The Myth of England', *Listener*, 81: 670–72.

Horne, A. (1989), *Macmillan 1957–1986: Volume II of the Official Biography*, London, Macmillan.

Horne, D. (1969), *God is an Englishman*, Sydney, Angus and Robertson.

Howkins, A. (1968), 'The Discovery of Rural England' in Colls, Dodd (eds), *Englishness: Politics and Culture 1880–1920*, London, Croom Helm: 62–88.

Hurd, G. (1984), *National Fictions: World War Two in British Films and Television*, London, BFI Publishing.

Hyde, H.M. (1953), *Carson: the Life of Sir Edward Carson, Lord Carson of Duncairn*, London, Heinemann.

Ignatieff, M. (1993), *Blood and Belonging*, London, BBC/Chatto and Windus.

Inge, W.R. (1927), *England*, New York, Charles Scribner's Sons.

Ireland, D. (1947), *Six Counties in Search of a Nation: Essays and Letters on Partition*, Belfast, Irish News.

Jackson, A. (1989), *The Ulster Party: Irish Unionists in the House of Commons 1885–1911*, Oxford, Oxford University Press.

——, (1990), 'Unionist Politics and Protestantism in Edwardian Ireland', *Historical Journal*, 33: 839–65.

——, (1992), 'Unionist Myths 1912–1985', *Past and Present*, No. 136: 164–85.

——, (1993), *Sir Edward Carson*, Dundalk, The Historical Association of Ireland.

Jackson, I. (1971), *The Provincial Press and the Community*, Manchester, Manchester University Press.

Jacobs, E. and Worcester, R. (1991), *Typically British?: the Prudential MORI Guide*, London, Bloomsbury.

Jay, R. (1981), *Joseph Chamberlain: a Political Study*, Oxford, Clarendon Press.

Jowitt, Visc. (1951), 'The British Constitution' in *Our Way of Life: Twelve Aspects of Our British Heritage*, London, Country Life.

Judd, D. (1968), *Balfour and the British Empire: a Study in Imperial Evolution*, London, Macmillan.

Kendle, J. (1989), *Ireland and the Federal Solution: the Debate on the United Kingdom Constitution 1870–1921*, Kingston Ont. and Montreal, McGill-Queen's University Press.

Kennedy, D. (1988), *The Widening Gulf: Northern Attitudes to the Independent Irish State 1919–1949*, Belfast, Blackstaff Press.

Kennedy, P. (1981), 'The Pre-War Right in Britain and Germany' in Kennedy and Nicholls (eds), *Nationalist and Racialist Movements in Britain and Germany Before 1914*, Basingstoke, Macmillan: 1–20.

Kennedy, P. and Nicholls, A.J. eds (1981), *Nationalist and Racialist Movements in Britain and Germany Before 1914*, Basingstoke, Macmillan.

Kiernan, V. (1972), *The Lords of Human Kind: European Attitudes to the Outside World in the Imperial Age*, Harmondsworth, Penguin.

Kirk, N. (1980), 'Ethnicity, Class and Popular Toryism 1850–1870' in *Immigrants and Minorities: Historical Responses to Newcomers in British Society 1870–1914*, Folkestone, Dawson: 64–106.

Kuklick, H. (1984), 'Tribal Exemplars: Images of Political Authority in British Anthropology 1885–1945' in Stocking (ed.), *Functionalism Historicised: Essays on British Social Anthropology*, Madison, Wisc., University of Wisconsin Press: 59–82.

Lacey, R. (1977), *Majesty: Elizabeth II and the House of Windsor*, London, Hutchinson.

Leacock, S. (1940), *Our British Heritage*, London, Right Book Club.

Lebow, R.N. (1976), *White Britain and Black Ireland: the Influence of Stereotypes on Colonial Policy*, Philadelphia, Institute for the Study of Human Issues.

Lebzelter, G.C. (1981), 'Anti-Semitism – a Focal Point for the British Radical Right' in Kennedy and Nicholls (eds), *Nationalist and Racialist Movements in Britain and Germany Before 1914*, Basingstoke, Macmillan: 88–105.

Lee, J. ed. (1979), *Ireland 1945–70*, Dublin, Gill and Macmillan.

Lee, S. (1925, 1927), *King Edward VII: a Biography*, London, Macmillan.

Leeper, A. (1937), 'Flags and Names', *Contemporary Review*, cli: 428–37.

Leslie, S. (1966), *Long Shadows*, London, John Murray.

Longford, F. (1974), *The Grain of Wheat*, London, Collins.

Loudon, J. (1951), 'The Festival of the Arts' in *The Festival of Britain 1951 in Northern Ireland: Official Souvenir Handbook*: 49–79.

Loughlin, J. (1986), *Gladstone, Home Rule and the Ulster Question*, Dublin, Gill and Macmillan.

——, (1990a), 'T.W. Russell, the Tenant-Farmer Interest and Progressive Unionism in Ulster 1886–1900', *Eire-Ireland*, xxvi, No. 1: 44–63.

——, (1990b), 'Some Comparative Aspects of Irish and English Nationalism in the Late Nineteenth Century' in M. Hill and S. Barber (eds), *Aspects of Irish Studies*, Belfast, QUB, Institute of Irish Studies.

——, (1992), 'Joseph Chamberlain, English Nationalism and the Ulster Question', *History*, 77, No. 250: 202–19.

Lowenthal, D. (1991), 'Heritage and the English Landscape', *History Today*, 41 (September): 7–10.

Lubenow, W.C (1988), *Parliamentary Politics and the Home Rule Crisis: the British House of Commons in 1886*, Oxford, Clarendon Press.

Lucy, G. ed. (1989a), *Lord Macaulay on Londonderry, Aughrim, Enniskillen and the Boyne*, Lurgan, New Ulster Publications.

——, (1989b), *The Ulster Covenant: a Pictorial History of the 1912 Home Rule Crisis*, Lurgar, New Ulster Publications.

McAulay, J.W. (1991), 'Cuchullain and the RPG-7: the Ideology and Politics of the Ulster Defence Association' in E. Hughes (ed.), *Culture and Politics in Northern Ireland*, Milton Keynes, Open University Press: 45–68.

McCaffrey, J.F. (1991), 'Irish Issues in the Nineteenth and Twentieth Centuries: Radicalism in Scottish Context' in T.M. Devine (ed.), *Irish Immigrants and Scottish Society in the Nineteenth and Twentieth Centuries*, Edinburgh, John Donald: 116–37.

MacDougall, H.A. (1982), *Racial Myth in English History: Trojans, Teutons and Anglo-Saxons*, Hanover, New England and London, University of New England Press.

Macintosh, J.P. 1968), *The Devolution of Power: Local Democracy, Regionalism and Nationalism*, Harmondsworth, Penguin.

McKenzie, C. (1938), *The Windsor Tapestry: Being a Study of the Life, Heritage and Abdication of H.R.H. the Duke of Windsor, K.G.*, London, Rich and Cowan.

McKenzie, J. (1984), *Propaganda and Empire: the Manipulation of British Public Opinion 1880–1960*, Manchester, Manchester University Press.

McLaine, I. (1979), *Ministry of Morale: Home Front Morale and the Ministry of Information in World War Two*, London, George Allen and Unwin.

McMahon, D. (1984), *Republicans and Imperialists: Anglo-Irish Relations in the 1930s*, New Haven and London, Yale University Press.

McNeill, R. (1922), *Ulster's Stand for Union*, London, John Murray.

Magee, J. (1970), *The Teaching of Irish History in Irish Schools*, Belfast, Irish National Teachers' Organisation.

Magnus, P. (1958), *Kitchener: Portrait of an Imperialist*, London, John Murray.

Manseargh, N. (1936), *The Government of Northern Ireland: a Study in Devolution*, London, George Allen and Unwin.

Marjoribanks, E. (1932), *The Life of Lord Carson: Volume 1*, London, Gollancz.

Martin, K. (1962), *The Crown and the Establishment*, London, Hutchinson.

Marwick, A. (1991), 'Britain 1951', *History Today*, 41 (April): 5–11.

Mee, A. (1941), *Arthur Mee's Book of the Flag: Island and Empire*, London, Hodder and Stoughton.

Miller, D.W. (1978), *Queen's Rebels: Ulster Loyalism in Historical Perspective*, Dublin, Gill and Macmillan.

Moloney, E. and Pollack, A. (1986), *Paisley*, Dublin, Poolbeg.

Morris, A.J.A. (1984), *The Scaremongers: the Advocacy of War and Rearmament 1896–1914*, London, Routledge and Kegan Paul.

Morton, H.V. (1930), *In Search of Ireland*, London, Methuen.

Mosley, O. (1968), *My Life*, London, Nelson.

Mosse, G.L. (1990), *Fallen Soldiers: Reshaping the Memory of the World Wars*, New York, Oxford University Press.

Moxon-Browne, E. (1991), 'National Identity in Northern Ireland' in P. Stringer and G. Robinson (eds), *Social Attitudes in Northern Ireland*, Belfast, Blackstaff Press: 23–30.

Nairn, T. (1977), *The Break-Up of Britain*, London, New Left Books.

——, (1988), *The Enchanted Glass: Britain and Its Monarchy*, London, Radius.

Nelson, S. (1984), *Ulster's Uncertain Defenders: Loyalists and the Northern Ireland Conflict*, Belfast and Syracuse, New York, Appletree Press and Syracuse University Press.

Newark, F.H. (1948), 'The Constitution of Northern Ireland: the First Twenty-Five Years', *Northern Ireland Legal Quarterly*, viii, No. 1: 52–66.

Newman, G. (1987), *The Rise of English Nationalism: Cultural History 1740–1830*, London, Weidenfeld and Nicolson.

Nicholson, H. (1952), *King George V: His Life and Reign*, London, Constable.

Nickolls, L.A. (1949), *Royal Cavalcade: a Diary of the Royal Year*, London, Macdonald.

Northern Ireland: Constitutional Proposals (1973), London, HMSO. Cmnd 5847.

O'Connor, F. (1993), *In Search of a State: Catholics in Northern Ireland*, Belfast, Blackstaff Press.

O'Faolain, S. (1941), *An Irish Journey*, London, Longmans/Readers Union.

Oldmeadow, E. (1940, 1944), *Francis Cardinal Bourne*, 2 vols, London, Oates and Washbourne.

O'Leary, B. and McGarry, J. (1993), *The Politics of Antagonism: Understanding Northern Ireland*, London and Atlantic Highlands, Athlone Press.

O'Leary, C. (1979), 'Northern Ireland 1945–72' in Lee (ed.), *Ireland 1945–70*, Dublin, Gill and Macmillan: 152–65.

Oliver, J.A. (1978), *Working at Stormont*, Dublin, Institute of Public Administration.

O'Malley, P. (1983), *The Uncivil Wars: Ireland Today*, Belfast, Blackstaff Press.

O'Neill, T. (1969), *Ulster at the Crossroads*, London, Faber and Faber.

——, (1973), *Autobiography*, London, Hart-Davis.

O'Nuallain, L. (1952), *Ireland: Finances of Partition*, Dublin, Clonmore and Reynolds.

Orr, P. (1987), *The Road to the Somme*, Belfast, Blackstaff Press.

O'Sullivan, D. (1940), *The Irish Free State and Its Senate*, London, Faber and Faber.

Panayi, P. ed. (1993), *Racial Violence in Britain 1840–1950*, Leicester and London, Leicester University Press.

——, 'Anti-Immigrant Riots in Nineteenth- and Twentieth-Century Britain', ibid.: 1–25.

——, 'Anti-German Riots in Britain During the First World War', ibid.: 65–91.

Pelling, H.Y. (1967), *The Social Geography of British Elections 1885–1910*, London, Macmillan.

Ponsonby, F.E.G. (1951), *Recollections of Three Reigns*, London, Eyre and Spottiswode.

Porter, B. (1982), 'The Edwardians and Their Empire' in D. Read (ed.), *Edwardian England*, London, Croom Helm: 128–44.

Price, R.N. (1977), 'Society, Status and Jingoism: the Social Roots of Lower Middle-Class Patriotism 1870–1900' in G. Crossick (ed.), *The Lower Middle-Class in Britain 1870–1914*, London, Croom Helm: 89–112.

Pronay, N. and Spring, D.W. eds (1982), *Propaganda, Politics and Film 1918–1945*, London, Macmillan.

Pronay, N. (1982), 'The News Media at War' in N. Pronay and D.W. Spring (eds), ibid.: 173–208.

Pugh, M. (1985), *The Tories and the People 1880–1935*, Oxford, Blackwell.

——, (1988), 'Popular Conservatism in Britain: Continuity and Change 1880–1987', *Albion*, 27, No. 3: 254–82.

Purdie, B. (1983), 'The Friends of Ireland: British Labour and Irish Nationalism' in

T. Gallagher and J. O'Connell (eds), *Contemporary Irish Studies*, Manchester, Manchester University Press: 81–94.

Purdy, A. (198?), *Molyneaux: the Long View*, Antrim, Greystone Books.

Ramsden, J. (1978), *The Age of Balfour and Baldwin 1902–1940*, London, Longman.

Reader, W.J. (1988), *At Duty's Call: a Study in Obsolete Patriotism*, Manchester, Manchester University Press.

Rees, M. (1985), *Northern Ireland: a Personal Perspective*, London, Methuen.

Richards, J. (1988), 'National Identity in British Wartime Films' in Taylor (ed.), *Britain and the Cinema in the Second World War*, Basingstoke, Macmillan: 42–61.

Riddell, P. (1951), 'Ulster Farm and Factory' in *The Festival of Britain 1951 in Northern Ireland: Official Souvenir Handbook*: 13–47.

——, (1970), *Fire Over Ulster*, London, Hamish Hamilton.

Robb, J.H. (1942), *The Primrose League 1883–1906*, New York, University of Columbia Press.

Robbins, K. (1988), *Nineteenth Century Britain: Integration and Diversity*, Oxford, Clarendon Press.

——, (1990), 'Varieties of Britishness' in M. Crozier (ed.), *Cultural Traditions in Northern Ireland*, Belfast, QUB, Institute of Irish Studies

Roberts, A. (1994), *Eminent Churchillians*, London, Weidenfeld and Nicolson.

Roby, K. (1975), *The King, the Press and the People: a Study of Edward VII*, London, Barrie and Jenkins.

Rockett, K., Gibbons, L. and Hill, J. (1987), *Cinema and Ireland*, London, Croom Helm.

Rodgers, W.R. (1947), *The Ulstermen and Their Country*, London, Longmans Green for the British Council.

Rodner, W.S. 1982), 'Leaguers, Covenanters, Moderates: British Support for Ulster 1913–4', *Eire-Ireland*, xviii, No. 3: 68–85.

Rose, R. (1971), *Governing Without Consensus*, London, Faber and Faber.

——, (1982), 'Is the United Kingdom a State? Northern Ireland as a Test Case' in P. Madgewick and R. Rose (eds), *The Territorial Dimension in British Politics*, London, Macmillan: 100–136.

Savory, D.L. (1947), *The War Effort of Northern Ireland*, Belfast, Ulster Unionist Council.

——, (1957a), 'Parliamentary Reminiscences 1940–55, I', *Contemporary Review*, cxxxxii: 76–80.

——, (1957b), 'Parliamentary Reminiscences II', ibid.: 137–40.

——, (1957c), 'Parliamentary Reminiscences III', ibid.: 196–200.

——, (1958a), 'The Partition of Ireland', ibid., clxxxiii: 12–15.

——, (1958b), 'The Irish Treaty Ports in 1938, I', ibid.: 119–22.

——, (1958c), 'The Irish Treaty Ports in 1938, II', ibid.: 177–80.

——, (1958d), 'The Republic of Ireland', ibid.: 292–5.

Sayers, J.E. (1969), 'Violence in Control', *Round Table*, lix (August): 401–4.

Scally, R.J. (1975), *The Origins of the Lloyd-George Coalition: the Politics of Social Imperialism*, New Jersey, Princeton University Press.

Schoen, D. (1977), *Enoch Powell and the Powellites*, London, Macmillan.

Schwarz, B. (1984), 'The Language of Constitutionalism: Baldwinite Conservatism' in *Formations of Nation and People*, London, Routledge and Kegan Paul: 1–18.

——, (1986), 'Conservatism, Nationalism and Imperialism' in J. Donald and S. Hall (eds), *Politics and Ideology: a Reader*, Milton Keynes, Open University Press: 154–85.

Searle, G. (1981), 'The "Revolt from the Right" in Edwardian Britain' in Kennedy and Nicholls (eds), *Nationalist and Racialist Movements in Britain and Germany Before 1914*, Basingstoke, Macmillan: 21–39.

Seymour-Ure, C. (1975), 'The Press and the Party System Between the Wars' in G. Peele and C. Cook (eds), *The Politics of Reappraisal 1918–1939*, London, Macmillan: 232–57.

Shannon, C.B. (1988), *Arthur J. Balfour 1874*, Washington DC, Catholic University of America Press.

Shea, P. (1981), *Voices and the Sound of Drums*, Belfast, Blackstaff Press.

Shearman, H. (1942), *Not an Inch: a Study of Northern Ireland and Lord Craigavon*, London, Faber and Faber.

——, (1949), *Ulster*, London, Robert Hale.

Simkins, P. (1988), *Kitchener's Army: the Raising of the New Armies 1914–1916*, Manchester, Manchester University Press.

Smith, A.D. (1983), *Theories of Nationalism*, London, Butterworth.

Smith, A.D. (1992), *National Identity*, Harmondsworth, Penguin.

Smith, C.F. (1925), *James Nicholson Richardson of Bessbrook*, London, Longmans Green.

Smyth, C. (1970), *Ulster Assailed*, Belfast, n.p.

Soffer, R. (1987), 'Nation, Duty, Character and Confidence: History Teaching at Oxford 1850–1914', *Historical Journal*, 30: 77–104.

Somervell, D.C. (1935), *The Reign of George V: an English Chronicle*, London, Faber and Faber.

Stead, P. (1988), 'The People as Stars: Feature Films as National Expression' in Taylor (ed.), *Britain and the Cinema in the Second World War*, Basingstoke, Macmillan: 62–83.

Stocking Jr, G.W. ed. (1984), *Functionalism Historicised: Essays on British Social Anthropology*, Madison, Wisc., University of Wisconsin Press.

Storch, R. (1982), '"Please to Remember the Fifth of November": Conflict, Solidarity and Public Order in Southern England 1815–1900' in R.D. Storch (ed.), *Popular Culture and Custom in Nineteenth-Century England*, London, Croom Helm: 71–99.

Street, P. (1979), *Arthur Bryant: Portrait of a Historian*, London, Collins.

Strong, R. (1976), 'Prologue' in Banham and Hillier (eds), *A Tonic for the Nation: the Festival of Britain 1951*, London, Thames and Hudson: 7–9.

Taylor, A.J.P. (1965), *English History 1914–1945*, Oxford, Clarendon Press.

Taylor, P.M. (1981), *The Projection of Britain: British Overseas Publicity and Propaganda 1919–1939*, Cambridge, Cambridge University Press.

——, ed. (1988), *Britain and the Cinema in the Second World War*, Basingstoke, Macmillan.

Tebbit, N. (1989), *Upwardly Mobile*, London, Futura.

Templewood, Visc. [Sir Samuel Hoare] (1954), *Nine Troubled Years*, London, Collins.

Thatcher, M. (1986), *In Defence of Britain: Speeches on Britain's Relations with the World 1978–1986*, intro. R. Butt, London, Aurum Press.

——, (1993), *The Downing Street Years*, London, HarperCollins.

Thompson, K. (1986), *Beliefs and Ideology*, London, Tavistock.

Todd, J. (1987), 'Two Traditions in Ulster Political Culture', *Irish Political Studies*, 2: 1–26.

——, (1993), 'Unionist Political Thought, 1920–72' in D.G. Boyce, R. Eccleshall and V. Geoghegan (eds), *Political Thought in Ireland Since the Seventeenth Century*, London and New York, Routledge: 190–211.

Tomlinson, R. 1994), *The Inglorious Survival of British Monarchy*, London, Little Brown.

Tudor, H. (1972), *Political Myth*, London, Pall Mall.

Tyndall, J. (1988), *The Eleventh Hour: a Call for British Re-Birth*, London, Albion Press.

Ulster Group (1971), *Recent Events in Northern Ireland: the Northern Ireland Troubles in Perspective*, Belfast, n.p.

Ulster Vanguard (1972), *Betrayal in Ulster: the Technique of Conservative Betrayal*, n.p., Ulster Vanguard.

——, (1972), *Ulster – a Nation*, Belfast, n.p., Ulster Vanguard.

Ulster Vanguard (Newtownards Branch) (1972), *Government Without Right*, Belfast, Ulster Vanguard (Newtownards Branch).

Urry, J. (1984), 'Englishmen, Celts and Iberians: the Ethnographic Survey of the United Kingdom 1892–99' in Stocking Jnr (ed.), *Functionalism Historicised: Essays on British Social Anthropology*, Madison, Wisc., University of Wisconsin Press.

UTDA (1984), *Sixty Years On: the Ulster Tourist Development Association 1924–1984*, Belfast, UTDA.

Utley, T.E. (1975), *Lessons of Ulster*, London, Dent.

Voices Out of the Air: the Royal Christmas Broadcasts 1932–1981 (1981), intro. T. Fleming, London, Heinemann.

Walker, G. (1994), 'Empire, Religion and Nationality in Scotland and Ulster Before the First World War' in I. Wood (ed.), *Scotland and Ulster*, Edinburgh, Mercat Press: 97–113.

Walker, M. (1977), *The National Front*, London, Fontana/Collins.

Ward, R. (1958), *The Australian Legend*, Melbourne, Oxford University Press.

Watson, G.J. (1989), 'England: a Country of the Mind' in R.P. Draper (ed.), *The Literature of Region and Nation*, Basingstoke, Macmillan: 147–59.

Webber, G.C. (1986), *The Ideology of the British Right*, London, Croom Helm.

Wheeler-Bennett, J.W. (1958), *King George VI: His Life and Reign*, London, Macmillan.

Whicker, A. (1982), *Within Whicker's World*, London, Elm Tree Books/Hamish Hamilton.

Wiener, M. (1987), *English Culture and the Decline of the Industrial Spirit 1850–1980*, Harmondsworth, Penguin.

Williamson, J.A. (1922/1964), *A Short History of British Expansion: the Modern Empire and Commonwealth*, vol. 2, London, Macmillan (5th ed.).

Wilson, D. (1993), 'Tourism, Public Policy and the Image of Northern Ireland Since the Troubles' in B. O'Connor and M. Cronin (eds), *Tourism in Ireland: a Critical Analysis*, Cork, Cork University Press: 138–61.

Wilson, J.C. (1981), *Conor 1881–1968: the Life and Work of an Ulster Artist*, Belfast, Blackstaff Press.

Wilson, T. ed. (1955), *Ulster under Home Rule: a Study of the Political and Economic Problems of Northern Ireland*, Oxford, Oxford University Press.

Winter, J.M. (1985), *The Great War and the British People*, London, Macmillan.

Wright, P. (1985), *On Living in an Old Country; the National Past in Contemporary Britain*, London, Verso.

Young, H. (1990), *One of Us: a Biography of Margaret Thatcher*, London, Pan.

Ziegler, P. (1978), *Crown and People*, London, Collins.

INDEX

Note: Page numbers followed by 'n' refer to notes.

8/09